EXPLORING THE PRODUCTION OF URBAN SPACE

Differential space in three post-industrial cities

Michael Edema Leary-Owhin

First published in Great Britain in 2016 by

Policy Press
University of Bristol
1-9 Old Park Hill
Bristol
BS2 8BB
UK
t: +44 (0)117 954 5940
pp-info@bristol.ac.uk
www.policypress.co.uk

North America office:
Policy Press
c/o The University of Chicago Press
1427 East 60th Street
Chicago, IL 60637, USA
t: +1 773 702 7700
f: +1 773 702 9756
sales@press.uchicago.edu
www.press.uchicago.edu

© Policy Press 2016

British Library Cataloguing in Publication Data
A catalogue record for this book is available from the British Library

Library of Congress Cataloging-in-Publication Data
A catalog record for this book has been requested

ISBN 978 1 44730 574 3 hardcover

The right of Michael Edema Leary-Owhin to be identified as author of this work has been asserted by him in accordance with the Copyright, Designs and Patents Act 1988.

Cover design by Policy Press
Front cover image: Michael Edema Leary-Owhin
Printed and bound in Great Britain by CPI Group (UK) Ltd, Croydon, CR0 4YY
Policy Press uses environmentally responsible print partners

Inspiration

I could be bounded in a nutshell, and count myself a king of infinite space, were it not that I have bad dreams.

(William Shakespeare c1599, *Hamlet*)

And over all the land, instead of trees,
Clean poles and wire will whisper in the breeze.
We'll keep one ancient village just to show
What England once was when the times were slow –
Broadway for me. But here I know I must
Ask the opinion of our National Trust.
And ev'ry old cathedral that you enter
By then will be an Area Culture Centre.
Instead of nonsense about Death and Heaven
Lectures on civic duty will be given...

(John Betjeman 1948, extract from, *The Town Clerk's Views*,
with the permission of Hodder and Stoughton Ltd)

It was from one of these soldiers that Obi had his first picture of Lagos.

'There is no darkness there,' he told his admiring listeners, 'because at night the electric shines like the sun, and people are always walking around, that is, those who want to walk. If you don't want to walk you have only to wave your hand and a pleasure car stops for you.' His audience made sounds of wonderment. Then by way of a digression he said: 'If you see a white man, take off your hat for him. The only thing he cannot do is mould a human being.'

(Chinua Achebe 1960, *No Longer at Ease*)

In part, we give things meanings by how we *represent* them – the words we use about them, the stories we tell about them, the images of them we produce, the emotions we associate with them, the ways we classify and conceptualize them, the values we place on them.

(Stuart Hall 1997, *Representation*, emphasis in original)

Contents

List of figures and tables

Figures

Tables

List of abbreviations and acronyms

AMNO	Acre Model Neighbourhood Organisation
A&N	Army and Navy Stores
BBC	British Broadcasting Corporation
BBCA	British Broadcasting Corporation Archives
BC	British Columbia
BCC	Business Community of China
BCG	British Colombia Government
BHP	Boarding House Park
BLNA	British Library Newspaper Archives
BMC	Boott Mills Company
BR	British Rail
CDBG	Community Development Block Grant
CII	Corporation Investments Inc
CJBS	Coastal Jazz and Blues Society
CLHA	Centre for Lowell History Archives
CMDC	Central Manchester Development Corporation
CMHC	Canadian Central Mortgage and Housing Corporation
CRC	Cordova Redevelopment Corporation
CTIG	Chinatown Improvement Group
CTNW	Civic Trust for the North West
DEM	Department for Environmental Management
DJC	Docklands Joint Committee
DNR	Department of Natural Resources
DoE	Department of the Environment
DRPA	David Rhodes Personal 'Archives'
DTES	Downtown Eastside
EIP	environmental improvement project
GLC	Greater London Council
GMA	Gastown Merchants Association
GMAG	Greater Manchester Archaeological Group
GMAU	Greater Manchester Archaeological Unit
GMC	Greater Manchester County Council
GMCRO	Greater Manchester County Records Office
GONWA	Government Office for the North West Archives
GRG	Georgian Group
GrGA	Georgian Group Archives
GTV	Granada TV Ltd
GTVA	Granada TV Archives
GWA	Groundwork Associates

HBC	Historic Buildings Council
HSC	Human Services Corporation
HUD	Department of Housing and Urban Development
IDEAS	Improvement of Downtown East Area Society
IRA	Irish Republican Army
L&C	The Proprietors of Locks and Canals on the Merrimack River
LCC	Lowell City Council
LDDC	London Docklands Development Corporation
LDFC	Lowell Development and Financial Corporation
LFF	Lowell Folk Festival
LHCDC	Lowell Historic Canal District Commission
LHPC	Lowell Historic Preservation Commission
LHS	Lowell Historical Society
LHSP	Lowell Heritage State Park
LNHP	Lowell National Historical Park
LNHPA	Lowell National Historical Park Archives
LRS	Liverpool Road Station
LSA	Lowell Sun Archives (Online)
LTI	Lowell Technical Institute
MA	Massachusetts
MCC	Manchester City Council
MENA	Manchester Evening News Archives
MLA	Member of the Legislative Assembly
MLSA	Manchester Local Studies Archives
MNB	Manchester No Borders
MOSI	Museum of Science and Industry
MP	Member of Parliament
MSCC	Manchester Ship Canal Company
MSIA	Museum of Science and Industry Archives
MSP	Manchester and Salford Inner City Partnership
MSPA	Michael Southworth Personal 'Archives'
MSWP	Manchester and Salford Officers Working Party
NAaB	National Archives (North East) at Boston
NAE	National Archives England
NoA	Newspaper Online Archive
NCTA	National Council for the Traditional Arts
NFF	National Folk Festival
NPA	Non-Partisan Association
NPS	National Park Service
NTDC	New Town Development Corporation
PABC	Provincial Archives of British Colombia

PCC	Project Civil City
PL	Public Law
quango	quasi-autonomous non-governmental organisation
RMPA	Robert Maund Personal 'Archives'
SCC	Salford City Council
TCIG	The Chinatown Improvement Group
TEAM	The Electors Action Movement
UBC	University of British Columbia
UDC	Urban Development Corporation
UHP	Urban Heritage Park
UrP	Urban Programme
VCA	Vancouver City Archives
VCAC	Vancouver Community Arts Council
VCC	Vancouver City Council
VPD	Vancouver Police Department
VSM	Victorian Society (Manchester)
WW2	World War II
YHA	Youth Hostel Association

Acknowledgements

Undertaking an arduous book project is an ambivalent experience. It is in turn exhilarating, frustrating and perplexing. At times it feels interminable. We long for it to end but when it does a chasm opens up in our life and we miss it. At times the voice of Nina Simone singing *Feeling Good* was uplifting and that of Bob Marley singing *Redemption Song* highly motivating. Writing acknowledgements is a delightful but doleful duty. It gives a pleasant chance to reflect properly on all those people who made the project possible in direct ways but also unknowingly. It signals the welcome end of a demanding task but instils a touch of mournful melancholy. It is hard to know exactly when this book journey began. A trip to Vancouver in 1977 stimulated a long-term fascination with that 'Dream City'. Years ago I wanted to cover just my home town, Manchester, Cottonopolis. Perhaps Michael Keith set this book ball rolling in 2004; if so we were unaware of it then. Lowell, Spindle City, appeared on the research horizon in 2008. Subsequently, the uncanny similarities with Manchester, according to Karl Marx but disputed by Charles Dickens, stimulated the international, comparative research perspective.

Editors at Policy Press supported the project from the time of the initial book proposal and I am happy to acknowledge their trust and encouragement. I am grateful they nudged me to expand the geographical reach of the research and resulting monograph. Laura Greaves, Laura Vickers and Emily Watt gave expert and precise editorial guidance and were accommodating with dates. Ultimately, their no nonsense style was good for completion. Special thanks to copy-editor Abi Saffrey – a critical friend – who offered expert editorial suggestions. Thanks also to the Policy Press graphic design team who created the strong book cover. It would be remiss of me not to record my thanks to the anonymous academic referees whose words of appreciation were important approbation. Perhaps more important were the thoughtful and informed suggestions regarding how some key concepts could be clarified and additional perspectives included.

Completing a long, intellectually demanding book journey can be lonely but one is rarely alone. Along the road family, friends, colleagues and acquaintances provide succour, support and welcome diversions too. Without their backing the task may still have been completed but at greater personal cost. Family involved from the start include: Emmeline, Melanie, Jude and Paulyn. Meg Oritsegbemi Owhin deserves thanks for always checking up on me in her inimitable way. Thanks to Rachel

Oluwaseyifunmi Owhin who provided a lavish (formal) dinner break in Oxford close to journey's end. Lene and Frederikke Christensen Kamm offered the zest of brain cooling sojourns to Copenhagen and Oxford. Lifelong friends Bolaji Lawrence and Glenn Blaylock – thanks again for the blasé expectations of completion. Elaine Blaylock in Toronto and John Blaylock in Abbotsford offered warm hospitality that will always be appreciated greatly. At Goldsmiths and later, the friendship of Sireita Mullings-Lawrence and Carla Diego-Franceskides have been special gifts. Rachel Dunkley-Jones and Nick Denes offered penetrating observations and erudite comments in the formative years of the research. Librarian/Scholar Liz Williams provided moral support. In the world of academia, insights and critical voices came from myriad directions. Since 2001, my intellectual development has been enhanced immeasurably by Michael Keith's astute comments on my work. Bev Skeggs' positive attitude and helpful hints were invaluable along the way. Brian Alleyne, Les Back, Ben Gidley, Sheila Robinson and Bridget Ward were highly supportive during my time at Goldsmiths College, London. Some of the arguments in the book were tested robustly by Sophie Watson and Fran Tonkiss and their comments helped greatly. Colleagues/friends at London South Bank University (LSBU): Neil Adams, John Adriaanse, Adrian Budd, Neville Kendall, Sonia Leeyou, Manuela Madeddu, Diane Paice, Phil Pinch, Tracey Reynolds, Shaminder Takhar, Duncan Tyler and Alan Winter were magnanimous in their willingness to listen to yet another Castlefield–Lowell–Gastown story. Duncan delivered forthright comments on an early draft of the conclusions, which after initial protest I accepted. In the LSBU Library Jane Haye afforded an unrivalled inter-library loans service. The nascent research may have faltered without the valuable support of Munir Morad, former head of department at LSBU.

The research depended crucially on access to the archives. And I will be forever in debt to the archivists for their keen interest in the research and their munificent willingness to share their deep archival knowledge. They facilitated the discovery of those crucial 'backstage revelations' that can induce Derrida's archive fever in the intrepid researcher. In Lowell, Manchester and Vancouver they are: David Blackburn, Robin Bray, Simon Currey, Katherine Davis, Crispin Edwards, Alison Gill, Heather Gordon, David Govier, Jan Hargreaves, Susan Hayes, Jack Herlihy, Jane Hodkinson, Simon Howles, Tony Lees, Rob Lewis, Martha Mayo, Paula Moorhouse, Paul Robertshaw, Helen Roome, Megan Schlase, Geoff Senior and Ian Smart. Similarly, the interviewees (including email and Twitter correspondents) gave their time generously and were willing to divulge new insights: Mark Arsenault, John Atkin,

Peter Aucella, Pat Bartoli, Howard Bernstein, Jim Cook, Ricky Gervais, John Glester, Jonathon Hall, Michael Heseltine, Kate Hudson, Harold Kalman, Lewis Karabatsos, Kevin Mann, Paul Marion, Warren Marshall, Robert Maund, Gary McClarnan, Lynda McLeod, Charles Parrott, David Rhodes, Ray Spaxman, Michael Southworth, Graham Stringer, Mike Webb and not forgetting 'Donna and Joe'. Memories of Paul Marion's hospitality in Lowell, Robert Maund's in Kilbirnie, Ayrshire and David Rhodes' in Harrogate are most dear.

Undertaking any long journey requires transportation and sustenance. Speaking of sustenance, I am grateful to: The Owl Diner, Ray Robinson Diner, Arthur's Paradise Diner (although I steered clear of the cardiologist's worse nightmare – the Boott Mill Sandwich), Cobblestones, Lowell Beer Works, The Acre Pub, Steamworks, Pane From Heaven, Juliet's Café, Belagio Café, The Oxnoble, The Britons Protection, Library Theatre Café, Shere Khan, On the Eighth Day Café, Jeff's Café, Chillies Café, Castle Fish Bar, Goldsmith's Café, Café Max Brixton and Café Amore SE17. Mentioning mileage; thanks to the train drivers and staff of the 06.17 to Manchester and 23.50 (sleeper) to Glasgow, out of Euston Station. Sustenance of a different kind was provided closer to home. Appreciation of the highest order goes to my mother, Margaret Lillian Leary, and father, Emmanuel Aghamadedeye Owhin, may they rest in peace, who furnished enduring, tough love and endowed me with cerebral competence and a resilient constitution. Such qualities facilitated completion of the journey. Blessing me with a unique name was further parental largesse. Finally, profuse thanks to the people of Vancouver, Lowell, and Manchester, a fraction of whose fabulous production of space stories I am privileged to divulge in this volume.

Foreword

Henri Lefebvre has become increasingly influential in the years since he passed away in 1991. Picked up in landmark books of Marxist (or Marxian) geographers such as David Harvey and Ed Soja, the work's insights have had a bracing impact on the study of the city and the discipline of geography in particular, witnessed in contemporary scholarship of a planetary urbanism or the diagnostic studies of the neoliberal metropolitan turn of recent decades.

Instrumentally, Lefebvre's work was taken up in the Anglophone academy for its particular recognition of the importance of the spatial in influencing the dynamics of social change. Lefebvre in some ways provided a figurehead, a social theorist of renown whose value was both symbolic and substantive. Symbolically, urban studies at times was often considered in the 1960s and 1970s as a less than favoured sub-discipline of the social sciences. But the city had proven to be a focus of political change, a dynamism that inspired a generation of writers whose interests were as much ethical and political as they were analytical and technocratic. Scholars such as Manuel Castells, David Harvey and Doreen Massey all saw the city as a crucible through which forms of class power were exercised and social injustice reproduced. As a leading leftist French thinker for much of the 20th century, a critic of structuralist and Althusserian Marxism and with an uneasy relationship with the Situationists, Lefebvre was nevertheless an author whose work reflected the spirit of the 1960s. His gravitas lent weight to the urban theorists whose Marxian provenance may at times have differed from his own but whose work increasingly was influenced by his insights. But the fact that Lefebvre's Production of Space was not translated into English until the 1990s and the sheer scale of his written archive and legacy meant that the work can never be understood purely in terms of coherent scientific scholarship alone. At times prolix, inevitably evolving over many decades, Lefebvre's own writing contains both puzzling contradictions and powerful insights. So in a sense it is perhaps more important to think of scholarship that is inspired by the work of Lefebvre, rather than work that is straightforwardly faithful to the detail of any particular paradigm.

It is perhaps in this sense that this work by Michael Leary-Owhin, *Exploring the Production of Urban Space*, makes a significant contribution to scholarship that draws on the inspiration as much as the writings of Lefebvrian urbanism, to generate scholarship that advances our thinking about the post-industrial and the comparative analysis of city change.

The sense in which all space is produced is the most fertile of Lefebvre's insights. In this particular volume this sense of production is used to compare the cities of Lowell, Vancouver and Manchester. If these are not the most normally compared sites of urban change they are nevertheless more generative for being so. The ability to combine historical narratives of urban change with theoretically sophisticated insights into the spatial fix of the contemporary city, provides a compelling source of analysis throughout this welcome monograph that builds on Leary-Owhin's previous published work.

Two areas of further study and one caveat come to mind in considering the whole monograph. The first is that through Lefebvrian analysis it is possible to move discussion of public space beyond the at times banal nature of much contemporary policy debate. As Leary-Owhin comments at one point 'public space should be regarded as a more complex, socially constructed entity than one characterised either by public–private or freedom–control dichotomies'. The multiple vectors of control and powers of freedom force the reader of this text and urge the readers of urban spatiality, to consider the city as more nuanced in its potentialities and devious in its designs than either the politically dystopian or architecturally more naïve invocations of public spaces would suggest.

This leads to a second productive axis and the potential caveat that works through the text. The sense that public spaces are indeterminate leads us to think more carefully about the propensity of the city to change, to mutate and to produce new combinations of immaterial capitalism, built environment and human nature. We need to consider critically the city's future as well as its past.

The author takes his inspiration from Detective Freamon, a protagonist in the popular TV series The Wire, searching the archive of the metropolis for evidence of its fabrication. In such a metaphor the researcher follows in the footsteps of those who have studied the streets of the industrial metropolis through a particular genre of knowledge production. The scholar as detective has a long and honourable genealogy. But if the scholar is a detective one is tempted to ask if the city should be understood as a crime scene. And if so then what might the crimes have been? For all his occasional critique of Foucauldian thinking the Lefebvrian tradition is very strong in helping us to deconstruct the city, its artifice and its hidden DNA. Lefebvre provides the template to answer Harvey's central question for urban studies when he asked in the book *Social Justice and the City*, in whose image the city was fashioned? In his own work this can make Harvey's thinking appear at times teleological, lending to a sense of inevitability to the mutations of a metropolis that appears to many eyes more contingent.

The detective looks to uphold the law. But what is the law? What kind of evidence does it demand and what kind of evidence is allowed to speak truth to metropolitan power. What kind of forensic urbanism might lead us to understand how we might build the city anew? In this sense we might look to supplement the insights of Lefebvre, both with a contemporary analysis of the combinatory forms of infrastructure, built environment and human culture. We might think again about the city's uncertain futures and consider also the sorts of evidence that might challenge the law in a forensic urbanism that opens a new politics of possibility of the city that is yet to come. This volume can hopefully contribute in this way to a body of Lefebvrian urban scholarship that develops as well as contributes to the tradition.

Michael Keith
University of Oxford
July 2015

ONE

Introduction: Cities and public space

[To reveal the production of space] we should have to look at history itself in a new light. We should have to study not only the history of space, but also the history of representations along with that of their relationships – with each other, with practice, and with ideology. History would have to take in not only the genesis of these spaces but also, and especially, their interconnections, distortions, displacements, mutual interconnections, and their links with the spatial practice of the particular society... (Lefebvre 1991: 42)

The slums are also crowded to overflowing with immigrant colonies – the Ghetto, Little Sicily, Greektown, Chinatown – fascinatingly combining old world heritages and American adaptations. Wedging out from here is the Black Belt, with its free and disorderly life. The area of deterioration while essentially one of decay, of stationary or declining population, is also one of regeneration, as witness the mission, the settlement, the artists' colony, radical centers – all obsessed with the vision of a new and better world. (Park 1984: 56)

Cities are the height of human achievement. Cities are fraught with ambivalence. We adore city life; it stimulates, entertains and excites. Conversely, urban experiences are scary, disorientating and may be physically and mentally deleterious. Cities are crucibles of democracy, yet remain cauldrons of inequality and injustice. Cities are open and tolerant, but perversely elitist and exclusionary. City streets present positive, unexpected encounters which can enrich our lives, but negative ones can disturb deeply. Ambivalence regarding the nascent modern industrial city was captured quintessentially in the visceral eloquence of Alexis de Tocqueville's disturbingly ambivalent assertion, that 1840s Manchester was a vile, filthy cesspit from which flowed pure gold, thereby allowing the attainment of civilisation while converting

1

men of all ranks into desperate savages. Above all, it is in the public spaces of cities – streets, squares, piazzas, plazas and parks – that some of the best and the worst characteristics of urban life and society are created, observed and reproduced. These sites are the geographical focus of this book and are interrogated drawing on the spatial triad ideas promulgated by the French, Marxist, sociologist-philosopher Henri Lefebvre. Looking at history in a new light in this book means exploring the histories of shifting representations of space and ascertaining the implications for the production of space and what Lefebvre called differential space.

I seek in this book to explore the production of space and in so doing stimulate a rethinking of Lefebvre's spatial theories and the essence of urban public space. From this overarching aim flow two research objectives: 1) to tease out the implications of the production of space for post-industrial city transformation; and 2) to unravel the role of differential space in such transformation. Empirically the research is grounded in three iconic post-industrial cities: Vancouver, Canada; Lowell, Massachusetts, US; and Manchester, England. Although strongly rooted theoretically, the book locates the conceptual ideas in the practice of urban policy making, urban planning and the politicised everyday use of public space, especially differential space – a surprisingly neglected concept in urban studies. The timescale is from the 1960s to 2010s.

Academic, journalistic and professional writing about cities has grown at a dizzying rate in the past few decades, following predictions in the 1980s that cities were about to wither away as new technologies created a revolutionary breed of dispersed ruralised, modem connected homeworker based in networked technovillages. On the contrary, cities strengthened their grip on global society, both in extent and intensity. New classifications in urban studies emerged to explain apparent city transformations. Cities acquired a plethora of prefixes such as: post-industrial, post-modern, global, mega, shrinking, rustbelt, creative, ordinary and imagined. Their ambivalence did not diminish either but, for academia, the media and politicians, the dark side of cities, their apparently insoluble problems and of course the threats to public space dominate literatures and debates.

Bodily presence in public space, particularly what might be called monumental civic space with inherent social meaning, has if anything grown in importance for people craving a variety of human and civil rights. Communities of interest wishing to express concerns and anxieties about a range of issues have taken to the streets in multitudinous gatherings, often orchestrated by social media and documented through the lens of the mobile (or cellular) telephone camera. Since 2011 mass demonstrations in public space – Tahrir Square, Cairo; Mong Kok, Hong Kong; Gezi Park, Istanbul; St Paul's Courtyard, London; Bolotnaya Square, Moscow; Times Square, New York; and Place de la République, Paris and many more sites of resistance – demonstrate that millions of people around the world, whether living in democracies or not, believe reports of public space death were a tad premature. What these marches, rallies, demonstrations and longer term occupations elucidate is the deceptively complex nature of public space. Here it is worth noting that in this book public urban space is not understood in purely physical terms. It is regarded as being produced by social interaction striated with power structures and influenced strongly by the political economy of the productive moment. Public space is always a work in progress and is never in any meaningful sense a finished product. Public space is constituted partly by bricks, stone, concrete, steel and glass, but crucially it is, to use Lefebvre's term, produced and reproduced continually through social struggle.

That said, this book is written against the grain of the slew of negativity and debilitating pessimism that characterises the majority of the public space debate in the Anglophone world. The book does not dispute previous research findings per se but rather seeks to enrich the appreciation of a critical historical period in the evolution of post-industrial urban transformations. And although this book was not conceived as applied public policy research, it does require a close, critical engagement with various urban policy and planning initiatives. Neither does the book seek to provide micro prescriptions for the improvement of public space, something done over several decades with considerable élan by the likes of Gehl (2011).

The book was stimulated by a number of academic offerings. Marshall Berman's (2006) exuberant, evocative exploration of New York's Times Square was particularly inspiring. A key conceptual thread in this book is the contention that understandings of public space should privilege a nuanced appreciation of its inherent complexity and the importance of recognising degrees of publicness and the differing social meanings (Light and Smith 1998). Similarly, the binary public–private space divide is eschewed here, following in particular Madanipour (2003), and Low and Smith (2006). The approach in this book sits readily within a more optimistic, but no less critically insightful, strand of the public space debate (see, for example, Amin and Thrift 2002; Madanipour et al 2013; Tonkiss 2013; Parkinson 2014). Regarding approaches to

Lefebvrian urban space investigation, I tend to follow Gregory (1994), Fyfe (1996), Hubbard et al (2003) and Groth and Corijn (2005).

Lefebvre problematised urban space, insisting it was not simply a neutral container, provoking its reconceptualisation as both material product and social process. In all due deference to Lefebvre, the general research approach in this book seeks of necessity to move 'beyond Lefebvre' (Merrifield 2011) in an attempt to integrate his differential space and right to the city ideas. The book seeks to extend and contextualise Lefebvre's ideas in the contingencies of the early 21st century city. There is a focus on the how representations of space are implicated in spatial practice that can lead to the production of differential space. Therefore, the research does not seek to reproduce what might be called a 'traditional' Lefebvrian analysis that counterposes repressive official representations of space against somehow more authentic quotidian spaces of representation. That said, the latter are not ignored completely and do figure in the ensuing analysis.

We live in an age when for many commentators, if it is not dead, public space is terminally ill and, if it was a species, extinction would be beckoning. I endeavour in this book to look through, between, past and under the apparently omnipotent forces seeking to degrade or destroy genuine urban public space. In doing so I provide concrete examples, some from unexpected quarters and trajectories, which demonstrate we can and should have a certain degree of optimism regarding the future of our cities (Lees 2004; Franck and Stevens 2006; Watson 2009; Hou 2010). The examples are explored through the case studies and focus mainly on how public space is produced through processes of urban regeneration (Leary and McCarthy 2013). Conjuring, as Robert Park put it in the opening quotation of this chapter, a vision of a new and better world, requires pondering from where might these visions originate and how might they be represented and implemented. I also build on my previous research that stresses the importance of civil society, civic values, spatial coalitions and what Lefebvre calls counter-projects (Leary 2013a), while not ignoring big institutional structures and ideologies, particularly where they coalesce in neoliberalism (discussed later in this chapter).

Lefebvre provided only tantalising glimpses of differential space, but it is clear that it relates fundamentally to his ideas about the right(s) to the city or the right to urban life. One of these rights relates to urban public space about which Lefebvre had deep concerns in the 1960s. Public space is the city synecdoche *par excellence*. It is the city sine qua non. In the 1930s Lewis Mumford stressed famously the centrality of public space for convivial urban life. In the 1960s and

1970s these ideas were affirmed by Jane Jacobs and Richard Sennett respectively, who also warned of possibly fatal threats to public space and therefore public life. Seizing on the more unpalatable aspects of the city, a pessimistic strand in the public space debate resurfaced in the 1990s focusing on various threats to public space due in part to the spread of neoliberal governance (elaborated later in this chapter). Proponents such as Davis (1990), Sorkin (1992) and Mitchell (1995) saw threats from the corporatisation, commodification and privatisation of public space. In the 2000s Keller (2011) feared that diverse, inclusive public space was being suppressed by neoliberalised urban governance. Rather than doxa, neoliberalism (and its cousin neoliberal urbanism) should be regarded as a highly emotive and contested term; various strands of the neoliberalism debate especially as it relates to public space are discussed later. Recurring shocks to public space from the 1990s onwards proved not to be fatal, partly because public space is impregnated with social meanings that are contested continually – a point stressed by Lefebvre. To misappropriate an inimitable quip from Samuel Clemens (Mark Twain); continual reports of the death of public space were exaggerated. The resilience of public space and resurgence of cities as places to live and as candidates for academic scrutiny are reflected in a blossoming of recent literatures about cities (see for example Eade and Mele 2002; Hall et al 2008; Bridge and Watson 2010; LeGates and Stout 2011; Mould 2015).

This substantial introduction to the book provides an overview of the substantive topic of urban public space and quasi-public space, followed by a brief overview of the different elements of the neoliberal debate. An elaboration of Lefebvre's spatial triad follows and the interpretations used in this book are explained. In addition, the importance of Lefebvre's ideas regarding abstract space, differential space and counter-projects are clarified. Following this, the rationale for the choice of the case study cities is elucidated. For each city, brief profiles are presented pointing to aspects of each city's history which became, I argue, significant decades later for the production of urban space. This chapter closes by mapping out the structure of the book.

Conceptualising public and quasi-public space

In the 21st century public space should be regarded as a more complex, socially constructed entity than one characterised by public–private, freedom–control or collective–individualistic dichotomies. Space in private ownership can and does exhibit genuine qualities of publicness. Urban space in public ownership can at times be overly controlled to the point of suffocation. I suggest public space should be conceptualised as being constituted by five interrelated attributes, shown in Figure 1.1. Spaces with characteristics clustered towards the left side of the axes will tend to be what we regard as genuine, inclusive public space. Relationships between the five axes can become complex, defying a simple public–private categorisation. Hence urban space may be publicly owned but access and performance may be restricted. Alternatively, space may be privately owned but have relatively open access and a high tolerance of performance including the expression of political views. In both cases I argue quasi-public space is created (discussed in more detail later).

Figure 1.1: The five axes of urban public space

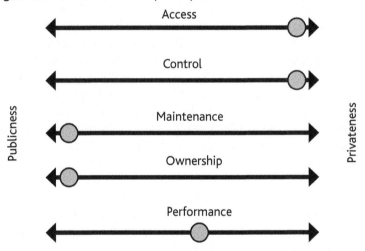

It is clear that public space is valued for a number of different reasons across a spectrum from the political to the ludic. Permanence is an obvious material characteristic of cities but temporary physical structures also endow a city with important social meanings. It is not just physical structures which can be temporary of course. Social interaction although constitutive of public space is inherently transitory. Its ephemeral nature does not detract from its potential power, particularly when the social interaction is dedicated to collective politicised expression. Indeed, it is often the sudden shock of a short lived politicised appropriation of public space which carries great power. Distinctly collective political acts in public space may be seen as the 'highest' activation of democratic rights. Such politicised activism in urban public space forms an important part of the empirical research in this book. However, in addition to being sites of formalised political expression and places of work, cities are sites of enjoyment, revelry and sheer fun, and have been since ancient times. Fairs, festivals, carnivals, street parties, block parties and a host of informal sporting and leisure or ludic events also characterise urban public space (Stevens 2007). These kinds of city sites constitute the other empirical research strand embedded in this book.

In the post-World War II (WW2) period, extensive redevelopment of city centres and downtowns increasingly blurred the distinction between traditional public and private space. To acknowledge and theorise this complexity the term quasi-public space has appeared in the literature, endowed with a range of meanings. In many cities in Europe and North America the classic public spaces of local authority adopted streets were redeveloped into enclosed shopping–commercial areas owned and managed by private companies. A large body of literature has emerged which concentrates on the privately owned and managed shopping mall, as a site of quasi-public space (see for example Gray and Gray 1999; Button 2003; Astill 2010). Staeheli and Mitchell (2007) see the quasi-public space of the shopping mall as a kind of genuine public space but I agree with Ranasinghe (2011) that the categories should be kept analytically distinct. Although privately owned and policed, the mall has come to incorporate a range of civic functionality as well as providing for sites of public assembly where consumption need not necessarily occur. In this sense the mall incorporates a blend of private space orientated exchange value and public space orientated use value.

Urban quasi-public space is understood in this book as having some of the characteristics of public and private space. Rather than the space of the shopping mall, the substantive focus here is on three related aspects of quasi-public space; first, the ostensible public space of the street which may in fact be privately owned and maintained land. Second, I focus on indeterminate urban space and space appropriated for its everyday use and politicised values. Third is the classic public space of streets and squares which are appropriated and in effect privatised *temporarily* by either the private or public sector. I argue that the first two can assume the character of differential space discussed in Chapter Eight. While not disputing the risks to open democratic societies posed by the mall, this book focuses on some of the more positive aspects of the first two kinds of quasi-public space which tend to be downplayed or ignored in the research literatures. In thinking through the complexities of urban public space and quasi-public space it will be useful to consider two remarkable events, both highly germane to the main themes of this book, which happened in London, England at the beginning and end of 2014.

On the night of 31 December at the River Thames in central London something strange and lugubrious occurred. On that night 100,000 ordinary city inhabitants and visitors were charged an entry fee to walk the classic public space of London's streets in order to experience the New Year's Eve fireworks display at close quarters. Payment of a public space entry fee became necessary through a £10 charge imposed by London Mayor Boris Johnson. He contended the fee was essential in order to ensure public safety. Putting aside whether it was really necessary, the question that arises from a Lefebvrian standpoint is how should this emolument and its implications be conceptualised? Publicly owned and maintained urban space with entirely free and inclusive access, in which people have rights to all manner of self and politicised expression, may be regarded as classic public space. When the public space of London's streets was enclosed, policed to restrict access, and a charge levied, that space was transformed into abstract space –the space of homogenised exchange value. It is space often brought into being through the operation of market forces in a neoliberal capitalist economy. Paradoxically, Johnson was at the time the democratically elected leader of Britain's foremost local government institution, the Greater London Authority.

In January 2014 in entirely contradictory fashion, Johnson announced his support for the retention of the informal skateboard park located in the undercroft of the Southbank Centre alongside the River Thames. The skateboard park is a site, not just for skateboarding, but for urban biking and high quality graffiti art. It has been use in these ways for several decades, but was threatened with removal if a redevelopment proposal by the Southbank Centre arts organisation went ahead. The £120 million scheme would see the area transformed into upmarket shops and restaurants. It is important to realise that the urban space in question is not what might be called classic public space in the ownership and control of a local authority. Rather, it is space in the ownership and control of a quasi-public–private entity (see Figure 1.1). Paradoxically, the Southbank Centre organisation is a registered, not-for-profit, publicly subsidised charitable trust. It is considered by many to be Britain's foremost civic, cultural institution. Johnson and other civic leaders opined that the skateboard park was: vibrant shared public space, a marvellous cultural asset, a precious much loved community space and a vital feature of the River Thames that helps make London a great city. Access to this Thames-side park is entirely free and inclusive, open to anybody 24 hours a day, seven days a week and therefore prized for its use value. It is classic differential space which the Southbank Centre wanted to transform into marketised, exchange value abstract space. After an 18 month struggle of resistance, led by the Long Live Southbank Campaign, the skateboarders won an impressive, against the odds victory, securing the long term, free informal leisure use for the site. See Jones (2014) for an extended discussion of the Southbank that is inspired partly by Lefebvre's spatial ideas.

Patently, this book is not about London, but the two examples of Mayor Johnson's spatial interventions exemplify several important conceptual strands permeating this book. Urban public space can acquire the characteristics of inclusive, diverse differential space, treasured by some for its everyday use value, which can be enjoyed without the need for financially based consumption; in that sense it is antithetical to the exchange value of what Henri Lefebvre calls abstract space. Public space is cherished by many people as a pulsating theatre of spectacular cultural action. It is a place of ludic value. It is a place of diverse encounter and cultural interaction. It is a community asset helping to secure social cohesion. Through social interaction, everyday material space takes on particular meanings. Through time, public space may come to occupy an important place in the social memory of a society. It may be regarded as part of a society's cultural heritage. Beyond this, it is a site of politicised expression and action. For many people public space rights connote democracy. All the more shocking then that, in a stable democracy such as Britain, these rights can be subjugated seemingly at the whim of one local politician. Corralling public space and charging a fee for entry into everyday city streets serves to privatise and homogenise urban space if only momentarily. Social diversity is reduced along the lines of social class, ethnicity and age for obvious socioeconomic reasons.

What emerges then is the realisation of the complexities inherent in the processes that render public space inclusive or exclusive. Boris Johnson is a politician firmly on the political right. He was elected to the House of Commons in May 2015 and is a leading member of, what has remained since the 1980s, a distinctly neoliberal government. He claims to be a libertarian and in favour of individual freedoms and reduced state interference in everyday life. The Southbank Centre is a multi-million pound quasi-public institution with a remit to foster inclusive cultural activity. London skateboarders and graffiti artists are mainly young people from a variety of social and ethnic backgrounds. Long Live Southbank is a not-for-profit single objective campaign with limited resources funded by small individual donations. Although this particular fight to defend the skateboard park from property development destruction was won in 18 months, this defence of differential space struggle had been ongoing for 40 years since the inception of the skateboard park. It is obvious that the campaign to defend the skateboard park was not just constituted by young skateboarders but by a broad coalition of interests.

In the case of the London New Year's Eve fireworks, restricting access, charging a fee and thereby creating a space of exchange value pushed the cordoned off streets and bridges into the realm of privatised space. On the other hand, the privately owned land of the skateboard park with its free access, freedom of performance and high use value rendered it quasi-public space. All cities are characterised by public space, but the important point to realise is that such space always exhibits degrees of publicness and degrees of privateness. In these two examples we see something of the complex impact of neoliberalism on public space. This manner of conceptualising public space in a complex neoliberal context is fundamental for a rounded appreciation of the case study empirical research presented in this book.

Neoliberal contradictions

Globalised neoliberalism, as it may be called, centres on the worldwide diffusion of a particular set of diverse, contradictory ideologies and practical approaches to urban governance, property development and public space. The debate is complicated by the fact there is no single agreed conceptualisation of neoliberalism. Apparently, it is a 'deeply problematic and incoherent term' (Venugopal 2015) but that has not hindered its continued use. For some it is a hegemonic ideology, a policy framework or a particular form of governance (Barnett 2010). Most commentators agree that it involves the Anglo-American post-1970s swing from a social welfare based political economy to one characterised by: reduced public borrowing and spending, low taxation, market dominance and an entrepreneurial city ethos facilitated by public–private partnerships (Harvey 1989a; Hall and Hubbard 1998; Harvey 2007). Occasionally, the term neoliberal is misconstrued in the North American context. Liberal in this sense does not mean the politics of the political left or libertarian. Neoliberal refers to a political ideology, rhetoric and governmental practice which favours reduced or minimal state intervention in markets and an expanded role for the private sector based on the privileging of individualistic over civic and communal values. Paradoxically, it simultaneously relies on an *enhanced* interventionist role for the state in facilitating and protecting market based economies nationally and internationally, even after periods of acute economic crises such as the 2006–08 credit crunch and its aftermath.

Ultimately, the intellectual roots of neoliberalism lie in the 19th century Manchester School laissez faire ideology. This version of Liberalism genuinely advocated a minimal state, market dominance and free trade, without the contradictions of neoliberalism. In addition, laissez faire Chartists, such as Richard Cobden and John Bright, campaigned for workers' rights and popular enfranchisement. They opposed the North Atlantic enslavement trade and supported freedom of the press. Post WW2 neoliberalism is based heavily on the ideas of Friedrich Hayek and Milton Friedman, who did use the term for a while in the 1950s. US President Ronald Reagan and UK Prime Minister Margaret Thatcher put a variety of contradictory neoliberal ideas into practice in the 1980s, although they never used the term. Instead they preferred political rhetoric around the concepts of freedom, enterprise and wealth creation.

There is not space here to pursue a lengthy elaboration of the neoliberal debate but its contours are outlined. For a useful discussion on the 19th century origins of neoliberalism and its ongoing political and economic mutations and manifestation after the Conservative-led coalition government came to power in the UK, see Hall (2011). Many writers in particular Harvey (2007) deploy neoliberalism as a set of coherent ideas and practices that tend to lead to increasing inequality, repressive state action and the privatisation of public assets, services and space. Economic priorities for capital accumulation are seen to subjugate civic values and social or cultural needs. Regarding its impact on urban public space and post-industrial city transformation several writers stress the manner in which a neoliberal political economy is used to create urban environments and public spaces conducive to commodification and capital accumulation (Brenner and Theodore 2002; Raco 2005; Lovering 2007). Atkinson's (2003) thought provoking contribution privileged what he called the revenge by cappuccino on public space of neoliberalised gentrification.

In a global context Davis' (2006) approach to neoliberal urban space in 'fortress' Los Angeles is taken even further by Graham (2011). He argues that military techniques, underpinned by sophisticated technological surveillance, developed for urban warfare in the Global South are being used against civilians in the cities of the Global North. Such interventions are driven by a desire to eradicate risks to neoliberal capitalism. At times it makes depressing reading but Graham is not fatalistic though and documents a wide ranging series of global counter-geographies of resistance. One of these is a reconceptualisation and reconfiguration of what he calls the public domain. It requires a rethinking from a static civic space to one which is 'continually emergent, highly fluid, pluralized', and organised by 'interactions among many producers and consumers' who must forge 'collaborations and connections across distance and difference' (Graham 2011: 349–50). In the chapters that follow it will become apparent how these kinds of ideas resonate with Lefebvre's regarding the production of urban space.

Peck (2010) stands at the end of the spectrum where researchers sometimes struggle to articulate an intrinsic essence at the heart of neoliberalism, despite its apparent ubiquity. They worry as to whether it actually exists as a useful analytical category, given its ability to mutate under local contingencies as it pervades the globe. This is not surprising given the contradictory imperatives of neoliberalism to roll back the state while at the same time relying on state power and public resources to defend private property rights and expand the penetration of markets. Despite the definitional problems, Peck tends to see neoliberalism as a set of dubious scientific, economic imperatives played out through sympathetic government policy diffused around the world since the 1980s from Ronald Reagan's US and Margaret Thatcher's UK.

Some of the subtleties inherent in neoliberal urbanism are highlighted in Mitchell (2013). He explains through empirical research in the US in the 2000s how the police target different urban locations for the deployment of two different strategies for the control and management of demonstrations in public and quasi-public space. Increasingly, under neoliberalism the state allocates increased discretionary power to the police for the control of public space. Escalated force is characterised by the police seeking to disperse demonstrators, even if peaceful, and prevent assembly and political expression in public space. Negotiated management is where the police negotiate with demonstrators before and during a political event in public space. This approach seeks to contain or even facilitate demonstrations and protests with minimal police interference.

An alternative conceptualisation is stressed by Larner (2000) who accepts the particular diversities of neoliberalism but wishes to understand the mechanisms through which it operates. She foregrounds neoliberal governmentality which seeks to produce individualised subjectivities. Neoliberalism is characterised mainly as a process which produces neoliberal subjects be they: consumers, entrepreneurs or empowered localised citizens. By diffusing power through a proliferation of governance structures and partnerships the economic imperatives of neoliberalism are bolstered.

Barnett (2010) takes a somewhat sceptical position. He sees in those who proffer neoliberalism as a critical term a degree of moralising over the defects of markets and capital accumulation, similar in kind to the moralising about the benefits of markets and a minimal state by the likes of Hayek and Friedman. Dualities such as public–private, state–market, individual freedom–social justice and profit–social welfare are found to be unhelpful by Barnett since they idealise and impoverish the actual richness and complexity of society and economy. Use of neoliberalism as a purely critical term conceals the potentials in different kinds of liberal thought and the manifest ways that neoliberal urbanism is resisted successfully. This strand of the neoliberal debate is illustrated in a variety of recent research. Several chapters in Leary and McCarthy (2013), and research by Pinch (2015) and Keith (2013) in the London context explain how benefits can accrue to ordinary or disadvantaged people in the face of powerful neoliberal urbanism during processes of urban regeneration. Living in Paris in the 1960s, Lefebvre witnessed first hand the impact of urban planning and what we now call urban regeneration on public space and social groups such as the working classes. What he experienced influenced his ideas about the importance of the social processes that create urban space.

Lefebvre's spatial triad: explication and interpretation

Lefebvre conceived his production of space ideas before the advent of the neoliberalism debate but understood well, from a Marxian perspective the problematic nexus of the state and the big corporate private sector. For Lefebvre, this nexus and the power relations of state and big business was the crucial context for the production of space. Lefebvre saw urban space, often regarded as empty and geometric, as replete with social meaning and power relationships which he conceptualised in a spatial triad. Urban space is understood as both outcome and process. Although a neo-Marxist, Lefebvre departed company with Karl Marx regarding the significance of urban space (see Lefebvre's *The Urban Revolution*, 2003). Lefebvre stressed the importance of urban space and its production for the maintenance of state regulated and implicated, neo-capitalist society, whereas Marx of course stressed the importance of land more generally, capital accumulation and dialectical struggle between the proletariat and bourgeoisie supported by a complicit state. For Lefebvre (1991) although class politics are important, the focus is on the relative power of those who create official representations of space and who deploy them to produce and reproduce the built environment. A defining feature of Lefebvre's theories is the importance of power relationships and the linkages between the private sector and the state, for the reproduction of neo-capitalist society. I would add that over recent decades the importance of civil society groups has become also become apparent. Urban space cannot therefore be produced without the formation of coalitions of interest, sometimes disparate coalitions. Although suffused with complexity, the spatial triad does have an intuitive simplicity (see Figure 1.2). The dotted lines represent the porous nature of the three elements allowing their interaction with each other and with the wider society/economy. At the intersection of the three spatial elements, urban public space is produced. My approach sees its elements as follows:

- spatial practice has three major elements: 1) the physical, material city and its routine maintenance; 2) major urban redevelopment in the context of existing neo-capitalist and state power structures; and 3) routines of daily life that conform with official representations of space. It is space directly perceptible through the senses – perceived space.
- representations of space: rational, intellectualised, official conceptions of urban areas for analytical, administrative and property development purposes. They are produced by technocrats: architects, engineers, urbanists and planners but also artists with a scientific bent. They are the dominant representations and may be in the form of the written word, for example in city-wide zoning plans and strategy documents, or quasi-scientific visual representations of various kinds such as maps, masterplans and design guides – conceived space.
- spaces of representation have two major elements: 1) urban everyday space as directly lived by inhabitants and users in ways informed not so much by representations of space as by associated cultural memories, images and symbols imbued with cultural meaning; and 2) emotional, artistic interpretations of city space by poets, writers and painters and other artists. These kinds of space overlay physical space and value places in ways that run counter to the dominant representations of space – imaginative and lived space.

Surprisingly perhaps, the term spaces of representation does not appear in Lefebvre (1991). Nicholson-Smith translated '*les spaces de représentation*' as 'representational spaces'. The term spaces of representation first appeared in Frank Bryant's 1976 translation of Lefebvre's *The Survival of Capitalism* (Borden et al 2001: 25) and is

Figure 1.2: Diagrammatic representation of Lefebvre's spatial triad.

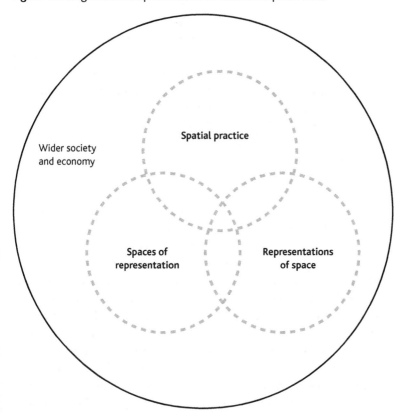

regarded as preferable because the original translation makes the triad 'more difficult to comprehend' (Shields 1999: 161). In addition to the triad, three other Lefebvrian spatial concepts are important for this book:

- abstract space: the urban spaces of state regulated neo-capital characterised by restricted access, restricted performance, commodified exchange value and the tendency to homogenisation.
- differential space: privileges inclusiveness and use value rather than the exchange value of abstract space. It is often transitory space which can arise from the inherent vulnerabilities of abstract space.
- counter-projects: initiatives in the urban environment promoted by civil society interest groups that run counter to official representations of space and are often resisted by city authorities, especially at the time of instigation.

For Lefebvre the production of a new space can never be brought about by any one particular social group and must necessarily result from coalitions based on relationships between diverse groups, which may include 'reactionaries', 'liberals', 'democrats' and 'radicals' (Lefebvre 1991: 380–1). It should be no surprise therefore when space-related issues spur collaboration between quite different kinds of interests and actors. The empirical research to be presented later certainly points to the importance of a variety of coalitions that were vital for the production of urban space. It becomes apparent that Lefebvre understood 'urban social space' to be composed of diverse structures 'reminiscent of flaky *mille-feuille* pastry than of the homogeneous and isotropic space' (Lefebvre 1991: 86). So an appreciation of social and spatial diversity is a key theme in the production of space.

Lefebvre developed his ideas about the production of space and, especially, abstract space while carrying out empirical research in the 1950s and 1960s related to the new town of Mourenx in the south of France. He compared the rapid creation of the new town unfavourably with the slow production of Navarrenx, the historic medieval town in the Pyrenees where he grew up. This unhurried production allowed for the emergence of diverse or differential space. Mourenx was built close to the site of natural gas deposits in order to accommodate the new industrial workforce. Abstract space was created and homogenised here in various ways: land uses, such as residential, leisure and commercial were segregated. Housing and streets were uniform, regimented and bland, and the population lacked diversity. Public space was homogenised also because according to Lefebvre it lacked animation through the performance of social relations in public (Lefebvre 1995). Life in Mourenx was boring in many ways, but particularly because the inhabitants seemed to lack the will to self-organise and resist, at least initially, the harm being done to them sociologically and psychologically by the new town (Stanek 2011: 106–19). Lefebvre was hostile to the new town urbanism that brought Mourenx into being through the collaboration of public and private alliances: the financial sector, big monopolist companies and the state (Stanek 2011: 116) – what I call in this book state regulated neo-capitalism, or just neo-capitalism.

It is evident that Lefebvre's often repetitive and at times convoluted presentation of his spatial triad concept in his book *The Production of Space* was interpreted by what might be called a first wave of urban theorists who engaged stoically with the ideas in the original French. David Harvey first brought Lefebvre's urban ideas, based on his reading of *The Urban Revolution*, to the attention of the Anglophone world with his 1973 book *Social Justice and the City*. Harvey was followed by others who read the French 1974 version of *The Production of Space* (Gottdiener 1985; Soja 1989; and Harvey 1989b). While they had their own particular interpretations, first wave theorists tended not to use the production of space as a framework for empirical research.

However, second wave urban researchers did, notably Fyfe (1996), McCann (1999) and Borden (2001). A third wave of writers tends to take a more intensely biographical and hermeneutical approach (Elden 2004; Merrifield 2006; and latterly Stanek 2011). Although there are differences in emphasis, commentators tend to agree that the triad relates to material, represented and lived space, that is, perceived, conceived and imagined space. It is easy to see though how confusion can arise since Lefebvre refers to at least 50 different kinds of space and favours at times a discursive, desultory literary style. None of the above (apart from Borden) engages much, if at all, with Lefebvre's claims regarding the importance of differential space; for them the spatial triad takes precedence.

Although Lefebvre's stimulating spatial ideas are at times complex and contradictory, there appears to be only one dismissive critique: Unwin's (2000) well argued, if somewhat polemical, provocation that Lefebvre's ideas are a waste of space. Unwin is particularly scathing regarding the implications 'for our empirical research practice', finding little methodological or empirical merit in Lefebvre's work (Unwin 2000: 23). Others disagree in ways elaborated later. Lefebvre is one of the few great 20th century urban philosophers to engage directly with city planning and what we now call urban regeneration albeit that he was rarely complementary. Lefebvre's production of space ideas remain highly relevant for the investigation of city transformation in general and issues of urban social justice in particular (Soja 2010; Harvey 2012). The utility of Lefebvre's ideas for urban planning practice and research has been observed recently in mainstream planning literatures (see Healey 2007; Fincher and Iveson 2008). Although it should be said that the urban theory and urban planning worlds more generally have been perplexingly reluctant to give Lefebvre the theoretical attention his ground breaking insights deserve. In applying a Lefebvrian theoretical framework to a historicised production of space investigation, the book seeks to avoid the danger of producing a caricature of those events which treats history as a form of political propaganda in a larger struggle.

Exploring how to explore the production of urban space

The dangers of 'presentism' in urban comparative research are well recognised (King 1991) and many urban researchers share Lefebvre's recognition of the importance of history. Rather than the 400 year longue durée of Janet Abu-Lughod (Brenner 2001), the historical frame in this book is the history of living memory, from the late 1960s to the 2010s. This timeframe coincides with the European and North American shift from a broad Keynesian political economy consensus to one that is distinctly neoliberal. During that time, in response to international industrial restructuring and recurrent public spending crises, a plethora of public policy interventions have been instituted to cope with the social, economic and physical consequences. Academic debates therefore resound with an abundance of different terms for these intervention strategies: beautification, urban renewal, urban regeneration, urban revitalisation and urban renaissance. There are subtle and not so subtle differences of approach elaborated in Leary (2013b; see also Couch et al 2011) that will not be rehearsed again here.

Several scholars in the urban studies and urban planning fields have recently employed a second wave Lefebvrian approach to empirical research (most notably Hubbard et al 2003; Degen 2008; Carp 2009; Lehtovuori 2010; Buser 2012; Halvorsen 2015) but there is no consensus about the best approach and methods for researching the production of urban space. Certainly, Lefebvre does not provide an explicit research toolkit. However, he does leave several significant ontological, epistemological and practical clues that steer the empirical researcher in certain fruitful directions. Merrifield (1993: 522) thinks that Lefebvre's framework provides a flexible device which can illuminate the nature of space and its relations with a broader social whole. Taking the history of representations of space seriously was for Lefebvre paramount as the opening quotation of this book demonstrates. Soja sees in Lefebvre the potential for a method based on "trialectics" that stresses the interweaving of the three spatial elements (1996: 10) and the history of representations (Soja 1996: 164–5). Kofman and Lebas (1996: 8–10) argue that being Lefebvrian 'is more a sensibility, rather than a closed system' and that many have found his theoretical insights difficult to apply due to the fluidity and openness of his thought. They are still able though to deduce a Lefebvrian approach to production of space research based on observation, investigation of concrete reality and historical analyses.

Borden (2001: 11–12) is the most explicit in divining in Lefebvre (1991) guidance for empirical research and postulates eight 'clues' which although useful are more conceptual than concrete. He is quick to point out that these do not constitute a patented system but are an approximation of a method that nevertheless keeps the researcher on the right track. In formulating his research clues Borden seems inspired by Lefebvre's claim that:

> The theoretical conception we are trying to work out in no way aspires to the status of a completed 'totality', and even less to that of a' system' or 'synthesis'. It implies discrimination between 'factors', elements or moments. To reiterate a fundamental theoretical and methodological principle, this approach aims both to reconnect elements that have been separated and to replace confusion by clear distinctions; to rejoin the severed and reanalyse the commingled. (Lefebvre 1991: 413)

These precepts inter alia proved effective in guiding the empirical research outlined in this book. Since this research is exploratory, rather than defining a rigid research design at the outset, the approach and methods evolved through a process akin to grounded theory (Bryant and Charmaz 2010). That said; the research process was framed within two theoretical parameters which shaped the production of knowledge: first the spatial triad of Henri Lefebvre; and second an approach to ontological and methodological issues influenced by the precepts of constructionism and interpretism (Bryman 2012).

Methodologically the research design was constituted by the following three elements: first, a comparative international case study which involved cognisance of the familiar dangers of case study research, particularly regarding validity (Yin 2013). Rather than being conceived in a single inspirational moment, the international case study comparison evolved over a number of years. Second, a mixed methods approach was used for the collection and construction of a range of relevant data. Mixed methods research has matured into a recognised approach (Bryman 2012). Its formalised origins are acknowledged to lie in the triangulation idea in Denzin's (1970) seminal text. He argues that research aimed at exploring complex social phenomena requires a range of methods and data to construct the most comprehensive and cohesive understandings. Third, archival methods and data form the foundation of the empirical research, supplemented and complemented by interviews, email exchanges, visual data and a Twitter exchange. All the face to face interviews lasted about one hour, were recorded digitally and then were transcribed. Notes were made during and after the telephone interviews. Emails were exchanged before and after each interview. Archival and other sources can be found at the back of the book, in addition to the list of references. Qualitative analyses only are used.

Comparative urban research

The overarching methodological framework for the empirical research is international comparative urban analysis and the book follows the tradition of comparing cities as simultaneously bounded and relational entities (Ward 2010). Urban studies may be regarded as an intrinsically comparative endeavour, in which researchers seek to explain distinctive outcomes in two or more cities through explicit comparison with reference to appropriate theory (Robinson 2011). Of course this is not straightforward or easy either theoretically or empirically (Dear 2005). Following Pickvance (1995: 36) urban comparative analysis is regarded as 'the collection of data on two or more situations' followed by efforts 'to make sense of them by use of one or more explanatory models'. Early comparative urban research from the 1960s tended to understand cities as bounded territorial containers. Consequently, individualising comparison sees the research goal as highlighting similarities and differences between cities as a means of grasping the peculiarities of each case but also as a way of illustrating the explanatory power of certain theoretical approaches (Brenner 2001: 138). Later researchers were inclined to comprehend cities relationally as constituted in and through social relations stretching across politicised space beyond a particular case study city (Ward 2010: 481). Rather than seeing the city as an isolated discrete phenomenon, an individualising *and* relational approach to comparative urban research is taken here.

Case study researchers are usually advised to choose cases rigorously based on objective selection criteria (Yin 2013), but as Healey (2007: 291) argues, the selection is often based on the requirements for research validity *and* pragmatism. In thinking about how to extend the research beyond Manchester, Lowell was an obvious choice. Both cities were the first and for a while the paramount factory-based manufacturing centres in their respective countries. Both had substantial textile industries. In both cities canals were important. Both cities had celebrity status, becoming startling tourist attractions in the 19th century. Over the decades they provoked continual comparison, with Manchester often being portrayed in an exceedingly bad light:

Celebrities, politicians, and foreign princes came to survey
the Camelot for themselves. Lowell had to be everything
that Manchester, England, that septic tank of child
enslavement was not. (Yafa 2005: 99)

And while Manchester does not owe its raison d'être to industry,
it was industrial growth that brought it fabulous, though hideously
unevenly distributed, wealth and worldwide fame, spiced with more
than a touch of notoriety. There is another important similarity.
Vancouver was laid out systematically in British colonial style. Lowell
was laid out and planned from the start as a modern industrial city.
Manchester grew haphazardly over the course of 2000 years. Despite
these differing origins, each city's 19th century development had
similar implications for urban public space. In Lowell and Vancouver
the industrial imperatives of the early settlement meant the provision
of public space was neglected. Lack of convivial public space was even
more extreme in Manchester.

If Manchester and Lowell seem an obvious research couple, Vancouver
– which never endured the opprobrium heaped on the two industrial
behemoths – appears to be out of a completely different mould and
in some ways it is. I contend this strengthens the methodological
approach, since any similarities in research findings serve to boost the
applicability of the theoretical framework. It was a visit to Vancouver
in 2010 that first triggered the idea that it might make an appropriate
third case study. Physically, Gastown has several similarities with
downtown Lowell and Castlefield in urban form and the three cities
have a variety of historic and other types of heritage legacies. It is
often not appreciated looking at Vancouver today that its raison
d'être was industry – it was an important industrial city until WW2.
Industry remains an important employer. Water was fundamental to
the industrial development of the city, hence Gastown's premier street,
Water Street, used to be on the waterfront. Initial secondary research
revealed quickly other similarities. Heritage revalorisation appeared
to have stimulated a post-industrial reimagining of the three cities.
This seemed to be facilitated by two other factors in common. In
each city historic preservation interests appeared to play a key role in
the production of space, as did various partnerships between levels of
government and between the public and private sectors. Each city
benefited from the designation of a historic protection zone in the
case study areas. Notably, each city suffered the threat of and actual
significant demolition of historic buildings in the early part of the
historical period with which the research is concerned. Ethnically and

culturally the three cities are and have been places of diversity for over 100 years. Each city for significant periods since the 1970s was governed locally by centre-left political regimes. Mancunians and Vancouverites share something else: perennially grey, damp and misty weather.

There are important differences of course. Vancouver was a British colonial possession. In the 1960s, unlike the other two cities, it was governed by an extremely conservative centre-right political party. Manchester and Vancouver are really city regions that draw on a catchment of several million inhabitants. They both have major international airports. Partly because of this they have been able to attract visitors from all over the world to significant sporting and other cultural events, such as the Commonwealth and Olympic Games. Vancouver and Manchester are significant regional centres of commerce, insurance and banking and their downtown or city centre areas survived the out of town shopping, commercial and leisure threat, resulting in abundant and pulsating nightlife. Lowell is part of the Boston city region and its downtown was affected badly from the 1970s by large out of town shopping malls. There is no need to labour the differences tediously here; they will emerge and their significance become apparent in the dénouement of the empirical analysis.

At times sitting among the spatial fragments and clues unearthed in the empirical research, I felt more like a private detective than a researcher. Maybe the two are not entirely dissimilar. In following clues and piecing together fragments of spatial production, I was reminded of the words of Detective Lester Freamon, a character in the popular TV police drama *The Wire* (Series One): "We're building something here, Detective. We're building it from scratch. All the pieces matter." Just as there are no agreed methods for researching the production of space, there is no readymade production of space archive waiting to be mined for revelatory data. Piecing together archival sources through the creation of what are called archival networks (Prior 2008) was a crucial element of the research strategy. Rather than simply being conceptualised as inanimate physical depositories, archival networks are seen as something more diffuse and animated: spaces of social memory (Ketelaar 2008). The networks therefore include archival data but also bundles of interactions between the academic literatures, the data, the archivists, interviewees' transcripts (where historical events are narrated) and of course researcher archival interrogations and interpretations. A purposive sampling approach was used to identify potentially relevant archives and appropriate interviewees on the basis of the substantive insights they might provide into the production of space. In the course of the research 14 physical archival depositories were visited and several more accessed online, and 21 interviews were carried out, of which 12 were face to face, three were by telephone and five by email. In the list of abbreviations and acronyms at the beginning of the book are the names of all the archives used. In the list of empirical sources at the back of the book, an abbreviation or acronym identifies the relevant archive.

In the case of some of the interviewees there were potential risks in requiring people to recall events from several decades ago. In practice their memories proved remarkably accurate and lucid, probably in part because are all still active in the field. However, a recognised strength of the mixed method approach is that it allows for corroboration of factual detail, a point made by Bryman (2012) and of course Denzin (1970). In addition oral history is accepted as a legitimate historical research approach. The archival research and interviews were carried out between 2007 and 2014. The archival data amassed are mostly from official institutional files and consist of a variety of types: official memoranda, official and unofficial minutes, formal and informal letters, public and private sector reports, briefing notes, hand written notes, policy documents, drawings, photographs, maps, architectural plans, leaflets, pamphlets, newspaper cuttings, flyers and other publicity materials. Some of these documents were marked 'confidential'. All relevant archival documents and images were photographed digitally. Several thousand jpeg files were created to form a substantial archival dataset.

In the field of historical analysis Samuel notes that photographs cannot be treated as "transparent reflections of fact" (2012: 329). Hall (1997) reminds us that photographs and other texts are representations on which we choose to impose meaning. And with this in mind photographs are regarded here as *representations* that always need to be interpreted. Lefebvre's warning, that space 'made to be read' rather than lived, that is, the photograph which gives the impression of transparent reality is a '*trompe l'oeil*' – is apposite here (1991: 143). He also warns that the surface appearance of public space, that which can be seen and photographed, is a trap which hides its complex production. That said, my own photographs are presented here mainly for illustrative purposes but also as analytical tools. They were all taken between 2008 and 2014. The intention is also to use these images to communicate the feel of the case study areas, or provide what Latham (2003) calls texture. In carrying out the empirical research, the ontological acceptance of urban public space as a complex amalgam of the visual, sensory, physical and social was a fundamental guiding light.

With typical acerbic humour Mark Twain seemed to relish an anti-reflexive research approach, advising Rudyard Kipling, 'Get your facts first' and then 'you can distort 'em as much as you please' (in Brooks 1969: 83). Getting the facts though can be epistemologically treacherous and Wacquant provides a useful interpretation of Pierre Bourdieu's take on reflexivity and his plea for it to be epistemologically grounded has certainly inflected the research underpinning this book. Bourdieu stresses that research reflexivity is not meant to encourage interminable egocentricity and entreats researchers to be self-aware at key stages of the research (Wacquant 1992: 46). Being born and raised in Manchester affected my position as researcher as it became evident that I was a partial insider (Lyser 2001): partial because I have not lived or worked there for 30 years. Insider status results from my Mancunian identity, my identifiable Manchester accent and knowledge of the city, its people and places. Partial insider status extends also to the subject matter and some of the institutions in the research field. I worked in local government town planning for five years and am familiar with its bureaucratic structures and jargon. My Nigerian-British identity could have rendered me an outsider in the predominantly white worlds of local government in the three cities and at the archives but in face to face encounters I never felt this, quite the reverse. Additionally, I always felt relaxed and at home in these three tolerant multicultural cities.

City profiles: Vancouver, Lowell and Manchester

The empirical research concentrates on Gastown, Vancouver; downtown Lowell; and Castlefield, Manchester. Although the three cities have been the subject of a variety of comparative urban research in the recent past, it would appear this is the first research where they constitute the principal empirical case study focus. Here I provide thumbnail profiles of each city, pointing to certain characteristics that will become central to the analysis and discussion. The intention is not to provide detailed histories or city descriptions; there are many easily available texts which achieve that eminently well. It is not the purpose either to document the economic growth and decline of the cities but pointers are provided to appropriate sources. The cities may be regarded as what Hodos (2011) calls second cities, that is, not capital, world, global or mega cities. In this respect, they have something in common with the majority of cities in the world.

Vancouver: Gas, Townsite, Alhambra

Vancouver is the largest city in the Canadian province of British Columbia, located 140 miles (225 km) north of Seattle, Washington. Vancouver nestles at the foot of the North Shore mountain range overlooked by Grouse Mountain and has long been famed for its stunning physical, coastal location with the waters of the Georgia Straight, False Creek and Burrard Inlet endowing it with postcard beauty (Figure 1.3). It is the youngest of the three cities but, with a population of about 600,000 in 2015, the largest. The city region or Greater Vancouver accommodated about 2.4 million inhabitants in 2015. Its location resulted from natural factors such as an abundance of high quality timber, vast fisheries' stocks and sheltered deep water anchorage. It also stemmed from the imperial expansionist ambitions of the late 19th century British government, hence the derivation of the name from the British naval captain George Vancouver (Figure 1.4). Rough logging encampments along the Burrard Inlet coast were consolidated into a township after the arrival of an Englishman, 'Gassy' Jack Deighton, so called because of his affable, loquacious character. He is said to have stepped ashore in 1867, with his first nation wife and a large barrel of whiskey before persuading thirsty loggers to build him a pub. They did so within one day and the makeshift wooden structure became known as the Globe Saloon. It stood at a crossroads by a large maple tree, which later gave its name to Maple Tree Square. In honour of Gassy Jack's cultural contribution to early community life, the township was named Gastown in 1867.

Before Jack arrived, in 1858 the Crown Colony of British Columbia was appended to the British Empire and in 1870 Gastown was surveyed by the colonial government. A larger townsite was laid out in the familiar grid pattern of British colonial settlements (see the visual representations of Vancouver space in Hayes 2006). Wide principal streets with narrow alleys running between were a notable feature of the planned layout. In honour of the Earl of Granville, then the British Colonial Secretary, the township was renamed Granville Townsite (and was still sometimes called Old Townsite in the 1960s). A small two cell gaol is said to have been erected conveniently close to the Globe Saloon. It was the potential for the creation of a deep water port which resulted in the township being selected as the terminus for the transcontinental Canadian Pacific Railway in 1884. When the railway arrived in 1886, the Granville Townsite was renamed Vancouver and incorporated as a city. Ironically, in June of that year, a devastating fire destroyed most of the wooden buildings that constituted the

Figure 1.3: The Vancouver postcard aesthetic, view from the VCA (photo © Michael Leary-Owhin)

Figure 1.4: Captain George Vancouver points the way to the place that will become Vancouver (photo © Michael Leary-Owhin)

settlement. Such was the economic potential of the area that it was not long before the township was rebuilt, this time of brick and stone. On completion of the transcontinental Canadian railway, hundreds of workers of Chinese descent were made redundant but granted a piece of marshy land adjoining Gastown by the Canadian Pacific Railway. They were soon joined by compatriot workers from other industries and the unemployed. Some of the buildings erected mimicked aspects of Chinese architecture (Kalman and Ward 2012). Eventually, the area, centred on what became Pender Street would become Chinatown. From this time Vancouver attained a cosmopolitan character as it attracted newcomers from the Americas, Europe, Asia and later the Caribbean and Africa.

Although based firmly on extractive and processing industries, by the 1920s Vancouver's economy had grown enormously and diversified into a variety of manufacturing industries, particularly iron and steel and later commerce, including insurance and banking (Mansbridge 2015). Gastown, originally located on the Burrard Inlet waterfront, found itself occupying an inland position as stretches of marshy coastline were reclaimed and developed mainly for railway infrastructure. Wholesale and retail merchandising grew in the late 19th century, when gold rush prospectors heading for the Fraser River and Klondike would stop off in Vancouver for provisions. A general store was opened at the intersection of Abbott and Cordova Streets in Gastown by Charles Woodward, creating the first Woodward's in 1892. To service the seasonal, itinerant and mainly male workforce a plethora of cheap hotels and rooming houses, usually with rather basic bars and cafés on the ground floor, sprung up all over Gastown in the late 19th and early 20th centuries. One of these was the Alhambra Hotel, which came to occupy the site of Gassy Jack's pub after it burned down in the Great Fire. Some say this hotel was built on the site of the first gaol. Other notable hotels included the Stanley, New Fountain and the marvellous flat iron Europe Hotel. Vancouver's growth and decline are well documented (see Vormann 2015). Over the decades the commercial centre of Vancouver grew and shifted westwards transforming Gastown into a more economically marginal area (Hardwick 1974) and leading to decline and some dereliction. Even more problematic was the post-WW2 emergence of Downtown Eastside (DTES) as a place of severe social and economic stress. DTES was also known in derogatory fashion as Skid Road or Skid Row. On the ground these three areas – Gastown, Chinatown and DTES – merged into one another in everyday life.

Lowell: espionage, acre, pianos

Lowell is located about 30 miles (48 km) north west of Boston and is the smallest of the three cities, having an estimated population of approximately110,000 in 2015. The population peaked at 113,000 in the 1920s, but declined in the 1930s, 1950s, 1960s and 1980s. The city is considered to fall within the Greater Boston area, home to approximately 4,680,000 people in 2015. Lowell has a unique place in US history. In the mid-19th century, it became the country's first and largest planned textile manufacturing centre. Consequently, it has huge significance as the birthplace of the US industrial revolution. Lowell is named after Francis Cabot Lowell. He was one of a group of a wealthy businessman based in Boston, later dubbed the Boston Associates. In 1810 he embarked on a tour of Britain with his family, ostensibly for health reasons. During the tour, he visited many cotton mills, including those in Manchester (Dublin 1992). This sojourn was prompted not by touristic curiosity but by a desire to garner intelligence about Britain's textile technologies. Plans and designs for textile machinery were closely guarded secrets and their export banned by the British government. Apparently, as a result of his industrial espionage Lowell was able to memorise the configuration of the machinery he observed. On his return, Lowell with engineer Paul Moody was able to manufacture replica machines.

The horrendous living and working conditions of the working classes in British industrial cities appalled Lowell and many Americans, provoking him to consider alternatives to the infamous Manchester model of factory organisation and worker exploitation condemned by Frederich Engels and many others. His 1810 visit to Britain allowed him to seek out a number of planned philanthropic model industrial settlements. These were factory 'villages' built by philanthropist mill owners, such as Robert Owen at New Lanark, Scotland. This breed of industrialist wished to create physically and morally healthy environments for their workers. They provided cheap, decent housing, and health and social facilities. Lowell did not wish to recreate Manchester in Massachusetts and what he saw of the British model settlements would influence greatly the arrangements for worker livelihood at Lowell. Ironically, another textile town was founded in New Hampshire and named Manchester.

Lowell, like Vancouver, owes its existence to water. Not the water of an inlet, but a river. Early in the 19th century the Boston Associates were searching for a suitable location to establish textile factories based on water power and build a town to service their capital investment.

They had previously established textile mills along the Charles River in Waltham MA but soon exhausted the water power available there. In 1821 they decided a section of the Merrimack River close to the small farming town of East Chelmsford would be the ideal location. Pronounced rapids at a bend of the river meant the 30 feet drop over a relatively short distance would provide ample water power for a huge concentration of textile production capacity. In a sense, the Boston Associates were production of space visionaries who imagined and produced an industrial complex and associated town on a grand scale. Earlier in the late 18th century, a waterway called the Pawtucket Canal had been constructed so that river based transport of timber could bypass the dangerous rapids. The company which built the canal was called The Proprietors of Locks and Canals on the Merrimack River (L&C) and it was this company the Boston Associates bought in 1821 to facilitate their enterprise. Lowell was founded at a site that later became known as Lower Locks, close to East Chelmsford. Here various industrial buildings were erected between 1813 and 1821. Small textile mills powered by the Pawtucket Canal and a machine shop were built. Some of these buildings were taken over by the Boston Associates in 1830 and incorporated into what became Middlesex Manufacturing Company. This complex was demolished in stages between 1930 and 1960 but the canal paraphernalia left intact.

L&C capitalised the construction of the power canals, the first factories, textile machinery and workers' accommodation. Kirk Boott, an English engineer, was hired as the company agent (chief operating officer). He laid out the settlement, designed the first factories, boarding houses and a mansion for himself. Manufacturing started in 1822, the year Lowell was founded officially. In a few short years 11 mill complexes, a huge machine shop factory, housing, and civic and commercial buildings sprung up. See the visual representations of space in Dublin (1992) and Marion (2014a) and the historical postcard collection in Lowell Historical Society (2005). Eventually, the original power canal system was extended into a 5.6 mile (9 km) network (Figure 1.5). Quickly too, Lowell was connected to Boston by railway. Huge profits were garnered in the early decades as the capitalist entrepreneurs exploited their US monopoly position. Although Francis Cabot Lowell died in 1817 the new town was named in his honour. In 1836 Lowell was incorporated as a city. Lowell's first chief hydraulic engineer was Englishman James B. Francis, who contributed significantly to the emerging hydraulic science of water power commercial distribution. In recognition of his importance to

Figure 1.5: Tranquil mill power: Pawtucket Canal at Central Street Bridge, Lowell (photo © Michael Leary-Owhin)

the whole enterprise, in 1832 L&C built a residence for the chief engineer: an elegant mansion located on Worthen Street.

It was the second chief engineer George W. Whistler who was to give the city its most famous son. James Whistler was born in Lowell in 1834 and became one of the most celebrated painters in US history. His painting style was controversial for his provocative use of colour, particularly black, hence the name of his most famous painting is *Arrangement in Grey and Black No. 1: Portrait of the Artist's Mother*, more commonly known as *Whistler's Mother*. He was born and raised in the chief engineer's house. Early in the 20th century, the historic importance of the house was recognised by the Lowell Art Association, founded in 1878. It acquired the property in 1908 and converted it into the Whistler House Museum of Art nearly a century before the mill buildings became objects of heritage adoration. In addition in 1868 one of the world's first city based institutions dedicated to local history was established – the Lowell Historical Society.

Following the paternalistic ideas of Francis Lowell, for the first few decades of production, all the textile workers were young women from Yankee farms and villages who became known as Factory Girls or Mill Girls. They worked long, arduous hours, disciplined by the factory bell, but earned cash wages and managed to save in bank accounts. They were boarded in large company dormitories or boarding houses where strict rules of behaviour and etiquette were imposed, but provision made for the health, education and genteel social development of the

Mill Girls. For example, the Girls attended lectures, plays, exhibitions and eventually published their own literary magazine, the *Lowell Offering*, and labour newspaper, *The Voice of Industry*. Lucy Larcom is perhaps the most famous Mill Girl, transcending her labouring status with regular pieces in the *Lowell Offering*, and eventually achieving renown as an accomplished writer. Lowell became a tourist attraction by the mid-19th century with a procession of dignitaries, journalists, writers and politicians all indulging in the 'Lowell tour'. Once they met the well fed, well dressed and well mannered Mill Girls they invariably offered high praise, in comparison with the savage criticism levelled at mill towns in Britain, particularly Manchester.

Charles Dickens was perhaps the most famous visitor. In 1842, after noting the cleanliness of the streets and workers' dwelling and the health of the Mill Girls, he drew attention to the morally and socially uplifting power of the piano placed in each boarding house. When *he* heard about Lowell's company boarding houses and pianos Karl Marx was sceptical that any paternalistic good intentions were being lavished on the Mill Girls by the capitalist mill owners (Ryan 1991). In *Capital Volume II* he criticises the boarding house provision for extracting excessive monopoly rent from the Mill Girls and converting necessary accommodation into a commodity. He criticises the pianos as cynical devices to ensure the Mill Girls remained subject to the bourgeois discipline of the factory environs even during their leisure time.

When it came to the supply of labour for building the canals and factories, as in Britain, Irish immigrants provided a ready and cheap source. They were initially allocated one acre of land, named rather prosaically The Acre, to the west of what would become the city centre, where a crude tented settlement grew up, spreading quickly until it became a city district. After the first few decades, the unprecedented profits generated by Lowell's factories began to decline as other mill towns were established in Massachusetts and elsewhere. Factory bosses reduced costs by cutting workers' wages, rather than reduce shareholder dividends. This tactic led to serious industrial disputes and Mill Girl strikes. In response, over the following decades the mill owners recruited cheaper labour with a variety of national and ethnic identities: French-Canadians, Greeks, Polish, Jews and Portuguese. Over time, they established ethnic neighbourhoods in various parts of the city. Progressively throughout the 20th century Lowell attracted other migrant groups from Africa, South America and the Far East.

Despite the best paternalistic efforts of the Boston Associates, Lowell became known as the Manchester of America. Alas economic success did not last, and there are many accounts of the rise and demise of the place that became known as Spindle City (Weible 1991; Gittell 1992; Minchin 2013 and see Figure 1.6). By the time Jean Louis 'Jack' Kerouac, Lowell's other internationally famous son, was a young man in the 1940s Lowell's economy was shattered. He was born in 1922 in a French-Canadian section of the city. His first novel *The Town and the City* published in 1950 suffered ferocious criticism but was dubbed 'The Great Lowell Novel' by *Lowell Sun* journalist Charles Sampas. Kerouac wrote the novel while living in the Queens borough of New York and, like many in the depressed post-war Lowell economy, felt obliged to leave Lowell in search of a better life. Certainly, this predicament was a cruel about face for a city that for a century *attracted* thousands of workers from distant lands, themselves seeking their own nirvana.

Figure 1.6: Abandoned and rejected: Lowell Mills (photo © Michael Leary-Owhin)

In addition to the personal decisions of individuals, there is no better testament to the sad degeneration of Lowell and the modernist rejection of its histories than the demolition in the 1960s of the Merrimack Mills complex. Also demolished were the associated boarding houses on Dutton Street, often called the Dutton Street Row Houses (Stanton 2006). It was the first of Lowell's textile factories to be built, being completed in 1822. After the Merrimack Mills were demolished, Boott Mills assumed tremendous importance as the most intact mill complex in the city.

Manchester: muck, brass, culture

Manchester too owes its founding to water; rivers rather than an inlet or canals. It is acknowledged widely as the world's first modern industrial city. From the 18th century industrial production was dominated by textiles, particularly cotton, earning the city the nickname Cottonopolis (Kidd 2006). For a time like Lowell it became a major industrial tourist attraction. The physician William Stukeley in 1725 called it the 'largest, most rich, populous and busy village in England' (in Bradshaw 1986: 10). At about the same time, Daniel Defoe added that Manchester is 'one of the greatest, if not really the greatest mere village in England' (in Bradshaw 1986: 11). One hundred years later the visitors had virtually nothing positive to say about the living conditions of the workers in the city. Charles Dickens visited several times and was in no doubt that what he had seen 'has disgusted and astonished me beyond all measure' (in Bradshaw 1986: 5). One voice did break step with the detractors when Benjamin Disraeli declared Manchester to be as great a human exploit as Athens, in his novel *Coningsby*. A counterweight is Elizabeth's Gaskell's 1848 novel *Mary Barton*, a sobering account of the tribulations of working life. Manchester is situated 30 miles (48km) east of Liverpool and lies at the foot of the southern slope of a range of hills (the Pennines) as Engels observed famously in his stinging critique, *The Condition of the Working Class in England*. His meticulous empirical research enabled Karl Marx to formulate his damning analysis of capitalism. Marx and Engels sat together day after day at the same window table in Manchester's Chetham's Library, founded in 1653, where they articulated the revolutionary ideas that would emerge as *The Communist Manifesto* in 1872.

Notably, Manchester's population peaked in 1931 at 766,300. It declined drastically after WW2 but has risen in recent decades, 510,000 being the estimate for 2015. Greater Manchester in 2015 accommodated an estimated 2.7 million inhabitants. Manchester is by far the oldest of the three cities. It was founded in AD 79 when a fort was constructed by the Roman general Julius Agricola in the place that would later be called Castlefield. The fort was built for defensive reasons on a red sandstone bluff at the confluence of the Rivers Irwell and Medlock. It was located strategically to guard the east–west routes across Roman England. After the Romans departed in AD 400, the fort and vicus were abandoned and Manchester refounded by the Anglo Saxons at the site of the Cathedral. Castlefield is located at the south western edge of the city centre and covers an area of about 150 acres (61 hectares). The area once housed 50,000 workers; by the 1980s those residents had been dispersed, leaving the area characterised almost entirely by industry.

Intriguingly, the name Manchester is shrouded in myth and mystery. Whitaker claims with some justification it was also called Mancunium and Mamucium in the Roman Itinerary, meaning breast shaped hill and that both were based on the Celtic name for the Castlefield area, Mancenion (Whitaker 1771: 2–5). Hence the first of the pre-Raphaelite painter Ford Maddox Brown's murals in the Great Hall of the Town Hall is called *The Romans Building a Fort at Mancenion*, rather than Castlefield or Mancunium – a puzzle to many visitors. Manchester's neo-classical Town Hall was found to be too small by the mid-19th century and was replaced by one exuding neo-gothic splendour. Its Great Hall has a high ceiling adorned with names of the cities across the globe where Manchester's businessmen established substantial trading links.

The startling growth from the 17th century of Manchester's population, industry and economy has been told many times (Briggs 1963; Kidd 2006; Hylton 2010). Manchester from the 1800s was more than just a cotton-based manufacturing town. The 'overworked sobriquet Cottonopolis' masked its importance for: coal mining, coal gas production, engineering, chemical industry innovation and technological advances (Kidd 2006: 22). Johnson and Nephew Wire Works Ltd provided the barbed wire which enclosed the American Wild West, bringing an end to the era of the cowboy. The world's first Rolls Royce car was built in Manchester and one of the first factories for the manufacture of aircraft by the AVRO Company was located here. Steam locomotives were sent from Manchester to India, South America, Africa and Australia. This concentration of industry gave Manchester a worldwide reputation for dirt and money, stimulating the proverb 'where there's muck there's brass'. The burgeoning industrial metropolis was awesome to flabbergasted visitors, prompting Briggs (1963) to declare Manchester the 19th century shock city of the modern age. It was the industrial epicentre of the Empire and the workshop of the world. It was a commercial centre for banking, insurance and commodities trading. It was and still is a nationally significant medical and scientific research centre of the highest quality.

It was also a place of radical Liberal politics. Intense industrialisation and urbanisation created a political ferment in the 19th century, centred on strident demands for social equity and political enfranchisement. Loathing of government import tariff policy led to the development of the 19th century economic laissez faire ideology of the 'Manchester School'. Public protests and demonstrations were commonplace led by radicals such as Richard Cobden and John Bright and suffragettes such as the Manchester born Emmeline Pankhurst. This truly Liberal city built the impressive Free Trade Hall in 1856 to commemorate its opposition to oppressive government, specifically the Peterloo massacre of 1819. The hall, located on the edge of Castlefield, subsequently became the home of the world's first municipal orchestra, the Hallé.

Watercourses influenced greatly the city's industrial growth and Castlefield's post-industrial reimagining. Britain's first entirely excavated canal, the Bridgewater, completed in 1765, brought coal from mines at Worsley and terminated at Castlefield. The oddly named Rochdale Canal, completed in 1804, linked Manchester with raw material sources and markets in Yorkshire and also terminated in Castlefield. The 'Great Ditch', the Manchester Ship Canal, opened officially by Queen Victoria in 1894, was crucial for Manchester's industrial prominence. It never reached Manchester, terminating at 'Manchester Docks' which somewhat perversely were located in the neighbouring city of Salford. When the Manchester Ship Canal Company bought the Bridgewater Canal Company in 1887 the cheque for £1,700,000 was the largest ever cashed. The smaller Pomona Dock, named for the trade with the Italian city, *was* constructed in Manchester on the western extremity of Castlefield.

Manchester has an ethnically and religiously diverse population but for different reasons than Vancouver and Lowell. This diversity is due in part to the many vessels that arrived at the docks crewed by sailors from the British Colonies. In the booming industrial metropolis many of them settled and raised families. Manchester's small, parochial local government was reformed in 1838 and the larger and more effective Manchester Corporation created. The township achieved city status before Vancouver but after Lowell when Queen Victoria used her royal prerogative in 1853. Many of its factories and warehouses exuded exuberant Italianate architectural motifs, becoming symbolic textile palaces (see Parkinson-Bailey 2000; Makepeace 2004; Hylton 2010 for many visual representations of Manchester space). The equally dramatic story of the city's post-WW2 industrial decline has been the subject of considerable research (Peck and Ward 2002; Mace et al 2004; Kidd 2006). Manchester is known throughout the world as the home of *Coronation Street* (or Corrie as it is popularly known), the world's first TV soap opera, which started in 1960 – though it is in 'Weatherfield'. Manchester United, the world's most famous football club, although founded in the Newton Heath district of the city in 1878, is now located in neighbouring Trafford Borough, from which the Old Trafford stadium name is derived. This Old Trafford stands half a mile from the Old Trafford cricket stadium, home to Lancashire Cricket Club.

It was in Castlefield in 1830 that the world's first locomotive hauled intercity passenger railway terminus opened at Liverpool Road Station: a name that no doubt raises ironic smiles in that rival city 30 miles to the west. This renders the world's first railway station Georgian, a point grasped easily when viewing the elegant frontage (Figure 1.7). Sadly, Liverpudlians demolished their historic terminus, Crown Street Station, in 1973. All manner of goods and produce moved through the elaborate Castlefield transport interchange, including: grain, sugar, wheat, potatoes, timber, chemicals and slate, but above all raw cotton and finished textiles.

Castlefield can appear mystifying at times. Certainly the dawn mist that enveloped the area in Roman times would have made it seem so and still does today (Figure 1.8). Even the etymology of the name

Figure 1.7: The Elegant Georgian Façade of Liverpool Road Railway Station (photo © Michael Leary-Owhin)

is uncertain and certainly misleading. It is thought by some to be a contraction of Castle-in-the-field. Whitaker (1771: 8–10) does not claim that he coined the name but he does claim there was an Anglo-Saxon castle on the site. Although Whitaker was a dedicated, knowledgeable scholar, he was at times fanciful and idiosyncratic in his assertions and

Figure 1.8: A misty, murky Castlefield dawn (photo © Michael Leary-Owhin)

his castle claim is rejected firmly by today's scholars (Nevell 2008: 17). Nevertheless, the evocative name remains. Four behemoth viaducts were built in the 19th century and came to dominate Castlefield, becoming blackened with coal soot; they appeared threatening before being renovated in the 1980s and perceived as historically important (Figure 1.9). Britain's first canal warehouse, with its iconic barge holes straddling the Bridgewater Canal, was demolished in 1960. Later, the remnants became the object of heritage adoration.

Structure of the book

The following six empirical research chapters consist of three pairs focused on production of space historicised investigations for each of the case study cities. Each chapter overlaps the other chronologically as they present different perspectives of concurrent times. For each city what is called the dominant academic narrative is outlined and used as a point of departure for the ensuing research. All six chapters reveal elided histories which, rather than overthrow entirely the dominant academic narratives, serve to enrich our understandings of the production of space at the practical and theoretical levels. Each chapter provides empirical evidence to support the argument that the production and enhancement of urban public space is integral to the reimagining and post-industrial transformation of the city. Through careful original research, new knowledge is constructed on several

Figure 1.9: One of Castlefield's behemoth railway viaducts (photo © Michael Leary-Owhin)

levels, including the roles played in the unfolding production of space dramas by characters absent from the dominant narratives.

Chapter Two provides a brief historical context for Gastown, explaining how the threat of demolition galvanised historic preservation society interests into initiating the Gastown heritage revalorisation project, through the accretion of a spatial coalition of diverse interests. The chapter documents empirically how understandings and representations of Gastown shifted in the late 1960s and early 1970s from those infused with a modernist planning ideology of demolition and clean sweep redevelopment to heritage inspired representations and post–industrial reimagining. A key beautification and revitalisation report produced and funded by a coalition of interests is shown to stimulate Vancouver's nascent liveability agenda, identifying specific locations for the production of new and enhanced public space. Chapter Three presents empirically informed analyses of a number of new public space projects initiated first as counter–projects and counter–spaces by a variety of community and historic preservation society interests. It demonstrates further that, Vancouver City Council (VCC) proved receptive to the counter–projects and provided an overarching strategic spatial framework within which the projects on the ground were devised and implemented. This chapter also introduces the importance of the social animation of public space, whether through politicised collective action or ludic enjoyment. Changing representations of space through time are shown to have implications for spatial practice on the ground, based on differences in the way social behaviour in public space is understood and interpreted.

Chapter Four shifts the geographical focus to downtown Lowell, Massachusetts, explaining the significance of the transformation of federal and local urban policy imperatives from demolition based urban renewal to heritage preservation, and sensitivity to history, and the valorisation of ethnic diversity. Reproducing the approach of the previous chapter, a number of public space interventions, initially emerging as counter-projects, conceived and delivered by a range of different spatial coalitions are analysed. The chapter also seeks to revisit the significance of Lowell City Council's (LCC) contribution to the heritage-led reimagining of urban space in the city. Having been elided in the dominant academic literature of Lowell's heritage-led revival, the importance of the Lowell Heritage State Park for the establishment of the Lowell National Historical Park (LNHP) is explained. In Chapter Five new research perspectives on the creation of LNHP are established, through the device of a truncated discourse analysis of a presidential statement in 1978. The chapter foregrounds contests over the naming of urban space and pinpoints relevant implications for the production of post-industrial Lowell. A range of alternative actors and agencies outside the dominant narrative emerge in the empirical research, which aims to describe and explain a number of major public space projects found once again to be conceived and delivered by a diverse coalition of interests. Another concept privileged in this chapter is that of indeterminate public space, which I argue encompasses the potential for the production of differential space.

Chapter Six documents the emergence of the Liverpool Road Railway Station counter-project in Castlefield, Manchester, and the alternative representations of urban space promulgated by the historic preservation societies that underpinned it. Evidence is presented of the contested nature of historic space within the public sector and the movement of the counter-project into the policy mainstream is specified. Several unlikely and surprising coalitions of interests, which struggled to assert the revalorisation of historic industrial urban space, are uncovered through archival and interview research. Castlefield's emergence from relative obscurity is illuminated using a variety of original data sources. Urban space in Castlefield is revealed to contradict any simplified public–private binary divide.

Chapter Seven takes a fresh look, through a Lefebvrian spatial lens, at the intervention in Castlefield of the Central Manchester Development Corporation (CMDC). The chapter reveals for the first time the struggle within government to establish the urban development corporations based as they were on a radical, neoliberal infused reading of urban problems and appropriate governance structures. Intertextuality emerges as a key concept for understanding how official representations of space were influenced by the decade long spatial struggles of the historic preservation societies described in the preceding chapter. Official conceptualisations of public space are exposed as vital for the strategic plans of CMDC, particularly the creation of new bridges and civic public spaces. These spaces and a strong civic ethos are shown to be decisive for creating potentials for the production of differential space. Chapters Six and Seven are based on my previous work: Leary, M. E. (2013) A Lefebvrian analysis of the production of glorious, gruesome public space in Manchester, *Progress in Planning*, 85, pp 1–52. (permission received from Elsevier). In addition these chapters incorporate further original research.

The last of the seven case study research chapters constitutes the empirical and theoretical culmination of the book in two important ways. First, Chapter Eight attempts to construct a meaningful association between differential space and the right to the city. In so doing it seeks to both flesh out Lefebvre's sketchy differential space idea and contextualise it in the contingencies of the 21st century. Second, it is the visual culmination of the book delivered through a series of images that add an analytical twist to the explication of differential space. This chapter differs from the previous six in that research material from all three case study cities is presented in order to demonstrate the divergent origins and various kinds of differential space, from ludic to politicised-democratic, that are produced through similar processes involving civil society engagement, urban policy, planning and regeneration. The chapter explains how understandings of differential space must be embedded within the historical moments in which such space is produced. Chapter Nine allows space for empirical and theoretical reflection on the key findings of the research. Important similarities and differences in the case study empirical revelations are emphasised. Methodological conclusions allow the assessment of a Lefebvrian approach to understanding the creation of urban public space and post-industrial transformation. In concluding, the book returns to the importance of urban public space for convivial urbanity and for democratic cohesion in relatively open and tolerant societies. Differential space is seen and comprehended in a new light.

TWO

Vancouver:
(Re)presenting urban space

... the production of a new space commensurate with the capacities of the productive forces (technology and knowledge) can never be brought about by any particular social group; it must of necessity result from relationships between groups – between classes or factors of classes ... Only a political party can impose standards for the recruitment of members and so achieve ideological unity. It is precisely the diversity of the coalitions just mentioned that explains the suspicious attitude of the traditional political parties towards the issues of space. (Lefebvre 1991: 380–1)

The objects of the past retain importance only in respect to the joy and instruction that they offer to the present. And we have no choice but to reinterpret them in terms of our contemporary understanding. However, there must be something there to reinterpret. Wipe the event away so that it leaves no mark and it can never be recalled ... Like a doll-faced, well-dressed, painted lady who has carefully and foolishly obscured the traces of the richness of her life, the city too without its history, may present a face that flashes prettily at first, but then seems vapid, dull and ultimately disappointing. (Birmingham and Wood et al 1969: 7)

Introduction

It was Lefebvre's assertions about the necessary role of spatial coalitions in the production of space that provided direction for an important stream of the empirical research documented in this book. Therefore, uncovering the history of those coalitions became a major imperative for the research. Another kind of history is shown in this and the subsequent empirical research chapters to be fundamental to understanding the production of urban space. Eloquently, but with perceptive precision Birmingham and Wood et al (1969) point to the importance of material city history and its contemporary interpretation in ways which Lefebvre would have perhaps found satisfactory. Vancouver needs scant further introduction. Since the dawn of the 21st century, the city has been deluged by superlatives from urbanists, city planners, politicians and millions of ordinary visitors. Depending on the particular proclivities of the writer, Vancouver is fabulously: sustainable, cultured, friendly, hip, trendy and socially equitable (Brunet-Jailly 2008). It is a place of pilgrimage, a dream city, more exotic than its west coast neighbour Seattle: a veritable utopia it seems. Sandwiched between swimmable sea and touchable mountains, its setting draws as much praise as the city itself. Its high density, public transport lubricated, family friendly form imposed through a series of city development plans is marketed as a model for aspiring city planners in North America and the rest of the world. Above all, Vancouver is the 'liveable' city. And even rumblings about it being Canada's unhappiest city (Slattery 2015) are unlikely to stem the adulation

How did an isolated, tough, masculine, nondescript logging camp with one rough and ready pub become transformed into an iconic world city? How did the neighbourhood 'written off in the early 1960s as a slum' that should be 'cleared to make room for a highway', become one filled with 'high-end restaurants, condominiums, offices, modern furniture' and men's clothing stores so 'hiply minimal that it makes a person's teeth hurt' (Bula 2011). A couple of chapters in this type of book cannot provide definitive answers to all these questions. The more modest objectives are to explore the recent histories of the production of urban space and ramifications for city transformation in that most iconic of Vancouver neighbourhoods, Gastown.

Startling growth in the late 19th and early 20th centuries, fuelled by abundant natural resources, its status as the terminus for the Canadian Pacific Railway and a huge port certainly helped to mould Vancouver into the economic powerhouse of British Columbia (BC) and Western Canada. However, by the time post-WW2 decline set in, exacerbated by industrial restructuring in the 1960s, Vancouver was drawing no plaudits from the world's academics, journalists and urban tourists. It is this post-war transformation from a fairly quiet run of the mill Canadian city to a fêted 'model of contemporary city-making' (Berelowitz 2010: 1) with which this chapter is most concerned. For many visitors to Vancouver, especially those who come for the International Jazz Festival, Gastown, Stanley Park, the sea wall and False Creek are Vancouver. Given the pre-eminence of the production of space ideas for understanding heritage-led revitalisation, it is surprising that no archival-based empirical research has explored Gastown's history in the vital decade from the late 1960s.

Vancouver's post-WW2 resurgence is well documented and a dominant explanatory narrative has emerged in recent years. That narrative usually starts with a revitalisation timeline from 1972, the year that a new radical political party gained control of Vancouver City Council (VCC). Liveability – understood as sustainable high density, people before property, respect for the past, the creation of inclusive public space, privileging of pedestrians over cars and a genuine ethos of social equity – is seen as the hallmark of the new era that created the wonderful city we can experience today. Credit for the city's startling transformation is usually given to local politicians and their professional planning staff. The dominant resurgence narrative is based on considerable credible research and has much to commend it. Certainly, it is not my intention to denigrate the excellent work of a variety of academics and journalists or indeed the integrity and effectiveness of the city's post-1972 politicians and planners.

While acknowledging the importance of these contributions to the academic debate and the building of a picture of Vancouver's recent history, in this chapter I draw attention to a range of actors, agencies and organisations largely ignored in the telling of the Vancouver transformation story. I argue that the production of urban public space was integral to that transformation. Furthermore, I present empirical evidence to support *and* contest Hutton's (2004: 1954) contention that 'public policy interventions have been important (and in some respects decisive) agents of transformation' in Gastown. In this and the next chapter I also pursue empirical investigations inspired by Berelowitz (2010: 1) and his proposition that Vancouver, the poster child of urbanism in North America deployed 'locally grown strategies' to reinvent itself and in the process instigated 'something curious, perhaps even miraculous'. Clearly, 1972 was a pivotal year, but I argue that the seismic urban planning shift from 1972 was made possible by the production of space of several years earlier.

Pre-1972 and a disparate coalition

Obviously 1972 was a cardinal moment in the city's history. It was the year that an emerging liberal/social democratic political force The Electors Action Movement (TEAM) wrested city government from the continuous 37 year control of the conservative, pro-development, business orientated, and ironically named Non-Partisan Association (NPA). Vancouver's political administration was reorganised with power being dispersed from the elitist three man Board of Administration to the mayor, city manager, departmental directors and newly established committees. Vancouver's eminent academic David Ley pointed to the year 1972 as ushering in a new era as TEAM politicians masterminded Vancouver's transition towards a service orientated post-industrial city:

> This group founded an urban reform party which assumed political power in 1972. They challenged the commitment to growth, boosterism, and the city efficient [sic] held by former civic administrations, presenting in its place a program of apparently humane, socially progressive, and aesthetic urban development. (Ley 1980: 238)

Bannerman (1974: 34), writing from a journalistic perspective, is also of the view that it was not until TEAM gained power in 1972 and Art Phillips became mayor that Gastown would 'no longer be the whipping post of civic authorities'. He argues that the relationship between Gastown and officialdom has been difficult at best. When Gastown was not being ignored, VCC was criticised for being ponderously slow or misdirected. From the beginning of this shift to post-industrial heritage preservation, local politicians were reluctant to become involved with the 'strange cluster of eager businessmen in Gastown' (Bannerman 1974: 25). Undoubtedly, property developers and businesses in Gastown did in the 1960s carry out do-it-yourself façade improvement and renovation of neglected historic buildings for at least a decade before the city formulated its restoration strategy. Bannerman characterises the pre-1972 decade as 'a struggle between youthful, innovative, and visionary forces of historical preservation' and 'the exhausted and outdated forces of the civic modernizers' (in Sommers 2001: 146). While informative, this oversimplification was perhaps influenced by Bannerman's close friendship with several of the young property development innovators, especially Larry Killam, one of Gastown's first heritage inspired property developers in the 1960s (Bula 2011). What emerges from the analysis of original archival data presented in this chapter is a more complex reality.

Punter (2003) supports the post-1972 dominant academic narrative but highlights also the significance of the appointment of Englishman Ray Spaxman as director of city planning. Spaxman's politically aware professional leadership enabled TEAM's new political priorities to be made manifest in a range of planning policies and concrete initiatives on the ground. Hutton (2004: 1954) contributes similar affirmations, arguing that post-1972 public policy and urban planning were important for Vancouver's post-industrial makeover. He sets them alongside processes of industrial restructuring and globalisation in their impact on the city in the period 1972 to the mid-1980s. In similar vein, Grant (2009: 359) foregrounds TEAM's liveability agenda and the 'significant step to the left' engendered by its electoral victory in 1972. Along with this, Grant sees TEAM's hiring of Spaxman in 1973, who began to overturn conventional planning wisdom, as a decisive moment. In addition to Spaxman, Grant gives credit to Larry Beasley and Ann McAfee, two planners hired in the formative stages of Spaxman's 15 year tenure, noting also the importance of Expo 86 for creating a more pedestrian and cyclist friendly city and the residential growth downtown. To his credit, Beasley (in Grant 2009) does acknowledge the contribution of Vancouver's various communities to the city's transformation.

The NPA is given short shrift by Punter (2003: 18) for whom it merely promoted business interests and downtown commercial development. He is scathing about long serving NPA city manager Gerald Sutton Brown for his support of massive road building proposals and major downtown redevelopment, made all the more unpalatable by his wielding of 'power verging on the absolute' (Punter 2003: 18). Brown, along with the director of planning, William Graham were sacked summarily by TEAM in 1972. Punter (2003: 24) is also critical of the NPA mayor, Tom Campbell, for orchestrating secret land deals and his notorious comment that major freeway proposals were being sabotaged by Maoists, Communist pinkies and 'hamburgers', that is people without a university degree. A note of ambiguity enters Punter's analysis when he accepts there *were* some VCC heritage-led beautification schemes pre-1972 but portrays them as a mixed blessing and condemns them for cleaving the historic district from mainstream city life and erasing most of its genuine urban character (Punter 2003: 52). Ray Spaxman during a research interview reproduced the post-1972 narrative:

> 'TEAM was the election action movement and it was clearly quite a radical move from the old politics to the new politics. It was led by a professor up at UBC by the name of Walter Hardwick, a major character in the evolution of this city. So Walter was on the council. They had a new bright very energetic finance orientated mayor. TEAM swept into power with only one member of the opposition in office when they came to power in 1972. They changed everything. The first thing they changed was, if you look at what they wanted to do in the archive, it ranged from everything like openness, transparency

involving people, decentralising and a very human attitude to design and architecture. There were major, major shifts and I was fortunate enough to be approached by them to leave Toronto and come here.' (Spaxman 2012, research interview)

To his credit he also recalls that before he went to Vancouver, Gastown's revitalisation was already underway, "maybe through local improvement schemes" that were "refinishing the street, putting cobbles in". There was a "very interesting street design done by a well-known local architectural firm". He concluded that "everything was not bad then obviously".

The massive 1960s downtown redevelopment and elevated freeway proposals supported for years by the NPA were part of a gigantic scheme – Marathon Development, better known as Project 200 – initiated by a consortium of major private sector entities: Marathon Realty, the development arm of Canadian Pacific Railroad company; Woodward Stores, the Department Store's holding company and Grosvenor-Laing, a British construction company. The primary purpose of the consortium was to promote Project 200 and the Hastings Street commercial corridor which in the late 1960s was still regarded as a lively, popular downtown shopping destination. In addition a group based on a loose coalition of business interests, the Improvement of Downtown East Area Society (IDEAS) materialised. Despite the altruistic sounding name, it was a property development, big business pressure group formed in 1966. Its single focus on Project 200 and Hastings Street is reflected clearly in the makeup of the all-male board of directors:

- President D. Lesser, LeRoy Jewellers
  - R. N. Bligh, Woodward Stores Ltd
  - J. Segal, Commercial Distributors
  - A. F. Joplin, Marathon Realty company

- Prominent Directors
  - J. F. Harris, Canadian Imperial Bank of Commerce
  - J. Cohen, Army and Navy
  - J. Hecht, Equitable Real Estate Corp

Consisting of 14 modernist high-rise waterfront office blocks and a huge elevated road, Project 200 would have carved through Gastown, Chinatown, DTES and the waterfront. It would have sliced Gastown in half thereby threatening its historic integrity. It proved highly divisive. The gargantuan proposals were hugely unpopular with a swathe of Vancouverites, including many businesses in Gastown, Chinatown, Strathcona and downtown (Gutstein 1975). Due to concerted opposition supported by the rise of TEAM, Project 200 was abandoned in 1971 (albeit that a few projects went ahead). With hindsight, there is no doubt that Project 200 would have been disastrous for Vancouver and in supporting this ill-fated scheme the reputations and credibility of the NPA, Tom Campbell, Sutton Brown and William Graham were certainly tarnished beyond repair.

Evident failings of the NPA regime in the years prior to 1972 do not mean it played no positive part in Vancouver's transition to the liveability agenda informed to some extent by respect for historic environments. In addition, this chapter explains, drawing on archival data, the important roles played by: small scale local businesses and trade associations, community groups, historic preservation groups and the federal and BC provincial governments. To date, the literature has ignored or downplayed the contribution of these actors and agencies. Finally, I argue that a coalition of interests, other than city planners and politicians, first conceived of Gastown, Chinatown and DTES as a coherent whole, where heritage and commercial opportunities had to be considered simultaneously with the longstanding serious social problems. The following sections of this chapter reveal with robust precision the spatial interactions between 1968–72 which triggered the first significant reimagining of post-industrial Vancouver in the city's oldest neighbourhood and point of origin – Gastown. Analysis and discussion based on archival data highlight the importance for the production of urban space of: the Chinatown community, the Vancouver Community Arts Council (VCAC), the Alhambra Hotel project, a 1960s restoration report and senior government interventions. These initiatives are regarded here as Lefebvrian counter-projects, which produced counter-space based on alternative representations of space.

Gastown meets Chinatown and Downtown Eastside

Gutstein (1975: 139) is surely correct when he says that when it comes to day-to-day and long term decisions about Vancouver, 'power lies in the hands of the 10 aldermen and the Mayor'. Add in powerful bureaucrats such as Sutton Brown, and the close family and friendship connections between corporate commercial interests and Vancouver's politicians, and it would be easy to surmise that until the 1970s the interests of small local business and communities were sidelined. Despite his condemnation of the big business/political nexus in Vancouver, Gutstein (1975: 152) does acknowledge that 'it hasn't been all bad' and he touches on several citizen victories in fights against City Hall before providing more detailed accounts of the successful Chinatown resistance to Project 200 and Strathcona urban renewal proposals. There is an extensive urban renewal literature (see initially Carmona 1999; Klemek 2012). Gutstein also provides insightful accounts of political and bureaucratic machinations during the rise of TEAM over 1968–74. It is all the more surprising, therefore, that he does not mention community campaigns calling for historic conservation or the creation and enhancement of public space in Gastown, Chinatown and DTES.

Hasson and Ley (1997) also provide an account of the Chinatown residents' successful opposition to the 1960s Project 200 proposals and document the contested Chinatown beautification programmes. They argue that it was the VCC in 1969 that started the promotion of 'ethnic neighbourhoods' and historic preservation by commissioning a consultants' preservation study regarding Vancouver's old Granville Townsite. Hasson and Ley argue that in 1972 Chinese property owners were dismayed at the prospect of having to contribute financially to Chinatown beautification schemes. According to Hasson and Ley the Chinese community, particularly property owners, always reacted rather negatively to VCC heritage preservation proposals. There is no hint from Hasson and Ley that Chinatown businesses or community interest groups were ever proactive regarding the preservation of aspects of Chinatown's physical identity. Similarly, Anderson (1991: 202) in her otherwise excellent work claims that it was only in 1967, when the prestigious Vancouver architectural firm Birmingham and Wood joined forces with the Chinatown protesters, that the Project 200 threat to the Chinatown's heritage and character was articulated. One Birmingham and Wood architect, Larry Killam, said 'it would be a tragic blunder if the City demolishes half of Chinatown for a freeway' (in Anderson 1991: 205). VCAC's president also opposed the proposals that would see a road 'slashing through the old city':

> ... we would again like to stress that it is our unchanging belief that massive changes in the area, resulting from major transportation developments, would damage the area beyond its potential for restoration into the beautiful and exciting precinct envisaged in the <u>Restoration Report</u> ...
> (Low-Beer 1969, underline in original)

Anderson (1991: 221) also notes the importance of a city-commissioned restoration report by Birmingham and Wood et al dated 1969 which called for the preservation and improvement of Chinatown, rather than its destruction. A detailed discussion is presented later of this seminal production of space moment, including its complex provenance.

In staking out the post-1972 origin of Vancouver's transformation, Punter (2003) also highlights the same consultants' report. Punter though dates the report 1972 rather than 1969. One would not expect an experienced academic of Punter's stature to have simply made a mistake but the confusion arises mainly because the report is not dated. Research at the city archives reveals the explanation for this puzzle. Both dates are correct. In fact two restoration reports exist in the city archives; both have the same title, *Restoration Report: A Case for Renewed Life in the Old City*. 'Old city' meant the three areas of Gastown, Chinatown and DTES. One of the reports is given as 'c1968' in the archival catalogue but my research dates it definitively as 1969. The second report has an additional three pages of introductory background and was published in 1972, due to the high demand. This three year discrepancy might seem trivial, but because it straddles the political transition from the NPA to TEAM it is imperative the date and provenance of this report are documented accurately. This report is central to the post-industrial reimagining of the city for a number of different reasons, not least because it signalled the intent of the NPA administration to pursue a revised approach to planning, urban design and economic revitalisation based on a heritage and culture-led restoration strategy. Given its importance in the Gastown production of space history, it is discussed in detail later in this chapter.

Instead of the Chinese communities being merely passive recipients of historic preservation and beautification initiatives emanating from VCC, the archival data reveal a different picture. In 1968 two Chinatown interest groups, Business Community of Chinatown (BCC) and the Chinatown Improvement Group (CTIG), took the initiative regarding the potential heritage-led beautification of Chinatown:

> We have arranged for the services of Birmingham and Wood, Architects and Planners as our consultants. We have space in the area that we are willing to commit for the duration of the project as a project office ... We are ready to go, and urge that the Council give us a green light on August 27th. (BCC 1968)

The point here is that it was not just positive *ideas* for a Chinatown preservation programme that were being proposed. Of greater significance is the decision of the Chinatown groups to appoint a well-respected Vancouver architectural practice to carry out a preservation study.

By January 1969 VCC had not responded positively to this Chinatown initiative. Another letter was sent to VCC by CTIG reiterating that Birmingham and Wood had been appointed as their historic preservation and restoration design consultants. What is striking here is how the Chinatown communities appreciated their efforts would require a long term commitment which necessitated coordinated collaboration with other preservation and development interests. The threat of the Project 200 freeway was clearly the initial spur but eventually a historic preservation coalition emerged:

> Our consultants have also been selected by the property owners of Vancouver's Maple Tree Square and Townsite areas to represent them as well and have been working with the IDEAS organization so that they can come up with a co-ordinated scheme for these potentially exciting parts of the city. As the magnitude of this task is very large they have offered to work in consortium with Hopping Kovach and Ginnel and a management and public relations specialists to be named later. (CTIG 1969)

It was not just coordination and collaboration in an emerging coalition that was suggested. CTIG understood that Chinatown should not be considered in isolation from Vancouver's other neighbouring historic areas, Gastown, and DTES:

> We are in complete agreement with this arrangement and further suggest that our consultants be in a position to coordinate the efforts of the IDEAS organisation on Hastings Street, who have named their consultant. These three areas must be considered in a coordinated effort ... (CTIG 1969)

Unfortunately, by 1970, VCC had still not given the go ahead for historic restoration in Chinatown and the impatience of CTIG members was growing. They hoped the implementation of the Report would 'correspondingly, speed up' (Mah and Chang 1970). Among other things, they wanted VCC to implement one of the Report's recommendations and set up an Academic Consultant Team to advise them on the complexities of historic restoration. It becomes apparent then that residents and businesses in Chinatown did not procrastinate while assuming others would act on their behalf.

It is also apparent that far from being parochial, Chinatown groups appreciated the importance of seeking support beyond Vancouver city limits. Several years before they visited Taipei in the hope of securing support for construction of a Chinese style Pagoda and Gate/Arch, but the projects had stalled. Thus they urged VCC to look into all possibilities to secure assistance from the BC government and Vancouver's centennial programme. Ironically, a reason the Chinese Pagoda and Gate had stalled was because of the uncertainty regarding the future of Chinatown created by Project 200 proposals. Before the *Restoration Report* was published, the government of the Republic of China (Taiwan) agreed to support the Pender/Carrall Street Pagoda and Gate (Figure 2.1) projects but it is interesting to note that the Consul General also supported Vancouver's preservation efforts, in principle because, 'it is this type of cooperation and good work that can further the understanding between our two countries' (Peng 1969).

Gastown: a mayoral walking tour

There is convincing archival evidence that historic preservation studies and projects in Vancouver were *initiated* by community interest groups

Figure 2.1: Chinatown Arch, Vancouver (photo © Michael Leary-Owhin)

other than in Chinatown, several years before TEAM came to power in 1972 and before the *Restoration Report*. It is well known that VCAC took an active role in promoting historic preservation in the 1960s, especially in Gastown. In order to draw attention to Gastown's historic value, VCAC organised a walking tour on Sunday 22 September 1968. With demolition threats looming, the objectives of the tour were: to have one last look at the buildings due to be demolished by Project 200; consolidate popular and official opposition to future freeway threats; and stimulate interest and active support for Gastown's historic preservation. The leader of the tour, Mrs Evelyn MacKechnie, invited Mayor Tom Campbell to attend. This was a mayor infamous for his contempt for community activists but, somewhat surprisingly, Campbell accepted. About 500 people attended the walk that day, which was a remarkable turnout considering that historic value of Gastown was not generally acknowledged in the city and Project 200 plans for the massive elevated road to rip through the area were still alive. The impressive turnout was remarkable because it was one of those typically miserable, wet, unpleasant Vancouver days. In thanking the mayor for his attendance, MacKechnie (1968) enthused:

> Indeed it was our pleasure and our privilege to have had you and Mrs. Campbell join our Sunday afternoon tour of "Gastown". The amazing response has been hard to believe. Letters and phone calls are still pouring in from a large cross-section of citizens, offering congratulations as well as assistance with our future plans.

MacKechnie's handwritten letter is shown in Figure 2.2. After the tour Campbell pledged his support for the restoration and rehabilitation of Gastown. It was his zeal for Gastown heritage that galvanised the growing patronage of VCC over the next few years until 1972.

Gastown tours had been arranged before, but never on this scale. And this tour was not a one-off event. Subsequently, VCAC held a series of tours, educational events and slide and film shows especially for VCC aldermen and professional staff. There were no precedents of any great merit for historic restoration and rehabilitation in Vancouver so VCAC looked further afield for inspiration. One of the films they showed documented a successful historic building rehabilitation scheme in Magdalen Street, Norwich, England, orchestrated by the not-for-profit Civic Trust historic preservation society. This scheme was completed in 1959 and VCAC had been showing the film in Vancouver since 1962. It had a big impact. One of the outcomes was

Figure 2.2: First page of letter from Mrs Evelyn MacKechnie to Mayor Tom Campbell (Mrs MacKechnie's address redacted by author, thanks to VCA)

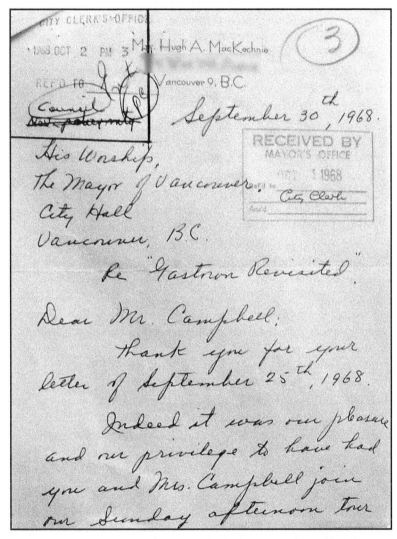

that a group of Gastown property owners came together to form the Townsite Association with the aims of rehabilitating some of Gastown's historic buildings and encouraging independent arts and craft shops and cafés to establish in the area (Astles 1972: 114). Townsite was a common name for Gastown in the 1960s and this Association should not be confused with the Town Group Ltd, Larry Killam's property development company. In 1962 the Townsite Association began to offer slideshows and guided tours to stimulate interest in and appreciation of Gastown's historic qualities. These were certainly the first industrial heritage guided tours in the three case study cities documented in this book, and some of the earliest in North America and Europe.

A measure of the role and influence of VCAC can be gleaned from comments made by the chairman of a city advisory body. Vancouver Town Planning Commission was established by VCC in 1926 and originally tasked with devising a city development plan but from 1960 its scope was reduced to advising VCC on planning matters. In a letter to the mayor, chairman Mr J. M. Lecky confirmed that:

> The Town Planning Commission was most interested in the recent walking tour of the Old Townsite area [Gastown] arranged by the Community Arts Council. Over 500 enthusiastic members of the public took part, which would indicate that the citizens are interested in the city's history and wish to preserve the area ... the Commission endorsed the following resolution: ... That the Community Arts Council be commended for its initiative in bringing this area to the attention of the citizens. (Lecky 1968)

This forthright praise for VCAC provides an early indication of the Gastown heritage restoration counter-project moving into the official mainstream. It was not only a concern to see individual historic buildings rehabilitated that was displayed by VCAC. In a thoughtful and profound letter to the mayor, the VCAC president provided a strategic rationale for the city to make a firm commitment to historic preservation. The letter demonstrates the emergence of alternative representations of space and a heritage valorisation counter-project. It is in fact a heritage preservation manifesto spelt out before TEAM embarked on its preservation and rehabilitation programmes:

> It is our belief that the preservation of Vancouver's historic area will play an important role in the city's future ... Vancouver has the potential to become one of the world's executive cities where the amenities of site and climate provide profound inducements to development of the city as a place of world importance in the post-industrial age now upon us. Within this context, the nature of the urban fabric become [sic] of supreme importance and the rich endowment of nature must be enhanced by a quality of urban development which will allow the city to compete as a world location for tourism... (Low-Beer 1969)

Project 200 and the eight-lane road proposals, through their immense scale and potentially devastating impacts, galvanised concerted opposition throughout Vancouver in campaigns well documented in the literature. However, important though this successful opposition was, it was largely reactive and negative in the sense that the opponents wanted to stop the proposals from happening. But in order for the post-industrial transformation based on heritage valorisation to occur, positive things must transpire through the deployment of real public and private sector resources. Such interventions constitute Lefebvre's spatial practice implemented through counter-projects.

Reinventing Alhambra: producing new public space

VCAC certainly played a leading role in the counter-project that reimagined a rather dilapidated and economically neglected Gastown as the premier built environment historic asset of the city. The historic valorisation of Gastown and the counter-representations of space they engendered had a powerful influence in instigating new understandings of the area's spatial meaning. Representations and ideas though can by themselves achieve little in the production of space as Lefebvre observed. It is spatial practice that makes a difference to the material city on the ground. At the time in 1968 when Evelyn MacKechnie was leading the mayor and 500 people around Gastown, four young developers were negotiating to acquire their first major historic building targeted for renovation and adaptive reuse – the Alhambra Hotel – located on a prime site at Maple Tree Square. The men were from prominent, well-to-do Vancouver families. Lawrence Killam, Howard Meakin, Ian Rogers and Robert Saunders formed the company Town Group Ltd and intended to convert the ground floor of the hotel to commercial with residential use on the upper floors. They bought the hotel, which had been a classic late 19th/early 20th century Gastown flophouse providing cheap single room accommodation for seasonal workers and unemployed men. Restoration took place in 1969 and the ground floor was let easily for boutiques, an art gallery and restaurant (Figure 2.3). Some of Gastown's old men and young hippies found low rent accommodation in the Alhambra's 32 renovated bedrooms. This was a primary demonstration project which helped establish the economic viability of historic building adaptive reuse in Gastown. Of more importance though was what Killam, who had emerged as the chairman of the company, did next. Originally the hotel had been built partly over an alley and later a building was erected in this alley. Killam demolished the building thereby creating a passageway from Maple

Figure 2.3: Alhambra Hotel Building, Gaolers Mews can be seen at the left hand side of the hotel (photo © Michael Leary-Owhin)

Tree Square that would eventually create a new public space linking Water Street, Carrall Street and Trounce-Blood Alley. He named it Gaoler's Mews believing the first city gaol was located there, although most local historians dispute this. VCC adopted the name officially in 1972. The Alhambra counter-project was a significant moment in the production of Gastown space in that, not only did it signal the heritage importance of historic buildings, it also privileged significant linkage between such buildings and the creation of public space.

A pre-1972 seminal moment: the *Restoration Report* 1969

Killham's Alhambra restoration project was one of a series of ad hoc rehabilitation initiatives by independent property owners in Gastown. Such projects were driven by historic preservation motivations but also by the search for profits. On their own they would not bring about a thorough post-industrial reimagining of Gastown. The importance of the *Restoration Report* for the post-industrial reimagining of Gastown and Vancouver should not be underestimated. It should be appreciated that it arrived when the massive modernist Project 200 was still supported strongly by the NPA dominated VCC. Often, the Report is cited as, Birmingham and Wood but because sections were written also by Hopping, Kovach & Grinnell, Design Consultants and Bing, Marr & Associates, Architects, it is cited here as Birmingham and Wood et al (1969). Although it is often claimed that VCC commissioned the Report (Anderson 1991; Punter 2003), it was in fact co-commissioned and funded jointly by the Townsite Committee (chaired by Larry Killam), Chinatown Improvement Group and IDEAS. And although he played no part in the report, the authors acknowledge the influence of urban designer Kevin Lynch (see Chapter Five).

Given the pivotal role IDEAS played in supporting Project 200 *and* historic restoration-led post-industrial transformation, it is strange that Guttsein (1975), Anderson (1991) and Punter (2003) do not mention it. Following prior approval by the other commissioning organisations, VCC in January 1968 gave final approval for what was known as the Stage 1 beautification studies. The following year the *Restoration Report* based on the Stage 1 studies was presented to VCC by the Director of Planning, Bill Graham. He provided a detailed summary of the approach and findings. Most notably, he outlined the relationship with Project 200 stating that 'the developers have indicated that the two can be complementary to each other' (Graham 1969); a view that with hindsight was wholly untenable. He noted the consultants' report recognised the existence of, 'difficult social problems in the area originally identified in "Downtown East Side", and more familiarly known as "Skid Road"'. Stage II was to prepare actual designs and implement beautification schemes in the three areas (discussed in Chapter Three).

The eclectic nature and differing priorities of the *Restoration Report's* commissioning bodies are reflected in the peculiar combination of views expressed, particularly regarding the potential harmony between the strong support for heritage preservation, and the promotion of the wholesale demolition and sweeping comprehensive redevelopment needed for Project 200. Old Townsite (Gastown) was regarded as complimentary to Hastings Street and Project 200, but it 'must be able to accommodate the itinerant population that now uses its indoor and outdoor rooms' (Birmingham and Wood et al 1969: 25). Although the concept of liveability was not mentioned expressly, it was certainly implied, given the stress placed inter alia on the importance of retaining the walkable character and pleasant public spaces. With strong advocacy for inclusive, democratic public space, 'for each person to participate and experience an urban life' (Birmingham and Wood et al 1969: 21), the emergence of a powerful strand of the pre-1972 liveability discourse is evident. There is resonance too with Lefebvre's ideas regarding the street, the right to the city and differential space.

Mostly the Report is a couched in staid professional language but at times the prose extolling the virtues of heritage preservation blossoms positively poetically:

> The city of Vancouver is only now beginning to mature. It still hovers on that fascinating threshold between naïve and reckless youth and the wonderful unfolding of its full adult potential. The city is at that stage where it still can choose to recognize the value and the beauty of its cultural inheritance. It has a very special and attractive human heritage, and though it has impetuously squandered some of it, and through ignorance and blindness has often pitifully neglected to take proper stock and care of its possessions, a substantial sum of them remain intact and only need to be revealed and cultivated to help Vancouver to refine and strengthen that character and personality which will make it great among great cities of the world. (Birmingham and Wood et al 1969: 7)

Such wonderfully powerful language (representations of space) was meant to inspire political and professional support for the cause. Another prominent feature of the attitude to historic preservation and its potential impacts on the city was the belief that the three historic areas must be treated as an integrated whole:

> It is within this precious piece of the city, encompassing Old Townsite; Hastings Street and Chinatown, that Vancouver has the very rare opportunity to achieve a wide range of exciting urban experiences. The harbour, the creek, the mountains, the new commercial project [Project 200] the historic Townsite, Hastings Street, (still Downtown to the majority of citizens), and the famous Chinatown – are all within short walking distances of each other; each is capable of enriching the other. (Birmingham and Wood et al 1969: 16)

When it came to making concrete suggestions for Gastown, the Report was adamant that the most significant space was the birthplace of the city, Maple Tree Square. An architectural artist's visual representation of how it might look after restoration shows high quality pedestrian friendly urban public space including brick paved surfaces, attractive trees and antique style globe street lights (Figure 2.4). In addition, attention focused on the close scale of the buildings, façades, streets and alleys which provided the area with a unique geometry. Throughout, the Report is unequivocal about the merits of heritage preservation *and* Project 200 in ways that, for the sake of compromise, are understandable but even at the time would have been extremely difficult to reconcile. It was however highly ambivalent about social problems faced in the heritage areas of Old Townsite (Gastown), Chinatown and by implication Hastings Street (DTES). At times a sensitive, caring approach is evident:

> It is a disturbing consequence that, as a declining area regains a new vitality, the transient and marginal population, having found support in such an area, are displaced. This population, a very visible but small proportion of our society, has not been understood and is largely unwanted. The old city is a living room, providing low-cost living, tolerance, companionship and anonymity. (Birmingham and Wood et al 1969: 28)

At other times a baleful attitude is taken to the social problems caused by the concentration of the elderly, poor and disadvantaged. A simple

Figure 2.4: Architectural artist's representation of how a beautified Maple Tree Square might look (Birmingham and Wood et al 1969: 33, thanks to VCA)

but Draconian solution was proposed, that of 'minimising the physical contact between shopper and the destitute' (Birmingham and Wood et al 1969: 37). One way to do this would be through the 'enforcement of existing bylaws' and the introduction of a detoxification centre to which street-dwelling alcoholics would be removed. It was felt that these measures would 'give immediate relief to the merchant and shopper' (Birmingham and Wood et al 1969: 39). Ironically, two years after the Report's publication, Maple Tree Square was brought to international attention not for the beautification scheme but for something entirely notorious – the 1971 Gastown riot. Paradoxically, this violent event helped stimulate the post-industrial trajectory of the city.

Reaction to the Report was overwhelmingly but not entirely favourable. A host of community groups, merchants and property organisations offered their fulsome praise including: the CTIG, VCAC, Gastown Merchants Association, Garden Club of Vancouver and the Architectural Institute of British Columbia. Speaking on behalf of the influential Townsite Committee, its chairman John W. Parker welcomed the Report and put on record his thanks to the city planners for their 'beneficial, encouraging, constructive and most appreciated' support (Parker 1970), sentiments which ran counter to the anti-city council rhetoric of Bannerman (1974). In the light of previous sporadic criticism of VCC for its tardy response to historic preservation issues by Gastown's property interests, Parker's praise is important and illustrates the variety of attitudes of the time. A number of delegations articulated their support for the Report in a series of VCC meetings in mid-1969. Mr D. Lesser (1969), President of IDEAS, said his organisation 'approve and heartily endorse' the Report. However, his statement is more of a diatribe than a reasoned response and continues in a tone that jars gratingly with the inclusive, democratic liveability rhetoric in much of the *Restoration Report*:

> For years we have suffered in this area [Hastings Street] from those unfortunates who have nowhere to go. This must not continue. We can harbour them no longer. With a beautified street and many renovations, the time has come when other facilities must be found elsewhere to house these people. We welcome strongly the Drunk Offenders Act ... We cannot have Pigeon [Pioneer] Square contaminated after it is beautified. We cannot have alcoholics, drug addicts, prostitutes and down and outs using one of our main thoroughfares for protection from the elements and to encourage their pilfering and molesting ...

Our eyes have been closed for too long. We can no longer push aside an acute problem which is a blight on a beautiful city. We do not have any miracle answers to this cancerous situation, but we will cooperate in any way possible in order to overcome it. (Lesser 1969)

Lesser seems not to notice the supreme irony of his closing comments when he says that members of IDEAS are proud of the part they have played in the beautification scheme 'which will benefit the whole of the City of Vancouver'.

Not everybody, however, endorsed the Report. Gerald Thomson, chairman of the Townsite Committee, reminded the mayor that for 20 years property owners in Gastown had been carrying out self-rehabilitation 'without civic input'. A comprehensive critique was levelled at the Report by two prominent Vancouver architects: Lawrence 'Chip' Barrett and James Wright. They stressed a number of technical defects regarding the poor use of statistics and the proposals to channel traffic to and from parking areas through pedestrian priority areas (the pedestrian alleyways). However, they reserve their most strident disparagement for the Report's failure to examine properly the potential beautification programme impacts on vulnerable citizens, and the shoddy treatment of serious social problems in the area. Barrett and Wright (1969) thought the proposals to be 'founded on little research' and as a result 'ambiguous, contradictory, superficial and generally misleading'. They challenge the representations in the 'The Argument' of the Report, which justifies beautification in the following order: cultural heritage, aesthetics and design, variety and diversity, distinctiveness of cities and tourism, arguing that:

If these are the priorities, where do the people of the area come into consideration ... Those elements that should concern us most – the very poor, the alcoholic, the criminal, the prostitute, the marginal and transient dwellers – these are only mentioned: "they could begin to find some resolution of their social problems in context with the new activities" the report states. One should ask how and where such resolution could occur. We are at a very low ebb when the tourist dollar and appearance replace base human requirements. (Barrett and Wright 1969)

Despite its good intentions, democratic liveability rhetoric and a desire to treat physical beautification and social problems in a holistic manner, the Report struggled to reconcile the competing demands of its varied commissioning bodies.

More than a city affair

Given the local business and community interests involved in commissioning the 1969 *Restoration Report*, it is not surprising that the focus was on particular historic areas and on possible city-wide powers and resources that could be brought to bear on heritage revitalisation efforts. Interestingly, there was no recommendation to seek a historic designation for the area; that would come from elsewhere. In affirming its support for the Report, VCAC urged VCC to declare Gastown a historic precinct so that future developments may be controlled (Low-Beer 1969). Bill Graham confirmed that, unfortunately, the city had 'no power to protect structures considered desirable for retention, other than by purchase' (Graham 1969). However, he indicated the BC government had an Archaeological and Historic Sites Protection Act 1960 which could regulate demolitions, development and alterations within any area designated by the Minister as a historic site.

Gaining provincial support for rundown Gastown would be a stiff challenge and a special committee of VCC was constituted to pursue the twin goals of historic designation *and* provincial funding. A delegation of VCC politicians and officers led by Alderman Edward Sweeney met with Dan Campbell BC Minister of Municipal Affairs, Wesley Black Member of the Legislative Assembly (MLA) and Herbert Capozzi MLA in December 1970. After hearing a strong presentation on the historic merits of Gastown, the Minister seemed well disposed to the historic area idea but he was less sanguine about funding which would be a more resistant nut to crack (Dan Campbell 1970). Tapping into a groundswell of support for historic preservation across North America, Gastown-Chinatown was formerly designated one provincial historical site in February 1971 under the 1960 Act. Nearly four decades later in July 2009 Jim Prentice, Canada's Environment Minister, announced the national designation of a Gastown only historic district.

Following concerted representations from VCC, the BC provincial government agreed in mid-1971 a beautification/restoration funding package to consist of $35,000 for the next five years but imposed a stringent condition. Only if this package was matched by funding from the federal government would provincial money be forthcoming. A convincing case would have to be put to the federal government, with no guarantee of success. Over the ensuing months VCC made intensive representations to the federal government. Interestingly, VCC hedged its bets with Mayor Campbell writing to Robert Andras, Minister of Urban Affairs and Housing, while Alderman Sweeney wrote to Ron Basford, Minister of Consumer and Corporate Affairs. Basford's response was less than encouraging. He advised that following criticisms of federal urban renewal schemes, no additional projects were being approved (Basford 1971). He was, however, interested in Gastown-Chinatown historic preservation and confirmed he would continue to seek alternative federal support.

In his brief to Robert Andras, Campbell noted that programmes of historic restoration would be considered for Maple Tree Square, Carrall Street, and Blood Alley but stressed that availability, 'of adequate funds is a critical consideration now facing the City' (Campbell 1971). Campbell requested $35,000 annually for five years towards the cost of rehabilitation projects, which would involve 'improvements of public areas, in some cases for the benefit of the community at large' and in other cases for the immediate area. Minister Andras was rather more optimistic suggesting in May a budget-swap deal, without being committed fully:

> If it were decided to reallocate to the Gastown/Chinatown preservation project $35,000 a year of federal funds for five years, for a total of $175,000 from the urban renewal funds available in British Columbia, I would be prepared to consider such a proposal. (Andras 1971)

Shortly after this the funding package was agreed formally. These public sector partnership funding arrangements became indispensable for a series of restoration and new public space projects in Gastown. Historic designation of Gastown by the BC government is mentioned frequently in the academic literature but this essential financial support for the city's historic restoration programme is barely acknowledged. Both $35,000 sources became of vital importance for one of the first and most iconic restoration-beautification projects in Gastown discussed later. News of the funding partnerships soon reached the Gastown Merchants' Association and the chairman expressed in blunt language his dissatisfaction with the slow progress of beautification schemes on the ground (Lefebvrian spatial practice):

> The recent expressed largess of the Provincial and Federal governments indicates to me that immediate action must be taken to obtain all the senior money available. Could the City of Vancouver not crash ahead with Gastown

Beautification Projects? Can't we get some action out of City Hall instead of the usual bickering and buck-passing? (Keate 1971)

This was not the only federal funding source which facilitated the preservation-improvement of Gastown and contributed to the production of new public space. Revealed in the next chapter is how, in providing a much larger tranche of cash, the federal government became embroiled in one of Vancouver's most contentious property scandals.

Conclusions

Over the last few decades Vancouver has become the subject of intense academic, journalistic and professional urban planning attention. A dominant academic narrative has been identified which privileges a post-1972 seismic shift ushering in the era of the liveable city. This chapter has revealed more complex production of space histories, which illustrate the importance of: the pre-1972 NPA regime, community groups, the not-for-profit sector and the private sector in the heritage-led reimagining of post-industrial Vancouver. Threats of historic building demolition in Gastown and Chinatown provoked a proactive response from community groups and property interests who formed a coalition with VCC to commission and fund jointly the single most important historic preservation treatise in Vancouver's history – the 1969 *Restoration Report*. It was this trenchant report with its cohesive commitment to historic preservation which galvanised politicians, professionals and community interests. It was both a strategic intervention concerned with whole areas but one also which pinpointed intelligently, historic spaces that would become vital to the future of Gastown, Chinatown and DTES. Its perspicacity and eloquence are testament to the literary accomplishments of the authors and we can only rue the day when such style faded from professional favour. Archival data analysed in this chapter throw light on the important but relatively unappreciated contribution of NPA Mayor Tom Campbell. He threw political weight behind the *Restoration Report*. His support was galvanised by the sensory experience of a Gastown walking tour organised by VCAC.

Private sector property interests are shown in this chapter to be concerned not solely with profit but also with historic preservation. Town Group's Alhambra Hotel restoration project was the first time newly emerging representations of space, that valorised culture and heritage combined with spatial practice to produce new urban public space which championed pedestrian mobility. It is surely no coincidence that the Town Group identified a property at Maple Tree Square, the place highlighted in the *Restoration Report* as the most historically important in Vancouver, for their first restoration project. It is evident that the strategic focus on areas, corridors and pedestrian routes in the Report infused it with a salience and durability which would have been lacking had there been an exclusive focus on individual buildings. However, the Report's authors looked inwards and concerned themselves solely with VCC powers and resources. Protective legislation and additional resources were essential if the richness of Vancouver's built heritage was not to be lost for ever. It was left to the VCAC to urge VCC to use its powers to value and protect Gastown for its historic importance. Lacking such legislative powers to protect the whole of Gastown, VCC's decision to petition the BC government to declare Gastown-Chinatown a historic site under their legislation was, with hindsight, a seminal moment in the pre-1972 struggle to reimagine Gastown through the lens of post-industrial heritage valorisation. Of equal importance, but largely ignored in previous research, is the five year tranche of beautification monies funnelled to Vancouver by the provincial and federal governments. How those resources and others were deployed in the pre-1972 production of Gastown space is elucidated in the next chapter.

THREE

Vancouver: Producing urban public space and city transformation

Later, however, perhaps towards the end of the period of accelerated growth, these same countries are liable to discover how [historic] spaces may be pressed into the service of cultural consumption, of 'culture itself', and of the tourism and the leisure industries with their almost limitless prospects. (Lefebvre 1991: 360)

The re-discovery of the street as a shaping element in the urban fabric – capable of giving joy and meaning rather than merely providing a right-of-way for the circulation of people and things – was a hard lesson for the city to learn ... As a result, the streets of Gastown and the related open spaces of Maple Tree Square and Blood Alley became a primary focus of the revitalization process. The proper design of the street and its furnishings became as important as the buildings defining them. (Parker in Vancouver City Planning Department c1978)

Introduction

Far from remaining trapped in the past, history has a knack of influencing and shaping the present. In Vancouver the presence in the late 1960s of cheap, long-stay hotels, dating from the late 19th century, occupied predominantly by single marginalised men, was still a notable feature of Gastown and DTES. In this sense the two places merged into each other and at their margins became indistinguishable. Many of these hotels suffered gravely from lack of maintenance by the 1960s. The westward trajectory of downtown functions had left commercial buildings crumbling, empty or underused and pushed Gastown into political obscurity. In the mid-1960s massive modernist redevelopment Project 200 proposals called for the bulldozer to flatten much of Gastown to make way for an elevated freeway, offices and apartments.

Such redevelopment would surely have confirmed Birmingham and Wood's worst fears and destroyed significant traces of the richness of Vancouver's heritage. It is apparent that the authors of the *Restoration Report* (Birmingham and Wood et al 1969) were acutely aware of the integral nature of Gastown, Chinatown and DTES, a theme pursued in this chapter.

Lefebvre's astute observation mentioned earlier about historic space and its relationship with cultural consumption and tourism has great pertinence for the examples discussed later, as Vancouver entered the era of post-industrial spatial production through projects and counter-projects on the ground. Allen Parker was one of Vancouver's most prominent and influential urban planners and his words quoted earlier, mirror uncannily Lefebvre's cogitations on the production of space and the social importance of the street. From the provincial and federal involvement and strategic historic preservation concerns of the previous chapter, this chapter turns to specific Gastown and DTES public space projects: 1) the Stanley and New Fountain Hotels; 2) Blood Alley Square; 3) Maple Tree Square; and 4) Carrall Street Greenway. In addition, the chapter reveals new insights regarding the controversial replication of heritage assets.

Two hotels, a scandal and a contested mortgage

The 1920s Chicago School of urban sociology provided fulsome empirical research data and analyses of urban form and growth which still resonate today. Rather like Vancouver, early Chicago was a place of hard masculine work and cheap accommodation. Robert E. Park noticed that such accommodation was neither evenly nor randomly distributed across the city, it tended to concentrate:

> In the zone of deterioration encircling the central business section are always to be found the so-called "slums" and "bad lands," with their submerged regions of poverty, degradation, and disease, and their underworlds of crime and vice. Within a deteriorating area are rooming-house districts, the purgatory of "lost souls." (Park 1984: 54–6)

In the 1920s of course such North American rooming-house districts were not regarded as valued heritage. Forty years later the richness of their historic value was beginning to be recognised just as the spectre of demolition loomed. This hotels case study resonates because it indicates how issues of historic preservation, social problems, social housing and coalitions of interest came together around a counter-project to produce new public space. In addition, it demonstrates how Gastown and DTES are intertwined both conceptually and spatially

An application to demolish the Stanley and New Fountain Hotels on West Cordova Street was made in April 1969. At the rear, the two hotels backed onto one of Vancouver's many pedestrian alleyways – Trounce Alley. At its eastern end it was known popularly as Blood Alley. Trounce-Blood Alleys run east–west linking Cambie and Carrall Streets. The hotels that formed one continuous façade were built in the 1890s, consisting of two-three stories. In the same block were the Travellers Hotel, the Manitoba Hotel and the Rainier Hotel, which gives an impression of the concentration of this type of accommodation in Gastown. Hotels like these provided short and long term accommodation serving mostly single men who worked in trades such as fishing and timber and in factories, construction and ironworks. This type of hotel, of which there were many in Gastown/DTES, tended to have lodging rooms on the upper floors and commercial services on the ground floor including cheap beer parlours, which contributed to the lively street life in Gastown.

The application to demolish was made by the owner of the hotels, Army and Navy Stores (Canada) (A&N), the discount clothing and household store chain, established in Vancouver in 1919. A&N acquired the hotels in about 1952 and granted the proprietors a lease until 1968. During those years the properties continued to provide rudimentary cheap accommodation for some of Vancouver's most vulnerable citizens, mostly middle-aged and elderly men, some unemployed, suffering ill health and drug addiction. By 1969, however, the buildings were unoccupied. After a fire the interiors were ransacked. Despite this, they were sound structurally. A&N wished to raze them to create a surface parking lot to service their flagship store located across West Cordova Street. Although built of brick in an attractive commercial turn of the century design, with segmented arched windows and elaborate cornices, until the threat of demolition the hotels were not considered architecturally or historically important by VCC. But it was thought demolition would harm the continuity of a historic street scene.

Shortly after the demolition application was made, VCC received a flurry of objections from a variety of interests. One objection from the Vancouver Antique Flea Market was accompanied by a petition. In a few hours on Sunday 4 May 1969, the organisers obtained 561 signatures. They were worried about these individual buildings but they had wider strategic concerns. They argued that the demolition would damage irreparably the comprehensive restoration plan for Gastown and that the people of Vancouver could expect more imaginative reuse of the buildings than a parking lot. They were also concerned that the demolition jeopardised 'the entire Blood Alley Development' (Hendricks 1969). This wonderfully evocative though slightly menacing name has a contentious provenance discussed later. Unlike in Lowell where the intention to demolish Merrimack Mills and boarding houses was supported by Lowell City Council, in Vancouver the council decided to delay making a decision on demolition, 'in order to provide details about the situation of these hotels in the proposed 'Gastown' beautification project' (Graham 1969).

This show of public (and civic) opposition to the demolition proposals was of course significant, but perhaps more so was the nature of another objection. Harold Kalman was a young twenty-something assistant professor in the Department of Fine Arts, UBC, specialising in architectural history. He was convinced that 'these two buildings play a uniquely irreplaceable role in the future of Gastown' (Kalman 1969). He was granted a delegation to appear before the city council in May 1969 and made an impassioned plea for the preservation of the hotels. Kalman went on to become one of Canada's leading architectural heritage experts but in 1969 he was a junior academic.

What made his intervention decisive was not his delegation but his subsequent direct financial involvement in the hotels project. Along with three others, Kalman set up Cordova Redevelopment Corporation Ltd (CRC) with the intention of buying the properties and restoring them for low rent social housing and commercial use. The four CRC stockholders were able to raise $300,000 to buy the properties and their offer to A&N was accepted. CRC partnered a not-for-profit social housing organisation, composed of a group of people living in Gastown–DTES, called the Residents of Gastown, known by the derogatory title 'Skid Road Men', which later became the Vancouver chapter of the Pacific Community Self Development Society. They commissioned a feasibility study carried out by Birmingham and Wood in June 1970. Their report is as much a moral oration regarding the desperate need for social housing, as it is a technical appraisal:

> At the present time there is an acute shortage of low rental housing in the area, and it is rapidly growing worse as Gastown is being developed as a fashionable "mod" precinct. What accommodation is available at low rents generally has substandard heating, plumbing, and ventilation, and

is commonly dirty and verminous ... (Birmingham and
Wood 1970 emphasis in original)

In the opinion of the consultants, the buildings *were* of historic value,
and ideally suited to the purpose of providing accommodation for the
Residents of Gastown. If the development went ahead 'they would be
protected against ruinous rent increases in the future' and they would be
able to control their own environment instead of 'helplessly accepting
wretched conditions on the take it or leave it basis their incomes
restrict them' (Birmingham and Wood 1970). In closing, the report
encapsulated succinctly the manner in which historic rehabilitation
and social problems in the area coalesced:

> This project provides an opportunity to deal with the
> housing problems of a group in urban society whose normal
> lot is to occupy the worst housing available in our cities, and
> to be forced out of any area which experiences revitalization.
> To give even a few of them the means to stand fast in their
> chosen area, and to have decent accommodation without
> the label of charity would be a significant contribution to
> humanizing the urban core. (Birmingham and Wood 1970)

What is also interesting about the feasibility report are the imaginative
visual representations of space. The architects chose to represent not
the West Cordova Street main entrance, but the rear aspect onto Blood
Alley (Figure 3.1). The image depicts how a pleasant new public square
might look after some appropriate demolition and a reorientation of
the hotels to the rear.

With the CRC and Residents of Gastown partnership in place
and a feasibility study completed, the next major challenge was to
convince VCC to issue development permits for the scheme. Bearing
in mind the unusual nature of the developers this was by no means
straightforward. Roy Coveney, a former cook, assumed the leadership
of the Residents of Gastown and did a 'tremendous selling job in the
council chamber' (Richardson 1972: 191). In an imaginative restoration
and refurbishment scheme the Residents of Gastown formed a not-for-
profit society – the New Fountain and Stanley Residential Society. It
would operate the hotel and receive 50% of the profits made by CRC
from the commercial development on the ground floor. Through this
financing arrangement over 100 marginalised people would be able to
live in rental accommodation of between $10 and $15 a week in a part

Figure 3.1: Architectural artist's visual representation of how the resorted Stanley and New Fountain Hotels might look (Birmingham and Wood 1970, thanks to VCA)

of town from which they would 'have been ignominiously driven by the normal course of redevelopment' (Richardson 1972).

It was the Vancouver historic preservation interests which championed the unusual scheme, about which VCC was initially wary. Hal Kalman recalls that Mayor Tom Campbell and the NPA had little interest in a scheme that would entrench over 100 economically and socially marginal people in a Gastown developing the potential for gentrification:

> That's why we moved in as advocate-entrepreneurs and did it beneath the political radar. When Art Phillips and TEAM came in, they gave us post-facto support. Art Phillips laid a bronze plaque into the pavement of Blood Alley. (Kalman 2014a)

However, CRC did not have sufficient capital to carry out the mixed use residential–commercial rehabilitation scheme. Fortuitously, two financial opportunities emerged that would facilitate the project. First, VCC in 1971 decided to buy from CRC a nondescript property at the back of the hotels. This building, a large ramshackle garage used for lorry repair, was slated for purchase and demolition by the council to facilitate a planning department scheme to transform Trounce-Blood Alleys into an attractive new public space for the city. A price of $60,000 was agreed. It should be noted that this purchase was funded by federal urban renewal funds. In addition, the intention was to create a new public space to be called Blood Alley Square as part of the Gastown beautification programme. Second, and coincidentally, the federal housing minister, Robert Andras, announced a $200 million fund to be channelled through the Canadian Central Mortgage and Housing Corporation (CMHC) and used for urban renewal-type innovative projects. Luckily, the project by architects Henriquez and Todd was considered innovative because it combined a cross subsidy mechanism of social housing with potentially high rental commercial floor space and the creation of new public space.

An application was made for CMHC funding and, despite the initial lack of political support, it eventually gained strong backing from the NPA dominated VCC, albeit with objections from the lone dissenting voice of political reactionary Alderman Edward Sweeney. Unfortunately, CMHC, which had no experience of this kind of mixed use housing–commercial deal and was sceptical of the CRC profile, rejected the loan application (Bannerman 1971). On hearing the details of the innovative scheme, Kingston Ganong, Vancouver CMHC manager, liked it and arranged a 95% low interest mortgage of $777,700. At that point things started to unravel. The CRC quartet doubted that they had the expertise and experience to deliver the scheme. In a research email exchange Hal Kalman explained that:

> When we started to get the [renovation] costs we got cold feet. None of us was experienced in projects of this scale ... And we didn't want to be responsible for the 95% mortgage with a high-risk project. So we sold Cordova Redevelopment Corp to, as I recall, two men from Winnipeg whom Richard Henriquez introduced us to ... Blood Alley was part of all this, intended largely to give the residents a place to hang out. (Kalman 2014b)

CRC partners decided to sell their interests in the scheme to two investors, Arnold Sigesmund and Alvin Zipursky, but CMHC insisted CRC retain a 25% shareholding, which they did until completion. Rumours in Winnipeg about the dubious financial track record of the two new investors caused consternation within VCC and at CMHC.

For five years in the 1960s a convoluted property based legal wrangle involving Zipursky and a property financing firm called Tri-State Acceptance led eventually to Zipursky being sued (*Province* 1971). How this dispute was resolved remains murky. Allegations were also made about the construction company for the Gastown hotels project called Total Construction Ltd which was not registered with the Workmen's Compensation Board and therefore should not have hired construction workers. Sigesmund and Zipursky were both shareholders in Total Construction Ltd. Accusations and counter-accusations were made between all parties involved. In July 1971, the *Vancouver Sun* and the *Province* featured long investigative articles questioning the financial probity of the scheme. It was alleged for example that the actual cost of demolition was only $2,850 rather than the $8,000 claimed by CRC (VCC 1971). By far the most serious allegation was that at the time the mortgage with CMHC was signed there was confusion as to the identity of the CRC principals. Similarly, doubts were raised as to whether Sigesmund and Zipursky were fit and proper characters to be party to any federal mortgage contract.

VCC was so alarmed by the alleged impropriety that the mayor petitioned Robert Andras, federal minister of urban affairs, to conduct an investigation with specific reference to allegations contained in the 17 July 1971 issue of the *Province* and the 26 July 1971 issue of the *Vancouver Sun*. Lawyers for CMHC were instructed to carry out the investigation. A disturbing possibility emerged, that the project would be swallowed by a hopelessly complex court case and eventually fail. It is important to realise that the hotels project was integral to the creation of new public space at Blood Alley Square. Vancouver City Commissioner Gerald Sutton Brown was distressed at the prospect that the problems with the hotels project could derail an important part of the beautification programme. He had a series of meetings with CRC and CMHC but was only reassured that the project was sound by a detailed report from Kingston Ganong. He assured Sutton Brown that CMHC had exercised due diligence throughout and confirmed the financial integrity of the developers, both in their relations with CMHC and all the construction contractors (Ganong 1971). Much to everybody's relief, the scheme was completed successfully, providing profitable commercial floor space on the ground floor, which subsidised the desperately needed social housing units above.

The creation of new public space and environmental improvements through beautification schemes can have unexpected financial consequences. At the interface of public and private space financial issues can arise. When the development was completed, including the creation of an entrance and frontage onto the new Blood Alley Square, all the abutting property owners were required to contribute two thirds of the 'local improvement costs'. CRC were dismayed at the prospect of these additional costs:

> Now in the Council's wisdom it feels that these improvement costs should be borne proportionally by the Residences of the Stanley & New Fountain Hotel Society in spite of the fact that the Council's original participating [sic] in the project was to benefit a low-cost accommodation for 103 men. (Sigesmund 1972)

VCC lawyers advised that it was unlawful under the Vancouver Charter to levy a local tax against only some occupants of a building. TEAM alderman Art Phillips (soon to be mayor) moved a motion that the council deem the New Fountain Residential Society to be qualified for a grant under Section 206 (j) of the Vancouver Charter. Furthermore, he moved that the Society should be advised to apply for a council grant annually to the value of the improvement tax demand. In a surprise move, the conservative dominated NPA city council agreed sympathetically to this arrangement. This action by CRC certainly portrays Sigesmund in more positive light, but Kalman explained that the two Winnipeg investors "didn't share our high-minded objectives and cut corners, but the project was completed as planned". In his opinion the Stanley and New Fountain episode was:

> ... a very important early step in addressing these problems, and one that has gone largely unnoticed and undocumented... So we gave birth to the first organization to represent the homeless and the disadvantaged. The social benefits of the project were, in my mind, just as important as the urban-architectural ones. (Kalman 2014b)

In 2001 the not-for-profit PHS Community Services Society took over the management of the residential accommodation and commercial space. Then in 2003 it was bought by VCC. Later in 2003 the New Fountain element of the scheme was placed on the Canadian Register of Historic Places for its heritage value and architectural importance, vindicating somewhat belatedly the opponents of its demolition in the 1960s. Through the decades, despite periodic crises (Mackie 2014) the Stanley-New Fountain Hotel has continued to achieve the social vision espoused so passionately by Birmingham and Wood and the original shareholders of CRC. Interestingly, when the 1970s restoration reconfigured the hotels the address was changed to and remains 36 Blood Alley Square, rather than West Cordova Street.

Blood in the alley

Without the active support of the city planning department buying land and property associated with the hotels and pursuing the Blood Alley Square project, the Stanley-New Fountain social housing project would never have been possible. Two different imperatives spurred the Blood Alley Square restoration and public space production project. First, and most immediately in 1969, it became clear that the proposed demolition of the hotels posed a serious threat to VCC's mooted Blood Alley Square scheme. In objecting to the proposed demolition, the Townsite Committee chairman appreciated the intimate connection between the hotels and Blood Alley:

> ... the buildings are required to protect the retail character of Cordova Street, to complement the historic Dunn-Miller (Lonsdale) Block and to preserve the intimacy of Trounce Alley and Blood Alley, important pedestrian activity areas under the Gastown Beautification scheme ... (Thomson 1969)

City planning officers understood that 'in order to preserve two adjacent buildings of historic value' public intervention was necessary and in 1971 approved the purchase of the land and property that would facilitate the creation of the new square.

Blood Alley so the story goes derives its startling name from its unsavoury, nefarious history. Many websites and tour guides claim that in the 19th century butchers' shops lining the alley would allow crimson waste animal blood to flow along the alley into the drains. Public executions were held in Blood Alley Square. Newly arrived gullible, drunken loggers and fishermen would be robbed and sometimes murdered if they ventured down the alley at night. Criminal gangs indulged in bloodcurdling battles here in the 1800s. John Atkin, one of Vancouver's foremost Gastown tour guides, sought to demystify the Blood Alley myths by claiming that it was part of Gastown's rebranding and revitalisation and the name was plucked out of the air by planners in the 1970s. They thought it 'sounded like a cool, folksy, Wild West name' (Atkin 2013). In fact the archives reveal the names Blood Alley and Blood Alley Square were in popular use in the late 1960s. What city planners did was to have part of Trounce Alley renamed Blood Alley Square by amending Street Name bylaw 4054 using bylaw 4636. Gaolers Mews was renamed at the same time (VCC 1970). To his credit Atkin (2014) confirmed this in email correspondence. However, the myths are so palpably enticing it is likely the guide books and websites that roister in the propagation of Blood Alley fables will continue.

It was the physical configuration of Trounce-Blood Alley which allowed its reconfiguration into Blood Alley Square. At the eastern end the alley widened out due to the smaller plot size of the hotels relative to the other buildings, effectively creating space with the potential to be a new civic square. In the 1960s this space was occupied partly by the large ramshackle garage that VCC wanted to buy and demolish. Strategic inspiration for a new public space at Blood Alley came originally from the 1969 *Restoration Report*. Trounce Alley was seen as an important opportunity to create intensive activity mews development and a 'pedestrian-oriented precinct' helping to create confidence for investment in Gastown (Birmingham and Wood et al 1969: 26). There can be little doubt that the purchase by VCC in 1971 of the land and vehicle repair garage at Blood Alley enabled the creation of new public space in an initiative led by the city planners:

> With the demolition of this structure an open area of City property approximately 40' x 215' was created. This area known as Blood Alley Square, the name 'Blood Alley' had long been popularly used to describe a private alley here, together with the adjacent Trounce Alley were considered to be ideal for development as a public pedestrian oriented open space in the preservation and revitalization of Gastown. (VCC 1973)

Note that the mention of Blood Alley here confirms that it was customary usage rather than city planners that bestowed the evocative name. City Planning Director Bill Graham certainly endorsed wholeheartedly the pedestrian-centred ethos of the *Restoration Report*, but also appreciated how improvements to the public realm and the production of new public space could be an economic stimulant and benefit city coffers:

> The use of the acquired lands as a public pedestrian thoroughfare and open space would be a major catalyst in the preservation and revitalisation of Gastown and would supplement private action already undertaken and

encourage further rehabilitation of surrounding buildings. The acquisition of these lands for use in conjunction with a pedestrian oriented development of Trounce Alley would create a more interesting and diversified space. Abutting restaurants and boutiques could lease back some of the area for commercial sitting out space, which might provide some financial return to the City. (Graham 1971)

In May 1972 VCC approved the appointment of architects Phillip Tattersfield and Associates to produce a design for the new city square. The brief specified paving, street furniture and street lighting to be based on that already used at Maple Tree Square (discussed later). A strategic purpose underlying the creation of the new Blood Alley Square was to complete a series of adjoining routes from Cordova Street on the south side through to Water Street on the north and eastwards to Maple Tree Square, as interconnected primarily pedestrian orientated public spaces. It was usual at this time for property owners to be required to contribute, through a local improvement levy or cost sharing scheme, sometimes as much as 80%. In this case Bill Graham was sensitive to the particularities of the Blood Alley location and felt that imposing a local improvement levy on the relevant property owners 'might jeopardize needed rehabilitation of adjacent properties, which in some cases operate on a small margin of profit'. With an eye to future beautification it was felt that the contribution of abutting owners to future improvement schemes for Water and Cordova Streets would be sufficient (Graham 1971).

Completed in mid-1974, the Blood Alley Square project was generally considered a great success (Figure 3.2). In September of that year the top historic preservation–restoration honours in the first Heritage Canada awards were presented to VCC for its role in the innovative Blood Alley Square scheme. After its completion, the development inspired a beautification scheme for Gaoler's Mews, which would allow pedestrians to move from Blood Alley to Water and Carrall Streets in a traffic free environment. These restoration initiatives sparked considerable commercial private investment in these new public spaces and a variety of boutiques, restaurants and studios quickly became established and continue to thrive. But rather than initiating total gentrification, these rather trendy activities coexist in reasonable harmony with the social housing of Stanley-New Fountain building whose main entrance is still off Blood Alley Square. Blood Alley set a positive precedent for reimagining these intimate, interesting but neglected city spaces.

Figure 3.2: Winter's evening at a snowy Blood Alley Square (photo © Michael Leary-Owhin)

In the 2000s Blood Alley was often cited not just for its putative infamous past but as the inspiration for the appropriation of Vancouver's urban alleys for alternative futures (Bramham 2011). When in 2010 Rob Sutherland organised a forum in Mount Pleasant called *Art in Unexpected Places* from which emerged the Vancouver Liveable Laneways movement (Hussain 2011), he was simply reviving, or rather reinterpreting, ideas based on the 1970s Blood Alley beautification reimagining of urban space. Drawing inspiration from the potentials presented is not limited to the public sector and commercial enterprises. Vancouver Public Space Network (2014) points to the increasing number of community and not-for-profit groups 'embracing these peripheral', or otherwise marginal, spaces. Alleys are increasingly being transformed temporarily into all manner of markets and street food orientated public spaces. Clearly, the unpleasant attributes of some alleys have not entirely disappeared and negative representations still exist, but it is apparent that a powerful positive discourse based on reimagined representations of space is at work in Vancouver and other cities.

Another kind of alleyway transformation leans more towards a positive reimagining of urban spaces that are often avoided. In recent years some of Vancouver's alleys have been transformed by artworks. At times the alley literally becomes the artist's canvas, or the stage for an installation. Vancouver alleyways have for decades attracted informal graffiti artists (Figure 3.3) but recently more formal, commissioned

Figure 3.3: Informal graffiti art in Trounce Alley, Gastown on a rare snowy night (photo © Michael Leary-Owhin)

artwork has appeared. An alley off West Pender in Chinatown-DTES provided the setting for an ambitious public art project featuring 100 photographs by Eyoälha Baker in her impressive 'Jump for Joy' photo mural. Murality, a not-for-profit arts organisation established by Amalia Liapi in 2013, sponsored Baker's innovative artistic project.

Artists have also been inspired by the public space of Trounce-Blood Alley Square as an arena for unique installations. A group of young Vancouver architects and academics calling themselves the Space Agency 'wanted to awaken an interest in public space in the city' so they commissioned a public art work competition for an alley installation (Rochon 2005). Winner of the competition was a Japanese duo, Satoshi Matsuoka and Yuki Tamura, and the organisers believed the artwork would 'awaken Vancouverites of all stripes to the vast but long-forgotten potential of this city's oldest back streets' (Rochon 2005). Their installation could be enjoyed by everybody and consisted of nine enormous translucent balloons suspended high over the ground and internally illuminated. Resembling puffy white clouds, the balloons floated above the alley for three days in August 2005. They were not simply art; they stimulated all kinds of formal and informal uses of the alley, including evening street parties and family-orientated events. So from being a place that decent people avoided, Blood Alley became civic space that benefited tourists and vulnerable people alike; a place to hang out or have a meal; a public art gallery.

Vancouver's spaces of representation

An unexpected consequence of the official naming of and physical signage for Blood Alley Square is the noteworthy impact on spaces of representation and the popular imagination, both of residents and people who do not know Vancouver. It seems that regardless of the facts related to the origin of the Blood Alley name, many people in Vancouver, Canada and round the world believe the lurid stories. Continuing entries in many Vancouver guidebooks and webpages attest to this. Perhaps, in this age of supposed post-modern, post-rationality, many people *want* to believe the gruesome stories. Perhaps more than any other part of Vancouver, Gastown and Blood Alley have been instrumental for infusing fiction literature with the shocking and disturbing Blood Alley of urban myth and legend. Filmmakers have been shooting in Gastown for decades with hundreds of scenes being shot here, including romantic scenes such as those seen in *Fifty Shades of Grey* (2015). There is not space to undertake an extensive analysis here of Lefebvrian imaginative, artistic spaces of representation, but two examples are particularly interesting and stimulating.

Stewart and Riddell in their teen noir adventure *Barnaby Grimes: Phantom of Blood Alley* present malevolent and disturbing spaces of representation. In their novel, a creepy district called Gastown:

> … was a sinister, brooding place, full of shuttered workshops and ominously boarded-up buildings, behind whose facades all manner of disreputable enterprises were rumoured to take place. And of all the tightly packed streets, Blood Alley's reputation was indisputably the worst. (Stewart and Riddell 2010: 25)

In reality Blood Alley, although it does have an edgy reputation, has never been considered Vancouver's worst part of town. Most Vancouverites would probably bestow that dubious accolade somewhere in the midst of DTES. What is interesting though, is how the authors draw on the mythical stories of Vancouver's Blood Alley to explain the origin of the name:

> Apparently, years earlier, tanneries had lined the Alley on both sides. The red dyes and acid chemicals of the so-called

'odiferous trade' sluicing down the gutters like blood. It was this vile effluence that gave the alley its name. (Stewart and Riddell 2010: 26)

The novel's first person narrator only knew Blood Alley by reputation but that was sufficient for a detailed insight into its unpleasantness and its geographical relationship with Gastown, "the place was notorious. It lay at the centre of Gastown, the dark heart of the grimy district" (Stewart and Riddell 2010: 25). Clearly, this is a case of art imitating life, imitating myth but with exaggerated salaciousness for increased literary impact.

Coincidentally, Eric Wilson's (1996) yarn *Vancouver Nightmare* is also aimed at the teen urban thriller market. This representation of Blood Alley Square is not only in Gastown, it is also located explicitly in Vancouver. There is even a fairly accurate map of the Gastown area with Blood Alley highlighted. Unlike the unremittingly scary Blood Alley in the previous novel, this one is a more ambivalent city space. While the characters do go there because it is a likely haunt of crooks and villains and they fear being mugged or stabbed, it is also a place of pleasant cobblestones and maple trees. It is a place where tourists wander perfectly at ease. Both novels combine fact and artistic fiction in sophisticated ways and while the Vancouver tourist office would be pleased with the fact that tourists visit Wilson's Blood Alley Square, they would perhaps be less than satisfied with the fearsome, brutish 19th-century Jack the Ripper, Whitechapel feel of the Stewart and Riddell novel. Incidentally, Wilson's reference to 'cobblestones' is interesting because Blood Alley Square was not resurfaced in cobblestones but brick paving of the same kind used in the beautification of Maple Tree Square – that most iconic of Vancouver places.

Smoke-in, riot, love-in

Rather like downtown Lowell and Castlefield, at the start of the 1960s few if any major films were being shot on location in Vancouver. It was regarded as a fairly quiet provincial city. Greenpeace had not yet been founded there. It was and is still not the provincial capital. More stagnating than stimulating, the city rarely featured in the national or international news. In 1997 a documentary film was made about the radical, left wing newspaper the *Georgia Straight*, founded in 1967 in Vancouver. According to the opening voice-over:

In the early 60s Vancouver was a sleepy little provincial centre going nowhere slowly. In many ways it epitomised the British in British Columbia. It was courteous and colonial with very few problems and even fewer ambitions. There was still an air of the 50s around. Tourism was basically non-existent and the city languished in its Pacific isolation. (Crighton 1997)

Increasingly though, as the 1960s became swinging and disobedient Vancouver began to change. The 1960s zeitgeist of free love, tolerance, rebellion against authority, alternative lifestyles and emerging recreational drug use among young people moved north up the west coast from San Francisco to Vancouver. Facilitated by low grade, cheap accommodation and a plethora of similarly cheap bars, cafés and restaurants, Vancouver began to attract increasing numbers of young people who some regarded as hippies (Aronsen 2010). Many of them gravitated to the Gastown-DTES area which by the late 1960s had the largest concentration of soft drug users in Canada. It was known humorously as Grasstown for that reason. 1970 saw a group of young people in Vancouver form an action group called the 'Don't Make a Wave Committee' – which later became Greenpeace. They were joined by another direct action group created by students of Simon Fraser University and trade unionists. Out of their discussions they formed a branch of the Youth International Party and became known as the Vancouver Yippies. They opposed what they saw as Canada's unreasonable anti-recreational drug laws.

Mayor Campbell had a proclivity for warning people to stay away from Gastown because of the perceived danger from drug users, alcoholics and panhandlers. He decided to sweep away the highly public and illegal displays of drug use, mainly cannabis, in Gastown and DTES with a high profile police action called 'Operation Dustpan' which commenced in July 1971. With hindsight this was a case of the use of what Mitchell (2013) calls escalated force (see Chapter One). Many undercover police were deployed some wearing hippie-style wigs, along with fake tans and scruffy clothes. Their intention was to infiltrate the Grasstown scene. There were over 100 arrests in the first ten days (Malmo-Levine 2007). Dustpan caused outrage among young people and many Gastown businesses and Vancouver citizens were also unhappy about the police action. A political protest was organised for Saturday 7 August 1971 by the Vancouver Yippies and the *Georgia Straight*. The newspaper advertised through the preceding week that the protest would take the form of a 'Smoke-In' *and* street jamboree,

Figure 3.4: Advertisement in the *Georgia Straight* for the 1971 Smoke-in at Maple Tree Square, Gastown (source: vancourier.com)

to be held at Maple Tree Square (Figure 3.4). Many sources refer to the Smoke-in but few mention the street jamboree. Although meant to provoke a carnival-like atmosphere and be fun, the event had two serious political purposes: to be a public display of civil disobedience against oppressive drug laws in general and a highly visible public denunciation of Operation Dustpan. In Lefebvrian terms the action constituted a temporary appropriation of public space in effect creating differential space, the subject of Chapter Eight.

Increasing numbers converged on the Square throughout the afternoon. Their behaviour was entirely peaceful: smoking pot, drinking beer, playing music, dancing in the street and just hanging out. There was free popcorn and a giant papier mâché spliff. By late evening about 2,000 people were enjoying the carnival atmosphere. Many tourists and locals enjoying a night out in Gastown watched the spectacle or joined in the fun. It was a warm summer's evening which added to the carnival atmosphere. Having anticipated trouble, the police were ready. At 10 pm on the orders of police Inspector Robert Abercrombie, but without warning, mounted police wielding heavy riding crops and police swinging riot batons attempted to disperse the crowds. What followed over the next two hours was pandemonium. Intense police violence was perpetrated on protesters, local residents and tourists alike. Two people were thrown by police through plate glass windows (Boudreau 2012). Thankfully, nobody was killed but many people were seriously injured, including some police officers. In total 79 people were arrested but only 38 charged with criminal offences. Interestingly, the disturbance was immediately given two names, the Gastown riot and more significantly the Battle of Maple Tree Square.

It quickly became apparent that the police violence was entirely unprovoked and indiscriminate. They attacked not only peaceful demonstrators but tourists and local people who happened to be in the area. During the riot, two city aldermen, Art Philips and Ed Sweeney, summoned to the scene by Larry Killam were so shocked by what they witnessed that their subsequent statements helped establish the need for a judicial inquiry (Bannerman 1974). The newspapers and the mayor, although he strongly supported the police, called for an inquiry into the disturbance. A commission of inquiry into the incident was conducted by BC Supreme Court Justice Thomas Dohm. He was highly critical of the organisers of the Smoke-in *and* the police affirming that the arrival of the riot squad had caused panic, terror and resentment. He concluded the police had used unnecessary and excessive force. Using a phrase that sticks to this day he labelled it a police riot.

It should be appreciated that the riot happened shortly after Birmingham and Wood had submitted their design for the rehabilitation of Maple Tree Square and the creation of new civic public space. Obviously, Gastown Merchants Association (GMA) was anxious for the scheme to go ahead despite the dismal implications of the riot. In the property damage and wreckage of the immediate aftermath, GMA realised that business may suffer and lines of credit and insurance would be impossible to secure unless something positive could be done about Gastown's image. Perhaps for this reason it organised and paid for what it called a 'Patch-Up Party' but everybody else called a 'Love-in'. Chapter Eight explains how the organisers of and participants in the Love-in inadvertently produced a kind of differential space.

Few would have guessed in the politically turbulent 1970s that the Gastown riot would come to be memorialised in one of the city's most imaginative pieces of public art. In 2009 innovative Vancouver born, African-Canadian artist Stan Douglas created a large scale artistic provocation, a photographic mural, called *Abbott and Cordova, 7 August 1971*. It hangs in the quasi-public space (see Figure 1.1) of the atrium of the newly redeveloped Woodward's building in Gastown (Figure 3.5). Clever use of digital technology reconstructs an imaginary but entirely credible scene from the night of the riot. He claims the image:

> ... is about the transition of that neighbourhood from one
> condition to another. It's about the beginning of the decline
> of the Downtown Eastside. It's also about how public space
> is used, and who controls it. (Douglas in Laurence 2009)

Perusing the image one would not guess that it is not a photograph from the night of the riot, that it is entirely a piece of imaginative art: a space of representation, which has the feel of a documentary moment, a factual record. In this sense it blurs the distinction between Lefebvrian rational representations of space and fictional spaces of

Figure 3.5: Blurring representations of space: *Abbot and Cordova 7 August 1971* (thanks to Stan Douglas and Linda Chinfen, photo © courtesy of the artist, David Zwirner, New York/London and Victoria Miro, London)

representation. Interestingly, the Woodward's redevelopment scheme included an element of social housing for the people of DTES and was designed by Gregory Henriquez, the son of Richard Henriquez who masterminded the restoration and adaptive reuse of the Stanley and New Fountain Hotels in the 1970s.

Post-riot beautification and the Teamsters

The *Restoration Report* regarded Maple Tree Square as the most significant space in the city as outlined in the previous chapter. In the Report it was considered to have a boundless future and superlatives were heaped on its public space potential. Given its location on the harbour's edge, its substantial handsome buildings and location at the confluence of five key streets, with careful design it would, 'rival the public spaces of the world' and it must 'inevitably fulfil its place as the civic and social platform of a great city' (Birmingham and Wood et al 1969: 26). Although the principal of a beautification project for Maple Tree Square was established in the Report, it was in fact a petition submitted in November 1969 from property owners in the area, which signalled the start of this important spatial practice project on the ground. Unlike the IDEAS men, the petitioners ran relatively small scale enterprises such as: property developers, local hotels, shops, restaurants, cafés and commercial services. This project would come within the remit of what VCC called Stage II East Gastown improvements. It was called East Gastown because it was still envisaged that the proposed freeway would bisect Gastown into east and west sections. Interestingly, the petition's signatories accepted that costs to them would be in the form of local improvement taxes of $5–6 per foot of street frontage annually for a term of 15 years (East Gastown Petitioners 1969). Even though they were hardly representative of the wider Gastown communities, which, at this time, still included a significant number of disadvantaged people, the VCC planning department agreed that a small committee elected by the property owners should represent the community's interests and aspirations. This committee, led by Lawrence Killam, met frequently with the city planners over the next year to work out the details of the East Gastown–Maple Tree Square scheme.

The project design objectives for East Gastown, as specified by the planning department in 1970, were to respect and enhance the historic architecture of the area and revitalise the environment with a pedestrian orientated emphasis. In recognition of its important historic and civic roles, the square was to be designed primarily as a symbolic space permitting vehicular movement, but maximising pedestrian circulation. On the basis of the preliminary design the cost was estimated at $273,000. Senior government (federal and provincial) agreed to contribute $35,000 each to the cost. BC Hydro and BC Telephone agreed to the undergrounding of their overhead lines at no cost to the city. It is important to realise that the scheme extended public realm improvements into Carrall Street, Alexander Street and Pigeon Square (known in the early years as Pioneer Square). A consultants' report submitted in June 1971 provided enticing visual representations of how the enhanced and new public spaces might look (Figure 3.6). It also specified cobblestones in a unique swirling design, to help recreate the 19th century ambiance.

The final cost was $329,395 and the budget overrun was attributed to higher than anticipated costs for: street furniture, some technically challenging paving work and most notably 'antique' street lighting (discussed later). Vancouver was praised widely for this project of public space creation and historic rehabilitation. Heritage Canada gave the city its top award in 1974 for the Maple Tree and Blood Alley Square initiatives. So powerful was the demonstration effect that the Water Street Improvement Committee, comprised of businesses in the area, requested a similar beautification scheme in a petition submitted in November 1972 by the chairman George Lee (1972). The committee did so in the full knowledge that its members would be required to contribute to the costs through a local improvement levy. This preservation and improvement scheme would eventually help establish Water Street as Gastown's main street and one of the most vibrant public spaces in the city, especially in the evenings under the characteristic incandescent street lighting.

Figure 3.6: Architectural artist's visual representation of how a beautified Maple Tree Square might look (Birmingham and Wood, Hopping Kovach & Grinell 1971, thanks to VCA)

Cobblestones, in fact brick paviours in this case, had not been used for a road surface for decades in Vancouver. Consequently, it was difficult for VCC to specify and source the bricks needed. Only one firm, based in the US, could meet all the specifications. This provoked a bizarre controversy in the city with the engineering and planning departments making confusing assertions about the quality or otherwise

Figure 3.7: Producing public space: architectural artist's visual representation of Maple Tree Square (Vancouver City Planning Department c1978, thanks to VCA)

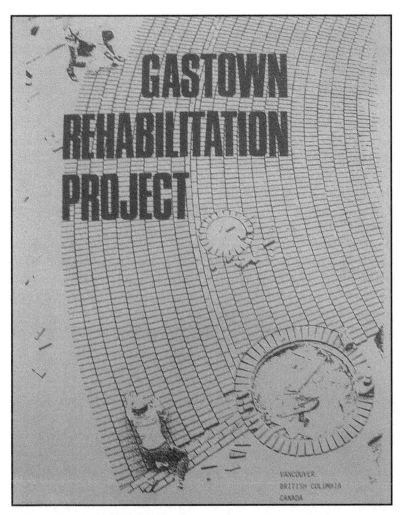

of Canadian versus US bricks and construction labour. Implementation of the project stalled and matters were not helped when the Canadian Teamsters Union made a spirited though ultimately futile demand that only Canadian bricks and labour be used (Bannerman 1974: 33). Finally, 160,000 bricks arrived from the US and were used for the Maple Tree Square public space restoration project. Several years later, the Vancouver city planning department (c1978) published a summary report entitled Gastown Rehabilitation Project – the front cover depicts the US construction workers laying US brick paviours at Maple Tree Square (Figure 3.7).

Fake kitsch versus authentic heritage

Several academics and journalists have been highly critical of what they consider the fake, kitsch, imitation Victorian streetlights in Maple Tree Square and other parts of Gastown (Punter 2003: 53). Some websites even claim they are imitation Victorian gas lights. Vancouver journalist, Robin Ward (1998) blasted the city council for its theme park approach to historic preservation in a major piece in the *Vancouver Sun*, particularly the Victorianesque globe streetlights and the Water Street steam clock. Claims about the dubious historical validity of the streetlights continue to be made. Kalman and Ward (2012: 15) assert that the 'globe clustered streetlamp is of 19th-century design, introduced as a 'heritage' feature in Gastown in the 1970s'. It is manifest that none of these criticisms as to the inauthenticity of Gastown's streetlights is supported by credible evidence. Given that these vilified street lights first appeared in Maple Tree Square and given that they are one of the most distinctive features of Gastown and appear in many publications and millions of tourist photographs around the world, it is worth setting the record straight as to exactly what they are and how the first ones came into existence. It will become obvious why the origin of the stigmatised streetlights should not be conflated with that of the Gastown steam clock.

It is well known that the Gastown steam clock is a 1970s antique style concoction based on a design by horologist Raymond Saunders and metalwork expert Doug Smith. It was the second steam clock in the world; the first was built by in England by publican John Inshaw in 1859 to attract drinkers to his tavern. Under the Vancouver downtown core runs a network of pipes, maintained by Central Heat Distribution Ltd, delivering natural gas fuelled, steam powered heating to many offices and public buildings. Where necessary the steam is vented through pavement grates and stacks. In addition to being a tourist attraction the Gastown clock has a practical purpose in that it stands over one such vent, preventing homeless people from sleeping on this soothingly warm spot. Gastown's clock was paid for by Lawrence Killam and his colleagues and erected in 1977. Given the provenance of the steam clock it would be reasonable to assume that Gastown's globe streetlights are simply fake Victoriana, dreamt up by urban designers and intended to create a historic feel – the reality is quite different. From my research, it appears that the story of how Gastown acquired its distinctive streetlights has never before been told.

Over the course of a few months, two unrelated things happened concerning a hospital and a young, heritage conscious property developer based in Gastown. August 1969 saw an unusual offer made by Vancouver General Hospital. Executive Director Kenneth Weaver wrote to VCC offering a number of antique, ornamental lamp standards, if a good use could be found for them. Eventually the informal proposal was formalised and Max Cross, deputy director of planning replied accepting the generous offer as, 'it appears that they will fit in perfectly with our Gastown beautification plans' (Cross 1970). At this point the planning department intended to deploy the streetlights as part of the beautification of Pigeon Square at Carrall/Hastings Streets. There the matter may have ended with Pigeon Square benefiting from some antique gas streetlights of unknown origin.

By a strange coincidence, an even more unusual but not quite so generous proposition was made shortly after VCC accepted the hospital's streetlights. Lawrence Killam, President of the Town Group property development company, wrote to the director of planning:

> We have acquired 12 antique English, gas streetlamps. The cast iron standards are 14 feet high, including a below grade base of 40 inches … Our cost, including complete restoration is approximately $200.00 each. We would like to sell three complete lamps to the City of Vancouver at our cost. (Killam 1970a)

Killam intended the streetlights would be erected in Maple Tree Square. It is not clear from the archives whether or not VCC accepted this offer. But Killam made another suggestion which set in motion an unexpected chain of events, as sometimes happens during the production of space:

> We have established a source in England for more of these lamp standards and will make this information available to the City of Vancouver on request. It is probable that the solution to a large supply of these lamp standards would be to have a *local foundry* sand cast the standards. (Killam 1970a, emphasis added)

Killam's suggestion for guaranteeing a steady supply of antique-style streetlights was acted on by the planning department but not in the manner he anticipated. The planning department working with the engineering department did some research and discovered that Gastown, decades before, did indeed have ornate, globe, *electric* streetlights, which seemed to originate from about 1900. They discovered particularly attractive streetlights dated to about 1925, which were all designed and made by local foundries. A search of local foundries was initiated to try and find the company that had originally cast these streetlights. By July 1970 it was not going well:

> At the meeting with the Planning Department regarding the East Gastown Beautification Project, Alan Parker asked us to find out whether the patterns for the castings, which were used prior to 1925 for supporting the five globes on a single upright street lighting pole were still being held by a local foundry. I am advised that neither Maclean and Powell nor Terminal City Ironworks, who did much of the department's castings, know of the existence of these patterns. (Nicholson 1970)

After nine months of fruitless searching for Gastown's original streetlight designs, city planner Alan Parker's quest took him to yet another Vancouver foundry:

> Locating the patterns for the original City of Vancouver streetlight castings (amongst many others of interest) in your pattern loft was a most satisfying experience. We had almost come to the conclusion that these patterns had long since disappeared ... As you will recall, from Messers. Parker and Adam's visit, the City is participating in a Gastown Beautification Project, aimed at capturing some of the atmosphere of the original townsite. Original streetlights certainly form part of the atmosphere. (Lawson 1970)

Lawson requested 300 five-globe, plus 25 nine-globe streetlights, of a 1912 design. In addition, the streetlights' team had tracked down a 1920s photograph of the lights in situ in a Vancouver Street which helped the foundry, Ross and Howard Iron Works Ltd, to retro-design accurate facsimiles or simulacra. It was not only the historical authenticity of the lamp standards about which the council took great care. A great deal of effort was dedicated to ensuring that the quality of light was as close as possible to the electric incandescent original. Incandescent light provides a more satisfying visual experience and photographic friendly yellow glow, in contrast to the harsh white or orange of other light sources. Within a few years Gastown's street lights came to be regarded as an iconic feature of the area's restoration and an important physical reminder of the city's history (Figure 3.8).

Figure 3.8 : Gastown's authentic replica globe streetlights on Water Street (photo © Michael Leary-Owhin)

With hindsight it is somewhat surprising that the myth of streetlight inauthenticity took hold, albeit that it has not detracted from the high regard in which Gastown's historic restoration is generally held. Certainly it was well known at the time that the globe lamp standards were cast locally using original moulds. Incandescent light bulbs, although they give a warmer light producing a better colour rendering of the surroundings, have a shorter lifespan and in the long term are relatively more expensive than the alternatives. In January 1980 VCC replaced them with more cost-effective mercury vapour lamps. Many merchants, residents and visitors were unhappy about the effect of the new lighting and in response the Townsite Committee instructed lighting consultants to investigate. They concluded that although mercury vapour lamps were slightly more cost-effective they, 'cannot produce a historically authentic appearance of the Gastown district in terms of lighting quality' (Munson 1981). It was not only Vancouverites who were unhappy. The BC provincial minister of government services was troubled by Vancouver's change to mercury vapour lighting in Gastown:

> Gastown is one of this Province's most important historic areas. We are proud that it was a Provincial heritage designation, which protected Gastown in 1971, and enabled the City's widely acclaimed revitalisation program ... There

are many things which contribute to the area's unique atmosphere. One of these has been the authentic lamp stands and incandescent lighting. We were very pleased with the City's choice of lamp-posts, cast from Vancouver's original 1912 molds [sic]. (Charlton 1981, emphasis added)

Subsequently, VCC did reintroduce incandescent lighting. Quite why the lack of authenticity myth emerged is hard to fathom, except that because the streetlights began to be erected at about the same time as the Gastown steam clock, perhaps it was assumed that the streetlights were also pastiche heritage frippery. Whatever the reason, Vancouver and Gastown owe their planning and engineering departments a debt of gratitude. Also of course the conscientious archivists at the Vancouver city archives deserve our thanks. Without their diligence and dedication, the real history of Gastown's streetlights would have been wiped away leaving no mark on the present.

Gas and more civic generosity

While the search for the original streetlight castings was in progress, Killam took the initiative once again. Being a prominent member of the heritage preservation group, the Townsite Committee, Killam was acutely aware of the significance of Gassy Jack Deighton for the founding of Vancouver and particularly for the history of Maple Tree Square where Deighton's pub, the Globe Saloon, once stood. One morning in early February 1970 Vancouverites awoke to find a visually impressive addition to Gastown's public art. Standing in front of the Europe Hotel was an imposing copper statue of Gassy Jack. While the statue would have come as a shock to most people in the city, its presence should not have surprised VCC. Killam wrote to the city's director of planning a month before, explaining that he and some fellow property developers had commissioned the large statue. He made a more generous offer this time but wanted a civic gesture in return:

> We would like to gift the statue to the City of Vancouver and would like to arrange to have the Mayor commemorate it on March 1, 1970, the one hundredth anniversary of the switch of names from Gastown to Granville. (Killam 1970b)

Killam and his colleagues wanted the statue, by Canadian sculptor Vern Simpson, to be located in front of the Europe Hotel facing across Maple Tree Square, from where Gassy Jack could direct his gaze, 'to the spot of his original saloon as indicated on the survey of Old Granville Townsite' (Killam 1970b). Given the March anniversary date, Killam hoped for swift official approval but in this he was to be disappointed. The director of planning's opinion was that it would be premature to decide on a location for a statue in advance of the Maple Tree Square beautification design. It was a matter though that came also within the jurisdiction of the city engineer, Randolph Martin, who was in no hurry to make a decision. His report to VCC explained the technical-legal issues, but still left the city council to make a decision about the 'statue illegally placed on a city street' (Martin 1970). Not only did the statue constitute a violation of Section 71 (1) of the Bylaw, Martin was unhappy about its location on the pavement and distressed that a field check indicated that the statue was poorly balanced, being 'propped up at the back with pieces of brick under the base' (Martin 1970). Any city council would have been horrified at the prospect of litigation resulting from an accident. Although Killam was prepared to gift the statue to the city, additional costs would fall on the council, principally related to indemnity insurance, which made the city engineer nervous about giving approval. Mayor Tom Campbell did not approve and used neither technical nor political language, telling Killam that he would 'have the statue hauled away to the city dump' (in Bannerman

Figure 3.9: 'Gassy' Jack Deighton watches over Maple Tree Square, Gastown (photo © Michael Leary-Owhin)

1974: 26) and for a time the prospects of official authorisation looked bleak. Eventually, after more cajoling from Killam the engineering, planning, financial and legal issues were resolved and approval given for the permanent placement of the statue in Maple Tree Square. It was placed appropriately in front of the site of the former Globe Saloon (Figure 3.9).

In the early 1970s few would have guessed that Maple Tree Square would become Vancouver's most iconic civic public space, or that Gassy Jack, the steam clock and antique streetlights its most (selfie) photographed landmarks. The fact that material enhancements and the production of new public space at Maple Tree Square were implemented after the Gastown riot, but before the change of city administration in 1972 is critical. It demonstrates the council's willingness in the pre-TEAM era to support fully the production of public space for its intrinsic societal benefits, its use value, rather than its exchange value. This attitude towards the use value of urban public space continued into the 21st century and it is pertinent to examine a direct public space descendant of the early 1970s restoration programme for Maple Tree Square.

Carrall Street Greenway: two contradictory initiatives

Maple Tree Square was of paramount importance because it signalled that the NPA was prepared to implement an urban liveability agenda through significant public investment. It was regarded in the *Restoration Report* as one of the main nodal foci. Carrall Street being a key component of Maple Tree Square was regarded as one of the principal axes running as it did from water to water: Burrard Inlet to False Creek. Carrall Street at its northern end was seen as a key part of the Maple Tree Square restoration. It was regarded as a major pedestrian link between Gastown, Hastings Street and Chinatown and any future restoration including the design of pavements or sidewalks should emphasise this important function.

In 2003 the city council first considered the Greenway idea. After extensive consultation and technical appraisal, an ambitious public realm enhancement scheme known as the Carrall Street Greenway was approved in 2005. This was to be part of the Downtown Historic Trail and was a continuation of the city's long-running Greenway programme which had seen 14 schemes developed, including False Creek to Burrard Inlet between Cambie and Main Streets. Interestingly, the Greenway objectives sought to combine public realm improvements per se with economic and business stimulation, provide employment opportunities *and* an improved quality of life for the disadvantaged residents of DTES (General Manager Engineering Services 2006). Carrall Street was characterised physically and socially in unambiguously positive terms, symbolically it was an:

> ... intersection of history and contemporary urban life in Vancouver and the DTES. It connects the City's historic districts of Chinatown, the Hastings Street corridor and Gastown, with the future development along north False Creek ... The street is lined with heritage buildings, dotted with parks, squares and other public realm spaces, and is now the heart of an emerging contemporary arts district. Within this intersection of historic places and built forms, Carrall Street is home to diverse cultures and economies. (General Manager Engineering Services 2006: 3)

The Greenway would cost $5 million and improve public spaces from Water Street–Maple Tree Square to Expo Boulevard. In design terms the Greenway was meant to reconcile the demands for stimulating economic activity and providing part of the pedestrian route from False Creek to Stanley Park, while simultaneously acknowledging and celebrating the diverse communities that lived in the vicinity. A Carrall Street public art programme was envisaged along with restoration and enhancement of Pigeon Square based on the same rationale. During the development phase, there were several rounds of meaningful community consultation. These facilitated several new community partnerships and bolstered community cohesion. In depth community engagement was thought to be a crucial element of the Carrall Street Greenway initiative. In a conference paper delivered in late 2009, Chow et al (rather ironically in the context of this book) note that the Greenway planners looked to Frederick Olmstead's linear parks in Boston, rather than 1820s Lowell for inspiration (see Chapter Five). They concluded that the Greenway was an excellent opportunity for Vancouver to 'explore ways of creating great streets that support transportation choices, community building and sustainable initiatives, both social and environmental' (Chow et al 2009). Construction began in January 2007 and was completed in autumn 2009. In keeping with the spirit of the *Restoration Report*, the Greenway is a direct descendant of the nascent liveability agenda instigated by the pre-1972 NPA city administration.

Simultaneously, and in rather schizophrenic fashion, another public space initiative was taking place in 2006 inspired by the successful bid for Vancouver-Whistler to host the 2010 Winter Olympics. Project Civil City (PCC) as it was called was part of a wider city programme to showcase Vancouver's liveability to a global audience (Boyle and Haggerty 2011). In addition, PCC was also promoted as an opportunity to accelerate programmes to reduce perceived public space disorderliness, particularly in DTES. With huge numbers of tourist visitors expected in Vancouver in 2010, Mayor Sam Sullivan was determined (in eerily similar fashion to Mayor Tom Campbell 40 years before) to reduce visible manifestations of social problems in public space:

> As the leader of the City, I have decided to set aggressive targets to reduce public disorder. In addition to tackling illegal and nuisance behaviours such as open drug use, aggressive panhandling and noise infractions we must also work as a community to find compassionate solutions to the root causes of poverty. (Office of the Mayor 2006: 3)

Despite the rhetoric of compassion, PCC was principally about trying to squash perceived unruly behaviour in public space. A range of initiatives were proposed for the downtown area including Gastown, Chinatown and DTES which would experience the bulk of tourist visits and spend during the 2010 Winter Olympics. Rather than a space of diversity to be celebrated, Carrall Street was reimagined under PCC as a corridor of transition between the affluence and attractiveness of Gastown to the west and the intense poverty crime, drug abuse and social disorder of DTES to the east. Under PCC a range of physical improvements went ahead: restoration of historic cobblestone paving, tree planting, lighting improvements, public art, small performance spaces and encouraging street facing patios. An overriding preoccupation of PCC however was, 'to reduce criminogenic situations by enhancing pedestrian presence and street vibrancy'. This would 'increase interpersonal surveillance that will make the streets safer' (Boyle and Haggerty 2011: 3192). Physical measures were also implemented in Maple Tree Square and Pigeon Park primarily to reduce the perceived incidence of social anarchy in public space.

For decades Pigeon Park on Carrall Street had been a meeting place and outdoor living resource for vulnerable and marginalised residents of DTES. Under PCC it was represented as a place of crime and visible social disorder. In the park, a large mural of memorials and locally meaningful graffiti was deemed inappropriate in public space. Here the aim of PCC was specifically to make Pigeon Park less attractive as a place for residents of DTES to congregate. The graffiti and murals were obliterated, bushes deemed to hide illicit activities were removed and benches and other long flat services were reconfigured to minimise opportunities for sleeping. Police were encouraged to issue more tickets for minor bylaw infringements such as jaywalking, loitering, begging, sleeping and even spitting. Predictably, the number of tickets issued soared compared with the previous year. Police acknowledged the recipients were unable to pay the fines. The intervention was seen more as a way of educating perceived ne'er-do-wells as to the limits of tolerable behaviour in the changed context of preparations for the 2010 Winter Olympics.

PCC was an exercise in reducing diversity in public space. In Lefebvrian terms it was an attempt to produce homogenous behaviours and abstract space. Although various PCC policy statements alluded to the need to address the causes of perceived social disorder and low-level urban crime, particularly in DTES, the vast bulk of resources were directed at trying to sweep away visible manifestations of deeper social problems. In terms of cost, PCC turned out to be prohibitively expensive, to such an extent that the Vancouver Police Department (VPD) filed a grievance against the city council. VPD maintained that it was inappropriate to spend scarce public money on certain aspects of PCC. In particular they and others objected to the pumping of public resources into the contentious public–private partnership, the Downtown Ambassadors, a joint hospitality and security initiative of the Downtown Vancouver Business Improvement Association.

Partly on grounds of ongoing, prohibitive cost, this experiment in heavily regulated public space was truncated. During the campaigning for Vancouver city elections the challenger for mayor had promised to abolish PCC on the grounds that the public money could be better spent elsewhere. Soon after the incumbent NPA regime was ousted from power in city elections of December 2008, the incoming centre-left council discontinued PCC. What the imposition of PCC illustrates with great lucidity is how certain citizens and certain forms of behaviour deemed unacceptable by regulatory authorities are put under the spotlight at certain times. In this case it was official concerns that undesirable use of downtown space would detract from the Vancouver touristic experience, sullying the Winter Olympics, especially for international visitors. Public space was represented by the city council not as an arena of democratic inclusiveness but as a space primarily for sanitised behaviour and exchange value consumption. PCC stands in stark contrast to the ethos of the production of public space emanating from the Carrall Street Greenway, the *Restoration Report* and related projects.

Conclusions

Two concurrent events in the production of Gastown space initiated dramatic spatial practice on the ground through a number of restoration-beautification projects in a place that in the late 1960s was a forlorn, neglected edge of downtown space. All the case study projects bar one illustrate for the first time the significant role of the NPA in pre-1972 production of post-industrial urban public space. This chapter has revealed how the demolition threat posed by Project 200 and the *Restoration Report* were spurs to the pre-1972 heritage infused (re)presentations and reproduction of space. A demolition threat also incentivised the counter-project of the Stanley and New Fountain Hotels restoration. A number of space-related coalitions were found to have been instrumental in conceptualising and delivering several of the public space projects examined through the analysis of archival data. Most notable of these was the coalition which conceived then implemented the hotels project which included: academic, city, federal, social housing, DTES residents and property development interests. Managing to survive the major financial scandal indicated the robustness of that coalition.

A strong theme of Lefebvre's spatial theorising argues that social relations produce and are created by urban space. An obvious example of this is the manner in which the creation of Blood Alley Square was integral to the hotels project which provided decent, affordable accommodation for many of Gastown-DTES's homeless and vulnerable men. In naming Blood Alley Square formally, VCC recognised the everyday spaces of representation of local people and bestowed an evocative epithet that inspired literary imaginative, artistic spaces of representation. Similarly, the increasing use of the name Gastown in the preservation policy process valorised the organic social relations and processes from which the city emerged in the days of Gassy Jack. And it was at Maple Tree Square, where Gassy Jack located the city's first pub, that the first and most important heritage-led public space project was located. Prefigured in the *Restoration Report*, it was facilitated by provincial and federal grant regimes which followed the provincial designation of the Gastown-Chinatown Historic Site. Similarly, Blood Alley Square was a project initiated by the pre-1972 NPA regime but completed under the post-1972 TEAM administration. Clearly, this fact tends to obfuscate where the credit should lie for early post-industrial production of urban space initiatives.

Despite the 1971 Battle of Maple Tree Square, a significant beautification project went ahead partly as a way of demonstrating the city had recovered from the trauma of the riot and that Vancouverites could enjoy high quality public space without perpetrating a riot. Maple Tree Square has double importance because it was here that antique looking streetlights were installed for the first time in a beautification project – an element of the scheme which has become synonymous with the heritage-suffused ambiance of Gastown. Evidence from the archives highlights the true provenance of these streetlights which have been disparaged for decades as tacky fakes by academics and journalists. Far from being Victorian pastiche they have been shown to be copies of original Gastown lamp standards retro-designed from original moulds and manufactured by the same Vancouver company that made the originals. Credit can now be bestowed on the city planners and engineers for persevering with the search for the original street light patterns, a search prompted by heritage conscious property interests.

In the *Restoration Report*, Carrall Street is seen positively as an integral constituent of Maple Tree Square. Concomitant affirmative representations of space underpin the ideas for the 2005–9 Carrall Street Greenway. This project had all the hallmarks of genuine, inclusive public space produced with the active involvement of the residents of DTES who were among the intended beneficiaries. In contrast, the panicky PCC response as part of the preparations for the 2010 Winter Olympics was predicated on representations of space which demonised the DTES population and rendered their use of public space a deviance to be eradicated. Rather than an intersection of history, culture and ethnicity, Carrall Street was represented as a spatial barrier to be policed in order to keep undesirable behaviours from being witnessed by Vancouver's Olympic visitors. If the principles underpinning the Greenway were reminiscent of the liveability rhetoric of the *Restoration Report*, then those of the PCC were more akin to the baleful attitudes towards DTES of the IDEAS big business hierarchy three decades before. Nevertheless the central conclusion of this chapter is that, despite big property interests and a pro-business city government, it is possible for spatial coalitions to germinate and see implemented Lefebvrian counter-projects where the production of space creates genuine urban public space and social benefits.

FOUR

Lowell: (Re)presenting urban space

Space is never produced in the sense that a kilogram of sugar or a yard of cloth is produced ... Does it then come into being after the fashion of a superstructure? Again, no. It would be more accurate to say that it is at once a precondition and a result of social superstructures. The state and each of its constituent institutions call for spaces – but spaces which they can organize according to their specific requirements. (Lefebvre 1991: 85)

'I grew up in the city, have lived in Lowell all my life. I've actually never lived anywhere but Lowell. If you had told me at seventeen that I was never going to leave Lowell, I would have been thoroughly depressed. I did not envision this as a place that I would stay, much less make a living in. It was a place that in my mind that didn't have a whole lot going for it; didn't have jobs, there was nothing to do at night. We left town to go and do something at that age in my late teens or early 20s, you get out of the city. If you had people my age that wanted to get out [in the 1970s], where was its future?' (Cook 2012)

Introduction

For Lefebvre, the state and its constituent institutions call for urban spaces but they do not act alone or with impunity in the production of space, and their specific requirements are often contested. This was certainly the case in Lowell as the city entered a critical phase of post-industrial reimagining and transformation in the late 1960s. If we are to take seriously Lefebvre's invocation to scrutinise the histories of the production of urban space, then of course the context in which the concept of the Lowell National Historical Park (LNHP) emerges in the 1970s becomes a critical historical moment requiring investigation. I argue in this chapter that this history was not an inevitable linear procession but rather involved a series of precursor projects and initiatives involving struggles of different spatial coalitions with greater or lesser support from the public sector. After explaining the emergence of Model Cities, in this chapter archival and interview data are used to dig beneath the surface of Model Cities to examine the importance of two neglected production of public space projects: the Western Canal beautification and Ecumenical Plaza. Lowell City Council (LCC) has been criticised for its complicity in the destruction of significant historic buildings through the urban renewal programmes of the 1960s, particularly the loss of the Merrimack Mills Company factories and the boarding houses at Dutton Street. This chapter examines a positive contribution of LCC to post-industrial reimagining; the establishment of a Lowell historic district commission, an idea rejected initially.

The Model Cities' initiative in Lowell is often seen as the moment when ethnic diversity, cultural histories and cultural events were embraced by various interest groups and LCC. And the initiative was of course important in these respects. This chapter, however, highlights three other initiatives usually mentioned in passing if at all in the consideration of Lowell's post-industrial transformation. The first, the Lowell Regatta, dates back to 1950s and was a unique fusion of sport, culture and ethnic diversity. The second, the Lowell Museum, provided a range of vital technical and collaborative experience that became critical in demonstrating the feasibility of LNHP. The third, Lowell Heritage State Park (LHSP) is shown in this chapter to be the most salient moment in the pre-LNHP era of Lowell's post-industrial reimagining. The emergence and significance of the LHSP is tied intimately to the most significant private company in Lowell's dramatic industrial growth and decline – L&C. Since 1792 this company has owned all of Lowell's canal water rights and significant land and property associated with the canals and mills. Once the most powerful entity in the city, by the 1970s it was experiencing financially tough times which would eventually threaten the whole LNHP project. Finally in this chapter, I examine the origin of the national park idea from a new perspective. The chapter seeks to make a vital distinction between the origin of an idea and its conceptual development towards feasibility. In excavating these interrelated histories, it is sometimes necessary, as in the other chapters, to jump back and forth in time and engage in chronological gymnastics which hopefully are not too disorientating.

Cultural innovations: welcome Model Cities

The Model Cities programme was a critical factor that helped to shape the post-industrial reimagining of Lowell, ushering in a concomitant production of public space era. It was important not just for its direct impacts but also for its catalytic effects which stimulated a range of subsequent interventions. While Lowell Model Cities programme is often mentioned in the research literature, researchers rarely present much by way of empirical analysis. Interest is usually limited to the role played by the Lowell Model Cities Education Component in generating the idea of a Lowell national park (see Ryan 1991; Stanton 2006; Marion 2014a). Without doubt the 1960s was a tumultuous decade for US urban society and federal politics. Federal urban renewal programmes, conceived in the 1940s, were sustaining intense criticism and the government needed a credible alternative. After the startlingly provocative claim by Senator John F. Kennedy in 1960 that 17 million Americans live in poverty and go to bed hungry each night, President Lyndon B. Johnson promised repeatedly in his 'Great Society' speeches to tackle the problems of poverty in the US. In the wake of serious urban unrest, continuing urban problems and perceived failure of federal urban renewal programmes, Johnson signed into law the Demonstration Cities and Metropolitan Development Act of 1966.

The Act was based on the recommendations of the Task Force on Urban Problems, chaired by Robert Wood, political science professor at Massachusetts Institute of Technology. Wood was tasked by Johnson with investigating urban problems and recommending solutions. The subsequent statue allowed for a multiplicity of initiatives and projects. Critically, for the key themes in this and the next chapter, the 1966 Act made provision for recreational and cultural programmes. These aspects of the legislation, often ignored in the literature, would eventually prove decisive for the creation of LNHP. It was hoped that the limited number of projects designated under the Act would be innovative and serve to demonstrate to cities nationwide how urban problems could be not just be ameliorated but eradicated.

Of course the focus of Model Cities' legislation was mainly economic revitalisation, the provision of new housing, improved health and reduced crime. Fatefully though, the 1966 Act contained provision not just for economic and social intervention but for historic preservation, which was to have profound implications for Lowell's Model Cities programme and the campaign to establish a federal historical park. Title V allowed federal grants to be disbursed for surveys of historic structures and areas:

... the Secretary is authorized to make grants to assist any city, other municipality, or county in making a survey of the structures and sites in such locality which are determined by its appropriate authorities to be of historic or architectural value. Any such survey shall be designed to identify the historic structures and sites in the locality, determine the cost of their rehabilitation or restoration, and provide such other information as may be necessary or appropriate to serve as a foundation for a balanced and effective program of historic preservation in such locality. (Demonstration Cities and Metropolitan Development Act of 1966, Title V, Section 604h)

Title VII relating to urban beautification and historic preservation resonated with the changing national mood regarding the switch from modernist planning's disparagement of the past to an increasing embrace and eventually adoration of urban material heritage:

The Congress further finds that there is a need for timely action to preserve and restore areas, sites, and structures of historic or architectural value in order that these remaining evidences of our past history and heritage shall not be lost or destroyed through the expansion and development of the Nation's urban areas. (Demonstration Cities and Metropolitan Development Act of 1966, Title VII, Section 605c)

Unfortunately, for those who drafted the legislation, demonstrations, often leading to major urban disturbances, violent confrontations and riots were commonplace in major US cities in the mid-1960s, whether provoked by anti-war or anti-Jim Crow sentiments. In this context the demonstration programme was renamed Model Cities by Johnson, in order to avoid political embarrassment and accusations from opponents on the political right that the money may actually be used to fund demonstrations and riots. Model Cities' federal funding was allocated through a process of competitive bidding organised by the Department of Housing and Urban Development (HUD), which would also disburse the funding. Cities had to identify one distinct area, a blighted neighbourhood, and propose a series of innovative initiatives and projects to combat defined urban problems, especially poor housing, poor health, unemployment and crime.

Lowell's Model Cities proposal focused on a neighbourhood called The Acre (400 acres, 13,000 people), which was and is a multi-ethnic neighbourhood at the western edge of downtown. A coalition of community groups was represented in Model Cities by the Acre Model Neighbourhood Organisation (AMNO). The Acre was chosen partly because it was where successive communities had long suffered from poor health, poverty and degraded environments, but there were other reasons. Patrick Mogan was a major advocate of The Acre. Mogan was a prominent educator and long range planner who was to play a pivotal role in Model Cities and the establishment of the LNHP (see Chapter Five). He claimed that the area was nominated because it is historically important and had enormous potential: 'All the ethnic groups had roots there, and it's also the core of the city – where the city started.' (in Black 1973).

From the start LCC showed intense determination to win Model Cities status. It was the first US city to have meetings with HUD officials in Washington. During the preparation of the bid document Lowell Mayor Edward J. Early managed to assemble not so much a team but an army of over 100 committed individuals across the spheres of: education, crime, urban planning, housing, community development, health, economics, local government, business, religion and civil society. In addition to paid professionals and local, state and federal politicians, the Model Cities core bid team was supported by hundreds of volunteers contributing either as individuals or through Lowell's many active non-profit organisations. This type of broad based coalition, in particular the local community elements, would later become vital during the campaign to establish the state and national parks. Mayor Early and a small committee, which included Patrick Mogan, assembled seven task forces to work on different aspects of the bid. Unsurprisingly, the taskforces focused on the obvious economic, social and physical problems facing The Acre, but most significantly taskforce six dealt with recreation, culture and preservation. Unlike urban renewal with its tight focus on demolition, economic and housing matters, it was realised at the local level that Model Cities was more flexible:

If a proper plan is drawn massive federal monies will be made available to build model service centers, model schools, new cultural facilities and much more. The government wants the 'Model Cities' communities to think big, to present bold ideas that will not only solve a neighborhood's physical problems but also to try and come up with solutions to the long welfare lists, to unemployment, to juvenile delinquency and crime. (*Lowell Sun* 1967)

The potential for cultural facilities to be included in Model Cities' schemes became indispensable for the campaign to establish the national park. William Nash, professor of city and regional planning at Harvard University, was the man entrusted by LCC to coordinate the bid process and oversee the production of the bid document. He did so with great aplomb. Lowell submitted the bid well ahead of the deadline. Hopes were high until a startling front page headline in the *Lowell Sun* screamed:

LOWELL LOSES MODEL CITY BID
Rumours that Boston, Cambridge and Springfield have been unofficially chosen as model cities in Massachusetts by the Department of Housing and Urban Development are apparently true, reputable sources admitted here today. (Washington Bureau 1967)

A Washington based journalist was obviously over reacting to rumours reverberating around Washington and Lowell. Despite reporting denials of the rumour by Bradford Morse and HUD Secretary Robert Weaver, the newspaper could not resist a headline that was bound to cause consternation in Lowell but would stimulate high sales. With a strong bid drawing House and Senate support, Lowell was always going to be a serious contender and punch above its population weight. In November 1967 HUD Secretary Robert C. Weaver named 63 successful city bids including Lowell. Lowell's success was a propitious achievement, especially since bigger cities such as Los Angeles and Cleveland were not successful: Los Angeles because its proposal did not meet the criteria and Cleveland because its proposal was deemed unimpressive

The Acre Model Cities programme ran for seven years and, although funding was cut drastically by the Richard Nixon administration from 1970, there is no doubt that the host of social, physical, economic and cultural projects improved greatly the lives of many residents. It is not the intention here to evaluate the Model Cities, nor is it to rehash the undoubtedly important role Patrick Mogan played in helping to initiate the LNHP in his capacity as the director of the Model Cities Education Component. Rather the focus is on neglected questions of the possibilities for historic preservation and cultural regeneration presented by Model Cities. Three projects are analysed. Two are physical projects: the Western Canal beautification (or environmental improvement) scheme; and the wonderfully named Ecumenical Plaza in The Acre. Despite the focus of Model Cities programme on housing, social, economic, health and crime issues, it should be noted that in dollar terms these were some of the biggest physical improvement projects undertaken. The third is not a physical project but the process through which Lowell Model Cities Agency was able to negotiate successfully easement and water rights from L&C.

The Acre and Western Canal

John Tavares, Lowell's Model Cities director, understood the importance of observable projects in The Acre neighbourhood as critically important symbols:

> ... visible results were necessary to keep interest in the program alive. Success is to a certain extent, in the eyes of the beholder and most Acre residents think of Model Cities in terms of its parks – particularly the 'big three': North Common, Bartlett School field, and Western Canal Beautification. It is easier to assign a tag to park benches and streetlights than to identify a teacher, a nurse or a meal as 'Model Cities'. (Tavares in Bohlen 1974a)

The Western Canal is important because it flowed through the densely populated, ethnically diverse district of The Acre. One of the educational aims of Model Cities was to reconnect communities with Lowell's industrial history using the city's historic built environment. Completed in 1831, the canal branches from the Pawtucket Canal at Swamp Locks and provided waterpower for the Tremont, Lawrence and Suffolk Mills (later renamed Wannalancit), before the used water was returned to the Merrimack River. The Western Canal beautification scheme was proposed in the Model Cities' second year action plan. Boston landscape architects Paul C. K. Lu designed the scheme in 1972 which ran from Moody Street to Broadway and had an initial cost of $352,000. It involved: grading the canal banks; clearing overgrown shrubbery; planting trees; repairing and updating canal stonework; installing benches; providing high quality paving for footpaths; and constructing an enlarged pedestrian walkway along the canal edge. Improved street lighting and car parking were also included. From day one Model Cities Agency encountered serious difficulties with implementation.

A major problem was the attitude of L&C. For a year before the design was drawn up, Model Cities Agency was in intense negotiations with L&C regarding access and water rights. L&C owned all the land alongside the canals in Lowell and wanted the sum of $5,000 per annum to grant access to the Western Canal through a legally binding easement. Eldred Field was a prominent Lowell attorney and one of the directors of Corporation Investments Inc., which owned L&C and Boott Mills. His attitudes exemplified the uneasy relationship that L&C had with the Model Cities Agency regarding work to create new public space along the canals:

> We are eager to see this beautification project go ahead and we want to sit down and work it out … [but] there were many technical problems involved in allowing the $352,000 beautification project on the section of the canal between Broadway and Moody Street … The directors have an obligation to the stockholders to insure the company is not giving anything away. (Field in Phillips 1972)

What he did not mention was that he was one of the three main stockholders in Corporation Investments Inc. Jack Tavares, Model Cities Director, was adamant that the project would not interfere with the operations of the canal and that they were only looking for 'permission to enter onto the property' (in Phillips 1972). Deadlock ensued putting the Western Canal scheme in jeopardy.

In late 1972 after much fruitless bargaining LCC voted to take the land by eminent domain (compulsory purchase). Whether this was a promise, or merely a clever bluff, it worked and L&C dropped spectacularly their easement price to $1 per year. Oscillating between support and fractious profit-centred obstinacy, the ambivalence of L&C is explored in greater detail later. Experience gained in negotiating with these savvy L&C businessman was crucial for later negotiations conducted by the state, LHSP and LNHP.

The Western Canal beautification scheme was not fully completed until 1976 at a final cost of $500,000 – it was one of the last projects finalised under the Lowell Model Cities programme. Most of the projects in The Acre did not touch in any direct way on the city's nationally important industrial legacies so the Western Canal had implications beyond the creation and enhancement of new public space. It symbolised the growing appreciation of the nationally important role Lowell played in the US industrial revolution, a point understood by Robert Heroux, AMNO assistant community coordinator:

The significance of the project is that it is essentially a pilot demonstration of what can be done in the future – in an urban national park – of how the city's 5.6 miles of canals can be best utilized to give distinction and beauty to the area. (in Flanders 1972a)

With hindsight the Model Cities bid team was wise to focus on The Acre, a place brimming with historical, ethnic and cultural richness. In focusing on the Western Canal, Model Cities turned attention away from the historic mills, important though they were, towards an even more significant historical asset, the intact canal system itself. Where the Western Canal passed through The Acre it divided the Irish and Greek communities who often did not see eye to eye regarding Model Cities, but that was about to change.

Ecumenical Plaza

The Ecumenical Plaza was the elegant name given to another major beautification scheme in The Acre section of the Western Canal. It was a 'long time dream' of the chairman of the AMNO Urban Design Task Force, John Tatsios (Flanders 1972a). By chance Lowell's two largest and most architecturally flamboyant churches were built just a few yards apart in The Acre: Holy Trinity Greek Orthodox Church and St Patrick's Catholic Cathedral, the original of which was the first Catholic Church in Lowell (Figure 4.1). However, the churches were divided by the barrier of the Western Canal. Architect Paul Lu of Belmont designed the scheme, the principal component of which was a wide bridge across the canal directly in front of the churches. The religious link was the centrepiece of the plaza scheme, which also planned for cherry trees, benches and new street lighting. However, the scheme proved controversial and was resisted particularly by the Greek Orthodox Church leaders who wanted more parking spaces for the congregation instead. Jack Tavares, Model Cities director, remembered some of the heated arguments involving the leaders of both churches:

> 'Father Gilopsis was the Pastor of the [Greek] church and he wanted to talk about the Western Canal. And he wanted uhhh, free parking for the church. Now we do that by filling in the canals. No, I'm not going to fill in the canal. Oh yes we are! Oh no we're not. Oh yes we are. And father John says, "Boys! Boys! it is the Christmas season!" [Laughing]

Figure 4.1: Two of Lowell's iconic churches in The Acre: Holy Trinity Greek Orthodox Church and St Patrick's (photo © Michael Leary-Owhin)

They were good times. You know, we had some battles, sure. They were good times.' (Tavares 1998)

It is interesting to note that even though the Model Cities programme was beginning to transform representations of urban space, there was still a legacy of the Urban Renewal mind set, which saw the canals as industrial relics and impediments to progress. Despite the quarrels, work started on site in 1974, cost $356,000 and was completed in 1975. While leading a tour for journalists around some of the major Model Cities projects in The Acre in 1972, John Tatsios 'could not resist the opportunity to plug his pet project' (Flanders 1972b). Tatsios demonstrated his keen appreciation of the cultural and community development importance of this physical project when he claimed the proposed Ecumenical Plaza would:

> ... unite – physically and philosophically – two churches, Holy Trinity and St. Patrick's. Under his task force's plans the two churches would be joined by a Plaza that would be built over the Western Canal that now separates them ... More importantly, Tatsios pointed to the Plaza as a project that emanated from a task force, gained the sanction of the AMNO board and gained approval of the city council

before going to the federal government for funding. (in Flanders 1972b)

The project provided new urban public space that was animated 'by a regular series of ethnic festivals' (Stanton 2006: 91). It was one of several such projects in the early 1970s which came to fruition as the national park campaign was gathering steam. Together they created a series of demonstration impacts which functioned to show the world, or at least Congress, that an integrated network of professionals, politicians, businesses, institutions and local communities had a viable vision for a post-industrial Lowell.

Model Cities: demonstration impacts

During the 1960s few people would have conceived of Lowell as an urban tourist destination. The times had long gone when politicians, dignitaries and other distinguished visitors came to marvel at the socially enlightened industrial powerhouse that was Lowell. A significant example of the demonstration impacts of Lowell Model Cities occurred in July 1976. Hundreds of the world's leading physicists from 50 nations were attending an international conference at the University of Lowell. A programme of events and entertainment was organised for spouses, companions and children of the scientists. Several years ahead of its time, the highlight was a tour of historical sites led by Patrick Mogan, who was at that time project director for the Lowell Historic Canal District Commission (more about this in Chapter Five). Some of the tourist attractions included the Northern Canal greenway park, Pawtucket Gatehouse, Guard Locks and the giant Francis Gate which saved the city from being inundated by floodwaters in 1852 and 1936. Just as important was a walking tour through The Acre, where the 'tourists' could appreciate the ethnic distinctiveness *and* the importance of the canal system which made Lowell the pre-eminent, textile manufacturing centre in the US.

One of the tour guides that day was Mel Lezberg, president of L&C, who organised a boat tour. This tour was made viable by two previous boat tours in 1974 and 1972. Gordon Marker, coordinator of the heritage park support campaign within the Human Services Corporation (HSC), led the 1974 tour, 'in a cavalcade of four motorboats', from Swamp Locks (Bohlen 1974b). HSC was established by Pat Mogan and close associates in 1971. It was a non-profit, community based think tank coalition set up to further the work of Model Cities, especially the national park idea. A group of Congressman from the House

National Parks and Recreation subcommittee visited Lowell in April 1974 to help them assess its credibility as a future unit of the National Park Service (NPS). Roy Taylor of North Carolina, the chairman, was not just impressed by the amount of local enthusiasm for the park project; he appreciated the historical importance of the city rendered intelligible by a guided boat tour of the many locks and gatehouses on the canal system (Figure 4.2). Certainly, the Congressional visitors'

Figure 4.2: LNHP tour boats at Swamp Locks about to go into action at the start of the season in the Educative City (photo © Michael Leary-Owhin)

appreciation of the national value of Lowell's historical assets would have been rendered far more coherent since they were accompanied by engineer and L&C President Mel Lezberg, a friend of Gordon Marker. In the context of the frequent claims about the often antagonistic relationship between L&C and LNHP, Lezberg's willingness to give his time freely is interesting. His words clarify that the relationship between L&C and Model Cities resembled ambivalent support rather than outright hostility:

'And we worked closely at that time with the city. And we would get Martin Welding to donate a crane, and a bunch of us would bring our own private boats and we'd sling them into the canals. And we'd take these dignitaries on tours. And you know, going by Western Avenue, Joan

Fabrics, we'd have to make sure all the boats came over to the opposite side of the wall because they had steam discharges that would suddenly [makes sound], you know. We had a lot of work, a lot of fun making that [boat] park up.' (Lezberg 1999)

Given that the year was 1974, and President Nixon was enduring an excruciating time trying to avoid impeachment, at the end of the exciting and informative canal boat tour, chairman Roy Taylor's quip was perhaps inevitable when he joked, 'Lowell has more Watergates than Washington' (in Bohlen 1974b).

Undoubtedly, the success of the 1974 boat tour was due in part to experience gained by a similar but more speculative boat trip two years before. Gordon Marker, HSC planning team director, along with other planners and architects boarded a boat in 1972 loaned generously by the L&C to assess for themselves the practical feasibility of national park guided boat tours. And in a show of even more largess, they were accompanied by Walter Coan, master mechanic of L&C (Parsons 1972). Perhaps Marker asked his friend Eldred Field, the intellectual force behind L&C, for a favour. It was this boat trip which demonstrated that such tours were feasible but only if a great deal of work was carried out to make the canals navigable in ways never intended for power generation waterways. Lowell's Model Cities (demonstration) programme was of course instrumental in supporting projects which helped establish the credibility of a Lowell national historical park, in the eyes of a largely sceptical Congress. Four other initiatives helped to provide the seeds from which a successful national historical park campaign would blossom.

The city reacts: a civic historic commission

Historic events have the inconvenient habit of occurring in parallel as well as sequentially. So it was that while Model Cities was helping to create new public space and signal post-industrial transformation, other distinctly less famous initiatives were activated. Although perhaps not so important on their own, taken together these projects did sterling work to establish the credibility of Lowell as suitable for a national park makeover. During the campaign to save the Merrimack Mills company boarding houses from demolition, M. Brendan Fleming, professor at Lowell Technological Institute, attempted in 1965 to establish a LCC historic preservation commission. He was thwarted by a particularly obstructive councilman, John Desmond. He led the animosity towards historic preservation in Lowell and opposed Fleming opining 'Lowell's past greatness is best forgotten' (in Howard 1965). It was not just the past that was still being disparaged a decade later. Lowell's present and future offered only bleakness as indicated by Jim Cook's painfully honest views at the head of this chapter. Cook stayed and was involved closely with Lowell's transformation, working for LCC, the Lowell Plan and the Lowell Development and Financial Corporation (discussed in Chapter Five).

Partly out of frustration with the failed attempt to establish a historic commission, Fleming ran for public office and was duly elected to LCC in 1969. Having judged a change of mood, in 1971 he tried again to establish a Lowell historic district commission. This time the proposal attracted widespread political and community support. Significantly, Arthur Eno, president of the Lowell Historical Society (LHS), in giving his backing drew attention to the power canal system as being of national importance, but 'close to crumbling' (in *Lowell Sun* 1973b). Fleming's proposition was approved unanimously and a Historic District Study *Committee* established in 1971. Its purposes were: 1) to conduct a survey of buildings to assess their historic value and recommend them for preservation; and 2) to advise LCC regarding the need for the identification of historic districts and appropriate preservation measures.

The creation of the Historic District Study Committee signalled a profound change in the perspective of Lowell's official representations of space. Being relatively inexperienced in the work of historic preservation, the Committee reached out wisely in an attempt to create a support network. For example, in early 1972 the secretary of the Committee, Dennis Coffey, wrote to the Smithsonian Institution in Washington DC, which responded with positive advice, while pointing to the recent frenzy of destruction wrought by urban renewal projects:

> You have taken on a task of vital importance in attempting to preserve the archaeology of Lowell. I only wish that you had started 10 years ago before so many of the major mills and the tenant houses were leveled by the city's Urban Renewal Program… Regardless of what else is done I would strongly suggest (and this will be necessary if HUD funds were to be sought) having the entire canal system, including the dam and all other appurtenances, placed on the National Register if you have not already taken steps to do so. (Vogel 1972)

Progressively over the years, many of Lowell's historic buildings and structures were registered. In particular, the canal system was added to the National Register of Historic Places in 1976, and declared a National Historic Landmark in 1977. Such designations obviously assisted with the campaign to establish a Lowell national park.

The Historic District Committee's draft report of the 1972 recommended the creation of six historic districts for Lowell, including: an Old City District, the Tremont and Suffolk Mills District and a Boott Mills District. In addition, a Locks and Canals District would encompass the whole downtown canal system. Significantly, this suggestion would bring strict development controls for the canal banks, potentially allowing the establishment of a system of green walkways and bicycle paths. Two years later, after an exhaustive survey of Lowell's historic built environment, the Historic District Committee's final report recommended the designation of two historic districts: City Hall and Locks and Canals. The latter would include the totality of the 5.6 miles of downtown canals along with all the associated locks, gates and mill complexes. Just as important was the creation in 1973 of a Lowell Historic *Commission* with strong historic preservation and protection powers. This local Commission should not be confused with either the federal Lowell Historic Canal District Commission established by the 1975 Act or the Lowell Historic Preservation Commission created in 1978 (discussed in Chapter Five). The city's Commission would scrutinise proposals for the re-development or alteration of important buildings within the historic districts. It also necessitated L&C seeking approval before making any changes to the canal system.

Rather than focus on individual canals or buildings, the Historic District Committee understood the importance of taking a strategic approach and gaining support from the wider community. Decisions should reflect the goals of the entire community in order to promote historic preservation equitably. Keeping an eye on the bigger picture, there was strong backing for a Lowell national park, with the Committee saying it 'strongly and ardently supports the Urban National Cultural Park proposal' (City Development Authority 1973). Gordon Marker showed an astute appreciation of the implications with his comment that the creation of the Lowell Historical Commission 'will demonstrate the strong local commitment to get federal and state funds involved in the preservation of the city's unique character' (in *Lowell Sun* 1973b). The City Hall and Locks and Canals historic districts were designated by LCC in December 1972. In response to federal requirements in 1978 that Lowell review its historic preservation regulations, the Historic

Commission was reconstituted in 1983 and renamed the Lowell Historic Board. Both Commission and Board worked reasonably amicably with Lowell Historic Preservation Commission (LHPC) and later LNHP on the historic buildings rehabilitation programme because any construction work or alterations to the historic buildings had to be approved by the Commission and later the Board. Although this was largely a rubberstamping exercise there were "some restoration projects that proved controversial" and needed serious negotiation (Parrott 2012a).

Lowell Regatta: ludic waterscape

Rather like Manchester, Lowell was seen as a city of industry, ingenuity, hard work and company profits but cities are also places of leisure, recreation and fun. If the search in the 1970s was for a new post-industrial economy for Lowell, in the wake of WW2 thoughts had turned to the city's ludic future in ways which would later resonate with the work of the city's two heritage parks. Surprisingly, it was in the 1950s that Lowellians began to promote completely different representations of Lowell than simply an industrial city. When the Boston Associates first came to what was then East Chelmsford in 1821 they gazed at the falls on the Merrimack River and saw only potential water powered energy and profits. While the River had been used for leisure purposes for centuries, it was not until the 1950s that it was reimagined as a space of large scale ludic potential. In 1958 Lowell's biggest motor boating event was planned. The Lowell Sun Company and the Lowell Motor Boat Club were the sponsors of a two day water-based festival in June to be known as the Lowell Regatta, located at what was then the municipal boathouse on Pawtucket Boulevard. Lowell residents showed their appreciation for the event which was attended by about 250,000 people.

It is important to note that the Lowell Regatta depended heavily on the active participation of the members of the Lowell Motor Boat Club and LCC with Mayor Samuel Pollard and city manager Frank Barrett being particularly supportive. Important for the national park campaign which followed were the volunteers and the diversity of ethnic communities which made essential contributions. Without this coalition of interests and popular support it is unlikely that the Regatta could have flourished. It was considered more than just a sporting event. Drawing on the city's ethnic diversity, the Regatta traditionally closed with a social event: a bean supper with dancing and live music, portents of greater cultural events to come.

Over the next two decades the Regatta grew in size and scope and eventually transmuted into a cultural extravaganza. Noon (1990) documents the pivotal moment in the early 1970s when the Lowell Regatta was transformed from a two day river based sporting event into a full blown week long multicultural fiesta. Xenophon 'Zenny' Speronis, a prominent Lowell restaurant owner, had the idea for a multicultural event allied with the annual Regatta. It became known as the Greater-Lowell Regatta, or Oktoberfest. Crucially, this much enlarged festival relied on greater numbers of volunteers and passionate popular support:

> At a meeting at the Speare House in March, 1974, the idea of a series of downtown events coupled with L.T.I.'s [Lowell Technical Institute] Regatta planned for May, August, and September was presented. According to Zenny, 'Within five minutes we had a spark. Out of that quick meeting came something alive that would eventually involve hundreds of volunteers from all walks of life working as a group to carry out the things necessary to bring people to Lowell' … The Regatta depends on services and supplies donated by local organizations and businessmen. It exemplifies a spirit of cooperation among governmental, business, ethnic, civic, and educational institutions. This principle of volunteerism and cooperation has its roots in the Lowell of the 1930's, 40's and 50's. (Noon 1990)

This spirit of cooperation between a coalition of diverse interests would later be of prime importance in convincing state and federal politicians of Lowell's national park credentials. Greater-Lowell Regatta was a three day event which showcased Lowell's ethnic diversity in highly positive ways and attracted crowds of about 400,000 people. It did this at a time when many commentators thought Lowell had no future. Noon displays an eloquent appreciation of how a festival or carnival can transform and animate public space into powerfully evocative and meaningful ludic spaces. Its transient nature contributes to the heightened sensory experience:

> A festival often happens in just a single day or weekend. To most of us, it comes and goes like magic. It can transform Lowell with crowds, drums, and flags, and then disappear just as quickly. But while it is happening, a festival is powerful because it animates and affects our awareness of

sound, smell, taste, color, and movement. The emotional response that results has a lasting effect on how the participants feel about the places and people of their own city. (Noon 1990)

The enlarged Regatta transcended the boating fraternity to embrace the range of Lowell's ethnically diverse communities. Noon offers perceptive insights into the cultural and post-industrial momentum it created:

> Today, the Regatta is most closely identified with the 1990 Lowell Folk Festival. It was co-sponsor of the National Folk Festival that came to Lowell in 1987, '88 and '89. This event has brought hundreds of thousands of people to Lowell. Each of the festivals has presented a national and multicultural view of traditional arts with a special emphasis on the arts of ethnic groups resident in the Lowell area. (Noon 1990)

It is important to appreciate how the Greater-Lowell Regatta grew out of the smaller Regatta. It is just as important to comprehend how the Greater-Lowell Regatta from 1974, based on its coalition of interests, began to demonstrate the community and business capacity to deliver large scale events, which helped to reconfigure, the production of Lowell's urban public space. The organisational capability and community support engendered by the Greater-Lowell Regatta Festival Committee was a key factor in the success of the National Folk Festival (discussed in Chapter Five).

A working mill and museum

Even in the 19th century Manchester was known for its culture as well as its industry. It boasted museums, art galleries, theatres, a municipal orchestra, debating societies, learned institutes and a world ranking university. Unfortunately for Lowell, the Boston Associates tended to bestow their cultural dollar largesse closer to their Boston roots, hence Harvard University has a *Lowell House* and a *Lowell Lecture Hall*. However, in the mid-1970s, there was a grassroots resurgence of interest in Lowell history, which LHS hoped to tap into with an exhibition called *Spindle City 1820–1940: Development and Evolution of an Urban Industrial Community* (Karabatsos 2014). Out of this exhibition came the idea for a full blown museum initiated by a group of likeminded citizens who formed the Lowell Museum Task Force, including representatives from: LHS, HSC, Model Cities, Lowell Tech, Lowell State College and the city library. Once again, a coalition of organisations and individuals came together to deliver a cultural project, including: Mary Blewett, history professor at ULowell; Dennis Coffey, development planner; Joseph Kopyeinski, librarian at ULowell and Patrick Mogan, director of HSC. Task Force Members gained experience in winning grant awards, attracting vital grant funding from the National Endowment for the Humanities and the New England Regional Commission.

For the sake of clarity, this museum should not be confused with the Lowell Museum (theatre). This was founded in 1840 by Moses Kimball, a rival and friend of illustrious impresario T. P. Barnum, at a time when theatre generally was frowned on in polite, sophisticated metropolitan society for its demoralising impacts. Kimball's museum was a multifunctional space in a building at Central/Merrimack Streets. Here were all manner of artistic and natural history exhibits, shocking curiosities, serious educational lectures, but also music and entertainment. Decent Lowellians, including Mill Girls, were far too refined to attend something that simply called itself a theatre, but would enjoy an evening's entertainment at the Lowell Museum. Unfortunately, the building suffered severe fire damage in 1853 and 1856; the latter inflicting complete destruction. There were suspicions at the time that the fires were set by anti-theatre zealots who had hired a torch to destroy this socially corrupting influence.

Wannalancit Mills on Suffolk Street (formerly Suffolk Mills) was the first home of the second Lowell Museum, which opened in late 1976. A fundamental aspect of the Museum was that from the start it should be integral to LHSP, for example, visitors could arrive at the Museum via the canal system in LHSP canal tour boats. In addition it was always intended that the Museum would be one of the attractions of the state park *and* the LNHP, a point made by one of the fundraisers Karen Carpenter:

> The theme is – what good is the museum unless we share it. We are hoping that the museum will become a focal point for the two parks and for the city, so that people will say the city is the Museum. (in Foreman 1976)

For a while the LNHP did have a positive impact on visitor numbers to the Museum. The Autumn 1978 Museum newsletter reported that visitors to its Spindle City exhibit were coming from all over the world in large numbers. However, after the opening of LNHP's own museum exhibitions Lowell Museum found it tougher to survive.

Paradoxically, it became increasingly difficult, "to raise funds for a small, non-profit when the state and federal governments were funding their respective parks" (Karabatsos 2014). Sadly, the Museum was forced to close in the early 1980s. For a while it seemed to epitomise all that was innovative and refreshing about post-industrial Lowell. In fact, the term post-industrial is misleading here. Up until the Museum closed Wannalancit Mills were still making textiles, with a large portion of the workforce hailing from Columbia. So in one original factory building there was in the basement a still functioning 19th century mill turbine, on the ground floor, the Lowell Museum and on the upper floors a functioning textile mill. What the Lowell Museum project demonstrated is the belief in a post-industrial future for Lowell, where the valorisation of history and heritage would play a leading part. In a final twist, LNHP located one of its own major museum exhibits, based on turbine-flywheel-power loom interaction, in Wannalancit Mills, where visitors can still witness for themselves the drama of canal water power on which the city's initial prosperity was built (Figure 4.3).

Figure 4.3: Turbine driveshaft gearing mechanism, Wannalancit Mills, LNHP (photo © Michael Leary-Owhin)

Show us you're serious: Lowell Heritage State Park

Researchers tend to focus almost exclusively on the importance of the LNHP for the post-industrial transformation of Lowell. I argue that LHSP played a fundamental role in encouraging a belief that a federal historical park was a credible possibility, not just conceptually but practically. Although former Governor Michael Dukakis (Democrat) is often credited with creating the LHSP, it was Governor Francis Sargent (Republican), Dukakis' predecessor, who first pledged the $9 million which allowed the park to be established. When Dukakis succeeded Sargent in 1975 he too supported the heritage park notion. Lowell's first historic park came under the aegis of the Massachusetts State Department of Natural Resources (DNR). And it was the assistant secretary, Michael Padnos, who was instrumental in coordinating the planning for the heritage park and persuading Governor Sargent to support it.

The heritage park idea was first floated in the early 1970s and should be perceived in the context of other state activity. The Commonwealth of Massachusetts had been active for some time in urban recreation initiatives in the Boston metropolitan area. Waterways were often the focus of these recreation initiatives. Another strand of state activity focused on efforts to revitalise mill towns struggling with deindustrialisation through cultural projects and the heritage state park programme was part of this wider suite of interventions. Ideas for a heritage state park emerged out of community participation in the Lowell Model Cities. With popular approval, a coalition consisting of LCC, Model Cities and HSC, lobbied for a state heritage park in Lowell. In response the DNR carried out a comprehensive feasibility study, supported by a Local Advisory Committee in Lowell: Mogan, Coffey, Tavares and Frank Keefe, a Lowell city planner, were among its members. Its report, *A proposal for an Urban State Park in Lowell, Massachusetts* published in August 1974, provided not just a wealth of important data but also a strong focus on the downtown canal system as the most important historic resource. Shortly after the publication of the 1974 report, the DNR became the Department for Environmental Management (DEM). The report set out two purposes for a future park: 1) the preservation of Lowell's cultural heritage; and 2) the development of the resources that comprise the area's industrial heritage to increase public appreciation and enjoyment (DNR 1974: 2).

This persuasive and comprehensive report was the start of the official intertwining of the planning for Lowell's two historic parks and the emergence of a strategy which began to differentiate responsibilities and functions between the Commonwealth of Massachusetts and the NPS. There is an explicit recognition in the DNR report that Massachusetts would play a leading role, not just of course in the heritage park but *also* in a future national park. Early in the report was the acknowledgement that some of the objectives for the national park already proposed at that time be included in the heritage park. DNR was explicit that the city's canal resources were the backbone of Lowell's cultural heritage and merited primary consideration in the development of the heritage park concept. In order to develop the canals as an economic, educational and recreational resource, it was recognised that there was an absolute requirement: to restore, maintain, and utilise sites and historic buildings associated with the canal system, and to restore and maintain the system of locks and canals. What this meant was the Commonwealth of Massachusetts through the DNR would take chief responsibility for the waterscapes of not just a heritage park, but by implication any future national park too. It also meant the DNR and a future heritage park would have to work obtain water rights from a formidable negotiating machine – L&C.

Massachusetts Governor Francis W. Sargent gave formal approval for the LHSP in August 1974, pledging an initial budget of $9.7 million, but he did not actually appropriate the money before he left office. Michael Dukakis included the initial tranche of $4 million in his first budget. It was the first of Massachusetts' urban heritage parks and the trailblazer in the US. It was a 'moment of triumph' for all those in the city who had worked with dogged determination to see a once-scoffed dream become reality (Sylvester 1976). Of course it took a while for things to happen on the ground and the park was not opened officially to the public until 1976, by which time Michael Dukakis, who was born in Lowell, was Governor – hence the confusion about who should receive the credit for LHSP.

Patrick Mogan was credited with conceiving the heritage park concept. However, in customary magnanimous style Mogan did not seek the credit, even though it was said that he had 'stuck by his dream through thick and thin' (Sylvester 1976):

> It's the result of an awful lot of teamwork … We had an idea that staff people, both state and federal, could support. Yes, there were a lot of skeptics. In fact, it was ridiculous. At one time we had to go underground, so to speak. It all started when the [Model Cities'] citizens group began to articulate their dreams, year after year. Without a groundswell of

popular support the idea could never have been articulated. (Mogan in Bohlen 1974c)

Gordon Marker reiterated that the long struggle to establish LHSP in the face of Lowell's extant industrial decrepitude was a significant moment for the city:

> Today is a major breakthrough, in terms of getting the state finally committed ... In the beginning, people didn't take to the plan. No one thought it was very likely that it would come through, especially given the history of Lowell, and its circumstances now, which are pretty dire ... (in Bohlen 1974c)

In complimentary fashion, Frank Keefe understood the importance of the state park as a demonstration of the emerging transformation of Lowell and the capacity to attract state and federal support, given that 50% of the initial $9.7 million came from the federal government:

> ... designation of Lowell as the first urban state park is perhaps the most manifest sign that Lowell has turned the corner and is on the way to becoming a cultural and commercial center ... Instead of being an old depressed mill city, Lowell will now be an urban park. Its image will be enhanced, the attitude of its citizens bolstered and the results will attract businesses and tourists and combine to substantially improve Lowell's economic climate. (in Bohlen 1974c)

While LHSP was to focus its major investment on the physical infrastructure of the waterways and the creation of new public space, the DNR also appreciated the importance of the social and cultural animation of urban space. In 1976 the city and state agreed to joint sponsorship of a concert series on the banks of the Merrimack River at Pawtucket Boulevard, site of the Lowell Regatta, including a variety of ethnic and musical events with historical themes (DNR 1976). Securing access to the riverbank was relatively straightforward but securing access to the canal banks was an entirely different matter. What also becomes apparent through the 1974 DNR report *A proposal for an Urban State Park in Lowell, Massachusetts* is the integral nature of the canals for any future heritage park in Lowell. Mel Lezberg was adamant that it was the experience of being on the water, of literally flowing through, Lowell's dramatic living mill histories which garnered backing from local, state and federal politicians. Patrick Mogan used to say, 'we'll put boats on the canals, we'll do all of this fun stuff' and a host of important people 'came and saw and looked, and had a good time' (Lezberg 1999).

At first sight, especially to the outsider, it seems odd even a tad pedantic that the Commonwealth of Massachusetts would create its own Lowell urban park when a national park was in the pipeline. The two urban parks, far from being separate in their conceptualisation and implementation were in fact developed in tandem. A rather broken down former industrial city was not an immediately obvious candidate for national park status. Protagonists in Lowell and Massachusetts knew that bringing Congress on board would require a considerable persuasive effort. Mel Lezberg was involved in the Lowell *national* park project from its inception. He is convinced that the LHSP was vital in demonstrating to Congress that Lowell *and* Massachusetts, the private sector *and* local communities could work in harmony to deliver a successful national park:

> 'And then the Feds said you know, "why the hell should we put in all this money in if the state's not putting anything in." So then the state assumed the responsibility of putting in I don't know, I think it began at eleven million dollars or something to match the Feds' forty million. And each of them got some tasks, one of the state tasks of course was the acquisition of at least the right to use the canals, and the acquisition of all the land that abutted the canals.' (Lezberg 1999)

Lezberg's first hand insights provide empirical corroboration for the claim that the state's heritage park financial commitment represented 'a crucial selling point in a campaign to convince a somewhat reluctant Congress to create the national park in Lowell' (Gall 1991: 400). This does not mean that both parks were developed under one strategic programme, although Patrick Mogan, various interest groups and a variety of local and state politicians did support both park projects. What it does mean is that the two parks were conceptualised and operationalised in tandem. Without the state park and the 1974 report which underpinned it, securing Congressional approval for the national park would have been infinitely more difficult if not impossible. Most research attention has quite reasonably focused on the importance of the historic mill buildings for Lowell's economic revival and the creation of the national park, with little attention given to the canal system itself. In the 1960s the whole canal system (173 acres) – including: locks, gatehouses, wasteways, dams, sluices and, intriguingly, three private streets – was still in the ownership of L&C. Therefore, an examination of the role the company played in the production of new public space in Lowell, prior to the advent of the national park, is crucial for a critically informed understanding.

Teamsters, tax and delinquency

By the 1960s L&C and the Boott Mills Company (BMC) were in effect one financial entity (referred to here as L&C). Due to the impact of economic recession and the devastation of textile industry decline, both companies started defaulting on their local property taxes in the late 1960s. By 1974 L&C owed the city $500,000 (Scholz 1974). For the state park (and any future federal park) dream to become reality there would have to be legal and financial arrangements with L&C which stood to reap significant financial gains in future canal related land and property transactions. This prospect was a source of trepidation and political controversy given the substantial tax delinquency. Five sites were earmarked for state park acquisition with the income accruing to L&C. It was the prospect of L&C deriving substantial profits from future deals with a state heritage park that exposed the substantial tax defaults to the intense glare of media attention. State Representative Philip Shea threatened to block the provision of Governor Michael Dukakis' $4 million allocation to create the state park. Shea insisted the back taxes must be paid before he would support any property deals with L&C. By 1975 L&C's property tax defaults had reached $700,000 and the company was in protracted negotiations with LCC to resolve the ongoing financial impasse.

With LCC considering initiating litigation that may have forced L&C into bankruptcy, an unexpected benefactor emerged bringing salvation of sorts. In April 1975 LCC, in a startling act of apparent munificence, received a cheque for $700,000 to cover the unpaid taxes (Phillips 1975). It was by far the largest single collection of back taxes in the city's history. Invoking consternation in many politicians and citizens was the fact that the cheque was drawn on a bank account of the pension fund of the International Brotherhood of Teamsters workers' union – the Teamsters – thereby raising the prospect that L&C would fall under the control of a labour union with a dubious past and murky present. A financially and politically savvy organisation such as the Teamsters would have known exactly what it was doing by:

... establishing some priority rights and the canal system, which has inflated in value as a result of the urban national park concept. The Teamsters, by paying the tax directly, may be putting themselves in the drivers [sic] seat in future dealings. (Wallace and Phillips 1975)

Why was the Teamsters Union connected with L&C in the first place? In 1959 L&C and BMC were bought by a New York holding company called Buckeye Corporation. Buckeye ran into financial difficulties and borrowed considerable amounts from the Teamsters using L&C and BMC property as collateral. Subsequently, a financial entity called the Lowell Holding Company Inc., based in Boott Mills at John Street, bought L&C and BMC from Buckeye in 1964. It had a small number of stockholders, including Lowell attorney Eldred Field, the company clerk, and George Horrocks of Pelham New Hampshire, the assistant treasurer. Eldred Field stressed the advantages of having L&C and BMC 'controlled by capital that is 90 per cent Lowell based', adding that 'the company will always cooperate with the city as good citizens' (Barnes 1964). Some years later, the Lowell Holding Company metamorphosed into Corporation Investments Inc. (CII) which coincidently was based at Boott Mills and had the same major stockholders. When CII came into existence it was of course liable for the Buckeye mortgage debt. It became apparent in the early 1970s that the creation of a state (and national) heritage park in Lowell held great potential for raising the financial value of L&C property assets. Unsurprisingly, not only did Eldred Field resist strenuously attempts by the Teamsters to take over CII, he was a supporter of the Lowell park campaigns and 'very chummy' with Gordon Marker (Lipchitz 2004).

Trustees of the Teamsters' pension fund named on the mortgage documents included the notorious Teamsters boss James Riddle 'Jimmy' Hoffa who became President of the Teamsters in 1957. He was reputed to have close links with mafia organised crime bosses in Detroit and New York and was investigated as part of the sustained FBI crackdown on organised crime wherever its tentacles reached. Despite being questioned relentlessly in 1957 by a young, inexperienced Robert Kennedy, chief counsel for the Senate 'Rackets Committee', Hoffa avoided indictment. However, Hoffa was sentenced in 1964 to 13 years in federal prison for jury tampering and misusing union pension funds. He served only three years from 1967 because his sentence was commuted by President Richard Nixon. Hoffa disappeared in Detroit in mysterious circumstances in July 1975, coincidentally at the time the

L&C tax scandal was approaching its unexpected dénouement. Foul play was suspected but his body has never been found.

In 1957 the Teamsters union was expelled from the American Federation of Labor-Congress of Industrial Organizations because its leaders were implicated in large scale corruption and associated with organised crime. That ban was still in force in 1975. It may well be that in saving L&C from catastrophic tax default and bankruptcy, the Teamsters inadvertently expedited the LHSP project. Had the Teamsters not paid the property tax debts but acquired L&C instead, the prospect of a state or federal agency handing over public money to a tainted labour union with shredded integrity would probably have scuppered the prospects of either park being designated.

Lowell's spaces of representation

A 1992 film of Hoffa's life starring Jack Nicholson, called simply *Hoffa* focused on his union and criminal activities. The film ends with Hoffa's freshly murdered body being driven away in a Teamsters' truck, presumably for disposal, into a pale yellow Detroit sunset. It is not known whether Hoffa ever visited Lowell alive or dead. Occasionally, though, corpses *are* recovered from Lowell canals and a lawyer, political activist and friend of Paul Tsongas commented wryly:

> 'Locks and Canals at the time had mortgaged a lot of their; had a mortgage with the Teamsters Union Pension fund. We used to joke that if they drained the Locks, the Canals they'd probably find Jimmy Hoffer [sic] down there someplace.' (Lipchitz 2004)

Hoffa's belligerent personality, shady dealings, dubious associations and mysterious demise narrated in *Hoffa* make for compulsive cinema. And the film blends factual representations of space with fictional spaces of representation to bring a touch of melodrama to Lowell's production of space history.

Lowell has provided the raw material for a range of cinematic and literary spaces of representation. Although there is not sufficient space here to pursue what would be a fascinating research investigation, one novel is worth mentioning for the imaginative use made by the author, journalist Mark Arsenault, of real Lowell locations (Tuttle 2005). Rather like the Gastown fiction mentioned earlier, there are grains of truth in the story, not just canal and mill locations but also in the heroin addicted characters, who were based on real people. Arsenault wanted to do an extended newspaper piece on them but it was spiked by his editor; instead, he wrote his first novel (Arsenault 2014).

In the neo-noir crime thriller *Spiked* the idea of Lowell's canals as a disposal site for an unfortunate murder victim drives the plot. Arsenault skilfully combines real places in Lowell with a dark and brutal story involving homeless drug addicts, local politics and a massive redevelopment scheme for The Acre. Journalistic corruption emerges involving a beautiful young Cambodian woman seeking lethal revenge on a former member of the Khmer Rouge. What ignites the plot is the discovery of a corpse:

> The Worthen Canal, which passes through some of the city's roughest neighbourhoods, was known to produce a murder victim on occasion. Since it flowed from the outskirts of the city to downtown, it was usually impossible for the police to pinpoint where a body had been dumped ... Two weeks of relentless cold had iced the canal at its edges, narrowing the flow of water to a channel down the middle. A body lay face down, partially trapped in the ice. It was a man, judging by the grey trench coat. He was maybe five-foot-nine, dressed in dark slacks and black-stocking feet. The left sleeve of his raincoat was torn off at the shoulder, exposing bare arm, ugly white and bent back the wrong way at the elbow. (Arsenault 2003: 13–14)

In the book the action moves through present day Lowell and the reader is held in suspense by a murder mystery while simultaneously learning something of the city's industrial growth, decline and heritage-led renaissance. Hoffa's disappearance in 1975 and the local tax difficulties of L&C may be completely unrelated, but rather like *Spiked* the embellishment of a few facts with imaginative fiction illustrates how elements of Lefebvre's spatial triad blur into each other imbuing the production of space with intriguing complexity.

In the campaign to establish LHSP, the press, politicians, professionals and community activists never failed to mention the LNHP proposals but luckily the involvement of the Teamsters never became a major impediment. L&C was free to play a significant role in the establishment and operations of LHSP. What is salient is that the inclusion of statements about LHSP in the ongoing campaign to establish the national park were not simply rhetorical. When it came to LHSP roles and responsibilities in the proposed national park, these would be stated explicitly in the Congressional report, the 'Brown Book', which became an adjunct to the designating legislation (discussed in the next chapter).

Origin of an idea: development of a concept

Conventional wisdom asserts that Patrick Mogan had the original idea for the Lowell national park which emerged out of his educative city work while teaching in the 1950s and 1960s. Without doubt Mogan played a pivotal role in generating the idea and developing the concept. He along with Paul Tsongas certainly provided inspirational leadership and worked tirelessly in the national park campaign. And it is not my intention here to diminish in any way their vital contributions. It is quite likely that a Lowell national park would have remained a presumptuous far-fetched idea were it not for the financial clout of the Lowell Model Cities Agency and Mogan's determination to pursue the idea. In addition to the Model Cities there were two other essential sources of funding for the development of the park idea: the New England Regional Commission and the National Foundation for the Endowment of the Arts.

One of the early historical accounts is a short handbook of the LNHP which names Patrick Mogan as the visionary (with others) who proposed 'a new kind of national park' (Dublin 1992: 86). Two of the leading authorities on the park's origin name only Patrick Mogan (Ryan 1991: 382–7; Stanton 2006: 86–90) although they both accept that many other people, albeit unnamed, played a part in the origin of the idea. In a major 30 year retrospective paper commissioned by LNHP, Frenchman and Lane (2008), credit for the park idea is given to Mogan along with Lowell Director of Planning Frank Keefe. For Gittell (1992: 73) the park was solely the idea of Patrick Mogan. Nevertheless, he is the only academic to acknowledge the involvement of what he calls tantalisingly 'students and academic researchers from Harvard and MIT', who were recruited by Mogan in the early 1970s to document the city's historic resources.

It is not just academic texts which identify Patrick Mogan as the source of the national park idea. During 1970s campaigning he was hailed by many politicians and journalists as the originator of the park. Several years before the national park was designated he was lauded as the 'father of the urban park' and a newspaper editorial declared unequivocally:

> Only a few years ago, an urban national park for Lowell
> was merely an idea belonging to one of the city's more

distinguished educators, Patrick Mogan. Mogan, who has since become known as the father of the urban national park, perceived more clearly than most, the uniqueness of Lowell's culture and heritage, and saw the creation of such a park as a way to preserve it. (*Lowell Sun* 1974)

Not surprisingly Congressman Paul Cronin was able to declare without contradiction that Mogan was the 'father of the urban park concept' (in Cook 1974). More recently, another recognised Lowell authority and enthusiastic blogger on the evolution of the park attributes the idea to Mogan. In a speech at an event to celebrate Mogan's 90th birthday, Richard Howe asserted with absolute conviction that Mogan was 'the visionary behind not only the park, but Lowell's renaissance' (Howe 2008). A former park superintendent in the 2000s, Michael Creasey would also regularly refer to Mogan as the father of the park. Another protagonist in the national park drama, Paul Tsongas, is often credited with having the original idea for the park. He certainly worked incredibly hard, arguing persuasively for the merits of the park, in Lowell and Washington. His close association with the later trajectory of the park campaign perhaps led the *New York Times* to proclaim that the national park was 'an imaginative scheme put forward in the 1970's by former Senator Paul Tsongas.' (*New York Times* 1992). In the face of such compelling claims, the evidence uncovered in the archives is even more startling.

The assertion in the *New York Times* article was contested in a subsequent letter to the newspaper. Professor Michael Southworth wrote the letter. Southworth was forthright and pugnacious, with the categorical declaration that, 'Senator Tsongas was an opponent of our concept in the beginning' but was helpful years later, after the project received wide recognition. He then makes an unexpected claim:

> I developed the concept for the national park and the Boott Mill Museum in the late 1960's and early 70's for the Lowell Model Cities Education Component when I was hired to explore innovative approaches to education, the topic of my Massachusetts Institute of Technology dissertation. A design plan, done with Susan Southworth, incorporated my idea of reusing the abandoned mills and threatened canals as a cultural and educational resource. (Southworth 1992)

Southworth's contention is all the more intriguing since he does not mention Patrick Mogan. In a subsequent email conversation

Southworth elaborates on his relationship with Mogan whom he first met in the late 1960s when Southworth was looking for a city in which to carry out empirical research for his PhD. Lowell with its nationally important industrial history and threatened present seemed the perfect location:

> I vividly recall my first visit to Lowell, arriving by train from North Station on a bleak winter day just before Christmas 1967 – a Dickensian experience. Trash littered the polluted canals, and one mill had been demolished recently to make a parking lot. Other mill buildings were largely abandoned and threatened. Pat Mogan, who was assistant superintendent of schools at the time (later he became superintendent), was immediately excited about the ideas I showed him and wanted to try them in Lowell. So that was the beginning of the Lowell Urban National Park. The story of its evolution is long and complex, with many twists and turns, but something actually came of it! In 1968 I applied for individual grants for my Educative City research from the National Endowment for the Arts and the National Science Foundation. I was fortunate to be awarded both grants in 1969 and 1970. (Southworth 2014a)

Interestingly, the National Science Foundation grant was for *Research on Children's Conception and Use of the City* and the National Endowment for the Arts grant was for *Environmental Design for Research on City Information Systems for Children*. On receiving Southworth's email I was fascinated as to why he contacted Mogan in the first place. Southworth admits he had never heard of Mogan but contacted him following a suggestion from Mike Spock, Director of the Boston Children's Museum, because Spock said Morgan was looking for new ideas (Southworth 2014b). It is clear from his letter to the *New York Times* that Southworth believes he deserves some of the credit for the Lowell national park idea *and* the subsequent development of the concept. He is, though, magnanimous enough to share the credit with Patrick Mogan. In 1970 Southworth was awarded a PhD entitled *An Urban Service for Children based on analysis of Cambridgeport Boys' Conception and use of the City* by MIT. His supervisor was Kevin Lynch. Although he did not base the empirical research in Lowell, the contacts he made there facilitated him being retained by Lowell Model Cities in a consultancy capacity. So the immediate question is, do the archival data corroborate or vitiate any or all of Southworth's claims?

Tracing the history of an idea is usually a difficult challenge. So it is important to listen to what the protagonists themselves say. A documentary called *Roots of an Urban Cultural Park* was filmed by the HSC (1991). In it several prominent campaigners for the national park active in the early 1970s, and all close to Patrick Mogan, give their slightly different versions of the emergence of the urban park idea. The campaigners were: George Anagnostopoulos, Mary Bacigalupo, Lillian Lamoureux, Peter Stamas and Marie Sweeney; Mogan was also interviewed. Interestingly, none of them claim the national park idea for themselves, nor do they attribute it to Patrick Mogan and Mogan himself does not assert ownership of the park idea. While they all accept that they were contributors to the idea, they acknowledge the contributions of others. HSC made a second documentary film in 1995 called *Patrick J Mogan: visionary and realist*. Here, Patrick Mogan addresses directly the question of whether the park idea should be attributed to one person – him. With characteristic humility, the man who undoubtedly did more than anyone else to bring Lowell's urban-cultural-historical park to fruition, says:

> 'Sometimes they talk about the park as if it was the idea of one person. It was the idea of a big group of people and some of those people had to have enough confidence to step forward and articulate and risk being called crazy, because you're putting a value on this thing which for years the conventional wisdom said had no value.' (Mogan in HSC 1995)

He expanded on this point saying that the idea originated in the firmament of an enthusiastic, knowledgeable, determined constituency of advocacy, made up of the various cultural community groups in Lowell that were part of the organisation of Model Cities.

In what is probably the first announcement of a possible national park for Lowell, the *Lowell Sun* makes no mention of Southworth's role but reported in October 1970 that Patrick Mogan and Peter Stamas, working for the Model Cities Education Component, had already drawn up plans for a national park based on preliminary research conducted by the National Education Association. Their proposal suggested the use of the outdoor environment for learning. They suggested a future national park could include the Lowell-Dracut Forest area, outlining three options: 1) an extension of Concord's Minuteman Park into Lowell; 2) a more extensive park along the route of the old Middlesex transportation canal stretching from Charleston

Navy Yard to Billerica; or 3) a Lowell only park (*Lowell Sun* 1970). Mogan during his time as a teacher used Dracut Forest as a teaching and learning environment in the 1960s, so that idea could well have come from him. Michael Southworth's PhD research concerned the idea of the educative city and how cities could be used to provide learning opportunities outside the traditional classroom. In December 1970 Southworth presented a report to Model Cities containing an inventory of historic resources in Lowell that may form part of an 'educational park' (Southworth and Balster 1970).

Given the lack of recognition of Southworth's role in the early planning of the national park, I asked him if he worked directly with Bradford Morse:

> No, we did not work directly with Brad Morse. As I mentioned, Pat Mogan asked us to draft the essential elements of legislation for the park, and Pat provided the draft to Brad Morse's office. I did talk with some of his staff a few times, and, of course, they had access to everything we had prepared for the Model Cities Education Component including an inventory of historic resources in Lowell, a narrative of the significance of Lowell in the history of the industrial revolution in the U.S., programmatic opportunities within the proposed park, and the physical plan for the Lowell Discovery Network. (Southworth 2014c)

Mogan and Southworth felt the city was rich in learning opportunities but because the environment was so distressed and forbidding such potentials were being overlooked.

By the time of the creation of HSC in 1971 Southworth with his wife Susan had established an architectural–urban design company based in Boston, Southworth and Southworth. They were commissioned by Lowell Model Cities to produce a more detailed proposal for a Lowell national park. The subsequent report was called the *Lowell Discovery Network: an Urban National Park*. They drew up a series of plans to convert some of Lowell's mill buildings and canal gatehouses into: information centres, shops, art galleries, educational workshops, restaurants and housing. Once again this important contribution to the development of the park concept has been ignored in the press and in academic literatures. Despite this, Southworth and Southworth did receive a design award for the scheme from the Italian Association of Design in 1972 under the heading 'City as a Significant Environment'.

Michael Southworth was also commissioned by Model Cities to conduct a feasibility study of the cultural reuse of Wannalancit Mills (Southworth and Zien 1971).

A variety of professionals were identified in the early 1970s as contributing to changing the park dream into reality (Papirno 1972). In addition to Mogan, Papirno identified: Elizabeth Schmidt, architect; Gordon Marker, urban planner; Arthur Flynn, information consultant; and Sandra Brawley, regional planner. Papirno also mentions a $30,000 grant to HSC from the National Endowment for the Arts. However, Black (1971) provides rare archival corroboration for Southworth's version of events with her assertion that the proposal for 'the park is based on the already completed projects'. One in particular by Michael Southworth, Gyoery Kepes and Kevin Lynch, all faculty at MIT, was called the *Lowell Discovery Network and Urban National Park*.

Another piece of urban design work by Southworth and Southworth focused exclusively on Boott Mills complex. Funded by a grant of $30,000 from the federal National Endowment for the Arts, this appears to be the same grant to which Papirno referred. It allowed the Boston based architects to produce a scheme for what they called a 'Boott Mill Cultural Center' – which would constitute an important element of the proposed Urban National Cultural Park. This report was commissioned by the HSC in association with the Model Cities Education Component. It is interesting to note this proposal included exhibitions and programmes which would communicate the importance of all ethnic groups to Lowell's development and to American industrial revolution history (Flanders 1973). An indicative scheme showed that the centre would include open access art workshops for ceramics, woodworking, ethnic cooking, photography and children's art. In Boott Mills courtyard there would be theatre, concerts, dance, cinema, ethnic and history exhibits and outdoor performance spaces (Figure 4.4). Flanders is one of the few *Lowell Sun* journalists to acknowledge how the Southworths' ideas contributed to the conceptual development of the national park.

The Boott Mill Cultural Center is of central importance because it detailed for the first time how adaptive reuse of a major mill complex might be achieved and it shifted the focus from the Model Cities' projects: the canals and churches of The Acre to the historically important downtown historic industrial buildings. Although the Southworths' contribution to the evolution of the LNHP has been barely acknowledged, it was appreciated by a prominent Massachusetts senator. Edward Kennedy's efforts in pushing through the national park legislation are well known of course. What has not been brought into

Figure 4.4: Boott Mills Courtyard wonderfully restored (photo © Michael Leary-Owhin)

the public domain, though, is his gratitude for Michael Southworth's early contribution. Southworth retrieved a letter from his personal archives in which Kennedy refers to 'your designs for the mills and canals' which were to form the basis for the 'Lowell National Cultural Park' (Kennedy 1972).

While it is obvious that Michael Southworth feels his work regarding the Lowell national park should be recognised, he is nevertheless unstinting in his praise of Patrick Mogan:

> Lowell would never have become an Urban National Park if it had not been for Pat Mogan ... He was the coordinator, supporter, and glue over so many years to bring the idea to fruition and pursued it relentlessly, never discouraged by opposition from the city council or state. My involvement was at the beginning, but Pat converted all the skeptics who were intent on demolishing the mills and the canals. Somewhere I have the first draft Susan and I wrote, at Pat's request, for legislation to create and manage the national park. He persuaded many decision makers and politicians to support the project and to make it a reality. He was a magician at getting funding for Lowell from every conceivable source! (Southworth 2014a)

In the 1991 documentary, *Roots of an Urban Cultural Park*, none of the HSC team acknowledge any contribution from Michael Southworth regarding the idea or conceptual development of the national park, apart from one – Patrick Mogan. He recalls that Michael and Susan Southworth helped them come up with the theme, 'that Lowell actually is a living exhibit of the processes and the consequences of the American Industrial Revolution' (Mogan, in HSC 1991). Mogan clearly respected the important input of the Southworths and was not afraid to put this appreciation on the record. After this chapter was first drafted I was pleased to see a brief allusion to the Southworths' work in the genesis of the LNHP in the book *Mill Power: The Origin and Impact of Lowell National Historical Park*. It is right that Marion (2014a) gives the Southworths some of the credit they deserve.

Conclusions

Henri Lefebvre's prescient comments about the role of the state in the production of space are illustrated in spectacular fashion through the analyses presented in this chapter. Whether it be government at the local, state or federal levels, this chapter has revealed how spatial coalitions brought counter-projects to the attention of the public sector that were then taken up in mainstream urban policy. These spatial heritage focused coalitions, as in the case of Gastown, were not just local but reached out to generate support in the state and national capitals. Through a detailed analysis of a variety of case studies it is apparent that the production of urban public space was a vital objective in the post-industrial reimagining of Lowell. What has also emerged in this chapter is conclusive evidence that the production of public space in Lowell, particularly ludic space, has a longer history than one might imagine. Archival data analyses have demonstrated how a variety of spatial coalitions coalesced around particular issues as Lowell entered a period of transformation from stagnation and economic problems to one of an optimistic heritage valorisation.

Fresh insights and perspectives have been brought to bear in this chapter on some of the familiar issues regarding Lowell's post-industrial transition in the 1960s and 1970s. In addition to confirming the importance of men such as Patrick Mogan the chapter has revealed the significance of a range of other prominent protagonists often overlooked in conventional narratives. Methodologically speaking one source in particular is worth highlighting. That source is the database of oral history interviews with Lowellians sponsored by UMass Lowell, Centre for Lowell History and LNHP. Official reports are of course often vital for constructing production of space histories but the UMass archival data help humanise history and provide unique insights, behind what may otherwise appear to be straightforward or uncontroversial events

The Lowell Regatta and Lowell Museum were important cultural precursors that demonstrated the organisational, community, business and local political capacity to deliver important cultural interventions. Significantly, the research in this chapter demonstrates how these and other projects became integral to the state and federal historic parks. In the 1960s most reasonable people would never have considered Lowell as a heritage centred urban tourism destination. Lowell's credibility as a state heritage and federal historical park was only ensured through continuous struggle and the persistent exertions of a variety of disparate coalitions and local volunteers. In recounting the history of Lowell's transformation, a pivotal but neglected moment was the creation by LCC of the Historic Commission. This was a strategic move which signalled a shift from an exclusive focus on individual historic buildings, to one encompassing historic areas and most importantly the intact 19th century downtown power canal network.

Lowell Model Cities is highlighted repeatedly in the literature as a wellspring which brought forth the impetus for a Lowell national park but Model Cities was important in other ways usually left unexplored in the literature. By using the Model Cities' legislation in the 1960 Act regarding surveys of historic structures and areas, funding was found for the first comprehensive surveys of the city's historical assets. These surveys provided valuable data in the campaigns to establish Lowell as a credible state and national park. What The Acre Model Cities programme also did was to build the political, professional and community capacity to form effective coalitions and work towards a common purpose. From a new perspective, this chapter has focused on the particularities of several significant public space demonstration projects. These public spirited interventions are shown to have provided vital visible manifestations of how a future national park could utilise Lowell's historic, cultural and ethnic diversity assets to restore confidence in the city, and provide everyday facilities for Lowell's ordinary inhabitants. The Model Cities' focus on the Western Canal in addition to the more familiar social, health and housing projects was an inspired and effective use of federal resources.

In accounts of Lowell's post-industrial resurgence LHSP is mentioned in passing if at all. It now appears that the state DNR 1974 report behind the LHSP provided the sharp and ultimately highly effective focus on the downtown canal system. It becomes apparent from the discussion in this chapter that the DNR report and LHSP had threefold significance. First, they generated valuable information regarding the state of the canals thereby giving a realistic indication of the costs of restoration. Second, they engendered skills and experience which would become important for the LNHP campaign. Third, they demonstrated how powers, responsibilities and resources for historical asset restoration and national park management could be allocated between state and federal parks. It was, however, the actual canal based operation of the LHSP, necessitating as it did tough negotiations with L&C, which demonstrated to the federal authorities competent financial park management at the state level and how the canal system could be incorporated into a future national park.

A notable revelatory moment in this chapter concerns the role played by the Teamsters Union and Jimmy Hoffa in the production of post-industrial Lowell public space. Using various archives it has been possible to piece together how L&C came close to catastrophic bankruptcy which would certainly have derailed if not annihilated the incipient state and federal historic park projects. In paying L&C's back property taxes, the Teamsters ensured L&C's wrangling with LCC did not become a thoroughly messy, ugly and destructive debacle. The apparent largesse of the Teamsters allowed LHSP to acquire, after protracted negotiation, the necessary land and water access rights. Without such easements the canal centred heritage park as envisaged by the DNR would never have been feasible. Archival data analyses in this chapter have helped explain the vital interweaving of the campaigns to establish Lowell's two historic parks and the fact the campaigns occurred in parallel is vital for a rounded appreciation of the shift in official representations of Lowell space.

Archival data offer compelling evidence to support Michael Southworth's assertions reported in this chapter. On the one hand, lack of recognition in mainstream academic and professional literatures is rather baffling. On the other, it is understandable. He was an 'outsider', only involved for a relatively brief period in the formative years. In contrast, those who have received copious praise, and rightly so, were high profile Lowellians, many of whom had extensive political connections and amicable relations with *Lowell Sun* journalists. They stuck assiduously to the task of reimagining a heritage focused, national park orientated, post-industrial future for a decade with admirable persistence. After his critical early contributions, Michael Southworth moved on – 3,000 miles to California. Nevertheless, his input undoubtedly provided counter-representations of space which illuminated and legitimised the national park project. His contribution deserves to be recognised widely in academic and professional circles.

This chapter touched on Southworth's work with Bradford Morse. The latter of course initiated the legislative struggle to establish LNHP and while his contribution is mentioned briefly in the next chapter the spotlight there falls principally on the civic minded creation of new public space.

FIVE

Lowell:
Producing urban public space
and city transformation

... countries in the throes of rapid development blithely destroy historic spaces – houses, palaces, military and civil structures. If advantage or profit is to be found in it, then the old is swept away ... Where the destruction has not been complete, 'renovation' becomes the order of the day, or imitation or replication or neo this or neo that. In any case what had been annihilated in the earlier frenzy now becomes an object of adoration. (Lefebvre 1991: 360)

'So I get there and they're telling me all about the design and they said we've only got one problem. I said what's that? We don't own the land. I said, you don't own the land and you're designing a park. And they said, we have money to acquire it. So they were spending money on design. Shortly after it [the parking lot] was appraised at $535,000, we had the money to make the purchase and they had $2 million to build it [the park]. So it was a pretty sad looking parking lot. I said, well how are you doing to get the land. And the staff said, that's your job.' (Aucella 2012a)

Introduction

A welter of frenzies of destruction was wreaked on Lowell for several decades until the 1970s. Coincidentally, just when Lefebvre's *The Production of Space* was published in the first French edition, the mood changed to one of historic adoration in Lowell. A pinnacle of this adoration was the designation of the LNHP. It is the quality of Lowell's downtown urban public spaces which in large measure provide for the social relations which make the park work successfully in multifarious ways. It was the fusion over three decades of a city based civic ethos with state and federal public spiritedness that facilitated the enhancement of existing and the production of new urban public space in Lowell. The purpose of this chapter is not so much to recount the history of the national park, that has been accomplished several times and there are several published accounts of its emergence (Gall 1991; Ryan 1991; Stanton 2006). The story of Lowell's post-industrial revitalisation continues to fascinate researchers and recently useful contributions have been made by Weible (2011) and Minchin (2013). Undoubtedly, the most comprehensive history of the national park to date is the NPS sponsored Marion (2014a).

Although it is necessary to present brief details of the genesis of LNHP, this is done only to situate and complement the presentation of new research insights which privilege a different set of protagonists and issues from those which tend to frame the dominant academic narrative. The naming and renaming of space and place are critical moments in the production of space. Places not named are 'holes in the net', they are 'blank or marginal spaces' (Lefebvre 1991: 118). Prominent protagonists in the struggle to establish the national park had implicit understanding of the salience of establishing credible representations of urban space. An alternative aim of this chapter is to focus on how the range of interests that promoted LNHP did so partly through attempts to impose a meaningful name through which they could gain leverage to appropriate and define its objectives. Lefebvre's spatial framework should be borne in mind, particularly as analysis of the three case studies presented in the second half of the chapter unfolds. In each case, as with the case studies in the other chapters, the state and each of its constituent institutions were involved deeply in the production of space. Additionally, what becomes apparent is the involvement of other actors and agencies across the private, not-for-profit and community sectors. The cases are based on three public space projects: Kerouac Park, the Canalway/Riverwalk and Boarding House Park. They allow examination of the coalitions, interactions and challenges facing the production of inclusive urban public space.

A presidential pen slips

On 5 June 1978 US President Jimmy Carter signed the bill which created PL 95-290 and made downtown Lowell a unit of the NPS. It is customary for presidents to make an affirmative statement when enacting legislation. Carter's statement affirms the pre-eminence of Lowell in the industrial history of the country. That was not contentious but the statement is intriguing for other reasons:

Today I am signing into law H.R. 11662, which establishes the Lowell National *Historic* Park. The city of Lowell, Massachusetts, was founded in 1822 at a site on the Merrimack River about 30 miles north of Boston. Over the next 50 years the city rapidly expanded to become our Nation's first great industrial city and the center of the Northeast's textile industry. This bill will permit the *restoration and preservation* of many of Lowell's historic structures through a cooperative arrangement with *State and local governments.* (Carter 1978, emphasis added)

Three things are striking about Carter's pronouncement. Each one is stimulating in its own way and they provide convenient vantage points from which to dive into the complex details of the post-industrial imaginings which helped transform the city of Lowell. US Presidents do not usually say much at such legislative moments – but they endeavour to capture the heart and soul of the legislation. On this occasion President Carter perhaps erred too much on the side of brevity at the expense of informative accuracy. With his succinct statement, Carter inadvertently highlighted three of the major issues which will be explored in this chapter.

First is the issue of the protracted contest to name and therefore define the heart and soul of the park. Carter names the park the Lowell National *Historic* Park. This may seem trivial, a slip of the pen, but the struggle to name the national park in the 1970s was a key arena for the assertion of differing representations of urban space. HR 11662 actually called for the establishment of the Lowell National *Historical* Park, which has been the name ever since. In the academic literature, various reports and the press over the course of the decade to 1978 the park was endowed with at least 17 different names (Table 5.1). Second, Carter refers to restoration and preservation. While these were important park objectives they are by no means the only or even the most important ones. Linked with the issue of naming, restoration and preservation go to the heart of park purposes. Third, Carter denotes a cooperative arrangement of state and local governments, as being the institutional partnership mechanism for the implementation of park objectives. These three issues: the naming of urban space, the purpose of public sector interventions and the means of implementation recur throughout this chapter.

Table 5.1: The disorientating array of names for Lowell national park*

1. Educational Park

2. Federal Urban National Cultural Park

3. Greater-Lowell National Park

4. Lowell Cultural Park

5. Lowell Historic Canal District National Cultural Park

6. Lowell National Cultural Park

7. Lowell National Historic Park

8. Lowell National Urban Cultural Park

9. Lowell Urban National Cultural Park

10. National Industrial Park

11. National Park at Lowell

12. Urban Cultural Park

13. Urban National Cultural Park

14. Urban National Park

15. Urban Park

16. Urban National Historical Park

17. Lowell National Historical Park

NB Names 6., 16. and 17. were names given by federal entities

* The startling variety of names for Lowell's national park hint at the ways in which various interests sought to conceptualise and own the city's downtown space, hinting at the park's future objectives

An 11th hour act

Congressman F. Bradford Morse (Republican) was convinced by Mogan and his team about the importance and feasibility of a Lowell national park. Morse submitted the first of several national park bills in April 1972. It sought designation of Lowell as an *urban* national historical park. The Morse bill only provided brief assertions as to the national historical importance of Lowell and provided some limited detail about how the park would function. His bill drew on Mogan's Model Cities idea for a diffused and extensive Greater-Lowell national park that would embrace the Dracut Forest and Middlesex Canal. Morse briefed Senators Edward Kennedy and Edward Brooke, who were supportive of the bill. This first Lowell national park bill should be perceived in the context of the urban remit of the national parks service, dating from 1968 and the policy of 'parks to the people' inspired by NPS director George B. Hartzog Jr. Like Hartzog, Department of the Interior Secretary, Walter J. Hickel was a strong advocate of the parks to the people principle. Hickel and Richard Nixon are often credited with the urban park idea and the notion of parks to the people. It was in the 1930s though that the concept of national urban parks first emerged, when NPS director Horace M. Albright persuaded President Roosevelt to designate several relatively small scale national urban historical parks (Sellars 2007).

For Morse and Lowell serendipity appeared to smile when Rogers C. B. Morton was appointed Interior Secretary in January 1971 after Hickel was sacked by President Nixon. Morton was an old friend and Morse, 'as a parting shot', promised to brief the Interior Secretary on the merits of the bill. It was a parting shot because shortly after filing the bill Morse resigned his Congressional seat to take up a post at the United Nations. With two urban parks already designated in New York and San Francisco, President Richard Nixon, with one eye on the federal budget, was not keen on a third (Foresta 1984) and the bill faced serious opposition in Congress. It also faced opposition from the NPS where it was felt that there were many crumbling neglected mill towns in New England, several with significant ethnic minority populations (Stanton 2006: 91). Unsurprisingly perhaps, although Morse's intervention was a seminal moment for Lowell history, this bill was never enacted.

Paul Cronin, a Morse aide, replaced him in the House. Cronin's team substantially rewrote the Morse bill focusing on the core canal system and related historic mills. He filed a second bill in February 1973. Rather like the Morse bill, HR 4514 asked ambitiously that Congress establish a national park – significantly the Lowell Historic Canal District National *Cultural* Park (Washington Bureau 1973). The canal district emphasis echoes the historic district identified by the LCC's Historic Commission (mentioned in Chapter Four). This bill too failed to attract enough support and was not enacted. Following these two unsuccessful attempts, a third bill (HR 14689) was drafted by Cronin and filed in May 1974. His adroit redrafting of his second legislative foray sought not a national park but a *plan* for one. This bill was to provide for a federal feasibility study, for the preservation of the historic, *cultural*, and architectural resources of the Lowell Historic Canal District. Convincing explanations, in what Marion (2014a: 46) calls Cronin's 'compromise bill', about the value of Lowell's unique intact canal power system and the opportunity for a comprehensive feasibility study alleviated NPS opposition (Stanton 2006: 91–2).

Although it fared better than its two predecessors, the passage of the bill through Congress was by no means smooth and success never guaranteed. Towards the end of the 93rd Congress it looked as if the bill would remain locked in the Senate Subcommittee on Parks and Recreation, chaired by Senator Alan Bible. He was not well predisposed towards the bill and was the chief obstacle to 'pulling the legislation' (Black 1974) out of the subcommittee. However, Bible's sudden resignation at the 11th hour of the 93rd Congress eliminated the main impediment to Senate passage of the bill. Senator Henry 'Scoop' Jackson, chairman of the Committee on Interior and Insular Affairs, did what is called 'pulling the subcommittee, to dredge the legislation out of the subcommittee hopper and onto the Senate floor' (Black 1974). On Tuesday 17 December 1974 the bill was passed unexpectedly by voice vote of the Senate and on Friday the 93rd Congress adjourned. The day after approval Senator Edward Kennedy recalled he was pessimistic, 'if you had asked me about it yesterday. I would have told you I was 99 per cent sure it wouldn't have made it this session' (in Black 1974).

Cronin's second bill was signed into law by President Gerald Ford on 4 January 1975 as Public Law (PL) 93-645. It is interesting to note the Act did not refer to economic revitalisation, instead its purposes were:

> … preserving and interpreting for the educational and inspirational benefit of present and future generations the unique and significant contribution to our national heritage of certain historic and cultural lands, waterways, and edifices in the city of Lowell, Massachusetts (the cradle of the industrial revolution in America as well as America's first planned industrial city) with emphasis on harnessing this unique urban environment for its educational value as well as for recreation, there is hereby established the Lowell Historic Canal District Commission … (Section 1)

Note that this commission should not be confused with the city of Lowell Historic Commission or the 1978 Act Preservation Commission (to be discussed later). In another compromise the 1975 Act ensured the Lowell Historic Canal District Commission (LHCDC) consisted of balanced membership nominated by LCC, the state, NPS and other federal authorities. It was chaired by Thomas P. O'Neill III and included Patrick Morgan and Frank Keefe.

Brown Book and the DEM

David A. Crane and Partners, a Boston architectural firm, won the competition to carry out the two year, $100,000 feasibility study on behalf of LHCDC. It would culminate in a detailed plan for how a

Lowell national park might function. Crane and Partners worked jointly with other specialist consultancies, calling themselves the Lowell Team. It is interesting to note that the Lowell Team began work just before the Lowell Museum opened and its significance for the national park was highlighted by Jonathan Lane of Crane and Partners who argued that the opening of the museum demonstrated to Congress that Lowell was serious about the national park (Schubarth 1976). In January 1977, the LHCDC presented its plan for a Lowell national park to the 95th Congress and because of the distinctive colour of its cover and text, it became known as the *Brown Book*. The 250 page report is a comprehensive, well researched and visually distinctive document. It is impressive in many ways but several aspects are particularly noteworthy.

The *Brown Book* praised previous heritage based revitalisation initiatives and investments by Model Cities, the city council, the state and community sector, thereby recognising implicitly the political, technical and community expertise available to a future national park. In particular, the report applauded the designation of the city's two historic districts and the creation of the Lowell Development and Financial Corporation (LDFC, more on this later in this chapter). In a powerful vindication of LHSP's focus on the canal network, the *Brown Book* delineated DEM responsibility for the canal system. What is even more striking in the report is the explicit specification that park operations and management would be *cooperatively* undertaken by the NPS and the DEM. Lowell based members of the LHCDC were no doubt shrewd enough to realise the formidable challenges, faced by any organisation tasked with acquiring the necessary substantial, complex property and water rights from L&C. However, the most remarkable element of the report is the specification of a unique federal entity – the LHPC – the first of its kind – it would:

> … supervise a broader-gauged preservation and revitalisation effort than would be feasible or desirable for an individual agency … This effort would include: … administering a preservation programme of facade easement purchases, grants, and loans; developing and assisting educational and cultural activities; and executing a renewal program to catalyse the private redevelopment of historic structures. (LHCDC 1977: 9)

The LHPC was to be unique in its commercial *and* cultural community orientation. Its first meeting was an informal one in December 1978. Some of the commissioners in attendance were Patrick Mogan, Frank

Keefe and George Duncan. Also present were Fred Faust, soon to be the first executive director, Senator-elect Paul Tsongas and several unspecified members of the community (Sullivan 1978). Other commissioners mandated by Congress represented various government departments including the Interior and the NPS. LHPC was to be a sister organisation to LNHP with a chain of management which reported directly to the Department of the Interior. Significantly, they would share the revenue budget in a 50:50 split.

In addition to providing grants for historic building restoration and cultural programmes, of which the NPS had little experience, the *Brown Book*, in totally unprecedented fashion, expected LHPC to provide cash to the LDFC for it to provide low interest loans for historic preservation. Although traditional national parks do of course contain historic buildings and cultural assets, it was not a major purpose of these parks to provide grant aid. This point is made forcefully by Paul Marion, LHPC Director of Cultural Affairs in the 1980s:

'I don't believe the National Park Service had ever ventured into the area of grant-making. This process for arts and humanities-type activity was reserved at the federal government level for the two national endowments: National Endowment for the Arts and National Endowment for the Humanities ... The power to make both cultural grants and building grants (up to $75,000 for private developers) was reserved for the LHPC, sister agency of the Lowell National Historical Park.' (Marion 2014b)

It was obvious to the Lowell Team that the purposes of the proposed park were not those of a traditional NPS unit. Such parks are mandated with managing either federally owned, large scale wilderness areas or smaller historically important urban sites and monuments usually consisting of a few buildings or structures. In such parks the NPS has a high degree of control over its physical assets and visitor access and egress to visitor attractions. In Lowell, LNHP would provide the traditional management of visitor centres and provision of tours and interpretation. It would in addition offer technical guidance to private owners considering preservation and adaptive reuse of historic properties and impose appropriate design standards. Given that some of the most important public spaces would be the canal and river banks, easy public access would be fundamental to the functioning of this new style urban park. Significant attention in the *Brown Book* was devoted to demonstrating, in logistical detail, how the thousands of daily visitors would access and egress the park but more importantly how they would circulate within the park between the principal historic visitor attractions on foot and by rail, trolley and boat. Several of these foci are named in the report and identified for federal acquisition, for example Boott Mills. Therefore, it becomes evident that park managers, rangers, visitors and Lowellians would be creating processes of social interaction in public space; in Lefebvrian terms, they would be producing space.

A proposal to reinstate part of Lowell's early 20th century trolley system was particularly innovative. From the 1880s until 1935 Lowell had an extensive trolley or streetcar system whereby coaches the size of a single decker bus ran on rail tracks powered by overhead lines. In 1982 LNHP and LHPC commissioned the Gomaco Trolley Company, Iowa, to design and build two replica open sided streetcars to a 1902 design by the J. G. Brill Company (LHPC 1983). They began operation in 1984, were instantly popular and have remained so. Lowell now has several miles of trolley tracks orientated to the needs of national park visitors but with plans, supported by a federal grant, for expansion and upgrading for general movement around the city (Welker 2014). Comparisons with Gastown's maligned streetlights are instructive. It appears nobody has ever accused LNHP of creating fake Victorian streetcars as part of a kitsch heritage theme park. This illustrates that Lefebvre was way ahead of his time with his remarks regarding imitation and replication quoted at the epigram of this chapter.

To achieve its multiple goals the park's geographical area was to consist of two zones: a smaller intensive use zone centred downtown and a larger preservation zone or district encompassing the whole 5.6 mile canal network. In addition an administrative distinction was made between the geographical area of the LNHP proper and a buffer area, the LHPC District. Hence, in the *Brown Book* one of the most important visual representations of space emphasises how the canal system can be conceptualised as two loops: the downtown canal loop, bounded by the Merrimack, Lower Pawtucket and Eastern Canals; and the outer canal loop, bounded by the Pawtucket, Northern and Eastern Canals. NPS would concentrate its major interpretive efforts within the intensive zone but the national park would also include the whole canal network. The majority of historic preservation and restoration projects subsidised by LHPC grants and LDFC loans would also be focused on the intensive zone bounded by the downtown canal loop. DEM would focus its efforts on the whole canal system particularly renovation of locks and gatehouses, the creation of new public walkways and securing park management and public access. Keeping the cultural focus, but choosing rather strangely to exclude 'historical' from the proposed name, the culmination of the *Brown Book* was a firm recommendation:

> This report proposes the creation, by Congress, of a Lowell National Cultural Park to preserve, interpret, develop and use, for the benefit of the nation, Lowell's historic, cultural and architectural resources. (LHCDC 1977: 5)

It was now for Congress to decide whether to accept this unequivocal recommendation but if so further legislation would be needed.

National park and plan amendment

Although he was not a member, Tsongas' influence on the LHCDC is evident, for example regarding the role of LDFC. While Tsongas did not conceive the Lowell national park idea, his powerful and unswerving support from 1974 was crucial. In that year he was elected to the House, riding the wave of Democratic Party success in the post-Watergate era. His defeat of Republican Paul Cronin did not diminish the power of the political coalition that would see a national park bill through Congress. Tsongas was re-elected in 1976 and elected to the Senate in 1978. From his days as a city councilman in the 1960s, Tsongas had his own ideas about how to bring about Lowell's economic revival seeing a central role for the private sector, in an early espousal of neoliberalism, rather like Michael Heseltine in the UK in the 1980s. In the early 1970s manufacturing jobs were minimal and dwindling and industrial investment seemed to be in terminal decline. Tsongas and George Duncan of Union National Bank in 1975 cajoled nine local banks into setting up a special economic development fund for Lowell:

> 'So George Duncan and Paul Tsongas came up with this idea, well if you got the banks to talk to each other, which at that time they weren't doing, and you got them to pool their money, now just to simplify things, if you needed $100,000 and you've got 10 banks to put up 10 grand each you've only got 10 per cent of the risk. So the idea of pooling bank money, private capital, was very unique and Lowell was one of the first to do it if not the first. And Paul used his stature in Congress as chairman of the [not clear] appropriations committee, so if they weren't going to do it he was going to play hardball.' (Cook 2012)

This initiative was to have far reaching consequences which could not have been appreciated at the time. An innovative aspect of the idea was that the funds were to be distributed via a not-for-profit organisation and by disbursing low interest loans rather than grants, the LDFC could operate indefinitely:

'So they created this corporation called the Lowell Financial Development Corporation with some assets from the banks. So the idea became, well if we are going to put this money out there and minimise the risk we want to attract development here, let's put this out at 40 per cent of prime, so now you had a good deal for the borrower as well as a minimal risk for the banks.' (Cook 2012)

Interestingly, a sister organisation to the LDFC called the Lowell Plan was initiated by Paul Tsongas and associates in 1980. It is a public–private partnership, but one dominated by the private sector, which acts as an urban policy think tank and lobby group for commercial interests, particularly related but not restricted to property development. It does however have a certain civic ethos and its not-for-profit status allows it to engage in a variety of worthy causes. When it came to drafting the 1978 bill, Tsongas ensured that the LDFC was the financial entity identified specifically to channel monies from the LHPC to the private sector for economic development, mainly heritage preservation, renovation and adaptive reuse projects.

A bill (HR 11662) to provide for the establishment of the Lowell National *Historical* Park was introduced into the House in March 1978 by Tsongas. This and the resulting legislation fused in the collective memory a profound association between Tsongas and the national park. Notice that the name had changed, seemingly under pressure from the Interior Department and NPS, with references to education, culture and urban being dropped. That said, education, culture and ethnicity all feature prominently in the various titles of the Act. Despite the name given to the park, the 1978 Act recognised the national importance of far more than Lowell's historical physical assets. Significantly, although the term, cultural was expunged in naming the park, Mogan and his compatriots were no doubt satisfied to see PL 95-290 declare Lowell was 'historically and culturally the most significant planned industrial city in the US' and that the 'cultural heritage' of many of the ethnic groups that toiled in Lowell mills 'is still preserved in Lowell's neighborhoods'. With its widespread cross party Congressional support, the bill's passage through Congress was not so tentative as Cronin's.

Significantly, the 1978 Act specified geographical areas different from those specified in the *Brown Book*. The LNHP area included the whole canal network and significant parts of downtown. That was to be expected but, in a far sighted representation of space innovation, Congress designated a concomitant buffer zone but one that included sections of both banks of the Merrimack and Concord Rivers and most of the rest of downtown – the Lowell Historic Preservation District (Figure 5.1). The 1978 Act contained another unusual provision: it required the national park to implement the recommendations of the 1977 *Brown Book*. In a real sense, therefore, unlike most legislation the detail was worked out *before* the act of Congress. Obviously, there was a requirement for LNHP and LHPC personnel to be thoroughly conversant with the 1977 LHCDC report. Since several members of the LHCDC would be involved actively in the national park (see Table 5.2), that allowed for seamless continuity, drawing on a decade's experience in reconfiguring Lowell space through heritage and culture-led interventions.

Figure 5.1: Boundaries of the LNHP and the LHPC Preservation District (thanks to LNHP)

Table 5.2: Organisational continuity over two decades in Lowell: Key Characters

LHCDC	LHSP Task Force	LHPC*
Roger S Babb	Dennis Coffey	Robert F Crecco
Carl J Byers	Michael Desmarais	Brian Delaney
Robert F Crecco	Frank Keefe	Chris Delaport
Leo J Farley	Joseph Kopycinski	Charles Donahue
F Ross Holland	Armand LeMay	John B Duff
Frank Keefe	Lillian Lamoureux	George Duncan
Patrick Mogan	Edward Lemieux	Frank Keefe
Thomas P O'Neill III	Patrick Mogan	Armand LeMay
Clarence C Pusey	Kurt Schork	Patrick Mogan
Antonia Uccello	John Tavares**	Robert Paquin
Gerry D Wagers	Michael Desmarais	William Whalen

Notes: *Membership of LHPC changed over the years; these were the members in the early years. **John Tavares and Patrick Mogan were also key players in Lowell Model Cities.

US national parks over the decades developed sophisticated planning, management and operational structures and tools which would guide the work of the LNHP. Central to this was the stipulation in the 1978 Act for LNHP to produce a General Management Plan. However, little of this traditional federal paraphernalia would be of use to the unique LHPC. Congress understood this and specified that LHPC must produce a Preservation Plan. LHPC did so in 1980. Its plan was focused on mandated projects such as Boott Mills and supporting community inspired cultural initiatives. LNHP and LHPC were endowed with different powers, responsibilities and orientations. They each responded in complimentary fashion to local and federal priorities. Different interests over the course of a decade held varying, sometimes contradictory, expectations and aspirations for a national park ranging from: economic development, educative city, celebration of ethnic diversity to historic preservation and restoration. There is no evidence that any of them were familiar with Lefebvre's production of space ideas. Despite this, Lefebvre's cogitations on the peculiar swing from historic destruction to adoration are echoed in the musings of a key player in Lowell's transformation efforts:

> 'Interestingly, what was looked at as a real negative, became a real asset. So the buildings that previously people wanted to tear down; there was now money to fix them up and restore them. That was huge, initially it was a $40 million commitment and it was in June 1978 that got approved. So all of a sudden you have identity, you have federal money

coming in, you have people wanting to step in and take advantage of that federal money and restore some properties so you had a hook, a marketing tool basically. And that is simply all it was because all of a sudden what was junk is now antique.' (Cook 2012)

Lefebvre himself could not have put it better.

Through the use of grants and loans a significant proportion of the $40 million was multiplied many times through private investment in a series of major projects often delivered through a coalition of public and private sector interests. Although not the focus of this chapter, LHPC's grant programme for the rehabilitation of privately owned buildings was, "an important initiative because that allowed the community to buy into the preservation ethnic" (Parrott 2012a). Over the years the programme led to the complete façade rehabilitation of Merrimack and other major streets downtown (see the before and after photographs in Parrott and Sanders 1995).

LHPC's *Preservation Plan* (1980) and more importantly its successor, the *Preservation Plan Amendment* (1989), would be decisive not only for generating important representations of space but also for influencing greatly the production of urban public space in ways which still resonate to this day. The remaining part of this chapter is devoted to an examination of how coalitions of interest collaborated regarding representations of space, investment decisions, and spatial practice to create and animate new public spaces in the city. In doing so they inadvertently provided the capacity for the production of differential space (analysed in Chapter Eight). Three public sector led projects epitomise the struggles and compromises necessary for the production of space: the Eastern Canal/Kerouac Park, the Greenway and Boarding House Park.

Kerouac Park: contested public space

Over the past 200 years in the modern city, urban space has been created by the public and private sectors, either for its use value, its exchange value or both. Pleasant public spaces, including parks of various sizes and formats, make cities more liveable for ordinary citizens *and* more attractive to investors. This was clearly understood by the Boston Associates who created the first pleasant linear parks in 19th century Lowell. Downtown Lowell, like Manchester city centre and Gastown, was developed at high densities as industrial capital sought to extract maximum profit from investments in manufacturing. The result in

Lowell was relatively little congenial public space. By the 1980s this was a disincentive for potential investors thinking about converting mill buildings for adaptive reuse.

Not all the mills and warehouses in Lowell were of historic value. One less than pretty and unloved building, dating from the 1920s and located at the intersection of Bridge/French Streets just across the Eastern Canal from Massachusetts Mills, acquired the name the Curran-Morton warehouse. It was nine storeys, constructed of reinforced concrete and so robust that at the height of the Cold War it was identified as one of Lowell's nuclear shelters. Being a 20th century warehouse not a 19th century textile mill, there was no requirement for large windows. Its potential for adaptive reuse was reduced further by the low floor-to-ceiling height of seven feet (two metres). In the early 1980s, Emerson College, Boston, was hoping to relocate; Lowell was one of the possibilities and a delegation from the college visited Massachusetts Mills in the company of Peter Aucella, director of city planning, and his assistant, Jim Cook. During the visit, delegation members pointed disapprovingly to the unsightly warehouse and asked about its future. In a research interview Aucella recalled that he discussed the possibility of demolition with city manager, Joe Tully, who did not object in principle (Aucella 2012a). The College did not relocate to Lowell, one of the reasons being that the chairman of the Board of Trustees was "never so depressed in his life as standing amongst the mills of Lowell, because it wasn't pretty" (Aucella 2012a)

However, the fact that Emerson College even considered the adaptive reuse of Massachusetts Mills prompted Tully to instruct Aucella to draw up a draft plan showing how the site of the Curran-Morton warehouse, if demolished, could be transformed into a public park. Significantly, Tully thought there was a good chance of funding through LHSP. At this time in 1984 the idea was for grass, trees and benches, all rather basic and no Kerouac memorial idea yet. A meeting was arranged with Frank Keefe, senior Massachusetts state planner and one of the original LHPC commissioners:

'So Frank Keefe got it right away and said ok we'll take the money from the Heritage State Park programme ... He was the money guy for the state, he controlled state budgets and was senior enough and had this good relationship with the Governor, don't forget Dukakis was born here. So there were all these connections. So he said absolutely we'll do it. So the city manager Joe Tully who was a character and a half leans over with his pen and says, Frank, or he would have called him Frankee because that's the way he talked. Let's just cross off that $3 million and make it $3.5 million and get this done right. Keefe says ok [Aucella laughs].' (Aucella 2012b)

Aucella and his colleagues included in the park design a stop for the proposed Trolley system being developed by LNHP and LHPC. Although the Eastern Canal Park scheme was presented to state officials as a piece of civic enhancement, Aucella and Tully realised its potential for enhancing the attractiveness of Massachusetts Mills for private investment and adaptive reuse. It became apparent that "getting that warehouse down opened up the development potential, it brightens up that whole area" (Aucella 2012b). Massachusetts Mills were being considered for residential adaptive reuse use in a $60 million private investment scheme. Tully was a shrewd city manager and apprehended the Massachusetts Mills proposal and the public park scheme had dual potential:

> ... from the City's perspective, this state funded project will not only assume a continuation of our revitalisation efforts by providing 3000 to 4000 new job opportunities for residents [by rehabilitating the mills into condominiums] but will also add a significant piece of new public open space to the Lowell Heritage State Park and Lowell National Historical Park System. (Tully in Pagano and Bowman 1997: 82)

Before plans for the new public space were finalised, Aucella left his job at the city council in 1986 to take up the post of executive director at LHPC. During the research interview I asked Aucella about the origin of the idea for the Kerouac memorial, since after his death the only thing with Kerouac's name on it was a gravestone in Lowell's Edson Cemetery. According to Aucella, Armand Mercier, a French-Canadian-American and LHPC executive director, conceived the Kerouac memorial. Mercier certainly urged the LHPC subcommittee on cultural affairs to explore the possibility. Another contender though is Brian Foye, LNHP exhibit specialist. He affirmed that he had the idea after a meeting with Kerouac's friend, beat poet Allen Ginsberg (*Lowell Sun* 1985). Tracking the history of an idea is rarely easy, as demonstrated in the previous chapter, and space does not allow further pursuit here. A triple benefit would accrue because: a Kerouac memorial would assist people appreciate Lowell as something other than a run down, sad former industrial city; the park would facilitate the removal of an ugly building; and it would improve the financial attractiveness of the Massachusetts Mills proposal.

It is remarkable, given his worldwide fame, that until the park was created, there was no official recognition of Jack Kerouac in Lowell. Perhaps this was because by the mid-1980s, Kerouac's legacy was still a divisive topic. Many Lowellians remembered him and were not particularly enamoured by the *enfant terrible*, preferring to erase his association with their still troubled city. He was for a time a youthful sports writer for the *Lowell Sun* before he was sacked:

> '... but you could most often find him in the bar. An awful lot of people at the time in the 80s said, I knew Kerouac he was a drunk, he was no good blah blah blah [sic]. Of course let's face it most people who read him, if you're not in the right frame of mind, you say, what is this junk? It's all stream of consciousness very avant-garde and whatnot but that's what makes it brilliant.' (Aucella 2012a)

Many literary critics share Aucella's view regarding Kerouac's 'stream of consciousness' junk and it may be a justified reaction to his second novel *On the Road* (1957), which first brought Kerouac worldwide acclaim. Such critiques though do not apply to all Kerouac's writing, especially the first novel *The Town and the City* (1950), set in Lowell which he fictionalised as Galloway, on the Merrimack River. Those who read only *On the Road* will develop a skewed appreciation of the canon of a multifaceted writer whose heartfelt autobiographical work is complemented by the enchanting magical realism of *Dr Sax* (1959).

Aucella recalled a rant by a city councilman, an implacable Kerouac opponent, M. Brendan Fleming. He was opposed to any type of publicly funded memorial which would glorify drinking and drug taking. Despite some strong objections the scheme for the park was approved by a vote of 7 to 1 within LCC: the only no vote was Fleming's. Funding came mainly from the LHSP. Rather than just have a commonplace plaque, LHPC initiated a public art solicitation for a full blown Jack Kerouac memorial with a budget of $1.1 million for the Eastern Canal Park, designed by landscape architects Brown and Rowe, and $100,000 for a memorial. Three finalists were selected but because of the highly constrained brief the designs were all criticised heavily. Mary Sampras, Kerouac's sister-in-law, was summarily dismissive, complaining "The models are just too blah" (in Britton 1987). Ben Woitena, an acclaimed sculptor from San Antonio, Texas was awarded the contract to design what became called the Jack Kerouac Commemorative. It was to consist of the eight highly polished three sided granite pillars, each one eight feet (2.6 metres) high and the plan was to have extracts from Kerouac's writings on two sides. The model of Woitena's design was exhibited in City Hall, becoming something of a popular visitor attraction in its own right

Unfortunately, an unanticipated impediment threatened to scupper this unique project. LHPC realised that approval from Kerouac's estate was needed to use text from the novels. For this, Paul Marion of LHPC contacted Kerouac's widow, Stella Kerouac in Florida. After several months there was no reply, and time was running out. Out of the blue, Stella Kerouac appeared unannounced one day in Aucella's office. After being shown the model of the proposed park and commemorative at City Hall, she gave consent for use of the words from Jack's novels. She felt that the model, and the reaction to it, was an important endorsement of Kerouac's value to the city; something the citizens embraced rather than the commemorative being forced on them by an insistent city council. June 1988 saw the official opening of the Kerouac Commemorative. The dedication ceremony was attended by Stella and Kerouac's first wife Edie Parker and was followed by a week long programme of artistic happenings. Evidently, the rehabilitation of Lowell and Kerouac in the 1980s was mutually reinforcing. Instead of disowning the unruly writer Lowellians could be heard claiming, "I knew him. I went to school with him. I had a drink with him." (Morissette in Lavoie 1988)

Needless to say not everybody delivered fulsome praise for the commemorative. George F. Will writing in *Newsweek* presented a piercing critique of the 'little park' and the sentiments behind it:

> Today "On the Road" is a period piece best remembered for Truman Capote's assessment: "[It] isn't writing at all – it's typing."... Lowell's little park is one more sign that America is making a cottage industry out of recycled radicalisms. There is a glut of media evocation of "60s" idealism.... These cloying, formulaic articles report on reunions of mellowed former "radicals" who now have children and the children have orthodontists ... Like sandbox radicalism these articles recall, the nostalgia that the articles chronicle is an exercise in smug narcissism. (Will 1988)

There may be a soupçon of truth in this but Will is rather missing the point. Kerouac's memorialisation in his home town was the catalyst not just for a beat generation commemorative but an impressive new slice of urban public space. Not only is the 'Kerouac sculpture carved into the landscape of Eastern Canal Park' (Marion 1988) it *is* the cityscape *and* assists decisively in the production of new public space. Kerouac Park remains an important element of use value urban public space in downtown Lowell (Figure 5.2). A variety of trees have matured into gorgeous specimens, especially the giant majestic willows (Figure 5.3). They provide shade on hot sunny days just as the elms, planted along Dutton Street by the Boston Associates, did in the 19th century.

Figure 5.2: Jack Kerouac Commemorative at Kerouac Park (photo © Michael Leary-Owhin)

The commemorative is not just lumps of inert granite in space, it has facilitated a range of social interactions. Visitors, particularly children, interact with it in a variety of imaginative ways: they like to feel the smoothness of the granite often putting their face against it on a hot summer afternoon. Residents and visitors appreciate the quiet haven of this highly accessible urban space in which they can contemplate not just the moving and inspiring quotations from Kerouac's varied writings, but their own existence. That would certainly please Woitena, who declared that his design was inspired by a Buddhist mandala, a structure that enhances meditation (Pizzi 1988). It may also have delighted Kerouac given his flirtation with Buddhism. People of all ages make use of the park, including the elderly and teenagers. It is thoroughly inclusive space, which at times provides somewhere for homeless people to socialise, relax or sleep. This collection of public artworks was just one of several commissioned by LHPC. Other notable public art sculptures in Lowell are *Homage to Women* by Mico Kaufman, a tribute to the Mill Girls, and *The Worker* by Elliot and Ivan Schwartz, a homage to the men who built the canals. Information on these and other public artworks was gleaned from an interview with Paul Marion as he guided me around downtown Lowell (Marion 2012). That said, LNHP has been criticised for 'relative silence of the permanent exhibits', regarding the central role of cotton in the conflict between the Union North and Confederate South that precipitated the Civil War (Goldstein 2000: 134).

Figure 5.3: Majestic shady trees at Kerouac Park

Unfortunately, in 1988 Joe Tully was found guilty of fraud and corruption in public office and sentenced to three years in federal prison. The case related to property development deals not connected with Massachusetts Mills or Eastern Canal Park. Despite this, those who knew him remained loyal and praised his contribution to the city's post-industrial transformation. After his conviction, Paul Tsongas remained adamant that "He was the best city administrator I ever ran into, and had it not been for him, there would not have been a Lowell Renaissance" (in Stanton 2006: 272). Tully knew the importance of high quality public space for enhancing development value. Before him, the Boston Associates appreciated the animation of public space.

Producing linear public space: Lowell Canalway

Boston Associates in the 1820s valued the importance commercially *and* socially of attractive, popular urban public space in Lowell. Ownership of the total 5.6 mile canal system, including all the canal banks and pathways provided L&C with the opportunity in the 19th century to create not just sporadic pockets and intermittent strips of attractive public space but a systematic linear Greenway for the whole canal network. This network was of course never completed but in the 19th century significant elements were constructed, particularly the Northern Canal (linear) Park and Lucy Larcom Park on Dutton Street, first planted with elms in 1825 and originally called Anne Street Canal Park. In Lowell, as in Manchester and Vancouver, there was a belief in the therapeutic and morally uplifting qualities of urban public space. It was never just something to move through to get somewhere. Lucy Larcom Park was considered a:

> … popular place for promenading, particularly on Sundays and holidays when the mills ceased work. Many of the so called Lowell "mill girls" took part in this outdoor activity. Nineteenth century social reformers, including numerous advocates of urban parks, believed that walking about in the fresh air was a restorative exercise that helped keep workers healthy. They also stressed the importance of bringing people of different classes together and inspiring urbane, cultivated behaviour through appropriate example. (Malone and Parrott 1998: 30)

Frederick Olmsted would become famous in the late 19th century for the design of such linear parks as Boston's Emerald Necklace. He is often singled out as inventing the greenway concept. It is less well known that Lowell already had a well developed system of canal greenways a decade before Olmstead designed his first park in 1858. Therefore, today's worldwide greenway movement may well have its origins in Lowell.

Rather than a Greenway, a limited 'Canalway' was envisaged in the *Preservation Plan* (1980). Charles 'Chuck' Parrott was the LNHP's chief architect in the 1980s in charge of the Canalway project. I interviewed Chuck twice in Lowell and supplemented these data with email conversations over the course of two years. Once the important preservation and adaptive reuse programme of the LNHP had achieved significant success between 1978 and 1985, attention turned to the ambitious objective of creating a Canalway for the entire 5.6 mile canal system. It was apparent that significant amounts of the land bordering the canals were by then in public ownership of some kind but the majority of necessary land was in private ownership. Even before the Canalway programme was fully operationalised, LHSP had in 1986, after several years of negotiation, acquired significant sections of canal banks and various easements from L&C at a cost of approximately $1.3 million (Lafleur 2006).

From 1983 LHPC's architectural and planning staff worked to secure official approval for the Canalway scheme, seeing it as a series of vital public spaces to be animated by festivals and other cultural events, which they called 'Folklife'. A Canalway Task Force was established and in June 1985 its report was published espousing a vision of the Canalway as the developmental focus for the next ten years. At about the same time it was decided to seek Congressional approval for an extension to the lifespan of LHPC for another seven years. It is essential to realise that only two reasons were given: one was the imperative to complete the Canalway and the other was focused on cultural activities and Folklife. The bill to extend the lifetime of the LHPC was submitted to the House by Chester 'Chet' Atkins in April 1987 and became PL 100-134 in October 1987. Armed with a Congressional mandate to create the Canalway and additional federal funds, LHPC devoted substantial energy over the next seven years to the delivery of this major but challenging urban public space initiative.

LHPC developed rigorous and enforced standards to ensure that new and reinstated Canalway sections were constructed to high environmental and historically sympathetic designs. The policy tool that ensured this was the *Preservation Plan Amendment* (1989). It argued for a variety of Canalway benefits:

> The Canalway is a proposed system of walkways along the canals that will make them more attractive and accessible. It will offer great opportunities for cultural and recreational activities and promote further historic preservation and economic development. Portions of the Canalway have already been built, but much remains to be done. (LHPC 1989: 7)

LHPC conceptualised public space, not just in a physical sense but as a socially constructed arena for achieving some of the wider social and economic objectives of the national park. The Canalway would reach into the neighbourhoods and reinforce the notion that the city is the park. The 1989 *Preservation Plan Amendment* costed the Canalway initiative at $12.1 million, including a cultural affairs programme and additional stops for the Trolley system. Generally, the Canalway proposals were well received by local communities and the press:

> Cynics could dismiss the Canalway as little more than a $12 million sidewalk ... But it is a sidewalk that can help transform neighbourhoods and commercial district into attractive spaces, that can help attract potential customers and tourists downtown and that can enhance the overall quality of life in Lowell ... Clearly, the Canalway is a major effort to benefit all sectors of the community. It is not just a tourist frill; it will be an asset to all members of the community ... [it] will enable Lowell to turn its long-neglected canal system to a waterfront showcase ... and help Lowell complete its dream. (*Lowell Sun* 1989)

Federal funds channelled through LHPC were deployed to design and build several segments of the Canalway during the next seven years, including at Swap Locks, Eastern Canal, part of the Lower Pawtucket Canal and part of the Western Canal. Significantly also, LHPC undertook sensitive adaptive restorations of the Northern Canal Park and walkway. PL 95-290, which created LNHP, gave explicit authority to the NPS and the Massachusetts DEM to create the Canalway. Unsurprisingly then, the DEM funded and constructed three prominent segments along part of the Upper Pawtucket Canal, Lower Locks and part of the Merrimack Canal.

Although parts of the canal frontages were in public ownership or owned by private companies, the vast majority of the strips alongside all the canals were still owned by L&C. Obviously, construction work to create the individual sections of the Canalway required access for contractors. Permanent easement and waterspace rights for boat tours, organised interpretive events and for informal activities were required too. Negotiations regarding these rights proved extremely protracted over the decades. Unfortunately, the problems experienced in the 1970s when the Lowell Model Cities wanted to carry out various canalscape-related projects were simply harbingers of the struggles to come in the 1980s and 1990s. By the mid-2000s a company called

Boott Hydropower Inc., which had bought hydroelectricity generation rights from L&C, was receiving a variety of strong criticism locally due to, for example, its hostility to volunteers cleaning up the canals but more importantly because of ongoing friction with LNHP and LHSP.

The Boott Hydropower chairman, Marshall Field (son of Eldred), asserted that the company's only assets were its right to sell water power and a lack of liquidity meant "We cannot obligate ourselves to spend money if we don't have it" (in Lafleur 2006).

In the blunt opinion of Mel Lezberg (1999), President of L&C in the 1980s, "the negotiations were horrendous". LNHP superintendent Michael Creasey found it "very frustrating" that the various entities with a stake in the canals had such difficulty ironing out agreements which delineated responsibility for canal system maintenance. Creasey added that "the primary stumbling block has been Boott Hydropower's reluctance to collaborate" (in Lafleur 2006). Chuck Parrott was candid enough to admit via email exchanges that the history is a little complicated and "will reflect the messy reality of the various interests" (Parrott 2014a). He avows that L&C, and its successor Boott Hydropower, now a wholly owned affiliate of the Italian energy conglomerate ENEL, "never offered any assistance in the work of developing or maintaining the canal greenway". Furthermore, since the 1983 sale of L&C, they "have actually been most non-cooperative beyond what they minimally have to do as required by their Federal license" (Parrott 2014b). His continuing exasperation born of years of dispute is palpable:

'… in practice they have been quite obstructionist when any Canalway development or public use of those waters or lands in any way affect their operations … ENEL has always placed onerous restrictions on construction access [and] access to the river reach of the Northern Canal Walk.' (Parrott 2014b)

Despite these forthright views, Parrott urged me "to use them any way you like", adding the assurance that nothing in them will get him fired. It is perhaps inevitable, given the amount of money bound up with land and property and the hydroelectric potential of the Lowell canal system, that various elements of the Canalway project would encounter challenges and conflicts. This often occurs at the boundaries between private land, public space and civic responsibilities. LHPC did not just encounter problems with L&C during the Canalway development period. The vignette that follows illuminates other complications and controversies encountered in the production of new Canalway public space.

Canalway blue dye and sun

Before the Canalway scheme was proposed by LHPC in the 1989 *Amendment Plan*, the *Brown Book* had identified the Lower Locks area where Lowell was founded (see Chapter One) as historically important and as an essential terminus for canal boat and rail based tours. With the locks and waterway configurations surviving virtually intact, it is easy to see why this area was considered by Parrott and LHPC to be one of the most historically precious in Lowell. By the 1980s much of the cleared land at Lower Locks was in use as surface car parking. Paul Tsongas, Joe Tully, Jim Cook and a group of community leaders were instrumental in persuading property developer Arthur Robbins to build a speculative hotel at Lower Locks. Hilton was the original occupier but it changed hands several times because of its financial fragility. Similarly, An Wang founder of Wang Laboratories was also persuaded by Tsongas and a $5 million low interest loan from LDFC to build a nine storey training centre across the Pawtucket Canal from the hotel site. On completion of these two major developments in 1985 LHPC anticipated high levels of pedestrian movement from this area, along the canal between the LNHP visitor centre at Market Mills and associated parking garage (or multi-storey car park).

A critical part of this Lower Locks public space scheme was a pedestrian route passing through the so called 'industrial canyon' where tall industrial buildings rose from the water and formed an impressive canal edge (Figure 5.4). One of these was built in 1883 by Hamilton Manufacturing Company. It consisted of four storeys and was used initially as a print works, hence the original name, the Blue Dye House. In 1929 a permit was obtained to convert the ground (or first floor) into parking space. A subsequent owner removed the two upper floors in 1958. By the 1980s it was still in excellent condition and retained many of its original historic qualities. It was being used to garage newspaper delivery trucks by the Lowell Sun Company, which owned the building – hence the new name, the Lowell Sun Garage. It was ranked by LHPC an 'A' quality historic building. It is not just the original name that is fascinating. Built in the historically important Italianate style, the building was double fronted, like the Stanley and New Fountain Hotels in Vancouver. One faced Market Street, the other helped create the Industrial Canyon. Viewed from the Central Street Bridge over the Pawtucket Canal, the 40 yard Blue Dye House

Figure 5.4: Lowell's Industrial Canyon with the Blue Dye House and Canalway on the right (photo © Michael Leary-Owhin)

frontage constituted an aesthetically pleasing 19th century architectural vista, that would be enhanced functionally by the public walkway.

Although in the early 1980s the comprehensive Canalway idea had not been developed, rehabilitating and creating new canalside public footpaths *was* a priority for LHPC. By late 1981 LHPC was about to commence a '$500,000 beautification project in the area of the Pawtucket canal' (Faust 1981). An element of the scheme was to provide pedestrian access between the Market Street parking garage and proposed hotel site. Faust, LHPC executive director proclaimed the project 'will also call attention to the Lowell Sun Garage on Market Street'. It is clear that in principle at least the management of the Lowell Sun Company was happy with the proposals and 'will make every effort to cooperate'. It was felt that 'some form of a walkway at the least, does not seem to pose a problem' (O'Hearn 1981). Their cooperation was vital for project implementation since the new public walkway would be attached to the building and overhang the water.

After the work was completed an acrimonious altercation erupted between the Lowell Sun Company, usually a supportive friend, and LHPC. General Manager James O'Hearn was incandescent with rage, declaring in a stinging but well penned letter to LHPC:

> As we have indicated to you and members of your staff, we are very, very, dissatisfied with our Market Street garage

project. We had felt it would be aesthetically pleasing when the outside rehab was complete and we see now we were ever so wrong. With the exception of the new windows, the building looks about as it always did. Cleaning and pointing of the brick caused little if any improvement ... We were never warned we would have to settle for a Spic and Span job. I shudder each time I walk up Central Street and see what a failure we are involved in. (O'Hearn 1983)

Significantly, O'Hearn's letter was copied to Paul Tsongas. But it is worth noting that O'Hearn is criticising the façade rehabilitation rather than the new public walkway per se. Fred Faust diplomatically acknowledged most of the criticisms, explaining for example, that the trisodium phosphate chemical used for the brick cleaning was chosen for its minimal environmental impact, rather than its stringent cleaning power. It was suggested that the Lowell Sun Company apply for a new round of LHPC grants, where appropriate, that could help resolve most of the issues. Faust certainly diffused what could have been a nasty protracted argument and ends his letter in a conciliatory tone, affirming how much the Commission appreciated the 'public spirit of the Sun's contribution' to the project and the personal assistance of James O'Hearn (Faust 1983).

Over the next few years LHPC and the Lowell Sun Company worked amicably to restore and maintain this historically important building. Unfortunately, the historically appropriate sash windows on the ground floor were smashed periodically by vandals. In 1988 LHPC agreed to repair a number of broken windows and protect all of them with lexan panels. Furthermore LHPC agreed to remove graffiti regularly until the building was sold. It was hoped that through 'this initiative that the longstanding maintenance problems along this portion of the canalway will be resolved' for the benefit of the public (Parrott 1988). Regrettably, maintenance issues continued. Three years later, Lowell's foremost property owner Louis Saab, who ran up massive property tax debts in the 1970s, bought the building from the Lowell Sun Company. He was evidently disgruntled about the lexan window coverings and the ongoing graffiti problems. At this point however, Chrysandra 'Sandy' Walter, LNHP superintendent, stood firm in responding to Saab's demands that the park continue to maintain the building:

I'm sorry that you are dissatisfied with our termination of graffiti removal, but our involvement in the building was done only as an emergency measure and was never meant to be a continuing obligation. It would be improper for the federal government to provide ongoing maintenance of a privately owned building. (Walter 1991)

Saab was a savvy businessmen and tough negotiator but he met his match in the implacable resolve of Sandy Walter.

Don't mention sport: Merrimack Riverwalk

In Lefebvrian terms the various visual representations of Lowell's national park space are fascinating per se, for the ways in which they emphasise different physical aspects of spatial practice. Such representations are crucial for how the Canalway was imagined and implemented. Hence in the *Brown Book* a visual distinction is made between two canal loops. However, the NPS official map makes an *administrative* distinction between the LNHP area and the LHPC District (see Figure 5.1). Crucially, this visual representation of space emphasises the inclusion of both banks of the Merrimack River. To some extent the text of the *Brown Book* underplays the importance of the Merrimack River and its vital relationship with Lowell's major facilities and visitor attractions. It also minimises the integral connections with the power canals and mills, physically and historically.

While, understandably, LNHP concentrated its efforts on the area of the downtown canal loop, LHPC devoted considerable staff and financial resources to the implementation of an all-encompassing Canalway. Initially, the idea was to allow public access so that people could appreciate the sweeping 'Mile of Mills' experience. Aucella, in his role as executive director of LHPC, played a pivotal role in making the Riverwalk a reality (Bernardo 2014). The story of the Riverwalk is significant not just for the creation of new leisure and educative public space but also for the insights it provides into how a coalition of diverse interests is necessary for the production of urban space in a post-industrial transition. In the early 1990s Paul Tsongas, the Lowell Plan, LCC, LNHP and LHPC came together around three major projects: first, an extension to the Canalway to include a Merrimack Riverwalk; second, the adaptive reuse of Boott Mills for condominiums; and third, a baseball arena close to the Merrimack River. It was eventually occupied by a Boston Red Sox Class A affiliate, opened in 1998 and named LeLacheur Park Stadium. Space does not allow a discussion of the last two projects but it is important to realise that they were integral to the creation of the Riverwalk.

Constructing a ballpark and associated Riverwalk brought not just technical problems but raised financial and political issues that would necessitate eventually the support of Senator Edward Kennedy and Congressman John Kerry with presidential help from Bill Clinton. To facilitate the ballpark and Riverwalk, LHPC did an unusual labour deal with LCC to enable Aucella to become project director:

'How that river walk came to be was in the late 1990s. What happened was the city wanted to build this arena and this ballpark and they were having trouble with the arena. So the Park Service loaned me to the city to run these projects. We [the Commission] were interested because we cared about the riverfront, we cared about the Canalway so we had some interest and we wanted them to be well designed as well. So I got involved with this very public bunch of issues, controversies …' (Aucella 2012a)

In order to be viable financially the ballpark project needed substantial public subsidy, particularly as the cost increased by $1 million when it was discovered the stadium would require a retaining wall along the river frontage section. In the 1970s, Lowell was required by the federal Environmental Protection Agency to build a major sewer that would take downtown waste instead of polluting the Merrimack River. The sewer was built in the late 1970s – nothing remarkable about that. Fortuitously though, one of the engineers had an inspirational idea, that the sewer's outside casing should be square instead of round, so that in the future it could be converted easily into a walkable surface.

So in the mid-1990s Aucella and his colleagues decided to build a new river walkway on top of that sewer. This project was priced at $5.7 million and it was an eligible activity for highway funding through the federal Department of Transportation. National, state and local politicians supported it. When a delegation went to Washington to argue for the grant, Aucella told them not to mention sport and "whatever you say don't let them know that part of the walkway is the stadium outfield wall, that's bad, it's a transportation project" (Aucella 2012a). Well, they went to Washington and the first thing they said was, we need this for the ballpark. Notwithstanding this *faux pas* they did secure the grant but they were awarded only $3 million and told to come back if they needed more.

A year later with the project partially completed, the other $2.7 million was needed and Aucella remembered it like this:

'... all the political people, Senator Kennedy, Congressman John Kerry were saying like, we've got to do this. Well there was an election coming up for the US Senate and the Governor of Massachusetts was a Republican, Bill Welt and he was running against John Kerry for his Senate seat and he was getting closer and closer in the polls. So finally Kerry called Bill Clinton's White House and said I need this. He said [in his campaign] the reason you should elect me, is because I'm close to the President and I can deliver for Massachusetts. Well the newspaper [*Lowell Sun*] was saying, deliver this. So the White House blessed the $2.7 million to finish the walkway. It was extraordinary but the newspaper turns around and endorses the other guy anyway, but the funding came.' (Aucella 2012a)

In a similar way to the Canalway proper, the Merrimack Riverwalk from LeLacheur Park Stadium to Boott Mills functions as freely accessible public space, a resource to enrich the everyday experience of Lowellians. What is also noticeable is that in parts its character is more tranquil-rural than frenetic-urban (Figure 5.5); like Kerouac Park it can be a space of tranquillity. Boott Mills courtyard restoration, although beyond the scope of this book, is one of the greatest achievements of

Figure 5.5: Rural tranquillity: Merrimack Riverwalk (photo © Michael Leary-Owhin)

LHPC (Parrott 2012b). It was a long term project involving several federal funding entities and four major private sector developments and it was undertaken in association with the Riverwalk. It is important to realise too that the Canalway including the Merrimack Riverwalk is an ongoing project and is still supported by federal, state and local politicians. Congresswoman Nicki Tsongas is a long time advocate of the LNHP and the Canalway in particular. In 2014 she helped secure a further tranche of $2.8 million federal monies to extend the Riverwalk from Boott Mills to Lower Locks. When making the funding announcement Tsongas extolled the Canalway as a true highlight of city transformation:

'I used to live next to the river and walk that walk, and I loved doing that,' she said. 'But there was always a vision to keep moving it across Bridge Street and around the corner, up toward the Concord River. This is just one more piece in advancing that vision and I'm glad the federal government and the CDBG [Community Development Block Grant] funds were able to play a role.' (in Lannan 2014)

The Canalway is a testament to the civic minded interventions of the various public sector agencies in Lowell and Massachusetts. It is equivalent to the Sea Wall in Vancouver. Having walked that walk I can only concur with Tsongas. There are few better sights in Lowell than watching a flaming ruby sun descend behind bridges and mill chimneys, while enjoying a Riverwalk stroll on a warm summer's evening.

Soul of Lowell: Boarding House Park

It is perhaps entirely appropriate that, in a city founded, planned and built by industrial capital, the dominant civic public space should showcase not City Hall but the city's most iconic mill complex. Boott Mills is justly famous for being the most intact textile mill complex in the US. Built in phases which mirror the expansion of the city, it constitutes not just a physical record of industrial growth in Lowell from the 1830s to 1900, but provides insights into important steps 'in the growth of American industry, technology, water power generation and scientific management' (Bahr 1984). The first mill buildings were built close to the riverbank and as more were added through the decades, eventually the complex of nine buildings formed a large enclosed millyard. In front of the mill complex the BMC built six, three storey boarding houses, set at right angles to the mills, to provide

Figure 5.6: The last surviving Boott Mills Boarding House (bottom left), 1985 (HAER MASS,9-LOW,7, Library of Congress, Prints and Photographs Division Washington, DC)

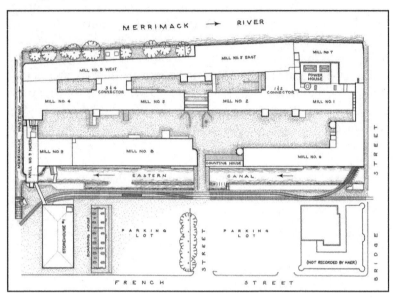

accommodation for the Yankee Mill Girls. Five were demolished in the 1930s leaving the westernmost building the only survivor (Figure 5.6). Paradoxically, the loss of these historic buildings provided the opportunity for the production of what was destined to become the most auspicious public space in Lowell – Boarding House Park. The project brought together a range of LNHP and LHPC objectives, particularly the relationships between historic preservation, the cultural remit and public space aspirations. Although PL 95-290 and the 1977 *Brown Book* identified particular buildings and structures where preservation and adaptive reuse were urgent, it did not specify particular cultural events or festivals that would be encouraged and supported nor, crucially, did it envisage the creation of new public space *where* such events might take place.

PL 95-290 required LHPC to produce a draft 'Preservation Plan' within one year and certainly before any major preservation or cultural grants could be awarded. In 1980 the final version of the LHPC *Preservation Plan* was published. It illustrated and explained how LHPC would achieve its major goals around three themes: preserving the 19th century setting, encouraging a variety of cultural expression and pursuing historic restoration projects mandated by PL 95-290. Clearly, cultural programmes were to be as important as physical preservation. Staff at the LNHP had a keen understanding that public space, whether it is streets, canalscape, parks or city squares, needed to be animated with activity. With this in mind, the *Preservation Plan* provided specific substance to the rather vague cultural aspirations of the *Brown Book*. Five site-specific projects were identified because, 'they best combined preservation and cultural objectives' (LHPC 1980: 40), including what was called 'Boott Mill Park'. The *Preservation Plan* was clear there were two aspects to its cultural remit: first, to prioritise the historical aspects of Lowell's industrial development and the role of ordinary workers in that development. To this end the LHPC would sponsor cultural programs and projects that 'use Lowell's significant structures as the setting in which the people of Lowell can tell their own story' (LHPC 1980: 3). Second, LHPC prioritised its wider cultural remit in terms of the valorisation of Lowell's ethnic diversity. In order to encourage cultural expression LHPC would:

> ... initiate a variety of projects and programs. These will include support of ethnic festivals, educational programs to portray cultural diversity, counselling in obtaining grants, scholarships, neighbourhood preservation grants, and creation of a multicultural center within the park. (LHPC 1980: 3)

Figure 5.7: Architectural artist's imaginative visual representation of a future Boarding House Park (LHPC 1980: 47 *Preservation Plan*)

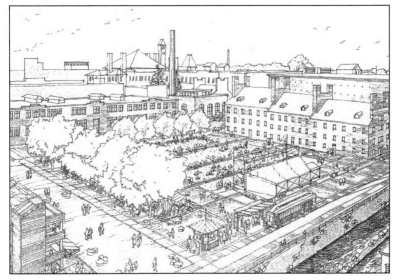

In an audacious civic minded move, LHPC promised to 'create a new civic open space' (LHPC 1980: 46) to be called Boott Mill Park. It was envisaged that the park would link the activities of the downtown commercial area with a proposed cultural centre/museum (to be housed in the remaining boarding house) and Boott Mills. Intriguingly, the 1980 *Preservation Plan* contained a remarkable visualisation of how the completed park might look (Figure 5.7). Regarding social interaction, the Plan proposed both a passive recreational area and a stepped open air performance centre, forming a terraced amphitheatre. In that sense it is reminiscent of the Castlefield Arena (see Chapter Seven). On the one hand, this was a bold proposal; on the other, it should be seen as part of the continuing project whereby new public space in Lowell is created *and* animated by social and cultural activities. While these are all important purposes for public space, I argue these production of space processes reveal the ingenuity and resilience of civic minded, public spirited intervention.

Although the idea of an outdoor theatre in downtown Lowell in 1980 seems innovative, this was not the first time this idea was mooted. Attention has already been drawn to the Southworths' 1973 proposal for a Boott Mill Cultural Center. It specified that the Center would see the conversion of the millyard into a 'festival courtyard', that would be the site for 'ethnic art, music festivals, as well as outdoor performances in warm weather' (Flanders 1973). It is worth noting that many LHPC minutes of meetings and reports refer to the proposed adaptive reuse of Boott Mills as the Boott Mill Cultural Center. The importance of the one acre site that became Boarding House Park cannot be overestimated. This derived partly from its downtown location and its being flanked to the north east by the magnificent Boott Mills. Challenges were presented by its sloping topography and its being flanked to the north west by the sadly decrepit Boott Mills' boarding houses, still displaying the livery of the H&H Paper Company. In addition, the public space of the park was to be connected into the trolley system with a stop at the Boott Mills by the Eastern Canal. Obviously, this combination of factors complicated the task of creating a new public space. More importantly though the project faced an even greater encumbrance, highlighted by Peter Aucella earlier – the privately owned site was in active everyday parking lot use.

Aucella joined LHPC as executive director in 1986. Over the next few years he became instrumental in seeing the Boarding House Park project implemented. Although Aucella evidently has a penchant for the melodramatic, as the quotation at the head of this chapter demonstrates, the crux of his sentiments is valid. His background in urban planning, project management and his keen appreciation of city politics unquestionably provided a welcome fillip for what was to become the Boarding House Park project. Certainly, the 1980 *Preservation Plan* gave high priority to the creation of a significant new public space in front of Boott Mills, but little progress was made on this project until 1986. Fortuitously, not only did Aucella have the skills and experience to tackle the complex new park project, he also knew the owner of the parking lot:

> 'Well fortunately once again Paul Tsongas a few years earlier had called me up and said there's this guy named Ed Barry who is working at mills in Lawrence Massachusetts, he's a client of our law firm, and other people in the law firm brought him to me and said, he should really be looking at Lowell. Paul said, so Peter would you give him a tour of the mills in Lowell. So I went to see him and said here's what the Commission wants to do. He said I think that would be fabulous but I've got one little problem I own 810,000 square feet of space [Boott Mills] and that's my only parking lot.' (Aucella 2012b)

Barry was understandably reluctant to part with the parking lot. Although it occupied a prime downtown location, in the mid-1980s the site for the proposed Boarding House Park was integral to the operation of Boott Mills, which at this time still provided space for hundreds of workers in a variety of commercial enterprises. Aucella explained what happened next, in an intricate deal involving: LCC, the state, the HUD, LHPC, LNHP and Barry's company, Congress Group Properties. Across the street from the parking lot was the John Street parking garage: a rather ramshackle affair with a shoddy one floor deck above the surface lot. Apparently, LCC aspired to redevelop it into a thousand car parking garage, but did not have the requisite $10 million. In effect, Barry was offering to swap the surface parking lot for a new parking garage built on the John Street lot. Aucella took the deal to the city manager, Joe Tully, confirming that LHPC would build the new downtown Boarding House Park and performance space for $2.5 million. Site acquisition would see Barry paid $0.5 million for the Boott Mills parking lot, but things grew more complex:

> 'I went to the city manager and said, we'll build a $2.5 million performing arts centre here if we can figure out how to get this land. So we are going to pay him $535,000,

my recommendation is we have him endorse the cheque to the city as payment for the broken down parking garage site. He'll renovate that as part of the financing for the whole project. But my advice is you take the $535,000 and don't just put it in the bank for the city, you put in a special fund to design a new parking garage. The city manager loved it.' (Aucella 2012b)

That still left the city needing $10 million to build a new parking garage on John Street. Fortuitously, in the 1980s Massachusetts had an off street parking programme providing 70% grants towards the cost of parking garages. LHPC and LCC convinced the state to award a grant. That was the last grant ever given in Massachusetts under the parking garage programme. With $3 million still outstanding, the city was able to secure a $1 million grant from HUD. So the city paid $2 million for a thousand car garage – an impressive piece of civic initiative.

Turning now to Boarding House Park, a design competition was initiated and three architectural practices shortlisted. In May 1985 the contract to design what was by then known as Boarding House Park was awarded to Brown and Rowe Landscape Architects. They would do the overall landscape design, with Rawn Associates engineers designing the steelwork for the performance pavilion. The creation of a new public space on this slightly sloping one acre site in downtown Lowell threw up a number of competing objectives set by LHPC. A major priority was to create a covered performance space and a seating area for several hundred spectators. Another was to memorialise the cotton industry and its workers. In addition, the new park was meant to provide an attractive low key setting for and access to the rehabilitated Boott Mills and the soon to be reconstructed Boott Mills boarding house cultural centre. On top of that, the new space was meant to be a place where residents, workers and visitors would want to spend time informally.

It is therefore easy to appreciate how LHPC's objectives for the project, the professional aspirations of Brown and Rowe and the budget constraints caused some tension throughout the design and implementation phases. Chrysandra Walter of LNHP was perturbed about how the various objectives of the brief were being prioritised. In a lengthy critique of the early design proposal she offered some support but pulled no critical punches:

Several significant problems remain with this plan, however. Most of them stem from the fact that the design's attention to the needs of a performance area have subordinated other critical agenda items. One of the most important of these is the need to serve park visitors and pedestrians by providing visual and circulation links between the restored boardinghouse and the Boott Mills complex. These links are essentially diagonal, whereas the present designs orientation is along the north–south axis features to stage, rather than the historic buildings. A row of trees effectively screens off the boardinghouse facade from the Park, instead of using the Park to feature this beautiful, restoration. (Walter 1986)

Brown and Rowe accepted most of these criticisms but remained steadfast regarding the trees in front of the boarding houses. Towards the end of the construction phase another issue of disagreement provoked a protracted exchange of correspondence. Brown and Rowe wanted to have the final say about the colour of the pavilion steelwork: red was their preference. This may seem a rather trivial matter but it sheds light on how the private sector was regarded in the design stage:

For the record, the color has always been tentatively a dark (NPS), green, or possibly a black. Chuck Parrott has explained to Mr. Rawn that one of his considerations in the color decision is the wishes of our abutting neighbor to the Park, Congress group properties, who are in the process of a $60 million development of Boott Mills. (Wittenauer 1989)

Clearly, Wittenauer, the LHPC construction supervisor, and Parrott felt that the interests of the developer Congress Group Properties needed to be given due weight in this decision and one can only speculate as to if and how Ed Barry influenced other design decisions for Boarding House Park.

In addition to the park and performance pavilion, a public art series was brought to fruition by LHPC. Sculptor Robert Cumming won the competition and designed a series of high quality textile industry themed polished granite sculptures, funded partly by the National Endowment for the Arts and located at the corners of the park. Cumming wanted people to touch them, walk on them, sit on them and he mused that the sculptures were "like brand-new sneakers that come out of the box a little too white" and he "wouldn't even mind seeing a little gum stuck to Francis Lowell's nose" before the summer is finished (in Francis 1990). In other words, he wanted the people of Lowell, including the children to use their imagination to make the park part of their everyday life. One critic thought the 'playful sculptures reflect the spirit of Lowell' (Unger 1990).

Despite a range of impediments and controversies the park was completed within budget and on time. Painted in NPS dark green, the performance pavilion creates an impressive focal point for the park, which was designed to seat 1,700 or 2,300 standing, in a sloping amphitheatre. It was opened officially in June 1990. In attendance at the dedication ceremony were State Attorney General James Shannon, Congressman Chester Atkins and former Senator Paul Tsongas. Tsongas said at the official opening that the park and the public art will provide an aesthetic boost to the city and, "I think what is out there will be considered the new soul of Lowell" (in Francis 1990). It is somehow fitting too that a Tsongas obituary starts by giving prominence to the park he helped create:

> When he stood in the raindrops at Boarding House Park, Paul Tsongas spoke of embarking upon his "journey of purpose" to become the President of the United States. We in Lowell knew better ... For Citizen Paul Tsongas, his journey to make his city and his world a better place began as soon as he was old enough to make a difference, and continued – with as much passion and purpose as ever – until it ended all too soon Saturday night. (*Lowell Sun* 1997)

Over the years, the park has hosted many wonderful large scale events and provided space for the tactile appreciation and quiet contemplation of Lowell's industrial past. Its multifarious attributes were recognised by the prestigious 1995 Federal Design Achievement Awards as a delightful example of civic architecture which encourages the kind of vigorous public life that is essential in a democratic society (Alexander 1995). That may well be so, but Boarding House Park also facilitated, inadvertently, the production of inclusive, differential space in Lowell, as discussed in Chapter Eight.

Conclusions

It would be astonishing if the process which brought LNHP to the statute books was either simple or uncontested. With 17 different names, three commissions and four congressional bills it is hardly surprising that President Carter and his aides should become discombobulated as to the correct appellation of the legal entity being brought into existence in 1978. This chapter has used the struggle to name the park, particularly in ways which would endow it with purposes beyond historic preservation, as a means to highlight key issues in the production of space. Naming the park is seen as a critical way of representing urban space and therefore a key aspect of the Lefebvrian production of space. The intention in this chapter was not to present an exhaustive LNHP history but to highlight key moments in the histories of the production of Lowell space either neglected or undervalued in previous research. History has tended to downplay the mutually reinforcing role of LHSP and LNHP, each supporting the campaign for the designation of the other. It is noticeable too that archival evidence has revealed LNHP was not solely a federal national park, it was and still is a multi–agency entity. It was LHSP which first emphasised the importance of the intact 5.6 mile power canal network. LHSP first secured, through difficult negotiations with L&C, water and property rights, later allowing LNHP to put the canal system at the centre of its vision for the park.

I conclude that it was the innovative triple agency structure of LHSP-LNHP-LHPC and the grant giving powers for both physical preservation and cultural events that created the potential for the enhanced production of new urban public spaces in downtown Lowell from 1978. By incorporating the recommendations of the *Brown Book* into PL 95-290, Congress gave either by design or accident, LNHP, LHPC and the DEM wide discretion in the subsidy and management of cultural activities which animated public space. It is apparent that the bills that went to Congress and the subsequent legislation bear the imprint of Patrick Mogan, his colleagues at Model Cities and Paul Tsongas. It is entirely fair that these two Lowellians take the lion's share of the credit; one for stressing the importance of Lowell's cultural histories and the other for amassing the political support in Washington necessary to see the 1978 national park bill enacted. Original ideas are powerful things. Ideas though will remain just that, sometimes attracting scorn and derision unless they can be fleshed out and infused with substance.

The three projects highlighted through the analysis of a variety of archival and interview sources have shed new light on the public space priorities of the public sector organisations involved. In a twist to the commonplace laments regarding the neoliberal privatisation of public space, the chapter has revealed the reverse. It has revealed what might be regarded as the public appropriation of private space for use value rather than exchange value. Federal, state and LCC politicians and officials are shown to have displayed acute awareness of the significance of attractive public space in its own right and as a stimulus to private and public investment. Much has been made in the literature of the role played by public–private partnerships, for better or worse, in Lowell's post-industrial economic transformation. What is evident from the analysis presented in this chapter is the seminal role of local, state and federal partnerships in the production of genuinely inclusive urban public space. Albeit that the Boston Associates 'descendants' in L&C did make it tough for the three-way coalition to pursue its public spirited remit. Through the lens of Lefebvrian spatial-historical analysis it is evident that where spatial coalitions emerge with a long term commitment and sufficient resources, urban space can be reconfigured in positive ways, of which the public sector can be proud and the private sector appreciative.

Kerouac Park is important then because it brings into focus several points made earlier in this book. It demonstrates the necessity of diverse spatial coalitions in order to produce new public space predominantly for its use value. In this case the project required LCC, LHSP, LNHP, LHPC, the private sector and historic-cultural preservation interests groups to bring this complex scheme to fruition on the ground. It demonstrates the relationship between attractive public urban space and private investment, hinting at the power of the private sector in ostensibly public projects. It is also important because it demonstrates how the cultural remit of the LHPC was crucial for transforming, with LHSP funding, a vague idea for a new public space into an intrinsically valuable democratic cultural asset for Lowell.

What is most conspicuous about the Canalway case study is the way it corroborates the testing issues that can arise in the production of space in the liminal edges between the public and the private realms. More positively it confirms how the various federal, civic and private interests could cooperate to create a significant addition to the Lowell's canalside public space. It elucidates too how, aspiring to create and maintain new public space requires a long term commitment, perseverance, good negotiating skills and strong nerves. The Canalway and Riverwalk function as an inclusive, totally accessible and environmentally friendly collection of linear public spaces. They connect a number of key points on the southern bank of the Merrimack River, within the Downtown Canal Loop, including: Boott Mills Museum, UMass Lowell, LeLacheur Stadium, Kerouac Park, Lucy Larcom Park and new communities at Massachusetts, Lawrence, Wannalancit and Hamilton Mills. Once again it is important to highlight these imaginative public space projects were produced through the concerted actions of diverse spatial coalitions. Rather like the Canalway, Boarding House Park demonstrates in compelling fashion what might be called the publicisation of private space. It is a small but significant victory in the production of public space based on an innovative and supportive partnership between public and private sectors. Significant though these achievements are, the importance of Boarding House Park for the production of differential space is explored in Chapter Eight.

SIX

Manchester: (Re)presenting urban space

Amid the various doubts and uncertainties with which ignorance and inattention have clouded the Roman geography of our island, no uncertainty has ever arisen and no doubt has ever been stated concerning the well-known claim of Manchester to the character of a Roman Station ... A Roman station has been acknowledged by all the antiquarians to have been constructed upon the bank of the Medlock and within the circuit of the Castle-field. And the station is considered by all of them to have been the denominated Mancunium of the Roman Itinerary. (The Rev John Whitaker 1771: 1–2)

The more carefully one examines space, considering it not only with the eyes, not only with intellect, but also with all the senses, with the total body, the more clearly one becomes aware of the conflicts at work within it ... Spatial practice is neither determined by an existing system, be it urban or ecological, nor adapted to a system, be it economic or political. On the contrary, thanks to the potential energies of a variety of groups capable of diverting homogenized space to their own purposes, theatricalized dramatized space is liable to arise. (Lefebvre 1991: 391)

Introduction

George Orwell nominated Manchester the belly and guts of the nation in his seminal text *The Road to Wigan Pier*, perhaps to echo the similar claim by Emile Zola for Les Halles market in his 1873 novel *The Belly of Paris*. With its slaughter houses and produce markets, Castlefield for a time was certainly the belly and guts of Manchester. In contrast, one of the world's first modern industrial city tourist guide books by James Ogden, *A Description of Manchester* (1783), urged visitors to begin in Castlefield, something which had become unthinkable by the 1950s, when the eminent historian A. J. P. Taylor (1977) condemned

Castlefield unflatteringly as the bottom of Deansgate. Two intriguing issues partially provided the springboard for the empirical research presented in this chapter. First, Manchester City Council's (MCC) official description of the Castlefield Conservation Area makes the interesting though apparently innocuous claim that 'The railway complex at Liverpool Road was sold to a conservation group for £1' (MCC 2008). Second, Degen (2008) cites a newspaper article that mentions a report by two historic preservation groups which proposed the establishment of a conservation area for Castlefield. Was one of these the same group that bought Liverpool Road Station (LRS)?

In this and the next chapter the focus is on providing a detailed explanation, across a decade long timescale, of how, why and by whom a post-industrial transformation involving the production of urban public space was instigated and achieved. To the casual visitor two aspects of Castlefield's spatial practice demand attention. These are the Castlefield Arena and LRS, the world's first railway station that eventually became the nationally important Museum of Science and Industry (MOSI). A number of not-for-profit historic preservation societies formed a unique series of coalitions and collaborations with the public and private sectors initiating production of space processes that contributed greatly to the post-industrial reimagining of Manchester. The next section provides a brief overview of the way Castlefield has been portrayed in recent academic literature, especially the contention that the area decayed in the 1970s and 1980s waiting to be rejuvenated in the 1990s.

The empirical research is informed by Lefebvre's claim that the three elements of the spatial triad should 'be handled with considerable caution' since to see them as separate and isolated would defeat the theoretical project (Lefebvre 1991: 42). An archival network was constructed during the research, which led to the discovery of two obscure historic preservation society reports, central for a rounded appreciation of the production of Castlefield space. The research leads in unexpected directions, uncovering linkages and alliances from Manchester to London and Granada. The research is not concerned with investigating the production of the MOSI as a collection of cultural artefacts per se. Neither is the concern with railways or LRS, per se. The focus, therefore, is on revealing the contested (re)presentations of space within the shifting coalitions created around the restoration of LRS site and the reimagining and production of urban public space. The intervention of the historic preservation societies can be understood as opening up the production of Lefebvrian 'counter-space' promoted by a 'counter-project' (Lefebvre 1991: 381).

Attitudes to Castlefield need to be understood in the context of the national mood in the 1970s. Although Stamp (2007: 138) claims that 'after the war, Manchester – like every 19th-century industrial city – began to hate itself', it was not so much 'the city', as modernist architects, planners, property developers and politicians who rejected Victorian city space in favour of orderly, clean modernist redevelopment. This disposition was captured evocatively by *Observer* journalist Stephen Gardiner (1973):

> The property developers have moved in on Manchester... Alarmed at the potential threat to a unique Victorian city, the Civic Trust for the North West invited Lucinda Lambton to make this photographic record ... "What's happening to Manchester! says the man behind the desk in the planning office. What's happening? Why it's going going gone." (What ever he may say in public this is how he talks in private.) ... "Things have changed you know. We aren't living in the nineteenth century now – you can't stop progress ...Why from what some of these preservationists on the conservation committee (that's what we call it up here) say, you'd think that Victoria was still alive. I mean one's got to be realistic. One's got to keep up with the times. Land means money. Not just money, it's a goldmine".

David Rhodes, who worked for MCC, had invited *Observer* journalist Gardiner and photographer Lambton to Manchester (Rhodes 2008). Unfortunately, Gardiner did not speak to any planners in Manchester. Rhodes was disciplined by his boss John Millar and a claim to the Press Complaints Commission by the Corporation against the *Observer* upheld.

Castlefield: a very lived upon place

Castlefield in the dominant regeneration narrative appears in the 1970s and 1980s as a place of dereliction and stagnation. Degen's comparative research features Castlefield and the El Raval area of Barcelona. She claims that Castlefield changed from a lively working class industrial neighbourhood to 'an abandoned place devoid of most of its population, a forgotten wasteland, filled with scrap-yards and derelict canals' (Degen 2008: 79). A quotation from the *Manchester Evening News* is used by Degen to emphasise the point that Castlefield was:

… a decaying little known backwater on the fringe of Manchester's city centre … Like a doormat trodden on by the passage of time, it lies now in Manchester's forgotten no man's land – a city's classic backyard … where the sun never shines beneath the stairway to the city's history. (in Degen 2008: 79–80)

However, this quotation is from an article entitled 'Treasures in city's backyard' which drew attention to the Roman archaeological value of Castlefield (Duffy 1979). He focused for the opening few sentences only on the wasteland trope, the rest of the article concentrated on the 'priceless historical connection' of the area. Degen (2003) draws on interviews with city planners to support the 'empty dereliction' representations of Castlefield space. Interviewees represented the space as an 'impenetrable area' dominated by scrapyards and concrete plants 'with Alsatian dogs prowling and barbed wire' (in Degen 2003: 871). Degen takes on these representations uncritically, stating that by the 1980s the area was gradually 'transformed into a no-go area' (Degen 2003: 867). For Degen this situation pertained until the regeneration of Castlefield 'commenced in the early 1990s' (Degen 2003: 867). Although in her research she does provide many important insights into the public sector role in the production of Castlefield space, her characterisation of the area before this time contributes to the dominant narrative and the idea that the production of space was somehow suspended until the 1990s.

Madgin (2009) in a comparative study of Castlefield and sites in Leicester, England and Roubaix, France, quotes from Duffy (1979) that Castlefield in the 1970s was pitted by crofts, crumbling buildings and silted waterways. Apparently, in the 1970s and 1980s only people working in the noxious industries and vagabonds entered the area. Castlefield was devoid of life, meaning and people. Dave Haslam, a Manchester based DJ turned writer, asserts that by the early 1980s in Castlefield 'the debris of industry and history piled up all around', the area was dead (Haslam 1999: 249–50). He recalls with aplomb that Castlefield in the 1980s would have made a superb 'gritty film set' with its 'rusty bridges and canals the colour of lead' making it the 'best example of urban dereliction you could find anywhere in the world' (Haslam 2007). His invocation of cinematic spaces of representation is a fascinating possibility explored in Chapter Seven. According to MCC (2004), Castlefield has been transformed from a derelict area into one of the country's most celebrated regeneration success stories. MCC reflects the dominant narrative with the claim that by the 1970s 'buildings had become dilapidated, piles of scrap metal and cars littered the land and the canal arms had become clogged and dirty' (MCC 2004: 54–5)

The process of reimagining and regeneration is said to have been led by the private sector in entrepreneurial city partnership with MCC, principally in the 1990s (Quilley 2002; Williams 2003; MCC 2004; Douet 2014). The result for the advocates of the traditional discourse is a successful regenerated city, an area 'dramatically transformed' into one of 'the most attractive and visited parts of the city' (MCC 2004: 54). It became a place reborn materially and in the popular and private sector investor imaginations. In the dominant Castlefield regeneration narrative, key enterprising elements of the private sector had the foresight to reimagine the city and lead its regeneration. Jim Ramsbottom, a Salford born millionaire bookmaker and founder in 1981 of a property development company called Castlefield Estates Ltd, is often seen as the pioneer of Castlefield's regeneration (Haslam 1999: 250; Parkinson-Bailey 2000: 289). According to Hebbert (2009: 58) Ramsbottom 'set the pace' when he bought up scrapyards and industrial slums 'and revealed the eighteenth century canal basin'. Ramsbottom's own view was that Castlefield in 1980s was 'a dump' and he is not bashful about his role in the revival of the area, claiming with energetic verve that he had a plan to bring the historic buildings back into use while 'resisting any quick fix solution' (in MCC 2004: 27).

Another fêted Castlefield entrepreneur is Tom Bloxham (a member of modernist architect Richard Rogers' 1990s Urban Task Force) who is seen as a private sector inspiration for the regeneration of Castlefield. In 1993 Bloxham founded the Manchester based development company Urban Splash, located in Castlefield. It carried out award winning conversions of mills, warehouses and new-build apartment blocks at the Pomona Dock area of Castlefield. Bloxham actively promotes a version of Castlefield's transformation that *begins* with the arrival of Urban Splash (Bloxham 2001). Noticeably, there is no role for historic preservation societies or the Greater Manchester Council in this recurring Castlefield discourse (but see Leary 2009; Madgin 2010).

In the post-WW2 period 'Castlefield' did not exist in official representations of space. It had been rendered invisible and ignored, its Roman, Georgian and Victorian historic value discarded in favour of a focus on the medieval Cathedral area. This attitude is typified in Manchester's post-WW2 reconstruction plan (Manchester Corporation 1945; Leary 2011). Rowland Nicholas, city surveyor and engineer and chief architect of the 1945 Plan, understood Castlefield as a place of industry rather than historic value. His preoccupation with sweeping away squalid, ugly Manchester and replacing it with the beauty of modernist order reached its zenith not in words but in a spectacular colour axonometric image spread across the pages of the back inside cover (Figure 6.1). This visual representation of Manchester by the year 2045 imagined most of the city centre redeveloped into regular modernist blocks of similar size, style, massing and orientation. It is a remarkable architectural rendering that offers no prospect of historic preservation, other than for the Cathedral area and a handful of buildings. In addition, the new roads and railways depicted would wipe away all material traces of Castlefield's historic significance. For good measure the north point sat resolutely on top of Castlefield! In the 1960 and 1970s Manchester's 19th century assets in the built environment, particularly its working class housing, brick-built factories and warehouses, were demolished en masse in urban renewal schemes similar to those in Vancouver and Lowell.

Figure 6.1: A modernist vision of the future: Manchester city centre 2045 (Manchester Corporation 1945)

Manchester Corporation's attitudes to the city's Victorian industrial and residential past should be understood in the context of the national mood in the post-war period. By the 1970s the canals which serviced the industrial revolution were dirty and neglected. Abandoned factory buildings were demolished or left to rot. Railway infrastructure was neglected in favour of road building. Denigration of the historic industrial built environment was a nationwide phenomenon. Post-war modernisation reconstruction plans for war damaged cities left little room for symbols of former industrial glory (Meller 1997). For example, despite a spirited campaign by John Betjeman and Nikolaus Pevsner to save it, the magnificent Euston Arch was demolished in 1962; the remainder of the station was demolished in 1964. Yet the arch stood at the entrance to London's Euston Railway Station, the world's first in a capital city.

There were two responses by the government and civil society to the apparently relentless destruction of built heritage. First, the Historic Buildings and Monuments Act 1953 established the Historic Buildings Council for England (HBC) within the Ministry of Housing and Local Government, which became the Department of the Environment (DoE) in 1970. The HBC's remit was to disburse grants to property owners for the restoration of important historic buildings, mainly large historic country houses. Government listing of buildings is a way of both recognising their historic or architectural importance and protecting them from demolition of unsympathetic alteration. Although ignored as unworthy of attention at first, in the 1970s historic *industrial* buildings were singled out increasingly for financial subsidy so that the HBC was better able to reflect the post-war growing public concern for conservation. The HBC grant regime was still in place in the 1970s and remained until the HBC was absorbed by the quango English Heritage in 1983. Second, the 1960s and 1970s saw a rapid growth in the number and visibility of British historic preservation societies as a general feeling of unease with the melting into air of familiar historic buildings exerted its influence. Historic preservation societies are important elements of civil society and their significance for public policy was beginning to be appreciated.

Contested spatial meanings

While the role of neo-capitalism, property speculators and the state in the production of urban space has been debated at length, the role of historic preservation groups has tended to be ignored (but see Madgin 2009). This section of the chapter explores how differing representations of space imbued LRS with conflicted underlying meanings that influenced the spatial practice of its transformation into the regenerated public space of the MOSI. Liverpool Road Railway Station was built in 1830 as the Manchester terminus of the Liverpool to Manchester Railway. Although not the focus of this chapter it would be remiss to ignore the implications of the source of Manchester's raw cotton, based as it was on the Transatlantic Trade in West African peoples, which was of course the same source as that used in Lowell.

Manchester's 19th century textile industry and that of the surrounding northern towns depended predominantly at the outbreak of the US civil war in 1861 on raw cotton grown in the Confederate States by enslaved West African peoples. Raw cotton was imported through the port of Liverpool then moved via canals and later railways into Castlefield. From there it was sent eastwards across the city to the factories. Finished textiles were sent in the reverse direction: a proportion of the 'Manchester cottons' being traded for more West African peoples. The story of Manchester's reliance on capital investment derived from the profits from the Transatlantic Trade although first asserted in Eric Williams' 1944 text *Capitalism and Slavery* and reiterated in Peter Fryer's 1984 *Staying Power*, is less well known but is an important adjunct to the traditional history which ignores it (see for example Kidd 2006). Williams claims that the Liverpool and Manchester Railway Company was funded partly by profits from the Transatlantic Trade (Williams 1994: 105). Williams' renowned book, based on his Oxford University PhD, was controversial for many years but its central thesis tends now to be accepted. President Abraham Lincoln's 1863 letter of thanks to the Working-men of Manchester for their anti-slavery stance and financial support during the civil war is one of the more honourable episodes in Manchester's cotton industry history. A dignified statue of Lincoln stands in Manchester city centre's Lincoln Square. In the 1980s the inscription at the base of the statue, to the Working-men of Manchester, was changed to the 'working people', in a nod at political correctness (Leary 2011).

Being the first building of its kind in the world, LRS looks more like a grand Georgian townhouse than a railway terminus. Its importance was recognised when the British Prime Minister, the Duke of Wellington, came to Manchester to open the railway formally in September 1830. Centenary celebrations in 1930 in Manchester and Liverpool were attended by civic dignitaries and thousands of people. In the following decades with the rise of the motor car, motorways and air travel, the station fell into disrepair and obscurity but continued to be used as a goods depot. Rather late in the day its historic importance was recognised when it was listed Grade I by the government in December 1963. This listing put the station on a par with St Paul's Cathedral and the Tower of London. By the 1970s the nationalised railway industry – British Rail (BR) created in 1948 – owned hundreds of listed buildings nationwide many of which were in a state of pitiful dilapidation. Under financial pressure from government, BR concentrated its resources on railway operations, not the restoration of historic buildings. Although it was Grade I listed, technically affording it the strongest protection, LRS was allowed to deteriorate badly. To prevent collapse it was supported in the early 1970s by massive wooden shoring (Figure 6.2).

Figure 6.2: Decrepit Liverpool Road Railway Station (MCC Local Images Collection, photo © Chris Makepeace, thanks to Jane Hodkinson)

In the early 1970s LRS began to attract national press attention but for wholly negative reasons. It was in a dreadful state of disrepair (Chippendale 1972). It was facing demolition by its public sector owner because it was being 'scandalously neglected by British Rail' and might go the way of other historic buildings that had been 'ruthlessly destroyed in the last few years' (Freeman 1972). Following this, two prominent London based historic preservation societies, the Georgian Group (GrG) and the Victorian Society, joined forces in 1973 condemning in a letter to *The Times* BR's disregard of LRS (Chance and Pevsner 1973). Nikolaus Pevsner of the Victorian Society is well known as the pre-eminent architectural historian of his generation; Ivan Chance, known to his friends as Peter, was chairman of the GrG and of Christie's, the London based international fine art auction house (McLeod 2008). The Group's patron in the 1970s was HM Queen Elizabeth the Queen Mother. It is now (in 2015) the Prince of Wales.

Despite the authors' proximity to the headquarters of BR and the British government, their plea went unheard but that was about to change. Rather than write to a national newspaper, another historic preservation activist wrote instead to the six Manchester Members of Parliament (MP):

> I am writing to you as the Georgian Group's representative on the Manchester Conservation Areas and Historic Buildings panel rather than as the Keeper of this Gallery ... Over the last two years members of the above panel have been extremely concerned about British Rail's shameful neglect of Liverpool Road Station, Manchester. (Hawcroft 1973)

Unearthing this letter in the National Archives (England) (NAE) was a pivotal moment for the research. The letter reveals how not-for-profit historic preservation interests constructed alternative representations of space, counter to official representations. Hawcroft's opinion was that the opening of the station was as historically important as the British victory at Waterloo in 1815. For Hawcroft and the historic preservation societies it was not the beauty of the building or its architectural merit that made it important. Its significance was a historical one at the national level and by implication critical for understanding the industrial revolution in Great Britain and the world.

Hawcroft was a prominent figure in the museums world, an expert in British water colours and curator of Manchester's Whitworth Art Gallery. His concern for the preservation of LRS grew into a passion. In the years that followed Whitworth Art Gallery would receive part of its funding from the Greater Manchester Council (GMC) and because of this Hawcroft was on first name terms with prominent councillors and officers. This insider status was used to good effect during the campaign to save LRS.

Given the lack of progress regarding the station site over the previous years, Hawcroft could not have expected his short letter to find its way to a senior Cabinet minister and kindle the eventual (re)presentation of the station site and the production of new urban public space. The letter and related archival documents underscore the potentially complex civil society networks and their intriguing interaction with local government, central government and the press that created the LRS counter-project.

Hawcroft's zealous promotion of the station's historical importance comes across strongly. His fervent representation of a building devalorised by its owners for many years is palpable and although he writes as an individual he places himself firmly under the mantle of the historic preservation societies. Four of the six Manchester MPs – one of whom was Charles Morris (father of Estelle Morris, who became important for the research as explained later) – were moved sufficiently by Hawcroft's entreaty to write to Geoffrey Rippon, government Secretary of State at the recently created DoE. Rippon became an LRS convert, embracing the preservation cause with alacrity. He requested civil servant advice on how to pressurise Sir Richard Marsh, Chairman of BR, assuring the MPs that:

> I have therefore instructed officials to seek an immediate meeting with BR, Manchester City Council, and the interested amenity societies in order that ways may be found to prevent further deterioration of the station and to secure in the long term its full repair, maintenance and use. (Rippon 1973)

Rippon used the term 'amenity societies' but the more informative label historic preservation societies is preferred in this book. Although Hawcroft's 1973 letter maps partially an initial political-spatial network centred on LRS, it was the decisive intervention of Geoffrey Rippon which activated the public sector element of the network, injected urgency and stressed the importance of preservation society participation. Through the archives it is possible to trace the web of power relationships between diverse groups and interests that revalorised the historic station. Through their counter-representations the station site became a Lefebvrian counter-space and counter-project. Records of two meetings prompted by Rippon's intervention survive in the NAE. Both meetings took place at Manchester Town Hall in June 1973 and 1974. For each meeting a set of informal minutes was produced where candid views about LRS were recorded. It is important to realise that these and all the minutes for the ad hoc LRS meetings were never made public, until placed in the NAE, because they were not records of a formal local government committee.

The first meeting following Rippon's 1973 letter to the MPs came after the failure of similar meetings the year before to achieve anything significant. In 1973 MCC was still known by its 1838 name, Manchester Corporation. Its Town Clerk (chief executive) was Sir George Ogden. Prompted by Rippon, Ogden organised the June 1973 meeting 'to thrash out what should be done about the station', inviting *only* representatives of the Corporation, BR and the HBC (Ogden 1973). Similarly, no preservation societies attended the June 1974 meeting. Ian Macpherson Glennie of HBC attended and was to prove instrumental in promoting alternative representations of LRS space. Glennie understood the political significance of the station's worsening state once the case had been embraced by the government in the guise of Rippon. In an unguarded moment Glennie strayed from the path of restrained official civil service language, expressing something of his feelings about the politicised nature of the station problem. He anticipated difficulties ahead in working with a recalcitrant Manchester Corporation and BR:

> Would you please see this correspondence [Rippon 1973]. This is a hot potato and I am under instructions to do what I can to make Manchester and British Rail do something about these buildings. (Glennie 1973)

The possibility of using the station as an annex for the Museum of Science and Technology, created in 1967 by the Corporation, Manchester University and Manchester University Institute of Science and Technology, was mooted but not pursued. The museum was outgrowing its premises because of the flood of acquisitions due to the bankruptcy of many factories in the area as the British economy restructured. The 1973 meeting signalled the start of a prolonged struggle to establish the meaning of and future for the station site and the wider Castlefield area. Even in the absence of historic preservation societies, their role in the emergence of LRS as a counter-project was acknowledged. At the 1973 meeting John Millar, the city's chief planning officer, was disarmingly frank about the preservation society role:

> The building had deteriorated and was now in a bad condition. There had been a national revival of interest in Victoriana. The Manchester Historic Buildings Panel had considered the situation – they being constituted of representatives of various groups and societies with architectural advisors had drawn the attention of the Planning Committee to its derelict condition. (Millar in Manchester Corporation 1973)

An important facet of the 1973 and 1974 meetings is the contested claims that were made for the historic meaning of LRS as the different branches of the public sector vied to impose their representations of space. Besant Roberts, Manchester Corporation architect, thought the only part of the building worth preserving was, 'the main entrance and first class staircase, the old platform and ticket office – with the sundial, clock and bell' (in Manchester Corporation 1973). BR's representative at the 1974 meeting, chaired by Norman Morris, a surveyor representing the BR Property Board, was implacable that 'only the station staircase and a small portion on each side' were worth preserving (Fulford in Manchester Corporation 1974). Fulford and Roberts' emasculated valorisation implied only grudging acceptance of the historic attributes of LRS but was applied consistently by BR. Articulating counter-spaces of representation at the two meetings were not historic preservation society voices but Ian Glennie of the HBC. He was adamant *the whole* of the Grade I station building was sacrosanct and of great historic and architectural importance. Regarding demolition, 'the Minister would never allow it' and 'the preservation of a small token area or shrine would not be suitable' (in Manchester Corporation 1973).

The two meetings demonstrate clearly the radically different representations of space promulgated by on the one hand BR and Manchester Corporation and on the other the counter-representations of Glennie acting effectively as proxy for the historic preservation societies. Furthermore, BR and the Corporation were conjuring up the dominant 1970s representations of historic British railway buildings: that most of them could be demolished as was the historic Euston Station in 1964. In addition, for BR and Manchester Corporation the edge of city centre station site encapsulated not historic but financial property development value. BR's property development commercial ethos explains its reluctance to invest in historic building preservation. Glennie wrote in exasperation after a year of deadlock for him but three years for the historic preservation societies:

> We are battling Manchester City and the Greater Manchester County over the restoration of the railway station. The matter is complicated by a private vendetta between BR and the City. (Glennie 1974)

It becomes obvious here that within the public sector there were conflicting meanings attributed to historic space, with Glennie being aligned firmly with the historic preservation societies. BR valued the station site financially rather than historically and the following year made a crucial distinction between the dilapidated station building, which it was prepared to 'dispose of for a nominal fee' and the value of the whole site which should 'be based on its prospective future use' (Fulford in MCC 1974). This comment seems to encapsulate unwittingly Lefebvre's claim that at certain times historic city space is blithely destroyed if property redevelopment will generate private profit or public surplus.

Francis Hawcroft continued with his behind-the-scenes insider campaigning but by 1978 was alarmed at the lack of progress, complaining to the GrG that 'British Rail and the local authorities have made no progress whatsoever with the negotiations' (Hawcroft 1978). Tensions between Manchester Corporation and BR about responsibility for repair and maintenance of the station were at the root of the impasse during the 1970s. Nevertheless, lack of progress seemed to galvanise the historic preservation societies. A series of meetings followed until 1980 in which the voices of the societies became increasingly strident and influential. In bare numbers, society representation at LRS meetings grew significantly from the mid-1970s. At one meeting in 1978 the seven amenity society representatives made up 40% of those present.

A Greater Manchester proposition

Created by the Conservative government's nationwide reorganisation of local government in April 1974, the GMC became responsible for strategic planning for the ten local authorities in the Manchester area (it was abolished in 1986). By late 1974 BR and Manchester Corporation after some minimal LRS repair expenditure remained united in frugality. And by 1978 merely a few hundred additional pounds had been spent on weather proofing repairs. What was required was a massive shift in representations of the station space that would propel forward into concrete spatial practice. Such a shift was instigated by GMC, the most significant addition to the core group of public agencies. Its first Chief Executive was George Ogden who moved across town from Manchester Corporation.

From the beginning GMC was anxious to establish its economic development credibility with the production of visible projects on the ground (spatial practice) and not just strategy documents (representations of space). The (second) chief executive hoped that, 'on issues like the acquisition of nationalised industry sites the County will be able to play a role' (Harrison 1978). Despite the apparent enthusiasm at the highest level within GMC, there was some reticence and at times progress was slow. It was GMC officers, especially Robert Maund (senior planner, who had moved from Manchester Corporation), who saw the potential of the station *and* the necessity of including the wider site in any acquisition deal with BR. Politicians were cagey about offering overt political support for what they considered a high risk venture:

> 'It was quite funny at the outset. There were going to be senior [political] people from GMC at the meetings. But both of them said at the last minute, "I've been called away and can't make it, good luck." [laughs], I think because it was very political at the time. I remember the County Secretary saying to me as he disappeared "do be careful" [RM and MLO laugh]. They could see that politically we officers would get a lot of flak if we couldn't deliver after rushing into commitments.' (Maund 2008)

GMC was keen from the start to buy the whole 2.5 acre (1 hectare) station site, not just the Grade I listed building. What was offered to GMC in 1975 was only the station building and platform for the nominal amount of £1, on condition that the station be restored fully. What BR was actually offering GMC was a six figure 'debt' of financial and moral responsibility for the station's restoration. Delay resulting from BR's dogged but eventually futile insistence on selling only the station building caused additional frustration for GMC and the preservation societies. Eventually, GMC prevailed but did not finally conclude the formalities of the 2.5 acre station site acquisition until mid-1978. It is important to realise that the meetings and negotiations took place 'behind closed doors' not reaching the public domain until late 1978 when the *Manchester Evening News* (14 September) proclaimed 'Historic station is saved for £1', given the actual timescale it is ironic that that the article added 'after a two year struggle'. On disposal of the station, track and adjoining Grade II listed 1830 warehouse (the world's first railway warehouse) to GMC, BR agreed to contribute £100,000 towards structural repair costs – a small price to pay for ridding itself of the growing burden of a troublesome building. While negotiations were proceeding, the Chairman of BR Sir Peter Parker did offer the station personally to Ivan Chance of the GrG for £1. The Group, comprehending the significant financial burden they would endure, declined politely citing 'financial constraints' (Murray 1977). Apparently, this fact has remained hidden from public view; the claim that LRS was sold to a conservation group for £1 could still be found on the MCC website in 2015.

Assistant GMC Planning Officer Robert Maund now signalled a major financial commitment on the back of GMC's acceptance of the historic preservation societies' initial revalorisation of the station.

The scheme was adopted also as a powerful symbolic demonstration of GMC's ability to deliver visible (spatial practice) projects on the ground. In February 1978 GMC felt confident enough to approach the HBC and gained an informal assurance that a grant of £23,000 towards structural repair and a massive one of £341,000 as part of the £2,000,000 cost of the first stage museum restoration and adaptive reuse would be forthcoming (Maund in GMC 1978). Spatial practice on the scale of LRS restoration and adaptive reuse had shifted from a historic preservation society counter-project to the public sector mainstream. The archive records this pivotal moment:

> He [Mr Maund] expressed the view that the only way in which the complex might be saved would be if the County Council could use the buildings to meet one of its major requirements. Museum policy might be just such an opportunity. (GMC 1978)

A 150th birthday party

In early 1978 when the fate of LRS hung precariously in the balance, several hundred Victorian Society, Manchester (VSM) members joined forces with railway enthusiasts to establish the Liverpool Road Station Society. Former British Prime Minister Harold Wilson agreed to be its first president. David Rhodes (whose pivotal role in the production of Castlefield space is discussed in detail later) became the first chairman. In a research interview Rhodes (2009) explained that he wanted a media friendly campaign to pressurise GMC and BR. The two societies organised a 148th LRS birthday campaign, giving out birthday cards at Manchester railway stations as a prelude to the grander 150th birthday celebrations. A range of events in Castlefield and the city centre drew thousands of people galvanising support for the campaign to save LRS.

A larger LRS party was organised in 1980, with the support of MCC and GMC, to celebrate the 150th birthday of the Liverpool to Manchester Railway. The highlight was the thunderous arrival at LRS of a magnificent steam locomotive. During a research interview David Maund remembered vividly the party climax:

> 'It was going to be a big day and they got a steam engine and they got the fog warning things on the tracks so when the train went over it went bang! You know, and they put a great sheet on a scaffolding frame blocking the view down the line. Everybody was assembled, you heard but couldn't

see the train going whoosh, tah tah, whoosh tah tah and the colossal bangs and it burst through the huge sheet. My son who was about four was sat on my shoulders and I thought he was going to go into orbit.' (Maund 2008)

And as Maund spoke he produced completely unexpectedly hundreds of 35 mm slides, documenting 1970s and 1980s Castlefield that had been ensconced in his personal archive for nearly 30 years. Two delightful slides capture the exciting moment when the steam locomotive appears (Figures 6.3 and 6.4).

Figure 6.3: Expectation mounts at the Liverpool Road Station 150th birthday party 1980 (photo © David Maund)

A financial impediment

A setback occurred, however, in early 1979 when the museum project was refused a crucial segment of the funding: a grant from the Urban Programme, by the Manchester and Salford Inner City Partnership. At the time the chairman of the Partnership, Reg Freeson, Labour DoE Minister for Housing and Construction said:

> ... this proposal cannot be said to make a direct contribution to the social and economic objectives of the partnership, however much it may further those ends incidentally ...

the benefits of this scheme are cast so wide that they could not be said to be of the particular local importance that would justify funding under Urban Programme. (Freeson in Corrie 1978)

Figure 6.4: The locomotive star of the Liverpool Road Station birthday party 1980 (photo © David Maund)

After the change of government from Labour to the (neoliberal) Conservative government of Margaret Thatcher in May 1979, the £100,000 Urban Programme element of the grant funding package was approved by Lord Bellwin allowing the project to go ahead thus securing the long term future of LRS and the creation of the MOSI. Urban Programme Partnerships were a central government initiative established under the 1978 Inner Urban Areas Act. In Manchester, the partnership consisted of MCC, GMC and Salford City Council. It was Michael Heseltine who reorientated Urban Programme in 1979, making the LRS grant possible (see Chapter Seven).

It had been a long haul since the early 1970s and at times LRS seemed doomed but the MOSI complex was opened officially by Her Majesty the Queen in 1982. It soon became established as a national museum run by a charitable not-for-profit trust, providing free access. One of the star attractions was the beautifully restored station building where visitors could once again climb the ornate staircase to the tasteful first class waiting room. And in a dual ceremony the Queen also opened the new outdoor set of the world's first TV soap opera, *Coronation Street* at the Granada TV studio complex located in Castlefield. While the future of LRS was still uncertain, during a meeting to discuss LRS, Castlefield is mentioned by name for the first time in the archival data encountered. A senior MCC planning officer indicated that the Council was 'looking at the whole of the Castlefield Area' which had the 'potential to become a showpiece of archaeological and industrial heritage' (Blackniki in GMC 1979). Castlefield was therefore rendered officially visible and its name reclaimed through a persistent historic preservation society counter-project. In 1978–80 the LRS counter-project gathered considerable momentum as large tranches of necessary funding were secured. David Rhodes was therefore able to turn his attention from the LRS site to the whole of Castlefield.

From Granada to Castlefield

One unexpected legacy of the Clean Air Act 1952 was that buildings blackened by two centuries of coal soot could be cleaned in the knowledge they would stay clean. In the 1960s, Manchester Town Hall was one of several wonderful historic buildings to benefit from a scrub down, revealing its exuberant, neo-Gothic splendour. In association with this effort a programme of blue badge walking tours was instigated which unfortunately proved rather unpopular. This is in stark contrast to the galvanising impact of the walking tours in Gastown arranged by the VCAC (see Chapter Two). A different kind of galvanisation in the 1970s offered glimmers of valorisation that began to shine on Castlefield. Research for the literature review revealed the existence of a potentially important report cited by *Manchester Evening News* journalist Michael Duffy. He claimed the report 'proposed the establishment of a [Castlefield] conservation area' (Duffy 1979). Research at the British Library Newspaper Archives (BLNA) revealed the article is in fact the first of a three part series. Duffy referred, with typical journalistic disregard for sources, to a report authored jointly by two historic preservation societies: the Greater Manchester Archaeological *Group* (GMAG) and the VSM. The GMAG was set up by GMC and included academics from Manchester University. It was tasked with advising the ten local authorities of Greater Manchester.

However, searching for a 30 year old report without basic bibliographic details is rather daunting. Searching for the GMAG led to a frustrating dead end because its name had changed to the Greater Manchester Archaeological *Unit* (GMAU) in 1986. Unfortunately, Greater Manchester County Records Office (GMCRO) archivists did not know of the report either. During the secondary research David Rhodes was found to be a member of VSM and agreed to be interviewed at his home in Harrogate. He revealed that he was the author of the elusive report and produced from his personal archive what may be the only remaining copy. Rhodes revealed that this was his *second* Castlefield report; he wrote the first several years before. Rhodes (2008) divulged that in the early 1970s two unlikely interests, a TV mogul and a historic preservation group, coalesced around the rather disparate subjects of company car parking and historic area preservation. In 1956 Sir Sidney Bernstein founded the Granada Television Company (GTV), which won the independent television franchise for the north west of England and began broadcasting in the same year. Sidney Bernstein called it Granada TV because he and his wife had an exceptionally enjoyable holiday in that Spanish city. In the days before mass package holidays, the name hinted at faraway, exotic excitement and romance.

He had state of the art offices and television studios built in 1962, designed by Ralph Tubbs. Bernstein wanted to make a pact with his employees that guaranteed them all a parking space. In order to keep his promise he imagined the rather nondescript industrial area from GTV down to the River Irwell and canals (Castlefield) would make ideal staff car parks. At the time it seemed a reasonable proposition. For many people including Rhodes the area was "a total knacker's yard everywhere" (Rhodes 2008). GTV commissioned a historic preservation group, the Civic Trust for the North West (CTNW) to undertake a pilot study exploring the feasibility of using the area for car parking. The CTNW was founded in 1961 five years after the Civic Trust was established in London. CTNW presented itself as a down to earth organisation, active on the ground with high profile, local preservation campaigns. This group was affiliated to the Civic Trust that inspired VCAC in the 1960s (see Chapter Two).

Rhodes worked for CTNW and was appointed to carry out the feasibility study. Clearly, Rhodes, an architect by training who was born and grew up in Ashton near Manchester, seems to have been unaware before the investigation of the historic nature of Castlefield. The report is not dated but Rhodes thought it was written in 1972, clues in the text support this so it is referenced here as Hall and Rhodes (1972), since it was in fact co-authored (more about that later in this chapter). Realising the historic importance of the area Rhodes took the opportunity to turn Sidney Bernstein's brief into a CTNW conservation research project:

'… and when I looked into it I discovered that it was where the Roman Fort was, it was where the first canal system in England, the first real canal in England – the Bridgewater – and the first real railway system in the world, so I produced this document which I called *Castlefield, Past Present and Future*, and this is the report [pointing].' (Rhodes 2008)

At this time the area was known mostly as Knott Mill or Saint George's. While there is no reason to doubt Rhodes' recollection of why the name Castlefield was chosen, it should be noted that the name was used in Frangopulo (1962), although to be fair to Rhodes this is a rather obscure book not available easily.

Visual representations of Castlefield

An integral part of the 1972 report are the maps and other visual representations of Castlefield space. Maps, especially those produced by professional cartographers, are of course not innocent reflections of material reality but are the subject of comprehensive selection and exclusion and can be overloaded with explicit and implicit meaning. Lefebvre shows a degree of scepticism about the maps and plans of expert urban planners and architects:

Some, such [representations] as maps that show 'beauty spots' and historical sites and monuments to the accompaniment of an appropriate rhetoric, aim to mystify in fairly obvious ways … The conventional signs used on these documents constitute a code even more deceptive than the things themselves, for they are at one more remove from reality. (Lefebvre 1991: 84)

In the case of Hall and Rhodes, their maps of Castlefield were hand drawn representations, annotated to pick out key historical features. It is clear the maps in the 1972 report were traced from an Ordnance Survey base map. This technique allowed Rhodes to exclude features considered irrelevant such as the Byrom Street site of working class housing, while simultaneously imbuing the maps with quasi-scientific cartographic legitimacy through the deployment of a 1:2500 scale. The visual representations follow the logic of the 1972 report's structure depicting Castlefield past, present and future.

Although in the first research interview Rhodes describes Castlefield as a complete knackers yard, the cartographic/architectural precision

Figure 6.5: Present apparent land use at Castlefield (Hall and Rhodes 1972)

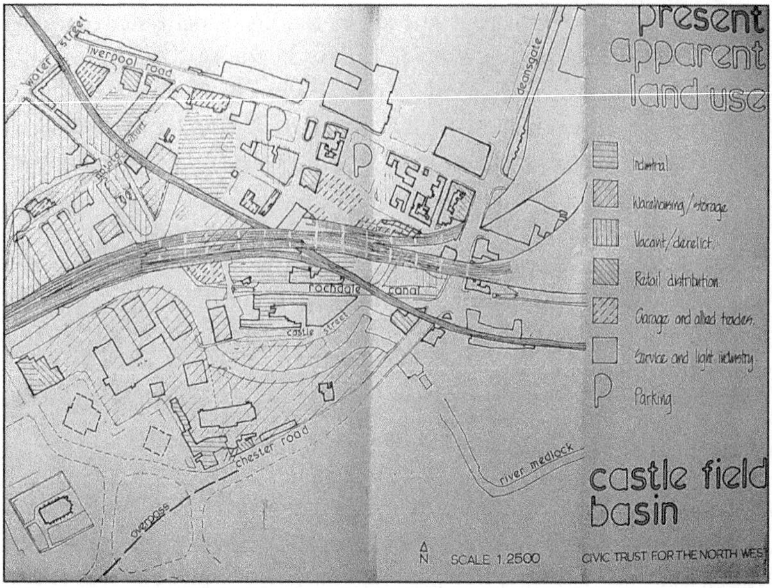

of the map of 'present apparent land use' (Figure 6.5) tells a different story. Only a relatively small part of Castlefield centred on the abattoir site was depicted as derelict. This presented a dilemma for Rhodes in that the abattoir was also identified a key historical component but is at the same time an aesthetically unappealing bad neighbour land use. The term 'bad neighbour' first appeared in British town planning legislation in 1947. It quickly became common planning jargon. It refers to industries which create high levels of noise, smoke, dust, smell, fumes or vibration, or those which use toxic or hazardous materials and included such delights as: scrapyards, blood boiling, glue making, bone grinding and the breeding of maggots from putrescible matter. Rather than reflect this complexity visually, the abattoir space is categorised simply as 'vacant or socially unpleasant'. A complex hybrid evocative space full of spatial memories was thus conflated and purged of spatial richness. The 'future development' representation introduced a range of aesthetic judgements about the quality of the Castlefield cityscape and categorised some land uses as 'unsightly and unused'. Through these representations Hall and Rhodes initiated the process of the devalorisation of Castlefield's *existing* industries. Devaluing present and past spatial practice, especially working class residential areas and industry, either to facilitate private sector property speculation or state led gentrification has become a well recognised tactic. A major difference here is that Hall and Rhodes championed the intrinsic historic value of Castlefield without regard for potential land prices and exchange value.

Through the device of zoning, creating eight distinct bounded areas, Rhodes inscribed CTNW's contemporary heritage values on to Castlefield space and an imagined future. In so doing these visual representations reveal the power of a socially constructed, heritage loaded past to inhabit the present. Zoning schemes have been a fundamental tool for the representation of modern city space since the early 19th century, allowing for the designation of homogenous spatial units and consequent spatial practice interventions through city planning and urban policy, a point stressed at length by Lefebvre (1991). Unlike some later representations of Castlefield that homogenise the whole area as a derelict wasteland, Hall and Rhodes (1972) presented a more complex understanding of Castlefield.

However, the 1972 report needs to be understood in its context. Castlefield had been an industrial district for the previous 200 years. The city plan of 1945 referred to the area in unflattering terms as 'Castlefield wharfage' (Manchester Corporation 1945: 188). Manchester was not perceived as a destination for mass historic tourism. A. J. P Taylor proclaimed that there are no sights for conducted tours in Manchester, 'no waiting coaches in Albert Square' (1977: 307). With no roads or pedestrian routes passing through it, Castlefield was literally invisible to most Mancunians. A variety of key local landmarks were located on the edges of the area, for example, GTV, St John Street, Central Station, a pretty Methodist Chapel, St George's Church and the attractive civic architecture of the municipal abattoir. It is hardly surprising, therefore, that Sidney Bernstein saw the area as prime car park land and probably expected rubber stamp approval for his car parking scheme. Unfortunately, for Bernstein the 1972 report did not even mention car park feasibility! In sharp contrast it did to Bernstein's chagrin reclaim evocatively a nondescript industrial city district and valorise its historical character. Little wonder that Bernstein, "was not very enamoured by it, he did not want to know that the area was phenomenally historic, so it went on the back burner" (Rhodes 2008). A few months later Rhodes started a historic conservation job in MCC's planning department. Castlefield was forgotten until it became a cause célèbre for another preservation society and Rhodes co-authored a second report.

Rhodes' ambivalent characterisation of Castlefield's industry sounded a curious note that deserved further exploration. In the second interview I pressed him on his 'knackered' characterisation of Castlefield. It is important to quote this conversation at length because it provides a complex appreciation of Castlefield as a liminal space somewhere between the aesthetic appreciation of history and gritty everyday reality:

Michael Leary-Owhin (MLO): When you went to Castlefield to do that first report, you described it as being in a horrible state but I notice that in 1982 GMC did an industrial survey of all the companies in Castlefield and 70 odd replied so there must have been a lot more. So I wonder what it felt like in the early 70s when you were there?

David Rhodes (DR): First of all if you go down Liverpool Road from Deansgate *all the shops are occupied*. City Hall is where the Air and Space Museum is and it's where the Ideal Homes Exhibition was and *similar things all year round* but that was the ultimate one. Before that in the 60s it used to be where they had the *Christmas circus* with elephants running round in a ring in the middle. The Upper Campfield building was always a bit more mysterious. I've got a feeling Manchester used that as a base. On the other side there were *pubs and all sorts of little businesses*. Now as you go through there, there's the St Matthews Church school rooms. There were all sorts of *genuine little businesses* going on around there. There was a car park between [pause]. What was the pub?

MLO: The White Lion?

DR: Yea, the *White Lion* is where the road goes to the Roman Fort. That was a municipal car park. Beyond that were *odd jobbing firms*. Every railway archway coming along until you get to the Roman Fort had *little car places*, you know where you can get your car repaired, things like that. And there'd be *a window cleaning company*. They'd be cleaning office windows and they'd have their ladders and their cart near there. So there's *all those sort of businesses going on*. The moment you go under the arches to come down to the canal then it was just knackers' yards and they ran quite a way through. Where the big [viaduct] bases come down, that was *real* knackers' yards and big Alsatian dogs that were ferocious when you walked through there. Of course it's all dripping [MLO laughs]. The water's dripping down all the time because when it stopped raining it'd still drip for days afterwards. So it had this grey overcast Manchester abandoned look about it. It was all chain link fences and bits of boarding and stuff. (Rhodes 2009, emphases added)

Rhodes' vivid, unembellished recollection of 1970s Castlefield is remarkably detailed and having explored the area many times in the last few years, I could follow his walk easily. His narrative resonates with Lefebvrian notions of gaining knowledge of the city through everyday sensory bodily experience. Note that Rhodes' 2009 account refers to real knackers' yards. What Rhodes clarifies is that it was only the spaces under the huge viaducts that were truly unpleasant and abandoned to the point of inducing discomfort, even fear. Far from revealing overly romanticised, nostalgic memories or unequivocal denigration, the 2009 interview constructs a dispassionate, account of bad *and* good neighbour activities in a city space of complexity. Rhodes' account contrasts with the blanket condemnation of the area encountered in the dominant academic narrative *and* in his own recollections in the 2008 interview

In this research dialogue, Rhodes speaks not just from the perspective of rational intellectual knowledge but with the benefit of careful first hand observation. He speaks from the direct, intense bodily experience of being in a space which stimulates a variety of senses and arouses emotional reactions. He provides a sophisticated ocular-centric, oral history appreciation of the complexity of Castlefield in the 1970s not encountered in the literature. One can hear the fierce dog barking, smell the animal intestines, feel the cold water's dripping down one's neck. One can feel also a touch of trepidation, leaving the bustle and activity of Liverpool Road for the empty darkness under the railway arches. Rhodes, along with other activists and much of the literature, tended to mask Castlefield's working class histories and the conflicts inherent in the struggle to establish its historic value based on a Roman and Victorian industrial past. Degen (2008) is one of the few researchers to appreciate Castlefield as a collection of sensory spatial experiences.

Only about 20 copies of *Castlefield: Past Present and Future* were ever made and the document does not exist in any library or official archives encountered in the course of this research. I chanced on the report at Rhodes' house in Harrogate, discovering it was co-authored by a Jonathan Hall, something Rhodes neglected to mention. Authorship of this report raises important issues. Rhodes spoke in 2008 as if he was the sole author. I raised this with him at the second interview:

MLO: I notice Jonathan Hall was one of the authors of the first Castlefield report we talked about. What role did he play in the report?

DR: When I was working for the Civic Trust he came as a student and worked for 2 or 3 months during the summer when I produced that document. He then went back to finish his degree. After he'd finished his degree he came and worked for the Civic Trust for a number of years. So he came back as a junior planner at the Civic Trust.

MLO: What was his input? Did he do the drawings?

DR: No. I did the drawings and the plans and everything. He basically, [pause] I put him down because I'm a generous person. He had worked on it with me, not just me. I don't know that he did anything specific on it but you know he'd worked on it with me. (Rhodes 2009)

Hall was clearly the junior partner in the production of the document and Rhodes, although slightly equivocal, is honest enough to accept his contribution. Establishing Hall's joint authorship is important for the historical record per se but also because, when he returned to the CTNW, Hall attended GMC meetings related to the LRS counter-project, something not mentioned by Rhodes. Hall is therefore one of the several likeminded activists who brought continuity and a professionalised heritage inspired vision to the reproduction of Castlefield space.

Rhodes' explanation as to why Bernstein should commission a historic preservation group to carry out a commercial feasibility survey was that it was cheaper than instructing a professional surveying company. A more plausible explanation is that Bernstein's motivation for the study and his brief to Civic Trust was more ambivalent than Rhodes indicates. It seems unlikely that the historic nature of Castlefield was completely unknown to CTNW at the time bearing in mind LRS was listed Grade I in 1963. I explored this issue in a telephone interview with Jonathan Hall, who claims more plausibly that GTV and Bernstein:

'… were interested to explore for generally philanthropic (but also obvious commercial) reasons how the area might be improved.' (Hall 2010)

GTV and Bernstein had been "stalwart supporters" of CTNW for years and realised that the area's edge of city centre location gave the dual potential for property development and historic value (Hall 2010). Bernstein probably wanted a CTNW seal of approval for his car parks. The commercial problem for GTV with its significant land holdings in the area was that there was little property development demand in a "grotty area that looked like a bomb site" (Hall 2010).

The Britons Protection incident

Throughout the 1960s and 1970s modernist city planning ideals were a wellspring for the erasure of large parts of Victorian Manchester and other cities in Britain and North America (Stamp 2007). Rhodes maintains that after the 1972 report went on the back burner he continued to champion the cause of the historic importance of Manchester's Victorian space and Castlefield in particular. Like many of the preservation activists in the 1970s he was professional, middle class and concerned more with historical and architectural merit than 'community history'. Rhodes became a leading figure in the VSM rising by 1978 to the position of chairman. Like the CTNW, the VSM under Rhodes' chairmanship tasked its most active members with finding projects around which the Society could build high profile publicity grabbing campaigns, rather like Patrick Mogan in Lowell and VCAC in Gastown. In 1980 Rhodes instigated a meeting of a handful of key VSM members. It took place one evening in the back room of a pub on the edge of Castlefield, The Britons Protection. Four other members attended, one of whom was Manchester University archaeology professor Barri Jones. They all put a 'fiver' (£5) on the table to pay for production costs of a report which would set out in detail the historic importance of the whole of Castlefield. Only 50 copies were ever printed (Rhodes 2008). The report was to be co-authored by Rhodes in his capacity of chairman of the VSM and Jones, a prominent advisor to the GMAG. This report was entitled, significantly, *Historic Castlefield*, therefore privileging a totalising look backwards. During the 2008 interview Rhodes had difficulty in remembering the year it was written, suggesting it was about 1975 but further research dates it to 1978; it is referenced as Jones and Rhodes (1978). It is more comprehensive than *Castlefield Past Present and Future*, running to 23 unnumbered A4 pages including significant visual representations. Madgin (2010) mentions this report in passing but there is no analysis and she does not examine its impact or refer to the 1972 report.

The different provenance of the *Historic Castlefield*, originating as it did entirely from historic preservation societies rather than a television company, is reflected in the forthright preservationist language of its opening:

> The area of Manchester known as Castlefields [sic] to the south of Quay Street ... has an historical importance which is only now being fully appreciated ... Moreover, Castlefield contains some of the most important features of Manchester's industrial revolution – a fine and accessible canal system, the earliest purpose-built passenger railway station in the world, churches, warehouses and factory buildings which are some of the finest examples of the ingenuity, wealth and confidence of our nineteenth century ancestors ... The purpose of this document is to present to the Local Planning Authorities proposals for a broad policy of preserving the essence of the area, to bring to public attention the importance of our heritage. (Jones and Rhodes 1978)

It is clear this is the report referred to by Duffy (1979). Its origin is important also because it drew intertextually on the 1972 report, as Rhodes freely admits "it is very similar to the first one" (Rhodes 2008). Use of the term heritage is important, signalling the deployment of preservation rhetoric that would become increasingly persuasive throughout the 1980s. *Historic Castlefield* provided a reasonably comprehensive, though concise account of the development of Roman, Georgian and Victorian Castlefield. Crucially the 1978 report depicted the location of the Roman Fort and vicus graphically plotting their relationship with the canals and rivers. The 1978 report urged that a range of facilities, under the heading of what is now called cultural regeneration, could be accommodated in the market halls and LRS buildings complex. The market buildings were recommended for conversion into a comprehensive heritage museum for Manchester, similar to the Museum of London. LRS was imbued with the potential for providing excellent facilities for a museum of transport and industry.

The 1978 report lamented the demolition of the abattoir which was structurally sound and an 'impressive example of Victorian civic architecture', insisting that the existing buildings could have been reused 'if a little more imagination had been employed'. Crucially, the 1978 report made visible the importance historically of the area as a residential site which incorporated 'a select residential area' and an 'extensive working class housing area' (Jones and Rhodes 1978). Significantly too, Jones and Rhodes signified the area as the site of the annual Manchester Fair or Carnival, a ludic event frequented by thousands of working class visitors. Originally, it was called the Knott Mill Fair and started as a celebration of the opening of the Bridgewater Canal in 1765, but by the 1850s it was being condemned stridently:

> It may with equal truth be said that among the great majority of the frequenters of the place, [Knott Mill Fair] there is to be seen a larger amount of brutality, roguery, and every other phase of human degradation, than could be found among an equal number of persons collected upon any other occasion, or under any other circumstances. (*Manchester Guardian* 1852)

It ceased to operate in 1878 partly due to these kinds of criticisms but mainly due to the commercial disruption and traffic congestion the event caused.

Figure 6.6: Future development proposals for Castlefield (Hall and Rhodes 1972)

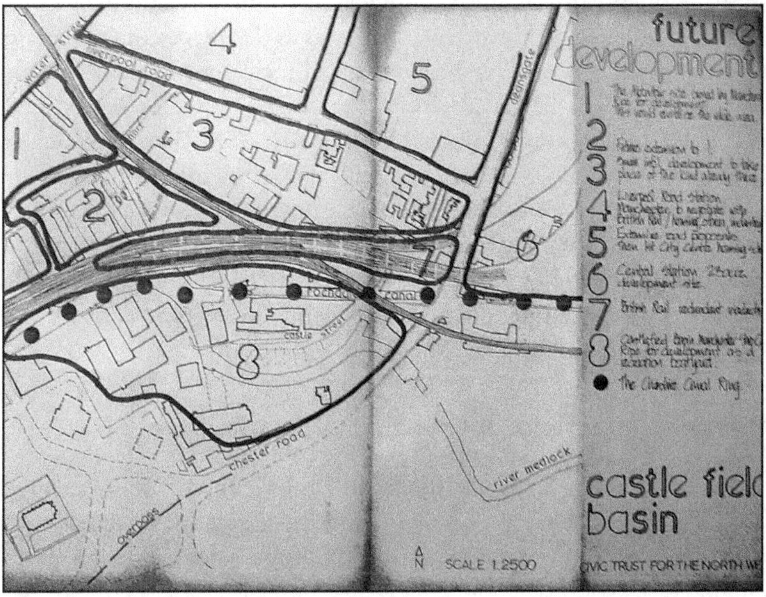

The 1978 report was forceful in its claims for a certain set of historically important Castlefield attributes and includes a number of unique visual counter-representations of space. Two in particular are important for the reimaging and reproduction of Castlefield at this time: the front cover of the report and a proposals map. Unlike the drawings in Hall and Rhodes (1972), the future proposals map (Figure 6.6) is an adaptation of an official UK standard Ordnance Survey 1:2500 map. Seven zones were defined, five are numbered and two are labelled. The abattoir site was sanitised into 'new industry'. Four images on the cover of the 1978 report manifest the way Castlefield was meant to be reimagined, highlighting the four key historic elements the area: the Roman Fort/ vicus (represented by an image of the 1978 archaeological dig), the Georgian LRS, canals and warehouses and the Victorian railways. Jones and Rhodes juxtapose cleverly the historical against the contemporary: a section of Richard Green's famous 1794 Manchester map and recent photographs respectively.

Whether deliberately or not the front cover of the 1978 report presents a more simplified version of Castlefield than is reflected in its richer written narrative. On the cover there is no place for representations of residential histories – exclusive or working class – nor for the abattoir, or what might be called everyday existing industry as opposed to heritage dominated views of the industrial past. The visualisations of space embedded in the front cover of *Historic Castlefield* speak eloquently in favour of a complete reimagining of the area. Jones and Rhodes privileged particular histories as *the* history of Castlefield that required 'a new awareness' of the historical significance of our environment 'so that its essential character can be preserved and protected for all to enjoy' (Jones and Rhodes 1978). The 1978 report has immense value as a piece of archival documentary evidence for the production of Castlefield, but it has greater significance because of what happened next. Unlike the 1972 report it was not relegated to the back burner. The 1978 report enjoyed a remarkable intertextual circular journey generating unexpected consequences that began to move the Castlefield counter-project from the margins to the mainstream.

Historic Castlefield: unexpected circularity

Although Rhodes co-wrote the report in the guise of the chairman of the VSM, his conservation officer job and the political connections of Barri Jones are critical for understanding the report's subsequent circulation and impact. Jones, a capable publicist, gave a copy of the report to the leader of MCC, Norman Morris, who he knew well. Morris gave a copy to Brian Redhead, a local journalist and BBC television presenter with whom he was acquainted. Redhead was so impressed by the historical qualities of little known Castlefield conjured up by the 1978 report and the compelling advocacy of Jones and Rhodes that, according to Rhodes, he decided to devote one of his Friday night BBC2 *Homeground* TV documentary programmes to the area.

Protracted enquiries about the documentary through the exasperating labyrinth of BBC archives were unproductive. A sliver of hope appeared when Redhead (1993) confirmed that the programme was broadcast in 1978. Crucially, I was told that if somebody or their relatives had appeared in a BBC programme, they were entitled to a copy. At this point serendipity intervened. My sister Emmeline Leary was a school friend of Baroness Estelle Morris (former Secretary of State at the Department for Media, Culture and Sport, which had oversight of the BBC). She was the niece of Norman Morris and kindly provided a DVD of the programme. Redhead's programme was called simply *Homeground Castlefield* and aired on Friday 15 September 1978 on BBC2 North West (BBC 1978) bringing Castlefield to the attention of a television audience of millions. In the programme Redhead interviewed David Rhodes, in his capacity as VSM chairman, Barri Jones and Norman Morris. In opening, Redhead confronted the studio audience with the question, "What is the most historic place in the north west of England: Chester, Lancaster [pause] or is it Castlefield in Manchester?" (Rhodes 2008).

That Castlefield was unknown to the audience is evidenced by Redhead answering his own subsequent question, "So where is Castlefield?", with the help of a map derived from Hall and Rhodes' report. The whole programme is a sustained attempt to valorise Castlefield and convince an incredulous studio audience of its historical credentials. Rhodes' remarkably accurate recall of the opening of the programme was confirmed by the programme itself. Much of the 30 minute documentary is shot on location in Castlefield making visible a declining industrial area in transition. It is a place Redhead refers to evocatively as "the grotty end of Manchester" but "a very lived upon place, though you might not think so at first glance" (in BBC 1978). The director chose to depict various Castlefield spaces including the LRS frontage, complete with BR 'Goods Depot' sign, the Roman dig, the canal basin, historic viaducts and warehouses. Televisual documentary history can be an important historical record in its own right. That said it is regarded here, like the other visual data encountered, as representations of space rather than a neutral, truthful window into past reality.

Redhead's programme includes a rare working class contribution from a man called Alf Hayman. Born in 1912, Alf started work for

Manchester Ship Canal Company (MSCC) in 1927 at the age of 14 and was still working in Castlefield for the Bridgewater Department of MSCC in 1978. He recalled Castlefield as a busy port in the 1930s handling hundreds of barges a day. When asked by Redhead while on location on the towpath of the Bridgewater Canal what kind of trade would have been going on in the middle of the last century, Alf replied "cotton, grain, rubber and foodstuffs of all descriptions" (BBC 1978) making him one of the few voices encountered in my research to associate cotton with the production of Castlefield. Hayman portrayed Castlefield as a space of everyday working life, neither nostalgicised nor a wasteland of dereliction and danger. His first hand account makes a new contribution to Castlefield's spatial history. He maintains something of a ghostly presence in Castlefield where his sign still warns 'No Tipping' (Figure 6.7).

Figure 6.7: No tipping in Castlefield: Alf Hayman retains a ghostly presence (photo © Michael Leary-Owhin)

It is not only as a historical record that the programme is important; it has major intertextual significance too. Redhead drew extensively on information and opinions fed to him by Jones and Rhodes. Redhead, prompted by Jones and Rhodes, was at pains to question Norman Morris about what was to be done in the future now that the historic value of Castlefield was recognised. Morris added weight to the shifting representations of Castlefield counter-project with his support for a policy initiative to secure the area's protection and improvement. Eventually, though not without equivocation, he became part of the coalition which drew the Castlefield counter-project into the mainstream. However, no acknowledgement was given in *Homeground Castlefield* to the work over the preceding eight years of the historic preservation societies, probably due to Rhodes' conflict of interests. No recognition was given either to the involvement of HBC or GMC, probably due to local government rivalries.

Before presenting the finale of the Redhead story, it is worth noting that another TV programme featuring Castlefield was aired in 1982. During the archival research a film script came to light unexpectedly: *Yesterday's Dust, Tomorrow's Dreams* (GTV 1981). It reveals that GTV was embarked on a secret project to produce a dramatised documentary film with Castlefield as the central protagonist. The area was to be extolled for the romance of its 2,000 year history, and "the excitement of Liverpool Road Station". The script articulates the history of the area, especially GTV and Castlefield's mutual interconnections. Dramas, such as *Coronation Street* "dovetail into the historic surroundings"; the drama of television and, "the drama of Castlefield's history seem to make good bedfellows" (GTV 1981). Eventually a copy of the TV programme *Yesterday's Dust, Tomorrow's Dreams* was acquired from the Leeds archives of GTV. One of Britain's most recognised faces, Annie Walker, landlady of the Rovers Return pub in *Coronation Street*, opens the film at the site where construction of the new full size *Coronation Street* set is underway, with the words:

> 'Well as Hilda Ogden said "We've had a lot of history in these parts and it ought to be a consternation area." But now thank goodness it's a conservation area."' (Doris Speed in GTV 1982)

The film entwines cleverly a number of histories: Roman, Georgian, Victorian, industrial and that of GTV. Archaeologists are seen excavating the site of the Roman Fort and the film provides information about the continuing 'reconstruction' of the Fort walls and ramparts, pottery kilns and iron smelting furnaces: the precursor to Manchester's industrial, scientific and technological greatness. Despite this no recognition is given of the conservation and heritage valorisation work of the amenity societies, HBC or GMC.

After the Redhead programme was broadcast the 1978 report followed a remarkable trajectory:

'Now the Leader of the council was called Norman Morris. He was only a very small chap. He was interviewed on the programme. I was filmed in Castlefield but not in the studio because they were interviewing the Leader of the council and I was working for the council. But Norman Morris gave a copy of the 1978 report to Brian Parnell the chief planning officer and said, "make that legislative". Brian Parnell gave it to Henry Blackniki and said, "make that legislative". I was in Blackniki's team and he gave it back to me and said, "make it legislative" [DR and MLO laugh].' (in Rhodes 2008)

By 'make it legislative' Morris meant create a statutory conservation area for Castlefield under the terms of the Civic Amenities Act 1967. By doing so the area would receive legal protection from inappropriate development, with MCC, property owners and developers having a duty to preserve and enhance the historic and architectural character of the area. Crucially though, conservation area status does not automatically release additional public sector resources. In Britain the power to designate historic areas, which receive statutory protection from inappropriate development, rests with local government. Rhodes only touched on the process of designation, which appeared to be uncontroversial and unproblematic. The story of how Castlefield became a conservation area is told somewhat differently by Warren Marshall. He was the city's leading architectural conservation officer for over 38 years and was interviewed by telephone in 2014.

Contested conservation: a minister's wife intervenes

According to Marshall, city Planning Officer Brian Parnell, after reading a report recommending designation drafted by Rhodes and Marshall, was entirely dismissive of Castlefield becoming a conservation area. He argued that if Castlefield was important enough to be a conservation area then so was the rest of the city centre. The young Warren Marshall agreed cheekily that was indeed the case (Marshall 2014). Months went by and Parnell would not budge from his obstinacy. Without his support a conservation area could not be designated. Then quite out of the blue Marshall received a phone call from Dame Mary 'Jennifer' Jenkins (Marshall 2014). She was the wife of Roy Jenkins the prominent Labour politician and one of the founders of the breakaway centre-right Social Democrat Party in 1981. Jennifer Jenkins wanted to know everything about Castlefield's historic credentials. She was passionate about historic building conservation generally and was the 'chairman' (as she insisted on being called) of the HBC. It is not clear why she became involved in the struggle to establish the Castlefield Conservation Area. She did though have a strong connection with Manchester because her mother was Dorothy Morris, née Hale, one of the first female journalists to write for the *Manchester Guardian* newspaper.

What happened next is rather murky but it is likely that Jennifer Jenkins had a quiet word with Brian Parnell. A few months later Parnell called Marshall into his office and asked "Why isn't Castlefield a conservation area?" An exasperated Marshall declared confrontationally "Because you've been refusing to approve my report for months." (Marshall 2014). Parnell told Marshall to go away and rewrite the report. He did so, the report was submitted to the appropriate city council committee and Castlefield was designated a conservation area in October 1979. That was not the end of the matter though. It appears that Jennifer Jenkins used her political influence to ensure that Castlefield was elevated to the status of an Outstanding Conservation Area in January 1980, which meant it became eligible for significant government funding.

Manchester has 35 conservation areas and there are thousands throughout Britain. While it is an important marker of historic value, Castlefield was just one of many. Henry Blackniki was always keen to generate not just local but national interest in Castlefield. In August 1982 a public–private delegation from the north of England visited former textile cities in Massachusetts, including Lowell, and drew lessons from the various policy initiatives that were "Transforming huge, disused cotton mills into offices, apartments, warehouses, and factories" (Willis 1982). Manchester Chamber of Commerce president Mr A. M. Toms said during the visit "You've done wonders with your old mills. We can learn a lot from you" (in Willis 1982). It was Michael Heseltine who commissioned the delegation and to whom it reported; a fact which becomes salient in the next chapter for the origin of the urban development corporation idea.

Although Blackniki was not part of the delegation, he was acquainted with Toms and was equally impressed by what was being achieved in Lowell through the federal and state parks. Blackniki desired that Castlefield stand out from other conservation areas and originated the idea of designating Castlefield the first Urban Heritage Park (UHP) in Britain (Marshall 2014). He persuaded MCC; designation was in December 1982. Rather bizarrely, the Castlefield UHP designation carries no statutory authority, does not result in additional protection or financing and remains the only one in Britain. That said, it is rather perverse that the UHP moniker is far more prominent across many internet websites than is Castlefield's statutory conservation area status. Remarkably, Blackniki succeeded in his aspiration to have 'urban' in the title, which Patrick Mogan and associates in Lowell had to let go.

Shortly after the conservation area was designated a public–private advisory body was created called the Castlefield Steering Committee (CSC). The first major report produced by CSC (1982a), the *Castlefield Tourism Development Plan*, gave unequivocal support for industrial heritage coupled with ambivalence towards everyday existing industry. The Tourism Plan constitutes a transitional moment in the area's representations of space. Castlefield was no longer valued historically for its own sake but instrumentally because the promotion of heritage tourism 'will bring vital economic benefits' not only to the area but 'to the inner city generally' (CSC 1982a: para 2.2). The Tourism Plan highlighted the annual Manchester Fair, drawing on Jones and Rhodes (1978), suggesting 'it would not be completely out of character' for fairground or carnival-type activities, Roman/Turkish baths, planetarium or market stalls to be located in Castlefield (CSC 1982a: para 5.6,). And for a few years in the 1980s an annual event called the Castlefield Carnival, sponsored by MCC and GMC, was held. It was a traditional working class fair with carousels (Figure 6.8), market stalls,

Figure 6.8: Working class fun, ice cream and carousel at Castlefield Carnival/Fair 1985 (MCC Local Images Collection, photo © Derek Brumhead, thanks to Jane Hodkinson)

jugglers, side shows, ice cream and toffee apples. Gentrification had to wait until the 1990s (Degen 2008).

Subsequently the idea of 'rebuilding' the north gate of the Roman Fort was proposed even though the original gate had been obliterated and no records of its structure remained. It proved controversial with some 'archaeological purist' arguing a replica could 'bear no resemblance to the original' (CSC 1982b). Opposition also came from members of the GMAU who claimed that it would be a 'Disney-ish hotch-potch' (CSC 1982b). Despite opposition the proposal was approved because it would give continuity to 'the theme of people living in the city over a very long period of time and would make the area more attractive' (CSC 1982b). The facsimile gate was 'opened' in 1986 and became a striking feature of the UHP popular with tourists but educationally vapid. The episode exhibits striking parallels with similar attempts in Vancouver and Lowell to create contemporary replicas of historical artefacts during the production of heritage infused public space. Castlefield's Roman gate, like Gastown's streetlights and Lowell's streetcars, remains a wonderfully irreverent and deeply encoded example of a simulacrum, à la Baudrillard, and a material manifestation of contested heritage-led production of space.

Conclusions

Another powerful vindication of a Lefebvrian inspired historical approach to the production of urban space has been presented in this chapter. In similar ways to Vancouver and Lowell, archival and interview research have demonstrated the critical role played by historic preservation interests in initiating the reimagining of urban industrial space in Castlefield. It is clear that such reimagining did not simply remain rhetorical; it produced counter-representations which in turn helped to produce counter-space and counter-projects. In significant ways the chapter has produced evidence to challenge the conventional wisdom of what is called here the dominant academic narrative, which depicts Castlefield as a dead wasteland in the 1970s, reinvented in the 1990s. Archival and interview data analyses reveal the substantial role played by GMC and the HBC in the initial stages of the post-industrial production of urban space in the city. Significantly, the chapter has demonstrated the unexpected and forgotten roles of GTV and the BBC in Castlefield's spatial history.

The LRS restoration project, driven initially by the historic preservation societies and from 1978 by the MOSI project, focused attention on the potential of Castlefield as an urban tourist visitor destination. The success of the station restoration and museum projects depended on the collaboration of a coalition of diverse actors and agencies in London and Manchester, from professionals and preservation activists to MPs, Cabinet ministers, journalists and railway enthusiasts. A similar pattern of heritage preservation activism and the building of spatial coalitions is evident in Vancouver and Lowell. Francis Hawcroft and David Rhodes used their privileged insider status and considerable determination to confront a public sector reluctant to accept the heritage value of the Victorian industrial built environment. Rhodes' architectural skills and appreciation put him in the category of what Lefebvre calls artists with a scientific bent. His noteworthy role in the creation of alternative representations of Castlefield that valorised its historic characteristics and pointed to an alternative post-industrial future is similar to that of the VCAC and the Southworth's in Lowell. At times, the spatial conflicts of which Lefebvre speaks are made manifest as when, for a brief moment in the 1980s, Castlefield was transformed from a space of industry, sweat and toil to a space of carnivalesque leisure and pleasure with the appearance of the working class Castlefield Carnival.

While the Lefebvrian inspired production of space literature tends to reveal dialectical tensions between representations of space and spaces of representation, this chapter has revealed contradictions within elements of the public sector, which applied different representations of space to Castlefield. The vital shift from reimagining and representations to material intervention through spatial practice was found in this chapter to be instigated by GMC and the HBC, rather than the private sector or MCC as in the dominant academic narrative. In ways similar to the unfolding of production of space events in Vancouver and Lowell, the counter-projects explored in this chapter are seen to build networks from the local to the national and international. These processes produced, after a certain amount of struggle, transformed understandings of urban space. With this acceptance, the designation of historic areas to be protected, preserved and enhanced was found to bring with it additional financial resources but only after counter-projects were shifted into the mainstream.

Historical analysis of the production of space in this chapter has uncovered unique and extraordinarily rich detail, allowing a greater appreciation of the complexities involved than was hitherto possible. Archival networks emerged in which archival, interview and visual data allow new histories to be uncovered with great significance for the production of urban space. Notable too is the way this chapter has brought into the public domain salient data from what may be called private archives. These sources mesh with the other data forming an archival network that paints a complex multi-layered production of space picture. Social relationships and interactions of many kinds are of course crucial in the production of space. In addition to highlighting the importance of big governmental structures this chapter has also made manifest the importance of interpersonal social interaction. In concrete ways the chapter has reconnected Manchester and Lowell through a certain circular archival logic. If Lowell's Boston Associates copied Manchester in the 19th century, then it is now apparent that MCC urban planners copied Lowell in the 20th. It is apparent that the methodological approach has succeeded in adding not just to our appreciation of the genesis of urban spaces but also to their mutual interconnections and links with the spatial practice of Castlefield. That said, there is no pretence here that definitive histories have been told. Archival networks that sometimes provide conclusive answers also throw up new questions, controversies and conundrums. A particularly salient question concerns the role of one of the largest investors in Castlefield's spatial transformation, the Central Manchester Development Corporation (CMDC), and its role in the production of space. It is to these issues that the next chapter turns.

SEVEN

Manchester: Producing urban public space and city transformation

As for spatial practice, it is observed, described and analysed on a wide range of levels: in architecture, in city planning or 'urbanism' (a term borrowed from official pronouncements), in the actual design of routes and localities ('town and country planning') in the organisation of everyday life, and, naturally, in urban reality. (Lefebvre 1991: 414)

'And we saw Castlefield very much as a sort of potential to be an international area of international renown, with principally leisure and tourism type activities with a bit of residential thrown in ... Castlefield was of real significance in terms of opening it up in terms of the canal basins and we were there to make a real difference.' (Glester 2008)

Introduction

This chapter contributes to a critical understanding of the production of Manchester space through an exploration of notable spatial moments in the 1980s and 1990s. In overall terms it explores the production of new public space in the Castlefield area focusing mainly on the decisive interventions of the Central Manchester Development Corporation (CMDC 1988–96), a third generation urban development corporation (UDC). This is not so much a case of the revisiting CMDC, but bringing a fresh perspective and a different theoretical lens to bear on a fascinating and vital moment in the production of space. In so doing the chapter argues that archival networks allow the further revelation of key moments in production of space histories. In order to contextualise the CMDC, a brief review of the 1980s reorientation of British urban policy is presented which explores the so far unproblematised emergence of British UDCs. One consequence of CMDC's intervention, the chapter argues, was the creation of the potential for the inadvertent production of differential space. Furthermore, this chapter explains why 'Castlefield' needs to be interrogated ontologically rather than accepted under this or that homogenous banner, for example privatised consumption (Mellor 1997), heritage tourism (Schofield 2000) or aesthetic exclusion through public space formalisation (Degen 2008; Kazimierczak 2014).

This chapter in common with the other empirical chapters weaves together the influence of alternative representations of space on spatial practice. Some of the counter-representations of space, which moved into the mainstream of city planning and urbanism in the post-industrial transition of the 1970s, are seen in this chapter to have continuing influence. Lefebvre's observations regarding routes, localities and everyday life resonate in the discussion of the empirical research findings in this chapter. In providing new linear public space routes through what was formerly private space, urban planners sought to provide physical access to sites of exchange value consumption. They certainly did this but in doing so they created other potentials. Castlefield's new bridges stimulated the production of significant new public spaces, in particular the Castlefield Arena. How these spaces, including quasi-public space, came about and how they assumed tremendous importance for the production of space is unravelled in this chapter.

Stubbornly, UDCs have retained their fascination and ability to generate simultaneously, awe and angst since the first ones were created in London and Liverpool in 1981. Academic researchers have revelled in the controversial UDC debate since the 1980s and it is perhaps not surprising that attention has continued to focus on the largest and most controversial UDC, the London Development Corporation (LDDC 1981–98) (Brownill 2011). The well recognised 1980s urban policy shift instigated by Michael Heseltine through UDCs was to involve private sector interests directly in neoliberal inspired public–private partnerships. In 2012 Lord Michael Heseltine was commissioned by British Prime Minister David Cameron to lead a study into how wealth might be more effectively created in the UK. In the ensuing report Heseltine is certain that the UDCs had critical impacts beyond the first two which he designated personally:

> In 1979 I launched the concept of the Urban Development Corporation (UDC) which led to a total of 13 being established. UDCs established the foundations for London's Docklands and were at the heart of a renaissance in several of our cities. (Heseltine 2012: 31)

His affinity with Manchester is evident throughout the 2012 report through the various references to the city. His decisive intervention in Manchester affairs after the Irish Republican Army (IRA) bombing of Manchester in 1996 is documented amply (King 2006). Heseltine's association with Liverpool after the 1981 riots is well known but his association with Manchester is perhaps stronger and goes back further, to the local government reorganisation of 1974. Furthermore, he has significant but less trumpeted associations with Castlefield at noteworthy points during its spatial production.

The LDDC has been the subject of a great deal of research attention over the decades that shows no signs of abating (Brownill and O'Hara 2015). However, there are other important UDC stories that deserve to be told, most notably that of the city centre located CMDC. Rather than extend the often polarised UDC debate, this chapter focuses on the significant impact of the CMDC on Castlefield and Manchester more generally, regarding the post-industrial reimagining of the city. The most authoritative CMDC research is Deas et al (2000) which approached CMDC from the viewpoint of an evaluation of outputs against its public (and private) sector resource inputs. Their paper is based on an earlier evaluation report commissioned by the DoE (Robson et al 1997). Despite UDCs' (and CMDC's) obvious potential for driving the production of urban public space, this aspect has received little research attention. A notable exception is Degen (2008) who contends that CMDC served, due to its property development remit and its close relationship with the private sector, to produce homogenised spaces of consumption which favoured the creation of upmarket middle class residential and leisure enclaves in inner city Manchester. Mellor (2002: 216) presents the least complimentary assessment of the social impact of CMDC maintaining that its regeneration efforts excluded poor inner city residents, creating instead a consumption orgy of bars, bistros and canal barges. More positive, though less comprehensive, evaluations of the CMDC are offered by O'Connor and Wynne (1996) and Williams (2003).

UDC context and precursors

UDCs need to be understood in the context of the powerful neoliberal turn of the 1980s (Harvey 1989a; Couch et al 2011; Tallon 2013). They should be comprehended in the longer historical timeframe of British urban policy stretching back to the 1960s. The dominant 'entrepreneurial city' neoliberal milieu is particularly important for understanding the modus operandi and impact of CMDC (Leary 2008;

Williams 2003). At its most extreme, neoliberal inspired planning and regeneration result in the purification of public space through the rejection of difference and the securing of boundaries to maintain the homogeneity of abstract space. Clearly, the state plays conflicting roles in these dramas through its need to provide welfare services for ordinary people and the manner in which, under neo-capitalist entrepreneurial regimes, it is implicated in subsidising the private sector. Lefebvre (1991: 375) makes this point arguing that, although the state claims to act in the interests of all users of urban space, its interventions tend to favour capital, especially property developers.

In the second half of the 20th century in Britain two quite distinct paternalistic, modernist approaches to urban problems operated. The first resulted in physical planning inspired comprehensive redevelopment programmes in major industrial cities which saw vast swathes of inner city working class areas reduced to rubble and rebuilt at lower densities. In the process thousands of families were dispersed to the urban periphery or to smaller towns. These comprehensive redevelopments were preceded by rationales bound up with classic Lefebvrian official representations of space in the 1940s city reconstruction plans (Clapson and Larkham 2013) and modernist planning rhetoric. The second approach, from the late 1960s, saw urban policy re-formulated with the aim of tackling urban problems in situ without comprehensive redevelopment and the dispersal of working class communities, that is, the focus shifted away from bricks and mortar to social needs.

Urban policy entered the UK political lexicon in 1968 when Prime Minister Harold Wilson, in response to J. Enoch Powell's bloodcurdling, racist diatribes, made his anti-racist declaration of a new Urban Programme (UrP) based on a social welfare model of public sector intervention. Housing, acute social need and the 'immigrant problem' would be the main criteria for assessing the need for intervention. UrP was set up initially not by legislation but by Home Office Circular 225/68. Thirty four English local authority areas were given UrP status: one of which was Manchester. The Circular allowed local authorities in England to tackle problems such as: deficiencies in the physical environment, particularly in housing; overcrowding of houses; family sizes above the average; and persistent unemployment. It added that a substantial degree of immigrant settlement would also be an important factor, but by no means the only factor, in determining the existence of acute social need. Many small scale intervention initiatives followed. Over time though, they were criticised for being ad hoc, lacking a strategy framework and for neglecting the causes of urban problems.

In response the government initiated a White Paper investigation. It is accepted widely that the 1977 White Paper *Policy for the Inner Cities* was the most comprehensive attempt by any UK government to understand the nature of the country's urban problems. In addition to (re)presenting the urban space problematic as physical, social *and* economic, the White Paper proposed a radical reorganisation of the local authority dominated institutional arrangements for the targeting, grant allocation and management of urban policy projects, giving increased control to central government. Inner city partnerships were to be established in areas suffering from the worst urban deprivation. Each partnership board was to be chaired by a government minister and each officer working party by a senior civil servant. In Manchester the partnership area boundary was drawn to include Frederich Engels' densely populated inner girdle of the two cities which still included the most socially deprived working class areas and huge amounts of decrepit industrial city space. Castlefield lay towards the middle of the partnership area. Although it contained large amounts of abandoned land and decaying industrial buildings it lacked significant population, 'immigrant', socially deprived or otherwise. Nevertheless, MSP came to be seen as a source of funding for Castlefield's urban regeneration as explained in Chapter Six. In contrast to the UDCs, the inner city partnerships have been subject to less academic scrutiny (but see Parkinson and Wilks 1983).

The professional work of the MSP was undertaken by the Manchester and Salford Officers Working Party (MSWP). In line with the 1977 White Paper and subsequent Inner Urban Areas Act 1978, the first draft of the MSP programme determined the decline of the economy of the inner areas 'is the major factor causing the inner city malaise' (MSWP 1978: para 8). Lack of private investment had resulted 'in the inner area containing the bulk of the two cities' vacant industrial buildings and derelict land' (MSWP 1978: para 4): a major issue was therefore, how to accomplish the 'renewal or refurbishment of industrial buildings and infrastructure' (MSWP 1978: para 8). In addressing the reconfigured urban problem the government allocated an annual budget to the MSP of about £10 million. A year after the creation of the inner city partnerships, the May 1979 general election brought Margaret Thatcher's right of centre neoliberal government to power. She appointed Michael Heseltine to the Cabinet post of Secretary of State at the DoE. Academic attention has focused on his UDC experiments (Imrie and Thomas 1999) but his creation of UDCs *and* his treatment of the UrP inner city partnerships were to prove essential for the production of public space in Manchester.

Clutching at straws: the 'private sector'

In the course of this research Lord Heseltine was interviewed in 2007 and 2009. Heseltine shared with his DoE predecessor Peter Shore a material understanding of the urban problematic, based on his first hand observation of the physical problems of dereliction in East London. Pragmatically, Heseltine approved of Shore's totally public sector inner city partnerships because "it was early days" and they "hadn't had time to work" (Heseltine 2007). Heseltine decided to chair the Liverpool Inner City Partnership as Shore had done. This was his first significant contact with that city. For Heseltine, the first Liverpool partnership board meeting was pivotal in changing the thrust of UrP nationally, for two reasons: first, because the change was immediate in 1979, while the UDCs took two more years to happen and longer before they had any impact on the ground. Second, inner city partnerships and the wider UrP affected many cities across England as opposed to the two UDCs Heseltine created. At the first meeting as chair of the Liverpool partnership, Heseltine announced that he had only one change to make. At this point in our conversation he was remarkably candid and self-deprecating:

> **Lord Heseltine (LH):** The initiative that I took at that first meeting is that I said, I'm going to continue with Peter's partnerships. I'm going to continue with the designation [of inner city partnerships] and I'm going to continue with ministers being in charge, one each, of these places: all very commendable. And the money's available. I only have one change and that is this. You will only get the money and spend it after consultation with the private sector.

> *MLO:* Ah.

> **LH:** That was revolution. There was no precedent worth the name of local authorities, if you like, working with the consent of the private sector: just did not happen. They didn't like each other. They didn't talk to each other. There was no relationship. So that was what I said.

> *MLO*: So how was that formalised within the partnerships, because they weren't members of the partnership boards were they, the private sector?

LH: That was the first question. After the stunned, horrified silence [MLO laughs] somebody said, well what is the private sector?

MLO: Yea.

LH: And there is no answer to that question in truth. But you can't be a Secretary of State and say I don't know [MLO laughs]. So there had to be an answer. So I clutched at the only straw that happened to be passing in the wind at the time and said, the local chamber of commerce.

MLO: Oh no, you didn't.

LH: I did, I did, I promise you I did. And as I did it, my reaction in seventy nine was precisely yours now. I knew this was ridiculous. You know, they just weren't up to it. But what could I have said? (Heseltine 2009)

This was a revelatory moment in the research, since the conventional academic wisdom is that the *UDCs* were the vehicle for the private sector reorientation of urban policy from 1981. Heseltine's exaggeration here in the context of the government's neoliberal politics is understandable but not excusable. MCC had worked in partnership with private sector property developers in the 1970s, providing £11 million for the £30 million scheme to build the enormous Arndale Centre, the UK's largest shopping mall at the time. Manchester Corporation had a long, distinguished history of working with the private sector and established Britain's first modern public–private partnership, the MSCC. It was set up by act of Parliament in 1885 as a private company capitalised at £5 million. The project went vastly over budget but was rescued, as the company teetered on the brink of bankruptcy, when Manchester Corporation invested a further £5 million, taking a 51% stake. MCC retained this stake and associated Board membership until being bought out by Peel Holdings in the late 1980s (the company is now called The Peel Group).

On the instructions of Heseltine, policy guidelines were produced for involving the private sector in urban policy but they left scope for local discretion at inner city partnership level about just how the private sector was to be involved and the extent to which partnerships should emphasise physical regeneration projects concerned with derelict land and buildings. I argue that this local partnership discretion was vital for the funding of LRS and MOSI projects (discussed in Chapter Six). Michael Heseltine's urban policy involvement with Liverpool is well known, especially in the aftermath of the 1981 riots. His involvement with post-1996 regeneration initiatives in Manchester generally is also well documented (King 2006). What has not been the subject of previous empirical research is the origin of the inner city UDC idea and Heseltine's long term direct and indirect involvement in the regeneration of Castlefield.

Representations of the urban problematic

Given the parlous state of the British economy and evident widespread industrial decline by 1979, it is rather mysterious that Heseltine only ever set up two UDCs. Importantly, his legislation in the Local Government, Planning and Land Act 1980 allowed UDCs to be created *anywhere* in England and Wales. All the research encountered in the literature views the policy process leading up to the first UDCs as unproblematic, typically 'UDCs were created by the 1980 Local Government, Planning and Act' (Imrie and Thomas 1999: 4). A number of academics claim the inner city UDC idea arose after the 1979 election which saw Margaret Thatcher triumph over Jim Callaghan (Barnekov et al 1989), but this confuses the origin of the idea with its public announcement in September 1979. While there is a great deal of literature on the private sector orientation and undemocratic nature of UDCs, there is little recognition that they were at odds with the neoliberal, anti-public sector ideology of the first Thatcher government, even accepting that neoliberalism contains major contradictions regarding the role of the state (Peck 2010). Consequently, it is claimed that Margaret Thatcher was right when she mused regarding Heseltine, 'he is not one of us' (Blowers and Evans 1997: 127).

Hence the provenance of UDCs raises an interesting question. If it was not from the Conservative government's neoliberal ideology, from where did the inner city UDC idea originate? Policy diffusion from the US is the conventional wisdom regarding the source of the inner city UDC idea, for example, 'hundreds of policy-entrepreneurs' from the 1970s made 'the pilgrimage to garner inspiration from the Baltimore model' (Quilley 1999: 190). Hambleton (1991) also points to the importance of the 'Baltimore model' in influencing British urban policy. Keith and Rogers (1991: 2) assert that 'American experience initially served as a model' for British UDCs. Haran et al (2011: 77) repeat the claim made by Parkinson (1993) that the UDC approach to inner city regeneration was an imitation of US strategy. Tallon

(2013: 45) affirms that UDCs were derived from the US model of entrepreneurial city regeneration. Apparently, the 'essential notion was American', according to Hall (2014: 429). Michael Heseltine did send a fact finding delegation to Massachusetts in 1982 to learn about US post-industrial city regeneration policy (Willis 1982) but that was after the UDC announcement.

Above all it is clear that Thatcher's neoliberal government was committed to reducing the size of the public sector, public spending, red tape and state interference in markets, but facilitating the expansion of markets and private sector wealth creation. Such a neoliberal orientated government was unlikely in principle to relish the prospect of establishing large property development non-departmental public bodies (commonly called quangos) funded lavishly with public money and endowed with strong intervention powers. Archival documents uncovered at the National Archives (England) (NAE) seem to support the notion that the inner city UDC idea did not originate with Michael Heseltine but came from two further possible sources apart from US policy emulation: first, a 1978 discussion paper entitled *Renewing the Inner Areas: The Task and the Means* (Roche and Thomas 1978). Second, the bizarre suggestion that the idea came from the London Chamber of Commerce, only to be seized on by one of the architects of Thatcherite neoliberalism.

UDCs are of course associated with Michael Heseltine's first period as DoE, Secretary of State 1979–83, and have probably attracted more academic criticism than any other single urban policy initiative. And while many journalists have interviewed him, no academic researchers in the urban policy field appear to have interviewed him on this subject. What is clear is that the character of UDCs was based on powerful political beliefs in the failure of local government inner city interventions and the concomitant need for private sector engagement in inner city revival. During the research interviews Lord Heseltine denied that he borrowed the inner city UDC idea from similar initiatives in the US, asserting that he had never been to Baltimore.

Roche and Thomas' 1978 paper was presented to the DoE's Property Advisory Group in March 1979 (Brown 1979), while Heseltine was still DoE shadow spokesman. Its authors were New Town officers Fred Roche (Chief Architect, Milton Keynes) and Wyndham Thomas (General Manager, Peterborough New Town). The paper advocated that inner city regeneration should be carried out not by local authorities through the city planning function but by bespoke, single-minded central government development agencies based on the New Town Development Corporation (NTDC) model. A year before

Renewing the Inner Areas appeared, its basic arguments were rehearsed in (Roche 1977). Responding to the proposition that the inner city UDC concept came from Roche and Thomas, Heseltine conceded only "their names I know" but that he could not recall such a paper (Heseltine 2009). This was the only point in the interview when I felt Lord Heseltine exhibited discomfort. He became mildly strident in defending his ownership of the inner city UDC idea.

Hearty laughter was Heseltine's reaction to the suggestion that UDCs were championed by a Chamber of Commerce and Keith Joseph despite the claim in a London newspaper that Joseph:

> ... is showing keen interest in a new plan for Docklands.
> The idea is to set up a high-powered independent agency
> to supervise the Docklands Strategic Plan ... like a new
> town development corporation. Sir Keith has asked London
> Chamber of Commerce, which dreamed up the scheme to
> fill him in on the details. (*Newham Recorder* 1979)

During the 2009 interview Heseltine claimed several times that, "it's all in the book". He kindly gave me a copy of the book he had in mind, his second autobiography, *Life in the Jungle* (2000). Only a small portion of the interview material is covered in this book and his first autobiography in 1987 *Where There's a Will*.

In defending his claims about the origin of the inner city UDC idea, Lord Heseltine did not date the inspiration to 1979 but much earlier. While a junior minister in the new DoE under Peter Walker in 1972 Heseltine became increasingly concerned about the terrible state of London's severely modernist Southbank arts and cultural complex built with public money for the Festival of Britain in 1951. It is an example of what Meller (1997: 67) calls the post-war 'golden age' of modernist planning, characterised by 'almost mystical belief' in public sector planning. Heseltine found the Southbank complex unacceptable functionally and aesthetically; it was impenetrable, ugly, depressing, decaying and deserted. His objection focused not only on the Brutalist modern architecture, "it was the buildings that had been put there that were so awful", but on the inefficient and ineffective Greater London Council (GLC) management and maintenance regimes (Heseltine 2009). He asked his senior civil servant, Ron Brain, to devise an intervention mechanism for him to take over the management and redevelopment of the Southbank Centre; something along the lines of a central government agency or quango. A report was prepared which recommended control of the Southbank Centre should be ceded to

Heseltine in the form of a dedicated quango modelled on a NTDC with full planning, redevelopment and compulsory purchase powers. A political irony is apparent here since the NTDCs were the result of the New Towns Act 1946: one on the most resolutely socialist, interventionist pieces of British town planning legislation ever enacted.

Heseltine liked Brain's proposals but was transferred suddenly to the Department of Transport where he took up the Aerospace and Shipping portfolio so the 'Southbank UDC' scheme was never operationalised (Heseltine 2007). However, during his time as aerospace minister, Heseltine spent many hours looking down on the East End of London as he flew to and fro to view the site of the proposed third London airport at Foulness, Essex. What he saw was the dereliction and hopelessness of hundreds of acres of deserted docks. The visibility of problematised material space, the spatial practice of Lefebvre's triad, is crucial here. He therefore had literally seen for himself the problems of material dereliction in London's working class East End and docklands. He had seen in two senses of the word: observed and understood. Heseltine's interaction with the perceived space of spatial practice at this juncture should be understood in the context of his rejection of the reports (the representations of space) of the Labour government created Docklands Joint Committee (DJC). It is would appear that the power of representations of space to exert influence rests to some extent on the ideological predisposition of the reader.

When in opposition from 1974 to 1979 Heseltine was shadow environment spokesman and he saw again the large scale abandonment of London's decrepit docklands which he believed was "one vast tract of dereliction, emptiness, rotting buildings, *public sector monopoly*" (Heseltine 2009, emphasis added), but this time, through the reference to the public sector, he indicates his concerns with urban governmental structures, that is, the local authority dominated DJC. The DJC was a statutory committee set up in September 1974, made up of the GLC and the London boroughs of Tower Hamlets, Newham, Southwark, Lewisham and Greenwich. It was charged with the unenviable task of regenerating London's East End. With hindsight its lack of visible projects on the ground by 1979 was a strategic error. On his first day back in government after the May 1979 election victory, Heseltine took his permanent secretary, John Garlick, to lunch and gave him a list of the ten priority policy agenda items, one of which was an inner city UDC for London. Heseltine told Garlick to find him the Southbank papers from 1972. He was at this point determined to create *one* UDC, not on the Southbank Centre "which would have been small beer", but for 6,000 acres of East London.

Heseltine wanted originally only one British UDC located in London Docklands. Even this raised strong resistance from his own civil servants and from powerful Cabinet colleagues, Keith Joseph the party guru and his friend Geoffrey Howe the Chancellor. Howe said "we haven't got the money" and Joseph resisted, "for ideological reasons because it was interventionist and we are a new type of government" (Heseltine 2009). Civil servants across Whitehall balked at the thought of having to put into place a new governmental agency reviled by local authorities because it stripped them of their planning and compulsory purchase powers and created a democratic deficit. Even John Garlick resisted because the civil service "believed they were the custodians of local government and we were taking powers away from local government" (Heseltine 2009). Heseltine felt cornered and decided to go to the Prime Minister and argue the case for a London UDC "which the three of us did one night in Downing Street". The three Cabinet Secretaries of State deployed their arguments and "she came down on my side" and that was how "the concept of an urban development corporation for London became real" (Heseltine 2009). Lord Heseltine admits the UDC was not an original idea, being based on the NTDC. However, he claims strenuously that he originated the idea of "taking it into the inner city" (Heseltine 2009).

John Garlick was effusive in his praise of this victory against formidable senior Cabinet opponents, but "produced with a flourish of triumph" another objection (Heseltine 2009). While admiring of the battle he had fought, Garlick announced there was an insurmountable problem: a London UDC would require hybrid legislation – an impossible situation. Hybrid legislation mixes elements of English private and public law and can have significant impact on individuals, groups or geographical areas. The problem with it is that all those individuals and organisations affected who oppose the measure have the right to be heard when the Bill passes through Parliament and debate cannot be guillotined. A hybrid London UDC Bill would have taken years to secure passage through arduous parliamentary procedures, with no guarantee of enactment. At that moment Heseltine asked, where is the second worst place in the country? Liverpool was the immediate answer. He would therefore have general legislation and designate London and Liverpool. He explains, "that's why Liverpool got an urban development corporation" (Heseltine 2009). Although Heseltine will always be associated with his regeneration work in Liverpool in the 1980s, he was adamant that his only concern in 1979 was London Docklands, if he could have had just this one UDC that would have been enough, "my intention was to restore London, Liverpool was included in order to avoid the risk of hybrid legislation" (Heseltine 2009).

Heseltine was fully cognisant regarding the strong civil service antagonism towards his UDC idea and wanted to make a public announcement with utmost speed. In a memo to the Prime Minister, he claimed that the Cabinet Ministerial Committee on Economic Strategy of 25 July 'enthusiastically accepted in principle my proposal for setting up UDCs' and that nothing in the detail to be worked out would change that decision (Heseltine 1979). However, Keith Joseph's measured reticence was still evident at the end of July:

> New legislation will be essential if we decide to take this further. But for the moment we have asked Michael Heseltine to arrange for urgent detailed studies by an interdepartmental group of officials with a view to enabling him to formulate detailed proposals ... Pending that further consideration, no public announcement will be made. (Joseph 1979)

Joseph stressed that, unlike NTDCs on which they were modelled, UDCs should be able 'to put real emphasis on private sector development' (Joseph 1979). A big part of Heseltine's dilemma, "cornered as I was by civil servants and senior Cabinet colleagues", was a need to placate these sources of opposition, through a "careful compromise" (Heseltine 2009). This led to UDC boards being private sector dominated but as a counter-weight local authority councillors, acting in a personal capacity, were allocated a few seats. It was not until September 1979 that Heseltine was able to make the UDC public announcement which, crucially for this chapter, included confirmation that UrP would continue but with significant private sector reorientation. Interestingly, two of the first LDDC Board members to be appointed were John Garlick and Wyndham Thomas! Lord Heseltine did not mention this during the interviews.

Of course having secured conspicuous amounts of scarce public money for two UDCs at a time of local government public spending cuts, Michael Heseltine was desperate to demonstrate rapid results on the ground. Unfortunately, for the first year Nigel Broackes (LDDC chairman) could only point to an output of consultants' reports, strategies and planning documents – classic representations of space. When Heseltine was about to leave the DoE for the Department of Defence in 1983, he was preoccupied by the urgent political need to demonstrate UDC efficacy. There was high unemployment and he "had the Tory Party round my neck" (Heseltine 2009). He met with Broackes, pleading for something visible and tangible to which he could point. Broackes suggested restoring some of East London's wonderfully historic but down-at-heel Nicholas Hawksmoor designed 18th century churches

Heseltine chuckled when recalling the other Broacke's suggestion: a request for £250,000 to restore some old dockside cranes. It was a potentially "career wrecking" gamble if the project went wrong. Heseltine worried what would happen "when Margaret got to hear about these cranes" (Heseltine 2009). A quarter of a million pounds was a large amount of money in 1982 for industrial heritage conservation rather than property development or direct job creation but the risks of appearing foolish and wasteful were considered worth it. The churches and cranes were restored and in the interview Heseltine was moved emotionally when remembering that these were the same cranes which bowed their heads in a mark of grieving respect as Winston Churchill's funeral cortège went by in 1965, it was tear jerking stuff. Heseltine and the LDDC, therefore, legitimised historic preservation in urban policy which would have great importance for Castlefield in the 1990s.

This was not the first time Heseltine was involved with historic preservation. Another important Manchester railway station was Central Station. It was the city's largest railway station and being built in 1880 it was of great historic importance. It closed in the mid-1960s and in the 1970s was threatened by demolition. Heseltine was keen to point out that before UrP was reconfigured and the first UDCs set up, "one of the first things I did in 1979 was to help fix the finance for GMEX" in Manchester (Heseltine 2009). GMEX (Greater Manchester Exhibition Centre) was a £20 million major urban regeneration project of lengthy gestation located in Castlefield and led by the GMC which resulted in the conversion in 1986 of Central Station to a nationally important conference and exhibition centre. In recent years it has been a popular venue for the Labour and Conservative Party Conferences. In 2008–10 it was refurbished by MCC at a cost of £30 million, extended and rebranded Manchester Central to acknowledge its former role.

During his second stint at the DoE in 1992 Heseltine supported strongly the CMDC-MCC Bridgewater Hallé Orchestra concert hall project with a grant of £10 million. This complex public–private sector regeneration partnership utilised a former bus station site on the eastern edge of Castlefield. The developer AMEC PLC rescued the precarious project in a depressed property market when they acquired the scheme from the Hanson Group. In redesigning the scheme AMEC increased the office element and created a new public space to increase the property values. Unsurprisingly, the difficult economic conditions of the early 1990s saw the scheme suffer numerous financial setbacks which threatened its survival. Heseltine's intervention was therefore crucial, not just for guaranteeing the necessary central government grant funding but for restoring commercial confidence in the scheme and Castlefield. More important was the designation of a Heseltine style inner city UDC for Manchester.

CMDC: a production of space investigation

Following the UDCs for London and Liverpool, a tranche of second generation UDCs on a similar large scale was created for various cities in England and Wales. In late 1987 Nicholas Ridley, DoE Secretary of State floated the idea of creating third generation city centre 'mini-UDCs', where he thought that tens rather than hundreds of millions of pounds could unlock potential private sector property investment and create new employment. John Glester, a senior DoE civil servant based in Manchester, affirmed during a research interview that Ridley was sympathetic to the prospect of a Manchester UDC partly because Glester had taken him around the area privately so Ridley had seen for himself the physical problems of derelict sites (Glester 2008). Ridley was enthusiastic too for Thatcherite ideological reasons, seeing a chance "you might say to take on the socialist municipal citadels" (Glester 2008), for example the 'radical left' regime of the Labour Party dominated MCC. Manchester made it on to the short list in 1988 following powerful advocacy from sections of Manchester's business community including the Manchester Chamber of Commerce. The suggested UDC area included the entire Castlefield Conservation Area with its deteriorating industrial buildings, unpleasant canals but important historical legacies too.

Nicholas Ridley was astute in his choice of CMDC chairman when he selected James Grigor whose appointment had to be approved by the Prime Minister. Grigor was boss of the Manchester based Swiss chemical engineering company Ciba-Geigy which first came to Manchester in 1911. Grigor was a well-respected businessman who, unlike the UDC chairmen in London and Liverpool, was seen as politically neutral rather than an outright Conservative Party supporter. "He wasn't part of the Manchester mafia" (Glester 2008). The Manchester mafia was a term used in the 1990s to describe the coalition of local business interests operating in the city, that for example promoted the Olympic and Commonwealth games bids (Peck and Tickell 1995). Grigor had argued strongly for the setting up of the

Trafford Park UDC in 1987 (partly out of self-interest as Ciba-Geigy had a large plant here). He knew and had good relations with Howard Bernstein, MCC assistant chief executive, and Graham Stringer, leader of MCC. Stringer and Bernstein were also interviewed during the research. Grigor's affinity for Castlefield may have attracted him to an agency dedicated to improving the area. Through his contacts at the Manchester Literary and Philosophy Society, he was aware of the rationale for and lengthy process needed to convert LRS to the MOSI.

Ridley was also politically deft with his appointment of the CMDC chief executive, demonstrating a willingness to listen to the views of Stringer and Bernstein. John Glester was appointed – he was no stranger to UDCs or Manchester politics. He was a career civil servant involved in setting up the Merseyside and Trafford Park UDCs having transferred from London to the DoE's North West Regional Office through promotion in the 1970s. Significantly, his ideological commitment to involving the private sector in urban policy to achieve inner city improvements dated back to his work with MSP in the 1970s when he was a DoE representative on the MSP officer group. Glester appears to share the views of the dominant Castlefield regeneration narrative when he says wittily of the place he first encountered it was, "clearly not a destination at that time, you know, apart from a day out amongst the pallets", it was just "a forgotten backwater" (Glester 2008).

Representations of CMDC space

Deas et al (2000) stress the importance of the impact of CMDC's private sector ethos on MCC. While not disputing these findings, evidence from interview and archival sources shows that influence was mutual. One major influence was MCC representations of space, particularly the 1984 *City Centre Local Plan*, which had of course been influenced by the same policy initiatives in Lowell that resulted in the Castlefield UHP designation (Bernstein 2015). Regarding representations of Castlefield presented in the 1984 Plan, it is evident they were influenced by the post-industrial reimagining of Castlefield instigated by Hall and Rhodes (1972) and Jones and Rhodes (1978). For the city's planners the eradication of inappropriate industry was a necessary precondition for the creation of heritage tourism friendly public space:

'... in Castlefield there had been a long term planning department view that the area should be de-industrialised. The mass of sort of scrap iron places, rendering plants; all those sorts of smelly bad neighbour kind of industries should be moved out and it had the potential to become a major tourist attraction.' (Stringer 2009)

Sir Howard Bernstein, MCC Assistant CEO at the time (and the Head of Regeneration, Pat Bartoli) reproduced this problematisation of industry during a research interview:

> **MLO:** But what do you think of the complete loss of all those jobs for ordinary working Manchester people in the Castlefield area from the 1980s?
>
> **Pat Bartoli:** I wouldn't say it is a complete loss because a lot of businesses were relocated because you had concrete batchers, breakers yards that relocated they didn't just disappear.
>
> **MLO:** Fair enough. But they disappeared from Castlefield.
>
> **Howard Bernstein:** But they disappeared from Castlefield because many of those industries were what I would call bad neighbour industries. You are not going to create a place where people are going to find attractive to live, if they're being asked to live next to a concrete piling manufacturer. So a lot of those industries were in the wrong place and as Pat rightly says a big effort was made in relocating them. (in Bernstein 2009)

Bernstein's sentiments highlight the genuine dilemmas faced by politicians on the left of the political spectrum who seek to improve perceived blighted city areas without engendering crass gentrification.

Glester accepts CMDC did not devise its development strategy in a vacuum; the Board and officers were influenced greatly by existing representations of Castlefield. During the interview Glester stresses that although CMDC employed consultants to produce its 1989 Strategy:

> 'The thing that was in existence, if you like, from the city council at the time was the City Centre Local Plan which covered this area, which was a very flexible document in many ways and in a sense we took that as our starting point.' (Glester 2008)

This attitude was fortunate because even before CMDC started work MCC's planners were adamant that there was already a salient planning framework – the 1984 Plan and, 'in only a few aspects does it need updating or fleshing out' (Kitchen in MCC 1988). Kitchen argued that CMDC could not operate in isolation and that the CMDC area should be seen in its local planning context. CMDC had only a small staff complement and contracted out most of the professional analytical and policy making work. ECOTEC planning consultants were appointed in 1988 to produce the first CMDC Development Strategy (ECOTEC 1988). Following the legal remit for UDCs the Strategy proposed four major objectives:

- bringing back into use existing neglected land and property
- the development of new commercial and residential property
- the attraction of private finance as part of these developments and redevelopments
- environmental improvement to the CMDC area

Protection and enhancement of the *historic* built environment is noticeably absent but would not remain so.

The irony of a Thatcher government supporting a staunch Labour local council is brought home by CMDC's tactics in its first few months. There was a ploy of "spreading the word about our intention to pursue compulsory purchase wherever appropriate and essential" (Glester 1989). CMDC used its compulsory purchase powers extensively, often acquiring sites from MCC thereby pursuing regeneration schemes initiated by the council such as Bridgewater Hall. A year later in 1989 CMDC refined its strategy emphasising the provision of financial 'assistance to encourage private sector investment' (CMDC 1989: 2). This time, echoing earlier historic preservation society and MCC representations of space, the 1989 Strategy was reconfigured by recognising that the Roman Fort, canals, historic warehouses and railway infrastructure created a 'Unique Selling Proposition' (CMDC 1989: 6). In the waterways CMDC saw great tourist potential to link centres of activity.

The 1989 Strategy is on the one hand an example of staid, rational, mainly written official representations of space. On the other hand, one of its striking features was the inclusion of artistic, imaginative colour visual representations of the future. While the written text kept faithfully to the script of private sector subsidy for urban regeneration (the creation of commodified abstract space), the images were more daring (Figures 7.1 and 7.2). They depicted new public spaces reverberating with animated throngs of people freely enjoying use value heritage tourism and leisure based consumption. However, two further points must be made. First, the use of these thoroughly artistic images in the 1989 Strategy blurs the distinction between rational representations of space and artistic spaces of representation. Second, these visualisations imagine Castlefield as a place of such high aesthetic qualities that artists would come to create visual spaces of representation: a sharp turn on Lefebvre's ideas. With the area run down in 1989 and still mostly privately owned space, the visions in the 1989 Strategy required significant imaginative leaps. It would be naïve to assume that these representations per se were directly responsible for the transformation of Castlefield. What they did was to serve as symbolic markers of alternative representations of future space which were weaved gradually into official urban planning policy.

Figure 7.1: Castle Quay, Castlefield: architectural artist's visual representation (CMDC 1989)

Using the 1989 Strategy to guide decisions making, CMDC awarded its first grant to GTV. *Coronation Street* in the 1980s was by far Britain's most popular TV soap opera. Cashing in on this popularity, GTV created the Granada TV tours experience in 1988. Paying visitors could enjoy the thrills of walking down Coronation Street and Baker Street, the set for GTV's *Sherlock Holmes* series. A grant of £2 million was made available to convert two derelict historic warehouses into an upmarket, canalside hotel to be called the Victoria and Albert Hotel. Visitors to the studio tours experience could stay in rooms

Figure 7.2 : Castlefield Canal Basin: architectural artist's visual representation (CMDC 1989)

themed for their favourite GTV drama. Although Stringer thought the hotel refurbishment and adaptive reuse proposal did not need grant aid, CMDC supported it because there was pressure to show results by spending its public money quickly. Another early grant for 'private sector' property development was made to the Youth Hostel Association (YHA), a registered charity, therefore a not-for-profit organisation. Their first venture was a hotel followed by a youth hostel. Unsurprisingly, the YHA pressured for the adjoining area to be improved and it became eventually the Castlefield Arena.

In addition to grant subsidy to the private sector for specific regeneration projects, environmental improvements were fundamental to CMDC's core strategy. By 1989 a package of environmental measures had been agreed by the CMDC Board, at a cost of £1.8 million (for 1989–90). Exaggerating somewhat, an excited Manchester journalist claimed it was a 'new vision of Venice' (Pugh 1990) echoing similar claims made repeatedly for Lowell in the 1970s. All these measures of spatial practice provided for visible impacts in the area. In 1989 CMDC indicated that environmental improvement was a major priority with the appointment of the not-for-profit Groundwork Trust's national commercial trading company, Groundwork Associates Ltd (GWA), to design and implement an environmental improvement masterplan for the Castlefield canal basin area. Their team was led by landscape architect Kevin Mann. The brief from CMDC required the creation of public access routes through the area. In addition Mann explained in email correspondence that the brief stipulated respect for the historical qualities of the area and the creation of high quality public spaces (Mann 2010).

Following the neoliberal turn, publicly subsidised environmental improvements were seen as a necessary prelude to major private investment in the area. Apart from Stringer, Bernstein and Grigor, the other significant player in the production of Castlefield during the CMDC years was local property developer Jim Ramsbottom. His affinity for Castlefield grew in the late 1970s when he used to enjoy taking long therapeutic walks in the area to dampen severe migraine (Glester 2008). In the early 1980s his restoration and redevelopment of historic buildings began when he converted a 19th century boat house, on the River Irwell in Salford, to the Mark Addy pub. The vehicle for his property developments was his company Castlefield Estates Ltd, established in 1981 and based initially in the Castlefield Lock Keeper's Cottage. However, plans for the redevelopment of his early 1980s property acquisitions in Castlefield stalled because of the banks' reluctance to lend for property redevelopment in the area. Although Ramsbottom's first property acquisition in Castlefield was Merchants Warehouse (Figure 7.3) bought in 1982 for a paltry

Figure 7.3: Merchants Warehouse from Merchants Bridge (photo © Michael Leary-Owhin)

£25,000, redevelopment of this and other projects in Castlefield had to wait for the arrival of CMDC and its crucial public sector financial subsidies. Ramsbottom applauded this policy intervention because CMDC 'rolled into town on a white charger, with saddlebags full of money' (in MCC 2004: 27).

This coalition triumvirate of Bernstein-Stringer, Glester and Ramsbottom was instrumental in bringing about large scale investment in Castlefield's spatial practice at a time of economic recession. During the research interview Glester alludes to the closeness of his working relationship with Ramsbottom, recalling that at a formal business dinner, "Jim said, you know one of the greatest things we've had recently is the arrival of Father Christmas in the guise of CMDC". So Glester sent him a Christmas card depicting a ruddy, genial Father Christmas. Glester provides insight too into how this informal but powerful coalition operated:

> 'Jimmy and I used to meet regularly with Graham Stringer and the chief executive who by this time was Howard Bernstein, who was the fixer [laughs]. Jimmy and I used to meet with Graham and Howard, maybe once every two months we'd have a *tour d'horizon* over dinner.' (Glester 2008)

Such coalitions and alliances are seen by Lefebvre as necessary for the production of complex and contested urban space. Undoubtedly, such informal arrangements served to build trust and probably contributed to a shared perspective on the future of the CMDC area. Cynics might worry, though there is no evidence that it ever happened, about the potential for corruption and the shutting out of proper, formal publicly accountable mechanisms. In any case CMDC was monitored closely by the DoE. In terms of bringing tourist-leisure related development and investment into Castlefield there was complete agreement. Ramsbottom worked closely with CMDC to restore and convert to alternative uses a number of historic buildings. Jim Ramsbottom's restoration projects were visible signs of private sector confidence in Castlefield and the work of CMDC. Such work proved important for the evaluation of CMDC success and the creation of new public space.

Bridges to multiple spaces

Spatial practice is a neglected element in Lefebvrian inspired research, with most researchers choosing to focus on imputed disjunctions between representations of space and spaces of representation. Heritage dominated representations of space influenced spatial practice and the production of Castlefield's distinctive public spaces. Bridges come into being not merely to connect separated places but to join spaces which are divided in our imagination (Simmel 1994). If we did not first 'connect them in our imagination', then the division would have no meaning (Simmel 1994: 6). Bridges become objects of beauty; aesthetic focal points for the eye, making abstract, imaginative connections directly visible. Bridges can serve many purposes, not just practical and technical but symbolic – 'the marriage of old and new' (Dennis 2008: 20). They symbolise too the imagined ability to make progress and enhance spaces. They embody people's hopes and fears as Dennis shows for Brooklyn and Tower Bridges. On a smaller scale the bridges of Castlefield, especially Merchants Bridge, had great importance for the production of space. Their designers tried consciously to instil the bridges with symbolic meaning in reference to either a heritage infused industrial past or an optimistic, modernist future.

CMDC's statutory mission was to subsidise private sector development in order to simulate further private investment in the area. Following this logic public space is regarded simply as a channel through which visitors flow to reach new points of exchange value, private sector consumption and new owner occupied apartments. This perception of space was rendered material through the many high quality bridges that CMDC commissioned and funded, most spectacularly, Merchants Bridge. For CMDC it was also important that the improvements created a 'dramatic visual impact' (Mann 1992: 35). CMDC also saw new bridges as essential, "if this area was to attract investment" (Mann 2010). CMDC problematised Castlefield instrumentally and imaginatively as a collection of isolated, divided areas that necessitated connection to stimulate private sector investment. However, through its spatial practice of public space creation and connection, CMDC also produced unexpected possibilities for the politics of encounter, political expression and the production of differential space, issues explored in Chapter Eight.

By the time CMDC took over, much of the Castlefield canal basin area was still owned by MSCC whose "customs police patrolled regularly with no public access, it was vacant, derelict and forgotten about" (Mann 2010). It was, therefore, an area into which the public would have had little reason, ability or desire to venture. Once there, it was difficult to navigate through the area because of the numerous watercourses which created isolated pockets of land. John Glester appreciated the need to create access routes through Castlefield to facilitate its role as a site of economic consumption:

'Our early works in Castlefield was [sic] to dredge the canals improve the tow paths, put in some bridges ... But what you couldn't do is [pause] if you came in on the A56, if you went in there, you came out there. You couldn't cross over and come out onto Liverpool Road so it was a question of putting bridges in, opening it up and we spent about, about six million of our budget over a period of about two and a half years doing a lot of those enabling works.' (Glester 2008)

A similar point regarding the commercial importance of Castlefield's bridges is made by Degen (2008: 106). Given the significance of bridges for the creation of commodified abstract space and convivial public space, it is surprising they have not stimulated comprehensive academic analysis. It is apparent from the Glester interview that the new routes and bridges were considered essential by CMDC for Castlefield's ability to attract private sector investment and realise its tourist development potential as indicated by this chapter's epigraph. CMDC's Board prioritised the improvement of pedestrian access into and through Castlefield from an early stage as a prerequisite for enticing the private sector to invest.

It is indisputable that the CMDC bridges did facilitate access to points of consumption: the bars, restaurants, offices, studio/workshops and private housing. In this CMDC functioned to produce functional abstract spaces of exchange value and commodified consumption. By the time CMDC was wound up in 1996 a further 11 bridges had been built. What goes unremarked in the literature is that five of the new bridges do not only lead consumers to sites of consumption. Rather they also provide north–south pedestrian routes which facilitated access to the free, not-for-profit MOSI and new public spaces of the Castlefield canal basin. Before presenting a more detailed analysis of the unashamedly modernist Merchants Bridge, it is worth considering how several other bridges acknowledged the past while encompassing the latest engineering techniques, heralded a brighter future and worked to produce new public space.

Architects Bridge commissioned by Castlefield Estates Ltd and completed in 1996 plays with the area's history in ways unlike the other bridges. Its 15 yard (13.7 metre) single span modernist engineered steel structure is hidden by a traditional aesthetic skin of red sandstone cladding – London's Tower Bridge is perhaps the best known example of this design approach (Dennis 2008). An outcrop of this strikingly ruddy stone, on top of which the Roman Fort was built, can still be seen at Coal Wharf. Cleverly then, the designers, through the visual aesthetic of its sandstone finish, point to Castlefield's geological and Roman histories. A steel plaque discourages casual access, declaring it to be a private right of way with no intention for seeking its adoption as a public right of way (Figure 7.4). That said the bridge designers did not incorporate gates to prevent access, so anybody who wishes can occupy the space at any time. Critics may argue it is privatised space but never having been public space this is not tenable, hence Architects Bridge is best regarded as quasi-public space (see Figure 1.1). Castlefield Estates Ltd also acquired the Castle Street access into the canal basin which leads to the two historic buildings that were converted to bar/restaurants: Duke's 92 and Albert's Shed. These access routes, once encompassed in the private space of the MSCC, were renovated with public money by CMDC and although they look like typical public streets and have completely free and open access, they are privately owned and maintained by Castlefield Estates Ltd, creating in effect more quasi-public space (for example, Castle Street at Coal Wharf – Figure 7.5).

Kevin Mann of GWA took a different approach for the foot bridges commissioned by CMDC and went to great lengths to ensure the new bridges respected their historic surroundings, drawing inspiration from extant historic canal bridges in Manchester. Originally, Mann wanted to reproduce Victorian-style cast iron bridges but this proved too expensive so he compromised with a combination of cast iron, steel and brick (Mann 1992). Structural ironwork is exposed and finished in

Figure 7.4: Merchants Bridge: technically no public right of way (photo © Michael Leary-Owhin)

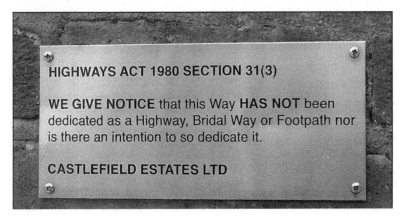

Figure 7.5: Dawn over quasi-public space: Castle Street at Coal Wharf, Castlefield
(photo © Michael Leary-Owhin)

traditional black and white canal colours. The result is elegant simulacra
that are perfectly at home among the historic viaducts, canals and
warehouses. Drawing inspiration from Castlefield's Victorian viaducts
was not straightforward since, in a double layering of symbolic meaning,
they too drew on historic elements, such as the Roman Fort, but
combined them with the latest Victorian engineering technologies.

A major problem confronting CMDC was the need for a north–south
link across the Bridgewater Canal from Coal and Slate Wharfs to the
Arena site and Liverpool Road. Unlike their Victorian predecessors,
which were massively over engineered, 20th century bridges became
lighter, sleeker, curvier and prettier. A design competition was initiated
by CMDC for a bridge over the Bridgewater Canal. It was run jointly
with Peel Holdings that owned (and still owns) the canal towpaths
and the Bridgewater Canal itself (Webb 2007). The brief stipulated
a striking structure that would offer the best of 20th century bridge
design and engineering excellence while complementing the attractive
awe inspiring, historic viaducts. Renowned engineers Whitby Bird and
Partners won the competition. Completed in 1996, Merchants Bridge
cost £450,000, is 71 yards long (67 metres) and curves seductively
in several directions, in a design not possible without sophisticated
computer modelling. It comprises a slender wedge-shaped, inclined
suspended structure and arch that lifts the bridge high above the canal to
allow boats to pass underneath (Figure 7.6). In form, style construction

and finish Merchants Bridge is self-consciously modernist. It signifies a break with the area's Victorian past, by embracing contemporary design innovations.

The bridge is a clever feat of civil engineering but what is more important here is its symbolic importance, and its role as inspiration for representations of space and spaces of representation. Whitby

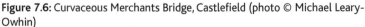

Figure 7.6: Curvaceous Merchants Bridge, Castlefield (photo © Michael Leary-Owhin)

Bird, writing just after the bridge won the Institute of Architects Excellence in Design Award 1997, drew attention to its symbolic meaning commenting, 'the bridge has become a focus and symbol of the regeneration of the area' (Whitby Bird Spokesman 2009). On completion the searing white finish and spectacularly confident optimism of the dazzling, curving structure contrasted markedly with the still run down appearance of the canal basin. Although with no means to restrict access, the bridge appears to be traditional public space it is the private property of Peel Holdings which is responsible for its maintenance (Webb 2007). Unmistakably, what CMDC and Peel Holdings produced here is another hybrid quasi-public space (see Figure 1.1). Through the provision of historically inspired bridges CMDC planners did more than simply consolidate the heritage valorised representations of space, they engaged in spatial practice on a relatively grand scale, linking new public spaces to points of consumption *and* points of historic interest per se.

Ludic space: Castlefield Arena

The challenge of animating the new large scale public space of the Castlefield basin was a major preoccupation of the CMDC and MCC planners, as it was for the Lowell city planners and national park regarding the new space of Boarding House Park. Castlefield Arena (also known as the Events Arena and Castlefield Amphitheatre) occupies a large site just south of Liverpool Road that in the 1980s was called Staffordshire Wharf. Two 'tuning fork' canal arms from the Bridgewater Canal reached into the Wharf over which was built in about 1790 the Staffordshire Warehouse, so called due to trade with the Potteries in the 19th century. After the warehouse was demolished in 1950 and canal arms filled in, utilitarian industrial sheds were erected and by the early 1980s the area was used as a tyre depot and waste dumping ground and in the late 1980s it accommodated part of the Castlefield Carnival.

It should be noted that the site had a difficult topography from a development perspective as it lies at the foot of the 20 foot high escarpment carved out of the red sandstone by the River Medlock. Vehicular access too was difficult, not being possible from Liverpool Road to the north or under the viaducts to the south, with the only vehicular access being from the east. Commissioned by CMDC and designed by the planning and architectural consultancy DEGW, the Arena covers an area of 37,800 square feet (3,512 square metres), accommodating 8,000 people with seating for 450 under the sweeping white canopy of what John Glester calls the grandstand (Figure 7.7). The designers took advantage ingeniously of the natural topography of the site and built the stepped seating area into the solid rock of the sandstone escarpment. In addition, the open air amphitheatre design is a nod of recognition towards Roman history. It was opened in late 1993 at a cost of about £2 million. According to Glester the rationale for the Arena and the steps down to it from Liverpool Road was that they were part of the CMDC public realm strategy. Additionally, there was "the need for an outdoor events space as perceived at that time" (Glester 2008).

It was Manchester's 2000 Olympic Games bid that pushed Castlefield's public space into the wider public sphere of the mass media. The private sector led 2000 Olympic Bid Committee with its 'unmistakable neoliberal undertones' (Cochrane et al 1996: 1325)

Figure 7.7: Castlefield Arena: at times politicised differential space (photo © Michael Leary-Owhin)

chose the Castlefield Arena as the venue for the Olympic Bid Decision Party. It was a highly organised, controlled and exclusive event accessible to invited guests only, based on a list drawn up by CMDC and Manchester's Olympic Bid team. The area was fenced off creating a kind of privatised space, and although admission was 'free', it was by ticket only. The Party was held on 23 September 1993 and saw the Bid team, members of CMDC, MCC and thousands of invited revellers assembled at the first live televised event in Castlefield. President of the International Olympic Committee, Juan Antonio Samaranch's announcement was relayed to Castlefield and the scenes there shown live on BBC TV to a worldwide audience of millions. Manchester first bid for the Olympics in the 1980s, when the Games were awarded to Atlanta. Manchester lost again in 1993 but the Castlefield crowd in true Mancunian style burst spontaneously into a rendition of Monty Python's sardonic song, *Always Look on the Bright Side of Life*.

In spectacular style the 1993 Olympic Bid Party demonstrated that Castlefield public space had relevance for the city beyond its industrial heritage and waterside environments. CMDC extolled the event to the DoE as another symbol of Manchester's regeneration success. This event was seen as proof of the viability of large scale formalised public space events in Castlefield which included the availability of alcohol. It seemed to confirm Degen's (2008) critique of the exclusionary, privatised nature of Castlefield's new public spaces. Despite its success the 1993 Games Party was a one-off event. Its importance is that it provided an organisational model for semi-privatised public events in Castlefield. The next major public event at the Arena followed paradoxically one of the most devastating events in Manchester's history. I argue it was this event which helped establish the Arena as a more indeterminate, diverse public space.

In June 1996 a huge IRA bomb exploded in the city centre. Nobody was killed but many people were injured and hundreds of buildings destroyed or damaged (King 2006). In the uncertain aftermath of the IRA bomb many Mancunians were keen to demonstrate the city's resilience and optimism after the shock and devastation of the June explosion. Several events were planned but the most ambitious was suggested by a music promoter, Steve Smith, who came up with the idea of a free pop music concert funded by grants and corporate sponsorship. 'Ear To The Ground', a local events company founded by Smith, promoted the event named Re.percussion, with the aim of highlighting the positive repercussions of the bomb. Interestingly, free music events and festivals were also part of the revival strategy in downtown Lowell and Gastown. After securing grants from MCC and CMDC and sponsorship from music companies, Re.percussion's organisers eschewed the traditional municipal public space of Albert Square and the event went ahead in August 1997 at Castlefield Arena. It attracted an impressive crowd of about 15,000. Ticketed access to the Arena site although free was managed strictly by fencing and roping; with entry and egress controlled by a large number of private security personnel supported by a prominent police presence. In 1998 the name changed to Dpercussion (for digital) and it became an annual free music festival for the next ten years (Ryan 2007) (Figure 7.8).

Gary McClarnan was involved in organising Dpercussion but in a telephone interview was critical, saying it was orientated to a "white hip hop youth audience" (McClarnan 2010). Others disagree, likening it to Notting Hill Carnival and arguing it constituted a multicultural space where difference was celebrated (BBC 2004). Dpercussion featured computer created acid house dance music and Steve Smith identified a link between what he saw as two revolutionary moments in Manchester's history:

> The Bridgewater Canal is where the industrial revolution started. Here we have a celebration of the second industrial revolution or the digital revolution. (in Haslam 1999: 256)

Figure 7.8: Dpercussion at Castlefield Arena: multicultural, free and inclusive (2006 Flickr photo © Lesley Campbell)

Dpercussion is significant because unlike the 1993 Olympic Party it was freely accessible to anybody who obtained a ticket beforehand. In that sense it inculcated Castlefield's public space with a greater degree of genuine publicness and a more diverse flavour than did the 'invitation only' 1993 Party.

Stringer from an insider political position offers a different rationale for the Arena from that of Glester. Stringer (2009) claims a psychologically centred logic for the production of the Arena propelled by a civic ethos. He argues that members of an unelected quango can be "a bit guilt ridden about what their relationship is with the public" and that they "have a sense of obligation to the public". For him if the "academic literature is saying it's only about property subsidy, it's got it wrong":

> **Graham Stringer (GS):** Oh yea. They [CMDC Board members] didn't have any people to consult because there was nobody living in the area. But they did have a sense of obligation to the public ... On Friday mornings there were hard headed debates about the money, whether a grant would make it work, whether it was the right thing to grant aid and all those other things ... [but a] community legacy, a public legacy was always part of the CMDC discussion.

MLO: Really? Was it anybody in particular in CMDC who was civic minded?

GS: No, it was the whole ethos really. The private sector people, this was their big chance to contribute. They wanted jobs and economic development, flats and office development and things but they also wanted something for the public whether it was subsidising art galleries or museums, the Museum of Science and Industry or the Arena. There was definitely a civic responsibility side to it … If you look for instance at one of the things I laughed at but they were absolutely committed to, was putting the bits of the machinery from the old gas works under the arches. And they saw that as public art. They wanted to both remember the gas works and have some public art that people would like. I mean some of the numbers speak for themselves but there's definitely a culture there of wanting to put something back for the public. (Stringer 2009)

Stringer has mellowed since his firebrand 1980s days but is still a staunch left wing back bench Labour MP and there is no reason to doubt his sincerity on this point about the importance of a *visual* civic legacy. It is worth noting that he was not implicated in the MPs expenses scandal of 2008.

Similar sentiments may well have persuaded the LDDC Board to back the restoration of the historic cranes and churches discussed earlier. When Glester says during the research interview, the Arena was built in such a way that it could be fenced off and a charge made for entry, he seems to confirm Degen's (2008: 122–4) criticisms regarding the neoliberal privatisation of space. However, for most of the year the public space of the Arena and bridges offer totally unrestricted inclusive access to everybody. Similarly, the Arena and other destinations are accessed via canal towpaths that are also in the private ownership of Peel Holdings and therefore constitute quasi-public space (see Figure 7.9). The area accommodates a range of informal activities *and* large scale highly organised politicised events as discussed in Chapter Eight. The striking visual impact of the Castlefield canal basin area per se, which is due in no small measure to the environmental improvements instigated by CMDC, also contradicts a purely instrumental reading of its production of space interventions. The result is a multifaceted and complex place which cannot sensibly be oversimplified and essentialised to commodified abstract space. With hindsight creating

Figure 7.9: Quasi-public space: the canal towpath at Dukes 92, Castlefield, (photo © Michael Leary-Owhin)

the public space of the Arena was a triumph of civic minded planning and urban regeneration but CMDC was evaluated officially for its economic impact.

Rational and imagined success

Through the lens of the spatial triad it is germane to consider how CMDC's intervention was perceived and evaluated. British governments since the 1980s sought to carry out independent evaluations of urban policy such as UDCs. There is no doubt that in 1988 Castlefield though not a wasteland was still a visually unattractive place with a neglected, rundown air; these perceptions took time to mellow. Many businesses had closed or been relocated, the sites left uncared for and dishevelled. CMDC spent £100 million of public money in its eight years of operation. The largest proportion was devoted to direct private sector subsidy but notably the next largest category was environmental improvement. A wide range of opinion over the years viewed CMDC as a dramatic success for rational reasons. In the House of Lords' debate for the Order to wind up CMDC, Earl Ferrers, Conservative DoE Minister of State, declared it such a marvellous success because so many achievements deserve recognition 'but I fear that, were I to mention them, I might weary your Lordships greatly, which would be distressing' (Ferrers 1996). A Labour peer was adamant that CMDC 'was in danger of giving development corporations a good name' (Dubs 1996). Similarly in the House of Commons it was claimed that CMDC 'has revitalised huge areas of what was a decaying city' (Dover 1996). Others saw CMDC going beyond the crude UDC stereotype of glorified estate agent, claiming it employed an expansive agenda leading a business growth coalition that helped restructure the city economy moving it towards services encompassing flagship projects, prestige events and visitor attractions including the marketing of historical assets (Deas et al 2000). DoE officials were satisfied from an early stage with CMDC success measured by economic indicators (Comrie 1991).

Pieda Ltd, the private sector consultancy appointed by the government to evaluate CMDC, was impressed. However, there were criticisms of the environmental improvement projects (EIP):

> The approach by CMDC has been to start work on improvements in the heart of the area and move outwards to the fringes. In consequence it is only recently that the full scale and standard of the EIPs has become apparent to passersby. A number of developers thought that the alternative approach of improving gateways and the outside edge of the site first would have meant that the EIPs could have had an earlier impact on potential occupiers/residents. In a sense the lesson here is that it may be possible to design a programme of EIP work so that the maximum visual impact is achieved as early as possible. (Pieda 1991: para 4.2)

Pieda, by focusing on the EIP programme, highlighted the importance of Castlefield's public spaces, especially where they abutted boundary roads, waterfronts, historic buildings and potential development sites. The production of space work of CMDC has spurred some imaginative ideas, such as the Castlefield Forum's proposals for a Manhattan style high line public park to be located on a disused viaduct (Shepherd 2012). Their plans did not pass the ideas stage but have been resurrected on an even grander scale (Fitzgerald 2015). Glester was of fully conversant with the Pieda report and with the official evaluation report by Robson et al (1997) but remembered other criteria, reminiscent of Lefebvrian spaces of representation, for the evaluation of success.

Castlefield's spaces of representation

Castlefield, like Gastown and downtown Lowell, is a photogenic place that has provided locations for many fiction films and TV shows. Here I touch briefly on how John Glester, the rational civil servant, deployed televisual spaces of representation in the research interview regarding the evaluation of success. There is not the space to pursue Castlefield's spaces of representation more generally (see Quilley 1999 for a brief consideration of the proliferation of Manchester based detective and gangster novels), but some intriguing examples are considered here. When he first encountered Castlefield, Glester recalls it was an unpleasant place drawing on a mixture of memories of routine working life and more unexpectedly, through macabre televisual spaces of representation:

> '… we got a lot of flak from people who wanted to do development in other parts of town where they were looking for city grant but we were saying you don't need city grant there or we haven't got the resources to give you there because we're spending it elsewhere. And people were saying well why are you spending it there on what was basically regarded as Granada's murder set, because it was where they filmed *Sherlock Holmes* and they filmed murders and things. And you know there were abattoirs at the bottom end of Liverpool Road with blood running down the streets.' (Glester 2008)

Glester's unexpected implication is that Castlefield could not be perceived a success while it was a grisly televisual murder location. Glester the rational civil servant therefore had a unique approach to the evaluation of success. His assessment was based on consultant's reports *and* his memories suffused by half remembered televisual spaces of representation:

> **JG:** I think that we realised we might have achieved something when Granada started filming their whatever it was called, their yuppie Manchester programme, what was it called?

> *MLO:* There were quite a few, *Cutting It?*

JG: Yea *Cutting It* and also the one with James Nesbitt in. Was it called *Best Friends*? Anyway when they started to film those down there rather than *Sherlock Holmes* [laughs] we knew. (Glester 2008)

The commercially and critically successful *Sherlock Holmes* detective series starring Jeremy Brett was made by GTV (1984 to 1994). In the final story, *The Cardboard Box* broadcast in April 1994, Jim Browner, a sailor who murdered and cut of the ears of his wife and her lover, is seen travelling at night from 'Dover to London'. In a foggy noir scene filmed in Castlefield, we see him walking across a black and white footbridge. The scene is one of dreadful foreboding as the audience knows he is on his way to commit a gruesome double murder. The 'Victorian' foot bridge was one of those built by GWA in 1990. Castlefield is the location for a grisly murder in GTVs *Cracker* (broadcast 1993–96), a violent psychological murder drama. In the 1995 episode *Brotherly Love*, a female sex worker is driven there against her will and is murdered brutally on a murky night under the gigantic, glowering iron viaduct which hovers over a slick cobbled street. Before producing these spaces of representation, GTV in the 1980s filmed scenes for the vicious police detective drama *The Travelling Man* (broadcast 1984–85). Castlefield is represented as a lonely canal-dominated cityscape. Alan Lomax the protagonist is a drug squad officer framed for corruption. Several scenes are shot in Castlefield; for example, in the episode *The Hustler* an aerial panoramic shot shows an extant industrial cityscape including timber yards and the huge corrugated iron sheds of Slate Wharf. More importantly, scenes of violence and torture, especially in the timber mill, are saturated with malevolence but, ambivalently, a deserted Castlefield provides a sanctuary for Lomax's home, a canal barge.

What Glester calls *Best Friends* was actually the comedy drama *Cold Feet*, staring James Nesbitt, broadcast 1997–2003, providing a timeline that seems to support Glester's interpretation. However, Glester's idea of a linear televisual transition is more complex that it first appears. The shift from *Sherlock Homes* to *Cold Feet* seems to herald a uni-linear transition from a dark scary, to a light pretty redefinition of Castlefield but such ideas of linearity are misleading. Castlefield, I would argue, *continued* in the 1990s and 2000s to be represented as a dark, lonely space of crime and visceral danger, for example in such television dramas as *Coronation Street*. In recent years under cover of a threatening night-time beloved of film noir directors: Steve Macdonald assaulted Vikram Desai in a canalside confrontation in Castlefield; Samir

Rachid (Deirdre's husband) was murdered in the Deansgate Tunnel of the Rochdale Canal; and Tony Gordon attempted to murder Roy Cropper by throwing him into the Bridgewater Canal (*Daily Mail* 2009). Castlefield was seen in a dark unpleasant light under the railway arches in the Channel 4 police drama *No Offence* broadcast in 2015.

In cinema too Castlefield was still in the 2000s embraced for its baleful qualities. In 2008 a film crew was busy in Castlefield working on a *Sherlock Holmes* film directed by Guy Ritchie, starring Robert Downey Jr, released in 2009. Its closing scenes, shot in Castlefield, portray a well-dressed woman pursued by an evil, murderous English aristocrat through a network of large tunnels under the 'Houses of Parliament'. Televisual and cinematic representations therefore continue to depict the chilling spatial excitement of dark representations *and* the romance and laughter of bright 'regenerated', commodified city space. Ambivalence is wrapped up in dialectal tensions that signify the complexity of Castlefield space. In an important sense too these spaces of representation contradict and *validate* the heritage representations of the amenity societies, city planners and politicians.

Conclusions

It is evident from the investigations in this chapter that the political processes through which Michael Heseltine sought to establish the UDCs were highly contested. Moreover, the inner city UDC idea was not simply borrowed from the US through processes of policy mobility. It is clear too that Heseltine's private sector focused reorientation of UrP predated the UDCs and was applied to the benefit of Castlefield, in conjunction with the private sector orientated urban regeneration work of CMDC. Following the welter of words that have cascaded from researchers examining the British UDCs, this chapter has explored the under researched impacts of CMDC regarding the production of new urban public space. Through a Lefebvrian theoretical research lens the chapter has elucidated a range of the intricate detail and social interactions which provide new insights into the processes and outcomes of the production of space. Archival and interview data analyses have shown how CMDC created abstract commodified space *and* new public spaces and routes with genuine use value characteristics. It is evident from the research in this chapter that policy document intertextuality continued to affect the development strategy of CMDC, based to a great extent as it was on the 1984 *City Centre Local Plan*, which in turn drew its heritage centred inspiration from Lowell and from the historic preservation society reports discussed in the previous chapter.

A public–private coalition was found to exist which facilitated the historic building preservation, adaptive reuse and the production of quasi-public space. Castlefield's new public spaces, bridges and routes are the most profound manifestation of this production of space episode. Not only do the bridges facilitate the kinds of commodified consumption criticised by other researchers, they also facilitate the everyday use value of Castlefield's significant public spaces, particularly the Arena. Through production of space processes CMDC succeeded inadvertently in creating genuine, inclusive use value public space. And contrary to some of the assertions in the academic literatures, there was not simply a unidirectional influence of a private sector ethos on the CMDC. Revealed for the first time in this chapter is the inculcation of a public sector civic ethos on the private sector members of the CMDC Board. Interestingly, this is a feature of the production of space, which was also evident in Gastown. Although there was not space to pursue the argument in any great detail, the chapter has found a distinct blurring in policy documents between semi-rational representations of space and imaginative artistic spaces of representation.

This chapter substantiates, as do other chapters, the utility of a methodological research approach, which privileged an archival centred excavation of relevant data combined with interviews to create an archival network. The application of an archival network for explicating the production of space is useful for the way the different sources of data formed a dense, coherent and mutually informative nexus. This network informed and constructed by mixed methods and mixed data allowed a richer picture to emerge along with concomitant appreciations, not possible with a more restricted methodological approach. Mixed methods research allowed the interrogation and corroboration of the interview data where they relate to events decades past.

Lefebvrian spaces of representation were found in this chapter to infuse the thinking of the CMDC chief executive as he pondered how to evaluate its success. Surprisingly, televisual spaces of representation are seen to play a part in how Glester of the CMDC evaluated its performance. Televisual spaces of representation imbued Castlefield with schizophrenic ambivalence for three decades. It becomes apparent in this chapter that MCC and CMDC understood the importance of not just creating public space but also of animating it with ludic events. In comparable fashion to the research findings for Gastown and Lowell, new public spaces in Castlefield were animated with free popular music festivals. Public space can of course also be animated by politicised collective action. In the next chapter the possibilities for the production of Lefebvrian differential space in the three cities are explored.

EIGHT

Venturing beyond Lefebvre: Producing differential space

From a less pessimistic standpoint, it can be shown that abstract space harbours specific contradictions. Such spatial contradictions derive in part from the old contradictions thrown up by historical time ... Thus, despite – or rather because of – its negativity, abstract space carries within itself the seeds of a new kind of space. I shall call that new space 'differential space', because inasmuch as abstract space tends towards homogeneity ... a new space cannot be born (produced) unless it accentuates difference. (Lefebvre 1991: 52)

The street contains functions that were overlooked by Le Corbusier: the informative function, the symbolic function, the ludic function. The street is a place to play and learn. The street is disorder. All the elements of urban life, which are fixed and redundant elsewhere, are free to fill the streets and through the streets flow to the centers, where they meet and interact, torn from their fixed abode. The disorder is alive. It informs. It surprises. (Lefebvre 2003: 18–19)

Introduction

Differential space is the conceptual culmination of the major spatial themes of this book. That said, I argue that it is essential to consider differential space and the right to the city as related intimately. Lefebvre developed both concepts in the politically volatile Parisian years of the mid-1960s. He did so partly in response to the evident political tensions and spatial contradictions impacting on France, especially Nanterre and Paris, in this turbulent epoch. Lefebvre developed the concept of the right to the city in his 1968 book *Le droit à la ville*: publication of which predated the May disturbances of that year. In the same year his book *L'irruption de Nanterre au sommet* was published in which he begins to develop the concept of differential space. It is unlikely to be coincidence that these books followed in close succession and I contend the right to differential urban space is a fundamental right to the city. Lefebvre counter-poses the abstract homogenised space of neo-capitalism against heterogeneous space of difference and the everyday lived space of ordinary urban inhabitants. Although the powerful spatial practice and dominant representations of space subjugate the urban realm through the production of abstract space, it is possible for differential space to emerge.

One of the key concepts Lefebvre associates with differential space is 'appropriated space' (Lefebvre 1991: 165) and it is the action of bodily appropriation that brings differential space into being. Both kinds of space stand in a mutually antagonistic relationship to abstract space. Lefebvre draws back from a tight definition of appropriated space, affirming that only by means of critical study can the concept be clarified. He is confident that appropriated space is urban public space seized and occupied by ordinary people for its use value. It may be a structure, a monument or a building but it may also be, 'a site, square or a street' (Lefebvre 1991: 165). Abstract space, appropriated space and differential space do not occur in isolation, but are found associated in dialectical tensions and it is the empirical exploration of these tensions with which this chapter is concerned principally. Although he does not refer to the right to the city per se in *The Production of Space*, Lefebvre puts the right to difference at the heart of his production of space thesis:

> One might suppose that little argument would be required to establish that the 'right to be different' can only have meaning when it is based on actual struggles to establish differences and that the differences generated through such theoretical and practical struggles must themselves differ both from natural distinguishing characteristics and from differentiations induced within existing abstract space. (Lefebvre 1991: 64)

A convincing case can therefore be made for understanding differential space as one of several possible rights to the city. In the pages that follow I explore what differential space might mean but before that it is necessary to consider briefly the concept of the right to the city.

The previous empirically orientated chapters point to the potential of differential space but have so far left its nature and processes of production unexplored. Following Goonewardena et al (2008: 13) who argue for the need to take Lefebvre's spatial triad and the production of space ideas as a point of departure and Merrifield (2011), who urges us to go beyond Lefebvre, this chapter seeks to do just that. It does so by incorporating a fusion of differential space and right to the city ideas into contemporary contexts and grounded empirical case studies in the three cities which are the focus of this book. What follows is a conceptual discussion of the nature of the right to the city and its relationship with differential space. Then an analysis and discussion of case study empirical research argues that, inadvertently, the potential for differential space was created through various heritage-led beautification and urban regeneration schemes in Gastown, downtown Lowell and Castlefield.

The right to the city

Many Anglo-American researchers, activists and social movements encounter right to the city ideas first through the English translation of a Lefebvre essay in Lefebvre (1996). This provides a brief but powerful explication of facets of the concept. Lefebvre always saw urban life and urban space through a neo-Marxian practico-theoretical lens. Importantly, his right to the city ideas have two aspects: first, abstract, theoretical or strategic rights; and second, concrete, practical rights (Aalbers and Gibb 2014: 208). They stress that chief among the abstract rights is the 'priority of use value' in the production of space, that is, in general terms cities should satisfy primarily the range of human needs of city dwellers rather than create excess profit through neo-capitalist accumulation. It is significant, but rarely remarked, that Lefebvre saw the right to the city being asserted in the context of the struggle for differential space.

The 1968 revolutionary moment in Paris notably brought together an unlikely coalition of: marginalised inhabitants, students, politicised workers, political activists, trade unionists, communists, the homeless and professionals. In Lefebvrian terms they all stood against the creeping hegemony of abstract space. The occupation of Les Halles, Paris' sprawling, historic, 19th century fruit and vegetable markets, was an act of political defiance in the face of the state and the property development interests, but as Lefebvre observed keenly it was also a space 'transformed into a gathering-place and a scene of permanent festival' and for a while became 'a centre of play rather than work' (Lefebvre 1991: 167). Les Halles became use value ludic space in distinction to abstract space of neo-capitalism.

Lefebvre presents a contradictory categorisation of ludic or leisure space suggesting at one point that it is a vast counter-space that escapes the control of the established order (Lefebvre 1991: 383) only to affirm that it is also the space of the leisure industry, through commodification and therefore a victory of neo-capitalism. However, leisure space bridges the gap between spaces of work and spaces of enjoyment and fun (Lefebvre 1991: 385). It is therefore 'the very epitome of contradictory space' or counter-space hosting exuberant new potentials. Lefebvre settles the ambivalent conundrum of leisure space with a masterful acknowledgement that this is where the production of space is at its worst and its enigmatic best – parasitic on the one hand and creating boisterous new potentials on the other, 'as prodigal of monstrosities as of promises (that it cannot keep)' (Lefebvre 1991: 385).

The 1960s was an era in Paris and other cities when ordinary working class people were effectively being forced from the central areas in vast state organised projects of so called slum clearance justified as urban renewal. Clearly, this remains a distressing phenomenon in the 2010s (Lees 2014). In this 1960s context Lefebvre articulates two key rights to the city: the right to inhabit the centres of cities (centrality); and the right to enjoy urban space for its use value rather than its exchange value:

> Among these rights in the making features the *right to the city* (not to the ancient city, but to urban life, to renewed centrality, to places of encounter and exchange, to the life rhythms and time uses, enabling the full and complete *usage* of these moments and places, etc.). (Lefebvre 1996: 179, emphasis in original)

Their right to live in or close to the city centre was stripped from them as they were pressed to the periphery of Paris and other cities. Hence Lefebvre stressed their right to urban as opposed to suburban life:

> The *right to the city* cannot be conceived of as a simple visiting right or as a return to traditional cities. It can only be formulated as a transformed and renewed *right to urban life*. (Lefebvre 1996: 158, emphases in original)

Lefebvre had in mind a range of rights related to urban life which may appear in the form of customs and prescriptions sometimes enshrined in legislation. Under this heading he included rights to: work, education, training, health, housing and the right to rest or non-work leisure (Lefebvre 1996: 157). In pursuing his right to the city concept, Lefebvre identifies a diverse range of social groups who are denied this elemental right. Unsurprisingly for a neo-Marxist, he points to the suffering of the working class and a 'new misery' imposed by the reordering of urban social space into abstract space which causes 'poverty of the habitat' and of the inhabitants whose daily life is subjugated to a 'bureaucratized society of organized consumption' (Lefebvre 1996: 178). This unwieldy phrase was shortened by his students at Nanterre University to 'consumer society'. Large scale urban planning projects in the post-WW2 period caused the working class to be:

> ... rejected from the centres towards the peripheries, *dispossessed of the city*, expropriated thus from the best outcomes of its activity, this right has a particular bearing and significance. (Lefebvre 1996: 179, emphasis added)

Lefebvre's concern did not stop with the working classes, he was aware that other city inhabitants may become ostracised and marginalised: youth, students, the colonised and semi-colonised, armies of workers with or without white collars and people forced to live in ghettos 'in the mouldering centres of old cities' (Lefebvre 1996: 159). He identified other rights under threat such as the rights of ages and sexes, by which he meant children, the elderly and women (Lefebvre 1996: 157). Urbanisation and urban renewal dominated by the profit imperative of neo-capitalism resulted in a functional separation of the city imposing an unpleasant and costly commuting regime on most workers creating 'generalized misery' (Lefebvre 1996).

By implication the right to the city includes individual access to public space but additionally encompasses: *collective* access, needs for adventure, similarity, difference, isolation and encounter. For Lefebvre it is clear that the right to the city is a collection of rights which have to be asserted by ordinary city dwellers. These rights will not be *handed over* to citizens by powerful neo-capitalist elites. Rather like differential space itself these rights are not to be *bestowed* on city dwellers through the largesse of landowners or the state. They have to be appropriated through active assertion of rights to urban space and everyday urban life. Lefebvre argued strongly that citizens must participate in the struggles to achieve the right to the city. Such struggles do not necessarily require violence, although at times violence erupts during the production of space. It can be provoked sometimes by elements of civil society or by agents of the state, especially the police. Inhabitants must participate actively in the production of urban space, must appropriate space through bodily presence and through the inhabitation of space:

The right to the city manifests itself as a superior form of rights: rights to freedom, to individualization in socialization, to habitat and to inhabit. The right to the *oeuvre*, to participation and *appropriation* (clearly distinct from the right to property), are implied in the right to the city. (Lefebvre 1996: 173, emphases in original)

The city as oeuvre, a complex totality, a work in continual progress through diverse struggles, is a key Lefebvrian construct. Urban space evolves from the myriad interactions of city dwellers when they engage actively in its production.

Lefebvre's unique understanding of the *denial* of the right to the city and the spatial subjugation of some citizens evolved from the events leading to the French 'revolutionary' moments in the commune of 1848 and more immediately from the French political confrontations of 1968 (Stanek 2011). It should be appreciated that Lefebvre's concern was not only with the city rights of the marginalised and vulnerable, important though they are. He was distressed also about ordinary working people's loss of the right to occupy the city. Lefebvre was Catholic in his understanding of the wide ranging nature of the right to the city which extended beyond basic needs and material rights into the realm of leisure and consumption, albeit without the necessity for monetary exchange. Concrete or everyday practical rights relate to security, creative activity, information, imaginary, sport, physical activities and play (Lefebvre 1996: 147).

Lefebvre is criticised for leaving the right to the city concept too under developed and fuzzy to be of theoretical or practical use, in particular by Attoh who believes Lefebvre's conceptual grasp of rights was 'sketchy at best' (2011: 674):

The right to the city framework offers us little help in navigating the way forward. Within the very openness of the concept of the right to the city we are sure to find a number of inconsistencies and sticking points. (Attoh 2011: 675)

Lefebvre's mission in his long project to formulate a schema for the production of space was aimed at the creation eventually of a general theory. We can surmise that this may be why his right to the city was not worked out in great specificity. So while Attoh (2011) is critical of conceptual looseness, he does acknowledge that Lefebvre's right to the city 'offers a great deal' partly because it specifies the right to inhabit and produce urban space and city life, 'on new terms (unfettered by the demands of exchange value)'. It signifies the right of inhabitants to 'remain unalienated from urban life' (Attoh 2011: 674). Lefebvre *does* provide clear direction for the right to the city, while avoiding prescription that would, with hindsight, have rendered the concept less durable and applicable.

Perhaps through a profound appreciation of the diversity of city dwellers and the urban milieux, Lefebvre deliberately left the concept malleable. The assortment of academic interpretations and the diversity of interest groups which have mobilised the right to the city can be seen as vindication of Lefebvre's reluctance to over-specify the concept. Since the city is a collective continuous work in progress, it follows that *all* people across the great heterogeneity of city dwellers have the right to participate (Mitchell 2003: 17) and the right to spatial justice (Fincher and Iveson 2008). Cities for people not profit is the right to the city plea of Brenner et al (2011). Soja (2010) applies right to the city principles in a study of low income users of public transport. Writing from his familiar neo-Marxist perspective, Harvey (2012: 5) is sure that the right to the city is a collective right to achieve democratic management of capital surpluses that accumulate in cities. In doing so ordinary working people, through social movements, rather than elite neoliberal private sector interests should claim 'some kind of shaping power over the processes of urbanization', in the interests of social needs and human development. Perhaps the most radical engagement with the right to the city comes from Merrifield (2011). He is an advocate but argues provocatively that it may well be time to ditch a concept that has been vitiated by embourgeoisement, while abjuring total rejection.

Since 1968 the concept of the right to the city has been in constant evolution around the world and urban citizenship is seen as practical rights involved with 'articulating, claiming and renewing group rights in and through the appropriation and creation of spaces in the city' (Isin 2000 14–15). In 2004 in Quito, Ecuador, a group of non-government organisations, Social Forum of the Americas, proposed the *World Charter of the Right to the City* which was refined at the Barcelona World Urban Forum 2004. An essay by Fernandes (2007) is much quoted; it explores Brazil's attempts to enshrine legally right to the city principles for urban dwellers, including local residents, street traders and the homeless. UN-Habitat following Fernandes argues that the right to the city involves:

- Liberty, freedom and the benefit of the city life for all
- Transparency, equity and efficiency in city administrations

- Participation and respect in local democratic decision making
- Recognition of diversity in economic, social and cultural life
- Reducing poverty, social exclusion and urban violence. (Brown and Kristiansen 2009: 3)

No single research project and certainly no one book of this size could possibly incorporate to any satisfactory extent the range of diverse interests and agendas promulgated by the right to the city discourse. Therefore, this chapter focuses on the right to participate in the production and appropriation of public space. In doing so it tends to encompass some of the concerns of: Mitchell (2003), the right to occupy the city; Tonkiss (2013), the right to design the city; and Harvey (2012), the right to participate in the shaping of urban space.

Differential space conceptualisations

Compared with the range of Lefebvrian innovative concepts embraced by academics, politicians and community activists, differential space is the Cinderella or poor relation, often overlooked and neglected in favour of the right to the city or the spatial triad. It is easy to see how the former has proved attractive in the post-WW2 era, particularly against the backdrop of: the 1960s civil rights movements in North America, urban rights movements in South America, the burgeoning human rights discourse and agitation for children's and women's rights in many countries. Furthermore, there is a certain amount of attractive mystique imbued in spaces of representation. They are the loci of passion and the 'clandestine or underground side of social life' (Lefebvre 1991: 33). Although for a host of researchers spaces of representation are the counterpoint to abstract space, a more logical and effective understanding of Lefebvre's ideas points to differential space as the counter-space to abstract space. While Lefebvre is not fulsome in his description and analysis of differential space, there is clarity and precision in his delineation of the concept's underlying structure. This precision provides hope in the face of seemingly omnipotent abstract space and official representations and most importantly it encourages a radical rethink of the nature of urban public space and urban life. Optimism is a salient constituent of differential space and in the opening quotation to this chapter Lefebvre maps out succinctly not just the germane characteristics of differential space but specifies how it may emerge in production of space dynamics.

That said, differential space does receive fairly cursory treatment by Lefebvre who is somewhat ambivalent, leaving the possibility of this alternative space 'frustratingly undefined' according to Harvey (2000: 183). Lefebvre is at pains though to stress that differential space is characterised by use value as opposed to the exchange value inherent in abstract space. Differential space, unremarkably, is the space where city inhabitants can happen on difference and enjoy spatial use value. Lefebvre summarises these two points in his 'right to the city' essay:

> It does not matter whether the urban fabric encloses the countryside and what survives of peasant life, as long as the 'urban', place of encounter, priority of use value, inscription in space of a time promoted to the rank of a supreme resource among all resources, finds its morphological base in its practico-material realization. (Lefebvre 1996: 158)

Under conditions of neo-capitalism, land and property is abandoned periodically by capital interests *and* the state. This withdrawal from space occurs continually in urban areas even in the centre of cities. From his neo-Marxist perspective Lefebvre highlights the potential for ordinary users of space to seize new rights to produce differential space from abandoned abstract space:

> An existing space may outlive its original purpose and the *raison d'être* which determines its forms, functions, and structures; it may thus in a sense become vacant, and susceptible of being diverted, reappropriated and put to a purpose quite different from its initial use. (Lefebvre 1991: 167, emphasis in original)

He then specifies, albeit briefly, how differential space, though inchoate, may be produced as demonstrated by the opening quotation of this chapter. Differential space may materialise in a variety of different geopolitical contexts producing different kinds of inclusive, use value urban public space. In doing so it engenders a reconfiguration of the power structures, democratic institutions and coalitions which work through the contestations of city space. Differential space may in the long term tend towards utopia or it may throw up rather more prosaic, everyday urban space. Lefebvre is ambivalent associating it with a utopian post-capitalist world, 'on the horizon' produced by social revolution that will result in a planet-wide space of 'transformed everyday life open to myriad possibilities' (Lefebvre 1991: 422–3), a kind of benign socialism. He detects differential space more prosaically in appropriated space such as the immediacy of Brazil's favelas (presumably before some of them became violent hotbeds of organised drug crime). Here urban space is appropriated and created by its everyday users to satisfy their needs. In a different context he detects it also in the 1968 student/worker occupations and political confrontations in Paris. So Lefebvre locates the right to the city and differential space temporally and geographically in the same Parisian space.

The most extended treatment of the emergence of Lefebvre's differential space ideas comes in Stanek's (2011) exceptional analysis. His impressive original contribution to the literature is a painstaking series of biographical revelations of how Lefebvre's empirical research expedited the construction of his production of space theories. Stanek devotes a hefty chunk of Chapter Four to a powerful explication of Lefebvre's empirical research regarding 'Nanterre as Differential Space' during the student political rebellion of 1968 (Stanek 2011: 165–92). The gist of a complex argument is that the potential for the production of differential space occurred because of a constellation of contradictions inherent in the location, design and function of the Nanterre University campus, to the north west of Paris. It was here that Lefebvre took up the post of sociology professor in 1965 and became a production of space instigator.

To make way for the University, the French government forcibly removed many inhabitants who had been living in shanty towns. In the mid-1960s such informal settlements were not uncommon and shared attributes with South American favelas. It is estimated there were about 120 shantytowns accommodating 50,000 inhabitants in the greater Paris area (Stanek 2011: 180). Specifically, the positioning of the Nanterre campus, in relation to both the neighbouring shantytowns and the centre of Paris, pointed at spatial and social contradictions of post-war French society (Stanek 2011: 186–92). Stanek then defers to Lefebvre's own empirical research regarding the student uprising at recently constructed, modernist Nanterre University. In his 1968 book, *L'irruption de Nanterre au sommet* Lefebvre provides precise insights into the nature of a certain kind of differential space:

> "Functionalised by initial design, culture was transported to a ghetto of students and teachers situated in the midst of other ghettos filled with the 'abandoned,' subject to the compulsions of production, and driven into an extra urban existence." Lefebvre writes that Nanterre became a *heterotopia* – "the other place," "the place of the other,

simultaneously excluded and interwoven," a place defined by differences. (Stanek 2011: 186, emphasis in original)

Lefebvre argues that the outcomes inherent in the location and design of the Nanterre campus produced effects different from the ones intended – they were *inadvertent*. This conclusion is only self-evident through the research lens of the spatial triad. This type of differential space phenomenon has been recognised in urban public spaces around the world where 'people pursue a rich variety of activities not originally intended for those locations' (Franck and Stevens 2006: 2). David Harvey prefers the term heterotopic spaces, about which Lefebvre (1991) says even less than he does about differential space. Harvey's preference for heterotopic space arises mainly from his reading of Lefebvre's *The Urban Revolution* and his distinction between isotopy (abstract space) and heterotopia. Harvey declares heterotopia to be simultaneously a utopian post-revolutionary space and a prosaic space of everyday life:

> ... where 'something different' is not only possible, but foundational for the defining of revolutionary trajectories. This 'something different' does not necessarily arise out of a conscious plan, but more simply out of what people do, feel, sense and come to articulate as they seek meaning in their daily lives. Such practices create heterotopic spaces all over the place. (Harvey 2012: xvii)

The teleological nature of Lefebvre's historical dialectic in which an inevitable transition unfolds, from the absolute space of nature to capitalist abstract space, finally reaching utopian differential space, has been observed several times (see Keith and Pile 1993: 24–5). Shields interprets differential space like Lefebvre as post-capitalist society and transformed everyday space (1999: 183) as does Kolb (2008: 95). 'Lefebvre's spatial code for socialism', an optimistic future 'always coiled in the belly of the capitalist beast' is Smith's (2003: xiv) evocative interpretation. Ruefully, he asserts that Lefebvre, 'allows little hint at all about how the differentiation of space is made and remade'. Merrifield (2006: 120) declares only half-jokingly that the project of differential space can 'begin this afternoon' through academics 'reclaiming our own workspace', by giving a nod to disruption rather than co-optation, a nod 'to real difference rather than cowering conformity'.

Rather than use Lefebvre's own term, differential space, Soja (1996: 35) uses a different one, 'Thirdspace', based on the perspectives of Michel Foucault. He defines it as a 'space of collective resistance'. It is a 'meeting place for all peripheralized and marginalized subjects'. This is rather at odds with Lefebvre's much broader social categorisation and more expansive conceptualisation of differential space, particularly its potential ludic qualities. Soja is closer to Lefebvre when he says 'Thirdspace is intentionally incomplete, endlessly explorable, resistant to closure' (Soja 1996: 36). Lefebvre's spatial ideas generally and his concept of differential space in particular, continue to resonate and infuse academic debate. Stanek et al (2014) seek to demystify Lefebvre and provide access to research investigating urban conjectures in a variety of global contexts. Brenner and Schmid (2015), drawing on Lefebvre, identify what they call differential urbanisation as a key component of a new epistemology of the urban.

Empirical explorations of differential space

Surprisingly, given its importance for Lefebvre as the counterpoint to abstract space, empirical researchers have tended to neglect the positive potentials of differential space. Iain Borden remains one of the few researchers to deploy Lefebvre's differential space concept in comprehensive, book length empirical research. He deconstructs skateboarding's history and explores the implications for the production of differential space, proclaiming that 'practices such as skateboarding may thus partially prefigure what this differential space might be.' (Borden 2001: 173). He argues that the creation of differential space through the temporary appropriation of space, even for a matter of hours, is a useful tactic but does not imply 'ownership'. Skateboarding through temporary occupation, or co-optation as Lefebvre calls it, is therefore more likely to be tolerated by powerful social groups (Borden 2001: 54–5). In the UK and North America, capital and state abandonment of space is associated with the cyclic, sharp economic crises and with long term structural changes in the economy in the fields of, for example, manufacturing industry and transport infrastructure. Lehtovuori (2010: 133) sees potential for the creation of differential space in empty buildings and urban wastelands where the 'machine of dominant space production comes to a temporary halt'. In an alternative conceptualisation of differential space he documents how the public space of Helsinki's Senate Square has in recent years been transformed, from a rather stale redundant municipal space into a vibrant differential space, partly through community centred carnivalesque leisure activities.

Oakley (2014) illustrates the creation of differential space through a case study of the redevelopment of derelict urban docklands in Port Adelaide, Australia. Along with the other researchers mentioned here she does a creditable job of interpreting this elusive, slippery concept. It is a space where voices and actions of a diverse range of interests including capital, the state and communities come together 'to contest and negotiate alternative landscapes' (Oakley 2014: 239). She too sees differential space derived from Lefebvre's right to the city. Disappointingly though, she concludes by conflating the exciting potential of differential space with the rather more prosaic processes of public participation. In one of the most thoughtful and insightful pieces of research, differential spaces of temporary appropriation are documented in comparative research focused on abandoned city space in Berlin (railway workshop), Brussels (railway station) and Helsinki (warehouse) by Groth and Corijn (2005). Theirs is a sophisticated, insightful here-and-now understanding of differential space which is:

> … space created and dominated by its users from the basis of its given conditions. It remains largely *unspecified* as to its functional and economic rationality, thus allowing for a wide spectrum of use which is capable of integrating a high degree of diversity, and stays open for change … a kind of 'urbanity' is produced in which the 'lived' and the contradictions that constitute urban life are nurtured, their deliberate juxtaposition allowing for a more complex vision of development than is evident in their immediate urban surroundings or in the unidimensional planning proposals to which these areas are subject. (Groth and Corijn 2005: 521 emphasis added)

Rather like the right to the city, differential space can be seen as a grand post-capitalist epoch or a call to immediate action at the local scale (Mitchell 2003; Harvey 2008; Soja 2010). Although the 'teleological prediction' (Howell 2001: 224) of forthcoming worldwide differential space has not been fulfilled yet, I draw on the following approaches to differential space in realising the empirical analyses:

- Lefebvre (1991: 52): appropriated space which accentuates differences
- Borden (2001: 55): tolerated skateboarding space
- Groth and Corijn (2005: 503): indeterminate space
- Franck and Stevens (2006): loose space

- Kolb (2008: 95): complex local places

Based on the literature and the empirical research of the foregoing chapters, I argue that counter-projects rooted in counter-representations may facilitate the eruption of spatial, dialectical tensions sufficient and necessary for the emergence of differential space. In previous research I reason that there are manifestly four critical aspects to differential space (Leary 2013a): first, its ludic characteristics result from the appropriation of space for its use value. Second is the ability to imprint meaning on abandoned or new public space. Third, differential space conjures up spaces where marginalised identities are made visible in public. Fourth, at its most democratically significant, however, it presents the full blown collective appropriation of public space for expressly politicised purposes. The rest of this chapter shows that the creation of use value ludic space and politicised spatial appropriative activity in Vancouver, Lowell and Manchester have produced spaces of difference akin to Lefebvrian 'here-and-now' differential space.

Riot, party, festival

We have seen how differential space can take different forms in different socio-political contexts. Existing urban space may be abandoned or new indeterminate public space created. In both contexts the appropriation of space by ordinary citizens can lead to the production of differential space. At the moment of its founding as a township rather than a logging camp, Vancouver materialised at the margin of industrial and leisure space with the building of Gassy Jack's Globe saloon in 1867. A number of other borders characterised Vancouver's city centre space as it developed in the 20th century, principally between Gastown and Downtown Eastside (DTES). There is also interesting liminality between Gastown and Chinatown but discussion of that is beyond the scope of this book. The analysis which follows concentrates on two manifestations of Gastown's differential space. First, the production of ludic differential space focused on Maple Tree Square. Second, and following on from Gastown's juxtaposition with DTES, is a deconstruction of the socio-spatial interactions of these two places in the production of tolerant, inclusive differential space. Heritage preservation efforts in Gastown since the 1960s improved the interior and exterior of many commercial and residential properties allowing the subsequent upgrading of the area as a visitor attraction for locals and tourists alike. While this was happening Gastown's public space was being reconfigured and new public spaces created.

I argue that one of the principal catalysts for the production of differential space in Gastown was the August 1971 Smoke-in which led to the (police) riot. After the violence, fear and destruction of the riot came an unexpected post-riot street party, imbued with some of the characteristics of carnival or festival. Certainly, Lefebvre was alive to the playful potential of the street and its potential for disorder and surprise as indicated at the start of this chapter. A moment's consideration indicates that the relationship between riot and carnival is a complex and contingent one. Riots, peaceful demonstrations, festivals and carnivals have a long history of association. Occasionally, carnivals deteriorate into riots but intermittently the reverse occurs driven by a conscious attempt to precipitate a process of cathartic healing in the wake of the injury and hurt that riots can inflict. In his analysis of the 1992 Los Angeles riots, Duignan (1993: 12) asserts controversially that:

> For uprooted urban people, rioting is fun for the participants, providing drama and excitement as well as loot. Riots may provide substantial gain for confirmed criminals, as well as a grand carnival for ordinary folk.

For some participants a riot may well unleash feelings of carnivalesque freedom; for the victims it is certainly not a fun event and the perpetrators of violence may be settled urban residents. Notting Hill Carnival, the biggest in Europe, has its origins in the reaction of London's Caribbean-British community following the dreadful racially motivated White Teddy Boy violence in August 1958 which led to a series of brutal riots. Similarly, Zukin's (2006) analysis of the post-riot production of space in Baltimore finds a connection between riot and festival. A spatial coalition emerged after major riots in 1968 consisting of: community committee groups, bankers, lawyers, downtown developers and well-intentioned social elites. This spatial coalition came together to reignite a sense of citizen pride in economically challenged and demoralised downtown Baltimore. Shortly after the riots the coalition organised a major free public ludic event – a city fair or street festival – to reaffirm the city's neighbourhood traditions which privileged public space use value. The fair attracted a wide spectrum of Baltimore's diverse inhabitants who demonstrated that they could revel in downtown space without rioting, it was:

> ... a novel experience that attempted to duplicate the excitement of a state fair in an urban context. It succeeded beyond anyone's expectations. In retrospect, that fair is

now seen as a watershed event that marked Baltimore's turnaround from a decaying smokestack city into a forward-looking metropolis. Above all, the event changed Baltimoreans' feelings about their hometown, instilling optimism and unity of vision at a low ebb in the city's history after the 1968 riots. (*Baltimore Sun* 1992)

I postulate that something similar happened after the Gastown riot with differential space consequences.

From pot party and riot to differential space

It should be appreciated that the August 1971 Gastown riot erupted shortly after Birmingham and Wood had submitted their design for the rehabilitation of Maple Tree Square and the creation of new civic public space. Obviously, GMA was anxious for the beautification scheme to go ahead despite the riot. Surveying the property damage and wreckage of the immediate aftermath, GMA realised that lines of credit and insurance would be impossible to secure unless something positive could be done about Gastown's image. They worried too about the possible long term economic harm to the area. In order to restore confidence they decided to hold a street party. It was meant to show the city and potential investors that it was business as usual in Gastown. Additionally, it was hoped it would initiate a process of healing and reconciliation between the police and the young people, and the Gastown residents and tourists caught up in that night of shocking violence after the Smoke-in. The merchants called it a 'Patch-Up Party' but everybody else called it a 'Love-in': an ironic reference to the ill-fated Smoke-in. An abundance of food and (alcoholic) drink was supplied for the partygoers free of charge by GMA.

Mayor Tom Campbell did not attend, explaining he feared there would be another riot if he did. In contrast to the demonstration, the Love-in which took place a week later on 14 August was lightly policed even though it attracted about 20,000 locals and tourists. VCC lent its support by closing all Gastown's main roads to vehicles. All ten city aldermen attended as did three police commissioners, a fact at odds with Bannerman's (1974) view that the VCC ignored Gastown until 1972. This second appropriation of public space for a political purpose was perhaps the street jamboree to replace the one that never happened. Ten times more people turned out for the post-riot Love-in than attended the politicised Smoke-in demonstration. Some police officers seemed to enjoy waving sticks of incense instead of riot sticks, and wearing flowers given to them by the hippies instead of riot helmets. Uniformed police mingled with crowds of revellers, singing, dancing and enjoying the free food and drink. Nobody was arrested despite obvious violations of drinking laws and the fact that the Gastown air was heavy with the aroma of marijuana. Crucially, for some of the major themes in this chapter, Ed Hicks, speaking on behalf of the GMA, called the event a festival and said it should be held every week (in Malmo-Levine 2007). That did not happen but there were significant consequences which cascaded from the Battle of Maple Tree Square which are important for the production of differential space.

In contrast to the riot of the week before, the Gastown free street festival demonstrated, rather like the Notting Hill Carnival and Baltimore city fair, that a variety of ordinary citizens, with a little help from the merchants, could participate peacefully in the production of ludic differential space. Although the post-riot Love-in did not stimulate a weekly festival it did provoke an annual public event in the mid-1970s called Gastown Days Festival. The first festival took place in 1975 over two days in late September in the streets and squares of Gastown. It was funded and organised jointly by the GMA and the Gastown Days Festival Committee of VCC. It included free music performances, carnival games, cavalcades, street theatre, cafés allowed to spill out onto the pavement and in 1977 a parade. Many people attended wearing Victorian fancy dress. Streets were closed to vehicular traffic to facilitate the ludic occupation of public space and, although marijuana was not legally available, the city council did grant licences for alcohol to be sold on the streets. In 1977 the Gastown steam clock dedication ceremony took place during the festival. Thousands of people attended and there are no reports of any public disorder or other problems.

Helped partly by federal support, the heritage-led revitalisation of Gastown, which made the festival possible, had become a nationally important exemplar of post-industrial restructuring. In 1971 Canadian Prime Minister Pierre Trudeau married a young Vancouverite, Margaret Sinclair. He appears to have established an affinity for the city because in 1975 he sent greetings to 'the Gastown Merchants Association and all those involved with and enjoying Gastown Days', continuing:

> When the problem of our city centres, and of how they should be designed and utilised, is becoming an acute one, it is invigorating to consider the Gastown example. You have brought both new life and a sense of history to your

area of Vancouver. Please accept my congratulations and my best wishes for continued success. (in Vancouver City Planning Department c1978)

If Trudeau was aware of all the other organisations, interests and individuals who contributed to bringing new life, a sense of history and new public space, he provided no acknowledgement in his letter. Trudeau's intervention is important because it highlights how the animation of public space and the creation of differential space serve asa fundamental signifiers of a vibrant, healthy city.

Free jazz in Gastown

Ten years after the first Gastown Days Festival, Maple Tree Square was chosen as the venue for an ambitious, free public space festival by a group of Vancouver jazz enthusiasts and a not-for-profit community radio station, Vancouver Co-operative Radio (CFRO). Co-op Radio has its roots in DTES community activism and was first established in 1974 in the semi-derelict Mercantile Bank building in Pigeon Park, at the intersection of Carrall and Hastings Streets. CFRO accepts no commercial advertising, is owned cooperatively by its 30,000 members with its programming produced by 400 volunteers. It seeks to increase community participation and positive social change by opening up:

> … the airwaves to more closely represent Vancouver's population, and especially to those who are denied access elsewhere by virtue of their race, sex, class or politics. (Kidd 1992)

In 1984 local jazz musicians, enthusiasts and CFRO formed the not-for-profit Pacific Jazz and Blues Association and promoted a community-focused free event located at Maple Tree Square, the Pacific Jazz and Blues Festival. Inspired by the ethos of CFRO, the festival was as much about representing marginal voices and communities and promoting community participation as it was about bringing jazz to the streets. Its initial success provoked a change of emphasis and a more expansive international flavour through the change of name to the Coastal Jazz and Blues Society (CJBS), also a not-for-profit that did however accept corporate sponsorship. The result in 1986 was the first Vancouver International Jazz Festival. Expo 86 provided a unique opportunity to boost the festival with world ranking jazz musicians including Miles Davis.

Over the decades visitor numbers have grown enormously to 500,000 jazz lovers over the ten days in June/July. It is the largest Jazz Festival in BC. On the one hand, the Jazz Festival is indistinguishable from any other major music event where tickets for the main acts can be expensive. On the other, it has remained true to its social and ethical roots. The festival opens with a weekend of free performances called Gastown Jazz. Two stages embrace Water Street at Maple Tree Square (Figure 8.1) and what is called the Steam Clock Stage. About 130 free performances are staged in a variety of venues across the city including public parks, community centres, concert halls, clubs, public plazas, and in streets of various neighbourhoods, including DTES. About 1,000 volunteers make the series of free events that appropriate public space possible. CJBS works with local schools and universities to encourage an appreciation of and participation in music of all kinds, running free workshops throughout the duration of the festival. The extraordinary combination of volunteer support, commitment to inclusive access, education, outreach and cultural diversity resulted in the award of Jazz Festival of the Year at the 2008 Canadian National Jazz Awards, Toronto.

Figure 8.1 : Free jazz creates differential space: Maple Tree Square, Gastown (2009 Flickr photo © John Whitworth)

Merging differential space

The historical trajectory of Gastown over several decades from the 1960s can be characterised as one of increasingly successful economic activity on the back of property investment and exchange value consumption. Processes of gentrification have resulted in the creation of upmarket bars, restaurants and apartment blocks. In contradistinction to this, DTES, although affected partially by such processes, has retained much of its 1960s character. It is still a place with relatively high levels of poor housing and areas of physical dereliction. DTES has been portrayed relentlessly for decades as Vancouver's and Canada's most deprived neighbourhood brimming with crime, addiction and a surfeit of unstable first nation peoples. It is important to realise, however, that most of the people living in DTES 'are not addicts, not missing, not aboriginal, not sex trade workers and not criminals' (Burk 2011: 146). What is undeniable though is that the area does have a high proportion of people who are poor, elderly, unemployed and living alone. It also has a sizeable stock of affordable social housing, vibrant arts and cultural scenes and strong networks of community activism that have delivered a range of enviable victories (Burk 2011: 145)

Three community centred production of space projects are particularly noteworthy. Each was a public art monument, conceived in the 1980s to honour and memorialise DTES residents and others. 'Marker of Change' memorialises the 1989 Montreal Massacre, when 14 women were murdered at École Polytechnique . The 'CRAB Park Boulder' is dedicated to the spirit of the people murdered in DTES. A totem pole in Oppenheimer Park called 'Standing with Courage, Strength and Pride' is meant to honour the sisters and brothers who have died unnecessarily and those who have survived in DTES (Burk 2011). These public space memorials politicise the personal and collective struggles and represent 'counter-monuments' because they critique the hegemony of dominant social narratives and have the potential to alter social relations through the processes of production and their defiant presence. They also convey the plight of excluded peoples into the political arena through 'a politics of visibility' (Burk 2011: 178).

DTES provides support resources and spaces often public in nature, where disadvantaged people can find companionship. Such spaces are crucial for people living in what may well be a small, unpleasant single room. Many long term residents of DTES have productive stable lives. They are not defined or bound by poverty or addiction. On the contrary they are empowered by a sense of community, kinship and an abiding sense of hope (Cran and Jerome 2008). Despite spates of fierce repression, such as during the lead up to the 2010 Winter Olympics, DTES is a space of relative tolerance. It is a space of diversity in terms of social class, ethnicity and culture. VCC, although partly responsible for gentrification, provides a supportive rhetorical stance, stressing that:

> ... there are many vulnerable people living in the DTES and negative effects of 'gentrification' are being felt through rising rents, displacement from homes and unaffordable restaurants and stores. However, despite these challenges, the diverse communities are resilient, caring, friendly and compassionate. (VCC 2013)

Unlike Gastown, DTES has to a large extent resisted the forces of gentrification (Ley and Dobson 2008). Nevertheless, gentrification has occurred. There is little doubt that the restoration and preservation of Vancouver's most important historic area, Gastown has been a great success in physical and economic terms. Ray Spaxman (2012) recognised this during a research interview:

> 'To be able to have preserved that is significant. It's wonderful to have Gastown. If you imagine the city without Gastown it would be a disappointing place. It's a major thing that we've kept it. It's a major thing that we continue to keep it alive and well economically and socially. The character of Gastown on an early morning with the sun rising looking down Water Street, it's phenomenal. There is a special turn of the century architectural ambiance so it's very important to us. It's like somebody you love has a particular shaped nose, it's part of our character.' (Spaxman 2012)

When pressed, however, he did acknowledge some negative outcomes of heritage-led post-industrial transformation, particularly in relation to gentrification in Gastown and DTES:

> 'It's getting the balance right between the economic, social and environmental aspects which is the challenge. The balance is always threatened. Like what's happening with gentrification. How the low income people feel when retail outlets that serve them are being altered to become designer dog stores. So there's this tension because people love the area for a variety reasons. One is that it's been a

place where they could get a decent meal at low cost but is now becoming a groovy place for the yuppies to move in and sit there having expensive dinners. There's only so much at that interface you can do and then it gets to become a conflict.' (Spaxman 2012)

Outright conflict does occur, of course, but it is fascinating to note how Spaxman's observations resonate with Lefebvre's ideas about spatial conflict and contradiction. Burnett (2014: 157) makes a similar point about the upmarket restaurants. At its margins DTES is becoming to a limited extent a 'dining destination' marketed dubiously as a space of 'authentic culinary adventures' and urban spectacle. In developing a complex argument, Burnett asserts that rather than low income people being displaced, their poverty is being commodified. There may be a grain of truth in this, but this argument about abstract space creeping into DTES is only part of what is happening. Lefebvre argues cogently that urban space is divided up into designated areas prohibited to one group or another (Lefebvre 1991: 319). Abstract space operates through a series of prohibitions rather than invitations. Such prohibitions are usually invisible. In addition to poverty and varying degrees of distress becoming commodified spectacle, DTES residents are not passive participants in a street theatre. They actively appropriate Gastown in everyday ways for its use value. In an inversion of the exploitative tourist gaze and associated commodification of poverty, DTES residents become visible in Gastown public space using middle class visitors and tourists as a survival resource.

Through the decades Gastown and DTES have been portrayed in official representations of space in five mutually contradictory ways. First, DTES was snubbed without specific mention in the *Restoration Report* 1969. Instead, the problem of a transient, marginal population in the Carrall Street area was regarded simply as largely unwanted. Second, the British Colombia Government's (BCG) delineation of the Gastown historic area in 1971 included Chinatown but excluded DTES (see Chapter Three). Third, in the 2006 Carrall Street Greenway Plan, this street was regarded positively as an intersection: a place where history and contemporary life meet in DTES. Fourth, the *Downtown Eastside Local Area Plan* (VCC 2014) delineation of DTES *includes* Gastown as one of the seven sub-areas but identifies the DTES Oppenheimer District as another one of the sub areas. Therefore, within the same representation Gastown is simultaneously part of and not part of DTES. Fifth, in recent times BCG advice to tourists is to be wary of Gastown's proximity to an unnamed DTES, a place imbued with implicit menace:

Gastown is within easy walking distance of downtown Vancouver. Be mindful of the fact that Gastown, while very safe, is partially located in a more graphic part of the city. (in Ferris 2015)

'Graphic' is clearly BCG code for dangerous. What is important here is that official representations of space tend to separate and isolate Gastown from DTES. Rather like the idea that Chinatown should be the domain of Chinese people (Anderson 1991), the implication here is that DTES is for marginalised, impoverished people. Under the representations of officialdom, particularly the PCC, there are implied subtle 'abstract prohibitions' inherent in the trappings of heritage preservation. In Gastown, such representations serve as signifiers to protect the 'spaces of elites' (Lefebvre 1991: 319) from intruders who do not belong.

In contrast, through a Lefebvrian lens what emerges is the active participation of DTES residents in the production of differential space through bodily appropriation. Carrall Street is certainly not perceived by them as a barrier to their movement westward into Gastown. It is fascinating to observe the intelligent, imaginative appropriation of space by people often caricatured as lazy, feckless and threatening. DTES residents occupy Gastown's public spaces visibly in a variety of ways. Of course they are often just passing through, resting or engaged in simple begging. What is highly prevalent, however, is the number and range of supposedly useless people displaying a plethora of artistic and craft skills. They provide spectacle and visual stimulation that is essentially free but they also interact in complex ways with Gastown residents, visitors and tourists. On any day of the week a multiplicity of scenes can unfold whereby singers, dancers and various performers are rewarded for their efforts with money from those who can afford it. More striking still is the range of painting, drawing and plastic artistry that DTES people bestow on Gastown. First nation peoples in particular sojourn their way from DTES to Gastown to deploy their stunning artistic skills such as carving (Figure 8.2).

Through their bodily presence in Gastown such gifted artists and artisans complicate the zoning and spatial division imposed on urban space by planners and city authorities, thereby creating differential space. Occasionally one can observe unique artistic products in the making in processes which contribute to the production of urban space, for example, intricate artwork where the sun's heat is the medium via a magnifying glass (Figure 8.3). Skilled musicians enliven Gastown streets in gentrification reversal (Figure 8.4). If Gastown chic spills

Figure 8.2: Appropriating the right to differential space: First Nation craft carving, Water Street, Gastown (2013 Flickr photo © Ted McGrath)

into DTES through creeping gentrification and the tourist gaze, then DTES residents contradict abstract space through their refusal to be corralled into a largely stigmatised DTES. In the process, they create a kind of differential space. Their presence blurs the distinction between the highly commodified abstract spaces of Gastown and the creation of everyday differential space which becomes a resource on which DTES can draw for sustenance. Although monetary exchange often takes place, underpinning this appropriation of space and providing its raison d'être, the social relationships created are not straightforward or simply based on exchange value. DTES residents are in effect living a subsistence lifestyle rather than engaging in marketised activities through which they seek to accumulate profit. They may well be part of a not-for-profit cooperative endeavour. Gastown residents, tourists and other relatively wealthy visitors are not buying the goods and services from street vendors and performers in a formal market transaction. Rather, they are involved in a transaction more akin to sympathetic charitable giving. Benefactors may well gain satisfaction from the fact, as a counterpoint to the consumption of poverty spectacle in which they and others might be engaging simultaneously. Gastown provides

Figure 8.3: A burning passion for art creates differential space in Gastown (2012 photo © Steve Blaylock)

rich and intriguing differential space of certain kinds. Lowell too affords a fascinating differential space case study, but for different reasons.

Lowell Folk Festival and differential space

Lefebvre was explicit that spatial practice, the material city, alone did not constitute urban space. It is through social relations and interactions that urban space is actually produced. Several significant challenges had to be overcome to create the new public space of Boarding House Park (BHP; see Chapter Five). Once constructed it became a rather undetermined space, a space whose purpose and meaning were essentially unspecified. It was urban public space not yet infused with everyday meaning. It was public space waiting to acquire social meaning and a repertoire of collective memories. The next challenge was to animate this indeterminate space with social interaction. Lehtovuori (2010: 128) calls the animation of public space through social interaction 'the event of assembly'. When it was conceived in the mid-1980s, the urban planners did not prescribe the kinds of individual and collective social activities that would bring a social buzz to BHP. What they did through their representations of

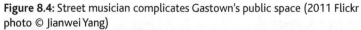

Figure 8.4: Street musician complicates Gastown's public space (2011 Flickr photo © Jianwei Yang)

space, public investment in spatial practice and the creation of a new public park was to inadvertently create the potential for the production of differential space, prioritising use value. This potential was realised when BHP became the primary site for the Lowell Folk Festival – an event of assembly – or rather a multicultural extravaganza, the history of which illustrates some of the intricacies of the production of urban public space.

In recent years over a long July weekend the Lowell Folk Festival (LFF) has attracted up to 250,000 visitors to BHP and many downtown city streets. When it started in 1987, however, it was a relatively small affair attracting 20,000 visitors. Its scale therefore was more in keeping with the cultural events of the previous two decades which demonstrated the local appetite for and community capacity to deliver such complex public space spectacles. Mention was made of the Lowell Regatta in Chapter Four. Pauline Golec, a Polish-American, worked at the Polish food booth from the Regatta's inception in 1974 and remembers the:

> 'Regatta Ethnic Festivals, the forerunner of today's Lowell Folk Festival. The Regatta was held on the banks of the Merrimack (Regatta Field on Pawtucket Boulevard) and, while it did have some music, it emphasized the various foods of Lowell's ethnic communities.' (Golec 2008)

Its unique blend of cultural offerings, supplied by Lowell's diverse communities, became a major component of LFF. Other small scale ethnic festivals took place in the 1970s during the summer and involved some of Lowell's distinctive communities including Irish, Greek and French-Canadian. Interestingly, the location was the linear, greenway of Lucy Larcom Park alongside the Merrimack Canal in downtown Lowell.

Celebratory public events in Lowell have a longer history though, going back to the 19th century and the Irish parades. Most notable of these was the Saint Patrick's Day parade when Lowell's Irish-American community marched through the nascent city, partly to show their resistance to Yankee repression. Less contentious were the public displays by the young Yankee female mill workers. Lowell Mill Girls, or Factory Girls as they preferred to be known, would promenade en masse after attending Sunday morning church services. Dressing up in a fine hat and bonnet to see and be seen in public was a favourite Mill Girl leisure pursuit and one which was viewed favourably by respectable society. They made a spectacular sight and influential Quaker poet and abolitionist John Greenleaf Whittier, who worked in Lowell before gaining literary fame, enthused that the streets blossomed as if 'the flowers in a garden should take it into their heads to promenade for exercise'. Thousands of women participated in this public display, 'who during week days are confined to the mills.' (in Malone and Parrott 1998: 30). These Sunday afternoon public space leisure spectacles were wholly unorganised, informal gatherings.

At other times the Mill Girls engaged in the organised politicised appropriation of Lowell's public space. In what may well have been the first substantial labour dispute in US history, hundreds of Mill Girls went on strike – 'turned out' – to protest a reduction in their wages. They marched through the streets joining up with other mill workers to attend rallies and hear speeches in support of their cause. In the strike of 1836:

One of the girls stood on a pump, and gave vent to the feelings of her companions in a neat speech, declaring that it was their duty to resist all attempts at cutting down the wages. This was the first time a woman had spoken in public in Lowell, and the event caused surprise and consternation among her audience. (Robinson 1898: 83)

When the Mill Girls appropriated the downtown streets and squares they produced differential space – a space for the articulation of political opinion that ran counter to the hegemonic opinions of Lowell's capitalist class and wider Lowell society.

By far the largest organised Mill Girls' politicised appropriation of public space was organised not by them as part of a labour dispute but by their employers. An enormous parade of Mill Girls occurred in June 1833 when President Andrew Jackson visited the country's premier manufacturing city. Every one of the 2,500 Girls wore a white dress, blue sash and carried a green parasol. 'Old Hickory' approved heartily and was heard to mutter frequently 'very pretty women'. His satisfaction with this public display of working femininity was appreciated by the mill owners and went some way to assuaging their distaste for Jackson arising from his ambivalent attitude to US protectionist policies, from which they benefited. At this early stage in Lowell's industrialisation, the city was widely regarded in the US and Europe as a model of enlightened, paternalistic industrial production. The mill owners showed a savvy appreciation that the parade of clean, fresh healthy and happy Mill Girls would provide a stunning visual vindication of their labour practices. In the decades that followed the Yankee female workforce was eventually replaced, first with Irish Labour then by immigrants from a host of countries and ethnic backgrounds. As migrants do, they brought their traditional folk music, distinctive cuisines and cultural traditions. They made music 'in the hyphenated-American social clubs that dotted the streets within walking distance of the factories' (Rahn 1997: 205). It was this cultural diversity that would eventually provide the raw material for a Lowell folk festival and a defining post-industrial moment for BHP and the city.

LFF emerged out of the city's hosting the peripatetic National Folk Festival (NFF) in 1987–89. This annual free festival was and still is produced by the Washington based not-for-profit National Council for the Traditional Arts (NCTA), the first one taking place in 1934. It traditionally takes place on the last weekend in July. The 'National' as it is affectionately known is a free, three day outdoor musical homage to history, culture and diversity. It celebrates the diversity and vibrancy of US and world culture through music, dance, storytelling, traditional crafts and international food. In its formative years the National demonstrated a radical inclusiveness and William Christopher 'Father of the Blues' Handy's first performance on a racially desegregated stage was at the 1938 National. In those early years the NFF promoters strove to deliver a musical event featuring local, national and international musicians but went beyond music to feature traditional crafts, food and drink. The NFF quickly developed its hallmark characteristic – diversity. Its eclectic sounds and cultures 'became appropriate representations of an immigrant city' voicing the experiences of both recent and long established settlers (Rahn 1997: 206). There was diversity not just in the eclectic range of music but also in the backgrounds, ethnicity and cultural distinctiveness of the musicians. Rather than one enclosed concert space, the format of the National features several stages in prominent city streets and squares that allows temporarily the public space of downtown to become sites of inclusive ludic space.

The idea to bring the NFF to Lowell was mooted in 1986 first by LNHP Superintendent Chrysandra 'Sandy' Walter. She observed astutely how the ethos of the National chimed with the cultural remit of the LNHP through its legislative mandate to promote and grant aid cultural programmes. Lowell's multicultural character ensured it had a head start in attracting the NFF. Celebrating Lowell's diverse communities and acknowledging their role in the industrial and cultural history of this city was a major preoccupation of LNHP inherited from Lowell Model Cities (Marion 2014b). Walter seems to have understood, without realising it, the Lefebvrian imperative that urban public space can only be brought about through social interaction. Walter and Paul Marion along with two LNHP staffers, George Price and Sue Leggat, flew to Washington in 1986:

> ... to meet with Joe Wilson, director of the National Council on Traditional Arts, and Vernon 'Dave' Dame, chief of interpretation for the Park Service. The purpose of the meeting was to convince Wilson to locate the annual National Folk Festival, which he produces, in Lowell for the next two or three years. We succeeded ... Joe and Dave were very enthusiastic about having the folk festival in Lowell. (Marion 2011)

Sponsors included LNHP and the festival was funded partially by Massachusetts Council on the Arts and Humanities and the federal

National Endowment for the Arts. Apart from the organisational capacity to deliver a major festival event, the other attraction of Lowell as the host city for the NFF was its own brand of distinctive ethnic and cultural diversity. In significant ways Lowell epitomises contemporary America: a nation of striking diversity, tradition and sometimes painful change. The American story of industrial growth and decline and the associated folk music traditions seem to coalesce in Lowell, a city which is undoubtedly 'a microcosm of the multi-textured and evolving American experience' (Rahn 1997: 205). When Marion and Walter were able to attract the National to Lowell in 1987, BHP was still in the developmental stage. Following its traditional format, the National performance spaces consisted of temporary stages erected in significant downtown public spaces including: John F. Kennedy Plaza, the city's premier public space, Lucy Larcom Park and Eastern Canal (Kerouac) Park. This spatial arrangement of scattered performance stages effectively transformed much of downtown Lowell into a post-industrial festival space in contrast to the wholly industrial city created by the Boston Associates for the generation of profit. After its three year run the NFF was declared a resounding success: by 1990, 186,000 people had attended.

Based on the success of the National, the four producing partners – the LCC, Lowell Festival Foundation, LNHP and the NCTA – agreed that Lowell should host its own folk festival. The first LFF took place over three days in the last weekend of July 1990. In its first year the LFF attracted 150,000 visitors and Lowellians have rock-and-rolled annually since. Although it provided one of the performance venues for the NFF, the Plaza would have a new role in LFF. One of the most distinctive traits of LFF was established quickly: the opening procession, or Downtown Parade of Nations that begins at JFK Plaza. It featured Lowell's diverse communities with flags of many nations displayed prominently. In carnivalesque style the parade is serenaded along the route by some of the festival musicians (Figure 8.5). An assortment of national flags denotes hyphenated American pride (Figure 8.6). From 1991 BHP assumed dual importance in LFF: it was the point where the parade terminated and the site of the largest outdoor stage. At BHP Lowell's leading local and state politicians welcome the parade in a volley of speeches which acknowledged the communities' contribution to the city's history and to the festival itself.

Like no other event in the city, the LFF provides the opportunity for Lowell's diverse communities to be seen downtown en masse in public in celebratory style. Joining the Irish-Americans and French-Canadian-Americans are: Armenian-, Cambodian-, Cameroonian-, Colombian-,

Ghanaian-, Greek-, Israeli-, Italian-, Lithuanian-, Nigerian-, Polish-, Portuguese- and Puerto Rican-Americans. Although not immigrants of course, First Nation Peoples are also represented. For a time those who are often peripheral and marginalised become the central focus of a positive gaze. Significant numbers in the crowds enjoying the spectacle hail of course from the same communities. It should be appreciated that the colour, music and multicultural excitement of the opening parade is entirely free – priority is given to use value over exchange value – and it assumes some of the qualities of multicultural carnivals seen in many cities around the world. Although this parade of nations is highly organised, for a while downtown is appropriated by orderly Lowell citizens who participate in the transformative production of differential space.

Figure 8.5: Inclusive public space: a multicultural parade opens the Lowell Folk Festival (photo © Michael Leary-Owhin)

Similarly, monetised consumption takes place, particularly consumption of food, but it is through not-for-profit community and religious groups, and ordinary Lowellians conjure up the food. This is in contrast to some festivals and carnivals where the (unhealthy) food and drink consumed creates profits for multinational companies. Apart from the parade and the ethnic food, the other unique characteristic of the LFF is the extent of volunteering generated and the sophisticated charitable fundraising machine that rolls into operation during the festival weekend. Teams of volunteers called the 'Bucket Brigades' patrol all

Figure 8.6: Politicised differential pace: flagging up multicultural hyphenated national pride at Lowell Folk Festival (photo © Michael Leary-Owhin)

areas of the festival and it is difficult not to contribute something when confronted by a fresh-faced eager Lowell High School student with a devilish smile rattling a bucket. Along with the Bucket Brigades, a host of other fundraising activities before and during the festival not only provide donations to worthy not-for-profit causes. They also help defray the $1 million festival costs, allowing it to continue as a free, inclusive event. LFF has become the largest free folk festival in the US. It necessitates careful, precise and expert organisation. That said, the LFF could not happen without the willing contribution of many volunteers of all ages and competencies. They are evident throughout the downtown and help provide the festival with a distinctly Lowell flavour.

Over the years the ludic differential space of LFF provides an arena for a wide range of free artistic performances, in downtown streets, particularly by local schoolchildren and Lowell's diverse communities. Erupting into the transformed downtown spaces also emanates a host of informal artistic performers and the omnipresent jugglers are joined by street buskers, singers and dancers taking advantage of readymade receptive audiences in relatively tolerant public space. Official hot food stalls and vendors of the usual festival clothing and bric-a-brac require a permit. This system of street vendor control is enshrined in the city regulatory code Chapter 167 'Hawkers and Peddlers', based on the rationale that sales during festivals 'are restricted to non-profit, volunteer supported organisations which annually support the festivals and ethnic activities of the City'. While restrictions on street vending in some countries denies low income people their livelihood, contributing to the production of abstract space, one can sympathise with the temporary restriction during LFF days.

In some ways the LFF achieves the vision of future local economic prosperity for Lowell based on an increasing middle class presence downtown and a lucrative heritage/cultural urban tourism sector (Norkunas 2002). Critics of the LFF, and of post-industrial Lowell generally, see increasing gentrification and a festival that succeeds only by drawing in 'several hundred thousand middle class tourists to the city' (Norkunas 2002: 42). My experience of the LFF is that it does attract significant visitors from across the class spectrum. Nevertheless, the defining features of the LFF – the fact that there is no charge and its location in public space – signify the emergence of differential space. It is a space though, if we accept Norkunas' critique, where continuing tensions and contradictions regarding the right to the city of working class people continue to be worked out.

It is evident that the multiple benefits inherent in attracting the NFF to Lowell were not lost on a major protagonist:

> When the National kicked off in late July 1987, the park and Lowell had their 'big bang' event, and every astute observer knew immediately that this venture was a keeper. Right off, the festival felt like a signature event, one that could define the city … Like the interlacing canals that converted the force of flowing river water to power for machines that turned raw cotton into bolts of cloth, the festival channels the expressive tributaries of the American experience into an urban-set performance and exposition whose end product is inspiration. (Marion 2014a: 201)

The park to which Marion refers is the LNHP rather than BHP and Chrysandra Walter was indeed shrewd to risk backing the event, which had it flopped would have left them facing severe opprobrium. They probably had the same excruciating stomach knots as Michael Heseltine did when funding a cultural heritage initiative in East London (see Chapter Seven). BHP and LFF are inherently important for the city. LFF represents a significant event of assembly; it animates and creates inclusive urban public space. For Marion, LFF "was a way to add vitality to downtown historic district at night". It was also "a lure to bring people into the historic district", which provided the context for the cultural experience (Marion 2014c). A tangible benefit spawned by LFF is the associated Lowell Music Series. This is a summer long weekend and evening collection of concerts, which were initially free but due to the constraints of the music industry a subsidised charge has been made in recent years. When access to BHP is restricted in this way, rather than being privatised, it assumes the character of quasi-public space (see Figure 1.1)

A three day event which attracts 200,000 people mainly from New England is unlikely to instil a worldwide redefinition of the city of Lowell. Interestingly, while in Boston, on my way to Lowell, I would mention my forthcoming visit and the reaction of Bostonians tended to be, 'what do you want to go there for, it's a really bad place'. Their opinions are informed one suspects more by the depressing, drug and crime infused spaces of representation in the Hollywood film *The Fighter* (2010) than by their direct experiences of the city. This gritty cinematic drama follows the boxing career of Micky Ward (Mark Wahlberg), a Lowell native, but it is the crack cocaine induced criminal antics of his brother Dicky Eklund (Christian Bale) which linger in the memory. Such an anecdote is not proof but it does indicate perhaps that LFF may have done more to change perceptions within Lowell rather than outside. Conversely, the comedy film *The Invention of Lying* (2009, starring Ricky Gervais) presents a sunny, irreverent depiction of Lowell, looking like an attractive place to live and work. In a Twitter exchange, I asked Ricky Gervais (2014) why it was shot in Lowell. He affirms "because it could be anywhere", in other words, any pleasant city in the US. Perhaps then Lowell's external image has improved significantly. Undoubtedly though, what the LFF did was to etch a highly positive and socially inclusive meaning onto the new public space of BHP and imbue it and surrounding streets with qualities of ludic differential space. At such times Lowell ceases to be a former industrial city that lost its way in a haze of factory closures and drug induced desperation.

Castlefield's diverse differential space

The third case study of differential space centres on the Castlefield area of Manchester. Here differential space manifests as ludic space but also as the space of politicised appropriation both informal and formal. Increasingly, in recent years with the absence of industry, Castlefield has become a space of informal leisure pursuits: narrowboat canal cruising, jogging, skateboarding, urban cycling, free running, picnicking, amateur photography, strolling and quiet contemplation. In addition to these ludic pursuits, however, there has been an ongoing politicised appropriation of public space. The expansive space of the Arena and the attractive canal watersides of the surrounding area have, during the 2000s and into the 2010s, been appropriated politically for diverse purposes. In this sense they assume some of the characteristics of differential space. Organised marches, demonstrations and protest rallies are key markers of genuine, democratic public space. In the case of Castlefield, from the early 2000s diverse people have chosen to express their identity, often related to sexuality, through the bodily appropriation of public space.

The annual Gay Pride carnival starts from Castlefield, which has also hosted AIDS vigils. On a smaller scale Castlefield was the venue for a photo-shoot for the 'Vanilla Girls'. Local photographer, Paul Jones chose Castlefield when asked by Steph Kay owner of Manchester's lesbian Vanilla Club to showcase some of the regular clientele (Figure 8.7). He selected Castlefield because it provides a spectacular, recognisable backdrop and the girls were comfortable there (Jones 2010). Many of these events are ignored by the mainstream media but are documented by 'alternative' media and urban photographers, many of whom post their images on social media photographic websites such as Flickr (Leary 2010). In 2006 Castlefield was brimming with narrow boats whose owners, members of 'Save Our Waterways', were protesting about the threats to Britain's canals from public spending cuts (Dowling 2006). Castlefield's diverse public space is often produced by local interests, most touchingly by Salford school children who in 2009 organised a rally at Castlefield to save their school, St George's, from closure. SCC's plan was to demolish and redevelop the site for private housing, thereby producing classic abstract space. Interestingly, the protest was held in Castlefield to avoid demonstration charges, after SCC billed the school for £1,000 when the protesters took to Salford's streets. The school won its fight to stay open.

Since the US and British led invasion of Afghanistan in 2001, collective political action has focused on the Castlefield area as groups such as the Greater Manchester Coalition to Stop the War have organised anti-war rallies (BBC 2001). The Campaign for Nuclear Disarmament too has organised marches that terminate in speeches and rallies in Castlefield (Hudson 2009). Anti-racism events have been a feature of the Arena since 2000 including 'corporate' events like that organised by the English Football Association's *Kick It Out* campaign. In 2003 a 'multicultural population flocked to Castlefield's Arena' to experience an event that wrapped up its serious anti-racism message in a day of music and entertainment aimed predominantly at young people (Kick it Out 2003). In the post-2008 era of public spending cuts, an

Figure 8.7: The Vanilla Girls' photo-shoot produces differential space in Castlefield (2009 Flickr photo © Paul Jones)

anti-austerity march and rally, the *Austerity Wrecks Lives Demonstration* organised by the Trades Union Congress, started and ended at the Castlefield Arena on 6 September 2014. In October 2015, 80,000 people converged again on the Castlefield Arena to demonstrate their opposition to the government's austerity policies, during an event organised by the Trades Union Congress and The People's Assembly.

Other event organisers have overlain political space with leisure space often as a strategy to avoid problems with local authorities or the police, who can be suspicious of purely anti-racism events because of the potential for violent confrontation with far right political groups. Manchester fire fighters joined a mass rally of colleagues from all over Britain to occupy the Castlefield Arena in 2002, in a prelude to the national strike of that year. This and similar appropriations of public space unify a number of important traits of the right to the city-differential space nexus. Here was a workers' collective made visible in public by the assertion of the right to a fair wage and the right to occupy public space for politicised purposes. In doing so they constituted a collective challenge to the hegemonic idea that space is a neutral container. It was the material space of the Castlefield arena which produced the social action of the strike rally. And in turn it was this social interaction born of industrial conflict that produced democratic, differential public space, albeit for a fleeting moment.

Production of autonomous differential space

Organised marches and protest rallies are important aspects of urban public differential space and the right to the city but some rights to the city cannot be gained by following rules formulated by those in authority. Drawing on ideas regarding the power of the peaceful bodily reappropriation or co-optation of streets, squares and abandoned space through *unauthorised* action, activists claim fundamental rights to the city. Manchester No Borders (MNB) was established in 2006 and I interviewed two of the founder members Donna and Joe (not their real names). It started as a friends' group until membership was boosted by a public meeting at the ironically named Friends' Meeting House. There are several hundred active members including local people and students. MNB has a clear philosophical position, "we understand ourselves as an action and theory group" (Joe, in Donna and Joe 2010). MNB wanted to broaden their work away from a focus on supporting refugees and asylum seekers, important though this was. The group did this principally by adopting European ideas of autonomous city spaces.

MNB's theoretical basis is about asking what is a right, Joe explained, "if it's abstract it's meaningless, it has to be connected with some material social gain". Rights have to be claimed by social movements in struggles for material things (in Donna and Joe 2010). MNB understood its mission in a global context and seems inspired, consciously or not, by the philosophy underpinning Lefebvre's right to the city:

> With sky-high rents forcing the poor to the margins, the creeping privatisation of public space, and a council willing to close down vital community services and simultaneously sell off swathes of the city centre to luxury property developers and retailers, there has seldom been a time when fighting for autonomous spaces in Manchester has been more important. (MNB 2008)

MNB announced a day of action in 2008 which expressed a desire to combine political action with leisure and pleasure: a cogent indicator of the production of differential space was reflected in the announcement:

> ... we are calling for a demonstration in Manchester for the FREEDOM OF MOVEMENT FOR ALL and to DEFEND AUTONOMOUS SPACES. This forms part of the international days of action in defence of autonomous spaces that have been called for this weekend. The day's

events will also include a fayre [sic] in the city centre, street parties, squat parties and workshops in occupied spaces. (MNB 2008, capitals in original)

MNB organised two events on 12 April 2008: a demonstration-cum-march and a symbolic squat, meant to signal how local people can assert their political rights to city space. The events were symbolic because they were always meant to be temporary, for a few hours. In a politicised appropriation of space, a group of activists from the MNB led a march through the city centre that terminated in the symbolic occupation of Jackson's Wharf in Castlefield (*The Mule* 2008). One of the organisers was candid enough to admit in email correspondence that:

To be honest the decision to occupy Jackson's Wharf was not the most politically thought out one we've ever done, but was partly dictated by practicalities. It was a good city centre location in a historical area which had become synonymous with regeneration success through posh bars and clubs and then in the last few years has gone downhill again ... (MNB Activist 2010)

The attraction of Castlefield for staging political protests is that it is free of charge and the police are relaxed about its use for organised rallies *and* spontaneous events. It is a highly flexible and indeterminate space in which a wide range of diverse people feel comfortable. Arriving at Castlefield, Jacksons Wharf was draped in the autonomous spaces banner (Figure 8.8), fairy lights were hung, bottles of beer passed around and the 'squatters' revelled in a party with music and dancing. Shortly after the squat started the police arrived, having monitored the march continually via city centre CCTV. They gave permission for MNB to continue to occupy the building but only until nightfall, when they had to leave. In terms of Mitchell's (2013) categorisation of police power highlighted in Chapter One, this is negotiated management. This intervention by agents of the state demonstrates how the right to occupy abandoned buildings and create everyday differential space is surveilled and constrained rather than utopian.

The occupation refocused attention on Castlefield as a node in a global network not so much of world trade but of the international movement of people, because activists feel that migrants and autonomous spaces face a hard time from the authorities, so squats, 'especially [for] some migrant communities, are the only alternative to homelessness' (Eliot 2008). There were ongoing squats in several parts of Manchester, so

Castlefield was not an obvious choice but Joe and Donna explained the choice differently from their anonymous MNB colleague mentioned earlier. Their explanation is worth quoting at length:

MLO: OK, but you did go to Castlefield so there must have been some reason.

Donna: A lot of demonstrations end there don't they in the [pause]

MLO: In the Arena?

Donna: Yea in the Arena and lots of rallies and marches end there. They are usually the most boring tedious ends to demonstrations ever because you get lots of socialist speakers…

Joe: And you are shut away from the public. You can say that there's radical stuff happening in Castlefield. If you have a more cynical view you would say that they don't want you

Figure 8.8: MNB's 'Symbolic appropriation of Jacksons Wharf, Castlefield (2008 photo © Donna of MNB)

in Piccadilly Gardens or Albert Square [two monumental civic public spaces].

Donna: Yea.

Joe: You are in this sanitised space where no one's gonna see you.

Donna: Yea, because if you're having a rally there then you're not bothering anyone but if you're trying to do it in the middle of Market Street then, they probably just wouldn't let you do it [laughing].

Joe: So that's why we wanted to start in a very public place but we also knew there were good reasons for going to Castlefield, which was the Jacksons Wharf.

Donna: Yea.

MLO: So you knew about that building before?

Donna: Yea.

MLO: How did you know about it?

Donna: It didn't come from me individually. I think it came from some of the people who had been involved in squatting in Manchester.

Joe: We wanted to do something public en masse so we wanted to do a mass action. The squat was symbolic and it's unusual for a large group of over 200 people to do a squat. It's usually a small group that cracks the squat. It's almost a bit elitist.

Donna: But I guess the end part of the day to occupy a building and to have a bit of a party was really for us, wasn't it? [looking at Joe] It was to bring together this group of 200 people, a bonding thing and working together. It definitely wasn't chosen for its visible location. We knew we'd be out of the way but I guess that made it easier for us. (Donna and Joe 2010)

MNB's choice of Castlefield emerges therefore out of complex interconnections of interlocking rationales related to visibility, invisibility, prior knowledge and an estimation of the probability that the squat could be implemented successfully. On the other hand St George's School protesters had pragmatic reasons for choosing Castlefield: it was free and convenient. However, of the activist groups only MNB imbued Castlefield space with political meaning per se and the fact that the group felt comfortable occupying the space is important. MNB's interventions are in one sense spontaneous unregulated triumphs for the production of differential space. However, the temptation to see Castlefield naïvely as some kind of post-industrial differential space paradise should be resisted. It is better conceptualised as a circumscribed differential space subject to the exercise of a certain amount of state surveillance, control and power, evidenced by the police presence at an anti-war/austerity protest rally at Castlefield Arena.

Figure 8.9: Police surveillance of an anti-war/austerity protest rally at Castlefield Arena

It should now be evident that the relationship between abstract space and differential space is a complex one. It is not simply that abstract space is always dominant or that differential space is achieved through a once and for all victory. Depending on the particular constellation

of spatial characteristics, opportunities and constraints, differential space can erupt into abstract space briefly or over a sustained time period. However, the reverse can happen. Progenitors of abstract space seek continually to overthrow differential space and return it to homogeneity and exchange value. It is better to think of the relationship between abstract and differential space as a continuous dialectical cyclical struggle. Figure 8.10 represents this cycle visually by what is called the differential triad. Several characteristics of the spatial triad and the production of differential and abstract space are implied here. This representation of an alternative spatial triad to Lefebvre's more familiar one has several key characteristics implied in the graphics. The visual symbolism should be interpreted as follows: dotted lines on some of the arrows indicate that process and outcome are uncertain and unpredictable but nevertheless non-chaotic and non-random. Differential space production is non-hierarchical, cyclical and therefore non-linear. The dotted lines of the three spatial moments of the triad imply that they are not bounded and isolated from each other or the social, economic and political context.

Figure 8.10: The differential space triad: a cycle of differential space production

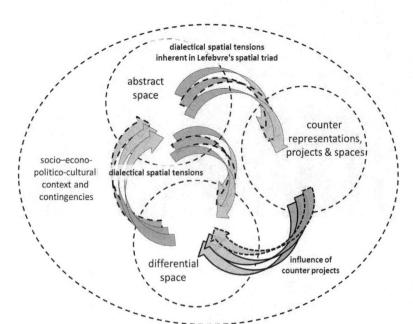

Conclusions

Differential space has been shown in this chapter to derive from diverse origins and manifest in varied appropriations of urban public space. Beneath the surface of abstract space, the chapter has confirmed the powerful potential inherent in the public spaces of the deceptively prosaic city streets alluded to by Lefebvre in this chapter's epigraph. This chapter has presented the finale of the major theoretical theme and the case study empirical analyses. Theoretically, the chapter goes beyond Lefebvre, presenting an innovative conceptualisation on the basis of a tight intimacy between the right to the city and differential space. In this understanding, differential space is not seen as a kind of third space nor is it seen as pre-existing, rather it is understood as the product of dialectical contradictions within abstract space arising from what may be called the publicness of public space. Differential space is seen to emerge inadvertently, once the conditions for its production coalesce. The theoretical power and empirical utility of differential space is shown to derive both from its ambiguous nature and precise characteristics specified by Lefebvre. Differential space is synonymous with a range of spatial interpretations and understanding and when viewed from this perspective it is apparent that a significant international research community is working within a Lefebvrian tradition, although some researchers may not be aware of the fact. If Paris May '68 was the inspiration for the right to the city, then Nanterre University in the same year inspired Lefebvre's conceptualisation of differential space.

Each of the case studies reveals a particular genesis and constellation of differential space characteristics dependent on local contingencies. In each case the production of space is by no means straightforward, obvious or inevitable. It is only through mapping out the intricacies and connections between the archival data, interviews and street level observations, that the processes which produce differential space can be understood. In the case of Vancouver, the ludic and politicised facets of differential space were present as the Smoke-in merged into riot. What the Gastown Days Festival did was to consolidate the post-industrial transformation of the area and valorise the use value appropriation of public space by a diversity of ordinary inhabitants. In raising awareness of the potential for the peaceful occupation of public space on a large scale, the festival also indicated the positive role such events play in the creation of improved place image. From the spatial contradictions inherent in the Gastown riot emerged a set of transformative spatial moments that produced the heritage-valorised differential space of Maple Tree Square and the free Gastown/Vancouver Jazz Festival. New insights in this chapter demonstrate how the official representations of urban planners can be disrupted as both wealthy tourists and poor marginalised people cross imaginary boundaries in the production of differential space with high use value.

In Lowell it is clear that a public sector civic ethos combined with the city's industrial history to produce a new public space animated by significant cultural events of assembly. A complex array of interlinkages between current and historical discourses and the aspirations of the public and not-for-profit sectors blended to privilege urban space use value over exchange value. In bringing the NFF to Lowell, the local protagonists drew on the positive attributes of the city's ethnically diverse communities and the cultural remit of LNHP and LHPC. In Lefebvrian terms the LFF transforms downtown Lowell temporarily into a site of ludic differential urban public space. That said, it is not claimed that a kind of urban idyll is produced. Rather the differential space of the festival is one held in continual dialectical tension. The putative middle class dominance and the use of the city's regulatory code indicate the homogenising potential which could be at work to vitiate the production of differential space.

Rather like the case of Gastown, differential space in Castlefield erupted subsequent to a traumatic act. In Castlefield the research in this chapter has revealed the creation of ludic everyday differential space and formal, politicised space. Rather like BHP, the public space of Castlefield Arena was at its inception indeterminate and flexible in character, awaiting the imprint of social interaction and meaning. Castlefield's unique history, topography and spatial meanings endow it with contradictory qualities and differential space potentials, which serve to facilitate *and* hobble political activism and efforts to claim rights to the city. On the one hand the Arena area is a large, well maintained, easily accessible public space where powerful institutions and state apparatus adopts light touch management strategies. On the other hand because it does not encompass traditional thoroughfares, Castlefield is understood as public space that activists are pushed into because they become invisible, shorn of political influence.

If space were only material this would be a problem but in occupying Castlefield's material public space, political activism occupies concomitant imagined and virtual spaces of representation. A great diversity of politicised interests therefore gain access to the wider public sphere of the internet where differential space is made visible through activists' own efforts to memorialise and preserve their ephemeral disruptions of abstract space. In common with other research, the case studies elucidate that the appropriation of public space and the production of differential space for its use value can be evanescent but of no less value for that. It demonstrates real possibilities for the overthrow of abstract space and the creation of a new urban reality, one informed by Lefebvre's ideas, but one rooted firmly in contemporary contingency.

NINE

Conclusions: Differential space implications

The hypercomplexity of social space should by now be apparent, embracing as it does individual entities and peculiarities ... The principle of the interpenetration and superimposition of social spaces has one very helpful result, for it means that each fragment of space subjected to analysis makes not just one social relationship but a host of them that analysis can potentially disclose. (Lefebvre 1991: 88)

All the same, the necessary inventiveness can only spring from interaction between plans and counter-plans, projects and counter-projects. (Not that such interaction should be seen as excluding ripostes *in kind* to the violence of established political powers.) The possibility of working out counter-projects, discussing them with the 'authorities' and forcing those authorities to take them into account, is thus a gauge of 'real' democracy. (Lefebvre 1991: 419–20. emphasis in original)

Substantiations, refutations, surprises

Public space may be the city synecdoche *par excellence* but it can also be deeply ambivalent. Without doubt the original research in this book exposes the importance of the production of urban public space for post-industrial city transformation. Case study research of three cities in three countries, big theoretical conjectures and a cornucopia of spatial fragments, rendered coherent through theoretically informed, robust analysis, have disclosed the importance of social relationships in the production of space. In so doing the book has brought forth a remarkable range of empirical data, leading to strong evidence for the production of differential space. The book contributes to the development of the debate by bringing into the public domain for the first time fresh insights arising from new and reinterpreted data. On this historicised, analytical journey, several of Lefebvre's important theoretical suppositions have been substantiated empirically.

Unexpectedly, a number of what might be called lost histories have been recovered, resulting in some surprising revelations. Empirical exposés extend the book's contribution into the realm of problematising what are called the dominant academic narratives.

The book encourages a radical rethink beyond the accepted ways of understanding the spatial triad and its relationship with abstract space, differential space and the right to the city. Differential space has been found to coexist through time with other Lefebvrian spatial moments. Therefore, the book makes noteworthy contributions through disclosures about hypercomplexity in the production of urban space; identifying spatial fragments and plotting their relationships and influences. This chapter provides space to reflect on the research objectives and gaze outward towards the wider academic world, the material city and the city of the imagination beyond.

To paraphrase Lefebvre, the research has reconnected elements that have been severed and replaced confusion with clear distinctions; it has rejoined the disconnected and reanalysed the commingled. On reflection one overarching conclusion can be stated succinctly before the empirical and theoretical elaborations which follow. It is that a theoretically robust, critical appreciation of the production of urban public space requires a careful engagement with the histories of the elements of Lefebvre's spatial triad. Analyses of the role of counter-projects in such an endeavour are vital. This engagement can best be achieved through the deployment of mixed methods research aimed at the discovery, interrogation and interpretation of differential space

This book set out to explore critically and unravel investigatively the production of urban public space focusing principally on the era of the 1960s–2010s. A range of implications for the production of differential space has been mapped for three iconic post-industrial cities. Methodologically, the mixed research methods approach based on a series of methodological clues provided by Lefebvre delivered a tough but flexible empirical framework allowing for qualitative analyses used iteratively throughout the research process. Through exploratory research the book has disclosed city centre space to be a highly complex, contested palimpsest produced by multifarious social relationships. Its complexity has compounded through time with the accretion of layers of subsequent spatial practice, and through the myriad official and unofficial representations of space. Complexity extends also to the imaginative, artistic spaces of representation and differential spaces that have defined the case study areas intermittently over the decades but particularly since the post-industrial reimagining and physical transformations of the 1970s onwards. Lefebvre's musings regarding the hypercomplex could therefore have been written with this research in mind.

Two critically informed theoretical relationships with the ideas articulated in Lefebvre's inspiring text *The Production of Space* have been developed progressively throughout the book. First, the research is grounded in the loose framework provided by the spatial triad. Second, the research of necessity moved beyond what Lefebvre admits is not a total system for researching the production of space, by asking fundamental questions about the nature of differential space, its relationship with the right to the city and its mode of its production in three specific contexts. In expounding the importance of the key research findings, this final chapter moves from substantive, empirical specifics to theoretical generalities. Before reaching this point, the implications of the research for the dominant academic narratives are elucidated. Reflections on methodological implications are presented. Suggestions for the praxis of those who would continue to research the production of urban public space are provided. Pointers to urban policy implications and suggestions for the future production of public and differential space are offered, caveated appropriately, given the qualitative case study methodology.

Empirical disclosures of similarity

Obviously, each of the three case study cities lies within a unique concatenation of historical, geographical, political, economic and social contingencies. What is remarkable, however, are the number of striking similarities in both the production of space processes and what may be called the spatial products. Chief among these revealed by the research is the existence and variety of differential spaces in each city. Lefebvre identified several types of differential space associated with different rights to the city. Ludic differential space of festivals, carnivals and concerts was found to exist in each case study area. Strong politicised spaces of demonstrations and rallies seeking either to claim various rights or offer resistance of various kinds were also identified. In Castlefield and Gastown, differential politicised space was appropriated spontaneously, informally and formally. A noticeable feature of all the differential space identified is its transient, fleeting nature. This should be viewed as a strength because such space is difficult to predict, difficult to control and probably impossible to eradicate in a democratic society. Hence, it appears there is significant potential for the production of differential space in the ordinary, everyday streets, squares and parks, but also in more monumental civic spaces.

Differential space therefore has the capacity to erupt and penetrate into abstract space at certain times. One of the more remarkable findings concerns the way differential space was produced in Gastown through the individual appropriation of space by residents of DTES. At such moments, there is a transient merging of the highly commodified spaces of Gastown and use value social relations centred on charitable giving and not-for-profit activity. Even where spatial appropriations are organised by civic authorities, I would argue they still represent a kind of differential space because they possess important freedoms, of access and expression. They are inclusive and available to anybody and everybody. Having said that, differential space is not a chaotic and anarchic free for all. It would be naïve to imagine that some kind of urban utopia is constructed at these moments. Everyday internalised societal rules apply and at times behaviour in public may well be surveilled by the police or private security agents. Nevertheless, politicised differential space happenings are an important democratic marker and demonstrate the vital importance of public space for an open, tolerant society.

Spatial collaboration conducted through diverse coalitions of interest characterise the production of space in the three cities. And despite increasing neoliberal hegemony, public sector coalitions and a civic ethos were also undoubtedly important. That said, the private sector played a noticeable role in the production of urban public space in the cities, sometimes in public–private partnerships. The research has revealed the key role played by historic preservation societies in conjuring counter-representations and counter-projects based on heritage valorisation as a basis for post-industrial futures. Lefebvre's observations that the production of space often occurs slowly is borne out by the empirical research. Heritage preservation advocates had to be prepared for a long haul in their struggle to challenge the dominant, official modernist representations which devalorised historic city space.

What might be called the 'will to demolish' spurred the construction of diverse spatial coalitions in each city, initiating struggles to establish alternative representations of space. In Lefebvrian terms the diverse spatial coalitions devised counter-projects based on alternative representations of space. Forcing city governments to recognise their legitimacy signified tangible democratic victories. Insider status certainly helped particularly with Patrick Mogan in Lowell and Francis Hawcroft and David Rhodes in Manchester. Each city saw the designation of a historic preservation area in the 1970s. That is hardly revelatory; what is important though is the fact that these designations brought with them important financial resources from national governments and other sources beyond the city. In the case of Gastown, archival data have revealed crucial provincial and federal funding, without which the production of Gastown public space would have stalled or been painfully slow.

In this era of apparently omnipotent neoliberalism, it is interesting to note the forging from the 1970s of *public sector* partnerships before *and during* the onset of the neoliberal milieux. Such partnerships offered resistance to powerful entrenched development interests especially in Vancouver and Manchester. Their pursuit of historic designation was not to further the production of abstract space. Indeed designation was far from unproblematic for downtown Lowell and Castlefield. Advocates in both cities struggled over time to establish the historic credentials of the area in the face of calls for modernist redevelopment

Policy intertextuality has been revealed for each city. Its characteristics are manifestly different from both policy incrementalism and path dependency. Archival and interview data have revealed that it was not just past policy and past decisions which shaped relevant urban planning policies, it was the also counter-representations of space, particularly those promulgated by heritage preservation interests. In each case study changes to urban policy were incorporated into official policy from unofficial reports and documents. That incorporation was not straightforward and simply imitative. Public sector, politicians and planners reshaped the reconfigured representations of space according to local priorities, funding and ideologies. And it was not so much past decisions that influenced urban policy development but rather past representations of space.

What was found to be constant across the case studies was a certain public or civic spiritedness which espoused tenaciously the importance public space. New, enhanced and beautified public spaces were regarded in each city as fundamental to post-industrial reconfiguration, particularly in the 1970s and 1980s. In the 1990s and 2000s, rather than an outright capitulation to revanchist neoliberalism, an uneven and complex spatial pattern becomes apparent with the emergence of what is called here quasi-public space.

Another common feature, historically and more recently, revealed by the empirical research is the importance of festivals, carnivals and ludic space generally for the animation of new and enhanced public space. Such space in the case of Lowell and Manchester was seen to be initially undetermined or indeterminate in terms of societal meaning. It was through festivals and carnivals that social meaning was imprinted on urban public space in the three case study areas. Traumatic events in Vancouver and Manchester were vital to the transformation of public space and the emergence of carnival, festival and public spectacle. One would not advocate trauma as a public policy trigger, but the 1996 IRA Manchester bomb and the 1971 Gastown riot did much to reconfigure post-industrial imaginations and initiate material public space projects on the ground. Regarding the politico-economic context for the production of space, it is important to realise that globalised neoliberalism is not the enemy of public space per se. In Vancouver, the development company the Town Group Ltd enhanced public space significantly, in conjunction with the restoration and adaptive reuse of the Alhambra Hotel. In Lowell the private sector collaborated in the creation of the significant public space of new parks and the Canalway. In Castlefield, the neoliberal orientated CMDC helped to produce new public space from what was formerly the private space of the MSCC and Peel Holdings. In Lowell and Castlefield, privately owned urban space exhibits some qualities of genuine public space – it is quasi-public space.

Emergent differences

Given the uniqueness of each city, it is unsurprising that significant differences in the production of public space emerged in the research. In Gastown the local, small scale private sector was instrumental in the 1960s in its efforts to endow the area with heritage value not so much through alternative representations of space but more through direct financial investment in historic adaptive reuse schemes which, crucially provided for new public space. Alongside this, the involvement of Chinatown community groups in the seminal 1969 *Restoration Report* was crucial. This was not a historic preservation interest group report per se, but a co-commissioned study and official VCC policy. While the boundaries of the designated historic areas for Lowell and Manchester excluded significant residential populations, in Gastown, a significant working class and marginalised population was included. Undoubtedly, this resulted in some degree of gentrification, which spilled over into neighbouring DTES. That aspect of the research findings is explored further in the next section.

In Lowell no sudden traumatic event catalysed the production of public space. On the contrary, a slower process led eventually to the acceptance into the federal mainstream of what started as a counter-project of heritage spatial valorisation. Unlike the other two cities, in Lowell the spatial coalition which reimagined a heritage-led post-industrial future was so successful that it transformed the federal understanding of a national park. Along with the creation of a unique sister organisation, LHPC, with its exceptional cultural focus and preservation grant remit, there are few clearer indications of Lefebvre's claims for the wider societal impact of the production of space. Local community roles in the production of space in each city are markedly different. In Castlefield there was no resident local community but this did not prevent a certain kind of spatially entrenched, civic spiritedness emerging within CMDC. In Vancouver community involvement was on the one hand mediated by local (not-for-profit) organisations and interest groups and on the other by concerned individuals. Broad based community support for the national park idea in Lowell was crucial for attracting federal support but more importantly the contribution of local community organisations to Lowell Model Cities public space projects had profound, positive ramifications for the campaign to establish a national park.

Recovery of lost histories

Recurring themes, actors, organisations and opinions shaped a dominant academic narrative regarding each city and though it was never the intention to dispute that research, what emerged through the archival and interview data were lost facts, new facts, new perspectives and a different range of important actors and influential organisations. Rather than only the usual suspects, new names must now take their place in production of space histories. In Vancouver Evelyn McKechnie helped achieve the near impossible by persuading conservative Mayor Tom Campbell of Gastown's historic credentials. Harold Kalman gained fame as a Vancouver architectural historian and heritage expert but he should also be acknowledged for his pivotal role in saving the Stanley and New Fountain Hotels from demolition, securing their adaptive reuse and facilitating the production of new public space at Blood Alley Square. Larry Killam ought to be remembered not just as the man behind the Hotel Alhambra restoration and Gassy Jack statue but also as the man who initiated the installation of Gastown's popular but often reviled 'Victorian' streetlights. Organisations such as the Vancouver Community Arts Council, the Gastown Merchants Association, the Pacific Community Self Development Society and the Pacific Jazz and Blues Association also played vital but neglected roles in the production of Gastown public space.

A notable contribution of the research is the recovery of lost spatial histories in the three cities. A name not associated before with Lowell's heritage-led post-industrial transformation is Jimmy Hoffa. Without a Teamsters' loan in the 1970s Lowell's path to national park status would have taken an entirely different trajectory and may have gone totally awry. Whether Hoffa will eventually be found in Lowell is something about which we can only speculate. Michael and Susan Southworth merit respect and a place in the public record for the role they played in reimagining and representing visually an alternative future for downtown Lowell. In Lowell, the role of certain organisations and institutions in the production of space have been ignored, particularly the Lowell Regatta and the work of Model Cities in enhancing and producing new public space. And although LHSP is often mentioned in passing in the literature, it played an absolutely vital role in focusing on the historic canals and conducting excruciating but ultimately successful negotiations with the sometimes cantankerous L&C. It formed with LNHP one of several neoliberal resisting public sector partnerships also ignored in the literature.

In Manchester the research has recovered lost histories relating to contributions to the production of space by the Greater Manchester Council, the Historic Buildings Council, the Victorian Society and the Georgian Group, although the latter *refused* to pay £1 for the Liverpool Road Railway Station. Manchester and Lowell have been shown to be connected, not just by the industrial espionage of Francis Cabot Lowell, but by a fact finding sojourn in the opposite direction by a delegation from England which included representation from Manchester. Michael Heseltine's critical but overlooked interventions in Castlefield have been elucidated by this research. More surprising, though, were the interview revelations which throw new light on the origins of the urban development corporations. Unpredictably, interview data have revealed for the first time the role played by Dame Jennifer Jenkins in (re)presenting Castlefield space and at 93 years old in 2015 she can still feel proud of that. The research has revealed the existence of two 1970s reports each produced in distinctly unusual circumstances. Appreciation of these reports is necessary for a fuller understanding of Castlefield's spatial history.

Urban planners and politicians in the three cities all resorted to what might be called the production of simulacra as part of their revitalisation strategies. In Vancouver, Lowell and Manchester there are significant similarities in the manner in which public officials devoted significant resources and intellectual effort to ensuring a degree of authenticity characterised the replica streetlights, streetcars and bridges respectively. If visitor and tourist reaction is any guide the simulacra are more real than the real thing. This finding adds another layer of complexity to the production of urban space. This is particularly ironic since Gastown's distinctive globe streetlights have been condemned consistently over the years as Victorian fakes by academics and journalists alike. The eliding of the historical provenance of Gastown streetlights indicates a quirkiness of history; it often clings to alluring myth with a tighter grip than it applies to fact.

Methodological reflections

A major theme of the book is the need for production of space research to take seriously the need for a rigorous engagement with the history of representations of space, spatial coalitions and counter-projects. The exploratory production of space research outlined here, concerned with the recent past of living memory, was eminently amenable to a mixed methods approach. This allowed the research to be both guided by the research priorities and an iterative, grounded theory approach. The power of mixed methods became apparent as the research progressed. Using a variety of sources, it became possible to correct some long established misinformation regarding the production of urban space, particularly regarding the 'fake' Gastown streetlights and the £1 Liverpool Road Station claim. Significant facts and opinions, brought to light for the first time, are endowed with greater credibility where they are corroborated by several sources in the data, allowing significant original contributions to be made in the field of production of space research. The range of research methods and sources deployed allowed for two way corroboration between archival and interview data. Perhaps most importantly though, the range of data allowed a far richer and subtly differentiated picture of urban space to be constructed for the case study cities than has hitherto been possible.

Two important kinds of networks have been revealed by and helped facilitate the research. First, what may be called the active archival network based on mixed methods research produced credible, robust data vital for the generation of new knowledge. Of most importance were the physical archival depositories. They ranged from the formal archives of public, private and not-for-profit institutions to the private 'archives' of individuals involved directly in the production of space. Second, interpenetrating coalitions of socio-political networks emerged as a key feature in the production of space and the research methodology was flexible enough to allow the mapping of the resulting spatial fragments and social relationships.

There is the potential for archival data to point dynamically to various relevant people, whether living or deceased. It became evident that archivists are dynamic catalysts which animate what some might regard as dusty old records by identifying relevant sources known only to them and by pointing to other relevant archives, archivists and other potentially relevant actors and organisations. Without the assistance of the archivists and interviewees and the discovery of the embedded networks of intertextualities, the empirical data would have not proved so rich or insightful. Archivists do not just assist with publicly accessible, catalogued data. There is always more in official archives than identified in the catalogue. Archivists have the power and discretion to make such data available if they so wish. Archivists provided access to boxes of relevant uncatalogued records at important key moments in the research, especially in Lowell and Manchester. Often regarded as a separate source, it became evident that research interviewees also help constitute the active archival network. They serve a similar research function as the archivists, pointing to other sources, including potential interviewees, and providing important interpretations regarding not just substantive issues but data sources too.

There is much to be said methodologically for interviewing research subjects about events long in their past since professional, political and other sensitivities have inevitably diminished allowing for more hard edged, candid 'backstage' revelations. Helpfully, the mixed methods approach allowed their memories to be corroborated by archival data. At times during the research the interviewees pointed to relevant archives and of course three of them have constructed their own personal archives. Easily available published research, usually regarded as secondary sources, also served a vital animation role in the archival network when it pointed to relevant archival sources and potential interviewees. Conceptualising all the data sources as constituents of an archival network and being open minded enough to follow potential research clues allowed the rediscovery of the diverse lost histories and fragments in the production of space alluded to earlier. Academics and researchers also constitute elements of the active archival networks. Finally, and reflexively, my different roles as an active element in what are undoubtedly socially constructed archival networks should not be overlooked: urbanist, scholar, detective, insider/outsider, provocateur and story teller.

Urban policy implications

To reiterate what was said in the introduction to this book, the case studies were not conceived or configured from an applied urban policy research perspective. Urban policy and planning are nevertheless undeniably implicated seriously in the production of urban public space. Offering policy and practice generalisations from qualitative research based on three case studies is fraught with conceptual and practical dangers. It would be naïve to suggest that urban policymakers, professionals and local communities should simply imitate some of the obviously successful spatial campaigns illuminated in these pages. There are particular reasons to be cautious about proffering glib prescriptions that would take the form 'to produce differential space one should…'

The three cities have their unique attributes, but shared a specific political and economic context at the start of the historical research period and that was a broad Keynesian consensus, by the end it was a broad neoliberal consensus. It would no doubt be possible to discover how the operation of neoliberalism differed in the cities but that was beyond the scope of the research. The economic and social trajectory of the cities went from industrial growth, to decline, to post-industrial reimagining inspired by heritage valorisation, only possible because of a significant stock of what became treasured historic buildings, structures, spaces and cultural assets. Strong relatively well resourced government from the local to the national also characterised the cities as did the active civil society institutions and networks. Before the internet, the press played its part in the production of urban public space, in ways which still remain to be elucidated fully. Finally, all the cities were in the Global North. The less these characteristics apply, the more caution needs to be exercised in generalising from the case studies.

Is any kind of generalisation impossible then? I would say not. Cities have universal characteristics. Chief among these is the presence, character and role of public space. This is one of the defining features of cities. Settlements not constituted at least in part by public space infused with abstract and differential qualities are in fact not cities. If they exist, and they probably do not, we do not yet have a name for them. Although outside the scope of the research, it is evident that even the highly regulated and controlled spaces of modern colonial and apartheid cities had to have 'public' space in order to function effectively, as do gated communities in the current era. In all cities urban public space is produced through dialectical tensions inherent in some variant of the spatial triad. Spatial contestations instigated and pursued by spatial coalitions across a broad spectrum exist in all cities. Everyday users of urban space and those who seek to instigate counter-projects that run in opposition to official representations exist in all cities. Demands for the right to the city are a globalised phenomenon which shows no signs of abatement. Such demands tend to be articulated in material public urban space through the production of differential space. These reasons to be cautious and reasons to be optimistic about generalisation should be borne in mind by readers of all kinds interested in participating actively in the production of urban public space.

It is clear that the empirical findings expose all kinds of possibilities in Lefebvre's production of space ideas which are usually overlooked in the literatures. While it would unwise to seek to specify a blueprint for how urban planners, politicians, local communities and the private sector should produce future urban public space, I do consider it legitimate at this point to offer some suggestions for the reorientation of urban policy towards Lefebvrian centred praxis. At the centre of this approach must be an understanding of urban public space based on the spatial triad. Urban public space particularly when it harbours differential qualities should be appreciated as both an incubator of democracy and a theatre where democratic values can be expressed, cherished and subjected to public scrutiny. Spatial coalitions pursuing counter-projects based on counter-representations are the keys to unlocking potential for the production of differential space. Such coalitions will be most effective and more likely to succeed in the necessary long run, when they include a diversity of interests across the spectrum of: professional, political, community, and public and private sector interests. That does not mean counter-projects for the production of differential space cannot be instigated by one particular interest group. What it does mean, however, is that because of the contested nature of what occurs in public space, without broader support counter-projects may well be unsustainable. It does not matter which sector initiates a counter-project, what matters is that stable, diverse and committed coalitions can be instigated with the tenacity to engage in long term spatial struggles to establish genuine public and differential space.

Those who would aspire to produce new public space and differential space should appreciate several factors germane to the process and outcome. Dedicated individuals and small groups backed by larger coalitions of volunteers can be successful even in the face of the state and neo-capitalist institutional structures. Most communities including diasporic communities have historical and cultural traditions on which they can draw to animate relevant spatial campaigns. A notable feature of the spatial campaigns highlighted in the empirical chapters is that they all started at the small scale with a few people. What offers hope and direction for future policy and production of space practice, is the wide and diverse range of interests that can potentially become involved in initiating counter-projects and counter-spaces based on the articulation of counter-representations of space. Willing collaborators should not be excluded simply because of their political orientation or because they happen to be based in the private, public or not-for-profit sector. Differential space is predicated on diversity so excluding collaborators on the basis of their age, gender, social class or ethnicity should be resisted. Compromise and negotiation are vital in the production of urban public space in two senses. They are vital because spatial coalitions are and should be as diverse as possible, so participants need to be able to resolve emerging internal tensions. They are vital because officialdom is likely to resist counter-projects at the outset and perhaps for years, so without compromise and negotiation spatial campaigns will tend to prove frustrating and founder on the intransigence of entrenched interests with allegiance to abstract space. In the early 21st century the internet and social media have obvious potential for the creation and maintenance of the spatial coalitions, in ways that obviously go beyond anything that Lefebvre could have specified. Activists, communities, politicians and professionals should devise imaginative ways to unleash the power of the internet for the production of urban public space. Anyone with a passing acquaintance with social media will realise that this is happening already, but the praxis will be stronger if it is overtly Lefebvrian.

Even under conditions of neoliberalised, state regulated neo-capitalism, the potential for the production of new urban public space and the concomitant use value, differential space is omnipresent. Unfortunately, what might be thought of as a spatial mirror reflects a rather unsavoury possibility. Just as abstract space harbours the seeds of its own vulnerability, so those who would engage seriously in the production of differential space should be aware that it too contains seeds which may erupt into forms of destructive homogenised, exchange value, abstract space. The consequences of this realisation for urban policy and practice and community activism are twofold. First, Lefebvrian spatial coalitions which do achieve some measure of differential space must appreciate the need for continuous vigilance and preparedness for continual struggle for its protection and enhancement. Second, a contrary strategy could be deployed based on the understanding that even temporary differential space is a precious, immanent constituent of urban life. The potentially painful implication here is that the cost of protecting some differential space might be excessive and it may be better to suspend the struggle and relocate it geographically or temporarily or both. Conceptualised in this way, it may be necessary for counter-projects to be organised metaphorically, along the lines of long term guerrilla warfare ready to pop up here and there as opportunities arise.

Future research possibilities

Although the research extended over a period of years allowing sufficient time to make significant empirical and theoretical contributions, it was over all too soon. I would not pretend the research outlined in this book is either definitive or exhaustive. Having tried for perfection, the research ultimately in its transparent, robust comprehensiveness merely flirts with it asymptotically. The future offers myriad possibilities. To invoke Lefebvre's prose-poetic metaphor, disconnected production of space fragments, like flakes of the *mille-feuille*, still abound in profusion and apparent spatial confusion, awaiting the intrepid researcher. Future research could be intensive or extensive in nature. Intensive research should focus on deepening our knowledge and understanding of the production of space in the three case study cities. Extensive future research would concentrate on deploying the kind of approach taken here to a range of different temporal, geographical and thematic contexts.

Intensive research concentrated on the three cities could search for different spatial coalitions using archival, interview and visual sources. Historical research could trace the rise (and fall) of counter-projects and spaces that may or may not have produced differential space. One would expect the relevant city council, state, provincial, national and federal archives to provide a rich source for this kind of research endeavour. There is potential too for production of space research in Vancouver to access non-public sector archives such as those of the Vancouver Community Arts Council, the Town Group, Woodwards and Canadian Pacific Railway. In Lowell researchers could turn to the archives of the L&C, the Lowell Plan and the LDFC. For the production of Castlefield, space researchers could interrogate the archives of Peel Holdings, Castlefield Estates Ltd, GTV (now ITV) and the Victorian Society. An expectation of being denied access should not inhibit researchers from knocking on archival doors beyond the more obvious ones.

Researchers could unearth further the spatial coalitions and processes through which the traumatic events of riot and bomb in Vancouver and Manchester respectively contributed to the production of ludic differential space. Following the research presented in this book, intensive research to uncover and explain the importance of the politicised appropriations of public space in the production of differential space is required. Occupations of public space and abandoned space, demonstrations and activist rallies are often transitory but their obvious importance for the production of space has barely been explored. And researchers in the three cities should focus on the spatial coalition dynamics and counter-projects which bring these spaces of resistance into being.

Production of space in the three case study cities is not bounded by their city limits or national geographies. Although it was not the focus of research for this book, a number of international spatial coalitions have been unearthed. It has been said many times before and quite rightly so that the history of Manchester for example is also the history of Lagos, Kingston Jamaica, Hong Kong and Kolkata. Future Lefebvrian orientated research ought to be developed, for example, into the spatial linkages between Vancouver and Beijing, Lowell and Québec and Manchester and any number of cities in the Global North and Global South.

In that respect researchers could start by walking into Manchester Town Hall's Great Hall, lifting their eyes to the ceiling and picking one of the cities depicted there. These are the great 19th century cities. They were Manchester's global trading partners in its heyday of industrial dominance. Such research offers the potential to transform radically our understanding of mutually constitutive linkages between cities in the Global South and North. Treating cities not as discrete entities but relationally and tracking global interconnectedness in the production of urban space would be a fascinating and insightful venture. Ethnic and class diversities as sources and resources for the production of space in the case study cities deserve further research attention. The roles played by people of colour, working class inhabitants and apparently marginalised peoples in the production of space in Vancouver, Lowell and Manchester merit being brought into the public domain through the Lefebvrian lens. Although to be fair, for Lowell it is evident a start has been made.

Extensive research holds myriad, mind boggling future prospects. Lefebvrian inspired research along the lines outlined in this book could be applied to any city for which substantial archival sources can be accessed. Useful archives may not of course be in the target city, for example substantial archival material exists in Britain which could form the basis for production of space research focused on postcolonial cities in the Global South and vice versa. Future research needs to give more attention than was possible in this book to everyday spaces which have historically and continue to resist the forces of abstract space. Future research should revisit the new town, condemned so thoroughly by Lefebvre but that condemnation was in the early stages of its production. It is highly unlikely that differential space has not been produced in maturing new towns of the Global North and South. In this book the focus is the inadvertent differential space potential of public space reimagined and produced through heritage-led revitalisation. Future research should explore in depth the public and differential space consequences of coalitions with different thematic substance, such as social housing, public transport, urban agriculture, pop up markets, festivals and carnivals.

Two violent episodes were highlighted in the research as being the catalysts, albeit inadvertently, for the eventual production of differential space. Lefebvre in the opening quote to this chapter does not rule out the use of 'ripostes in kind' to the violence of the state. Future research should seek to address the rather unsettling question, of whether there are any systematic, causal relationships between violent counter-projects and the successful production of differential space. Researchers in the future should now be less burdened than I was by the need to work out for themselves how to construct new, historically grounded, theoretically robust explanatory narratives for the production of urban public space. Similarly, through iterative processes akin to grounded theory, the empirical findings were of great help in clarifying and refining some key theoretical issues in ways which take Lefebvrian research into new terrain appropriate for the 21st century.

Theoretical implications and conjectures

Lefebvre asserts that when counter-space inserts itself into spatial reality, it has the potential to create differential space. From the 1970s this occurred in the case study areas. Through urban planning, beautification, regeneration projects and private investment, public space was created or enhanced. At times new public space lacks firm social meaning. At times it is undetermined or indeterminate space. Through time, it is possible to identify a cycle of differential space production. Under conditions of state regulated neo-capitalism, urban space is impregnated with exchange value creating abstract space. After a while conditions emerge amendable to the production of differential space – the space of use value – which intrudes into abstract space. This can happen spontaneously and unpredictably, or it may be regular, formal and organised. And although differential space has a robustness, it is also paradoxically fragile. This vulnerability results in abstract space being re-asserted through the actions of the private and/or public sectors. This cyclical process was seen at Castlefield and Boarding House Park.

Understanding the production of space through a differential space – right to the city nexus – is a useful way of infusing Lefebvre's sketchy outline with empirical substance. Each differential space occurrence can be thought of as lying somewhere along a spectrum with the democratic spaces of politicised appropriation at one end and ludic spaces of leisure and enjoyment at the other. Wherever they lie, they constitute 'real democracy'. Somewhere in between can be placed appropriated spaces of group or personal identity expression, be they around issues of sexuality, ethnicity, gender or lifestyle. What characterises the production of differential space more than anything else is geographical and temporal complexity. It can pop up here and there unpredictably or with annual regularity. It can have a kind of robust permanence, or it can exhibit transitory delicacy. It is also complicated by the nature and intent of the bodies in public space. So in the case of Vancouver, deliberate political subversion was evident through illegal activity – smoking pot in public. A week later property developers, hippies and police were all complicit in the production of a kind of differential space.

I have noted *en passant* the distinct blurring of representations of space and spaces of representation. Although hinted at with his reference to artists with a scientific bent, this idea is noticeably underdeveloped by Lefebvre and subsequent researchers. The potential blurring facilitates the creation of more powerful representations. In adopting hybrid representations of space, CMDC was responding to the twin art–science foundations of architecture/city planning and following a line mapped out in the florid rhetoric and imagery of Ebenezer Howard and Le Corbusier; rhetoric which empowers the quasi-scientific rationally for which they are better known. Blurring of representational categories in the spatial triad occurred also with the Southworths' imaginative architectural drawings of a heritage orientated future for Boott Mills. Blurring of representations of space and spaces of representation was evident in Gastown where remarkable circularity was evident, reflecting the popular idea of art imitating life and vice versa. The name Blood Alley was conjured out of everyday imagination and an intriguing but licentious mythical rationale generated, again spontaneously. Later the name Blood Alley was incorporated officially into city council representations of space. The mythical rationale later became incorporated into social realist fiction novels. In these novels, the actual details of the material spatial practice of Blood Alley Square appear as social realist 'faction'. A similar circularity of interaction, between the nitty gritty of the Gastown riot and the artistic representations in *Abbott and Cordova 7 August 1971* is evident. Unfortunately, there was no space to pursue these issues in this book, although they would certainly provide a fruitful avenue for future research. Theoretical boundaries in future research should be pushed to explore how artistic spaces of representation have and could influence the production of public space and differential space.

Towards the end of Lefebvre (1991), the implication is that like Marxist post-capitalism, differential space becomes inevitable and universal. However, the research findings here demonstrate that differential space can *co-exist* in dialectical tension with abstract space rather than negating it entirely. Politically appropriated differential space has appeared, disappeared and reappeared in the 2000s in the case study cities and probably in many other cities, which suggests it is not so much teleological as irrepressible. Where urban space is abandoned by capitalist interests and state enterprises, differential space can potentially be produced. Through the lens of the spatial triad, differential space is constituted by and constituent of social relations. Differential space confirms the unquenchable thirst of the human spirit for an urbanism of tolerant, diverse public space – the ultimate city synecdoche – not quite utopia but cause for sanguinity.

In this era when it is easy to lapse into neoliberal provoked fatalistic pessimism, it is important to stress that the production of space, inspired by a public spirited civic ethos can still create city spaces of intrinsic use value – public spaces of hope. Lefebvre posits a utopian post neo-capitalist, urban-centred world order on the horizon: it may emerge eventually. In so doing he highlights the importance of urban space and its production. In this book the research intimates that cities remain as they were in the 19th century, crucibles of societal convulsions and gentler every day, transformative spatial rhythms. Both transformations produce democratic differential space through collective politicised action. It is differential space that erupts through the vulnerabilities of abstract space. It is differential space that becomes the desired outcome of the production of urban public space in the 21st century. So the next opportunity you have to join the throng and participate in the politicised appropriation of city streets – seize your right to the city and revel in the production of differential space.

References

Aalbers, M. B. and Gibb, K. (2014) Housing and the right to the city: introduction to the special issue, *International Journal of Housing Policy*, 14 (3), pp 207–13.

Amin, A. and Thrift, N. (2002) *Cities: Reimagining the Urban*. Cambridge: Polity Press.

Anderson, K. (1991) *Vancouver's Chinatown: Racial Discourse in Canada, 1875–1980*. Montreal: McGill-Queens University Press.

Aronsen, L. (2010) *City of Love and Revolution: Vancouver in the Sixties*. Vancouver: New Star Books.

Arsenault, M. (2003) *Spiked*. Scottsdale, AZ: Poisoned Pen Press.

Astill, K. (2010) The right to protest in a quasi-public space, *Guardian*, 28 October.

Astles, A. R. (1972) Evolution and role of historic and architectural preservation within the North American city. MA Dissertation, Simon Fraser University.

Atkin, J. (2013) Vancouver demystified, *The Source*, 13 (19), accessed online at thelasource.com.

Atkinson, R. (2003) Domestication by cappuccino or a revenge on urban space? Control and empowerment in the management of public spaces, *Urban Studies*, 40 (9), pp 1211–45.

Attoh, K. (2011) What kind of right is the right to the city? *Progress in Human Geography*, 35 (5), pp 669–85.

Bannerman, G. (1974) *Gastown the 107 years*. Vancouver: Lagoon Estates Ltd.

Barnekov, T., Boyle, R. and Rich, D. (1989) *Privatism and urban policy in Britain and the United States*. Oxford: Oxford University Press.

Barnett, C. (2010) Publics and markets: what's wrong with neoliberalism? in: Smith, S. J., Pain, R., Marston, S. A. and Jones, J. P. (eds) *The Sage Handbook of Social Geography*, London: Sage.

BCG (2014) *Vancouver Neighbourhoods*. British Colombia Government, accessed online at http://au.britishcolumbia.travel/vancouver/neighbourhoods.aspx.

Berelowitz, L. (2010) *Dream City: Vancouver and the Global Imagination*. Vancouver: Douglas & McIntyre.

Berman, M. (2006) *On the Town: One Hundred Years of Spectacle in Times Square*. New York: Random House.

Bernardo, C. (2014) Speech by Lowell National Park Superintendent Celeste Bernardo as Peter Aucella received the Thomas G. Kelakos Community Spirit Award, accessed online at www.richardhowe.com.

Bernstein H. S., Sir. (2014) Research email communication with MCC CEO, 7 October.

Blowers, A. and Evans, R. (1997) *Town Planning Into the 21st Century.* London: Routledge.

Bloxham, T. (2001) Creating an Urban Splash: Rehabilitation of Central Sites, in: Echenique, M. and Saint, A. (eds) *Cities for the New Millennium*, London: Taylor & Francis Ltd.

Borden, I., Kerr, J., Rendell, J. and Pivaro, A. (eds) (2001) *The Unknown City: Contesting Architecture and Social Space.* Cambridge, MA: MIT Press.

Borden, I. M. (2001) *Skateboarding, Space and the City: Architecture and the Body.* Oxford: Berg.

Boudreau, M. (2012) The Struggle for a Different World: The 1971 Gastown Riot in Vancouver, in: Campbell, L., Clement, D. and Kealey, G. S. (eds) *Debating Dissent: Canada and the 1960s*, Toronto: University of Toronto Press.

Boyle, P. and Haggerty, K. D. (2011) Civil Cities and urban governance: regulating disorder for the Vancouver Winter Olympics, *Urban Studies*, 48 (15), pp 3185–201.

Bradshaw, L. D. (1986) *Visitors to Manchester: A Selection of British and Foreign Visitors' Descriptions of Manchester from c1538 to 1865.* Manchester: Neil Richardson.

Bramham, D. (2011) Alleys are cities' unexplored, unused treasures, *Vancouver Sun,* 29 July.

Brenner, N. (2001) World city theory, globalization and the comparative-historical method: Reflections on Janet Abu-Lughod's Interpretation of Contemporary Urban Restructuring. *Urban Affairs Review*, 37 (1), pp 124–47.

Brenner, N., Marcuse, P. and Mayer, M. (eds) (2011) *Cities for People, Not for Profit: Critical Urban Theory and the Right to the City.* London: Routledge.

Brenner, N. and Schmid, C. (2015) Towards a new epistemology of the urban, *City: Analysis of Urban Trends, Culture, Theory, Policy, Action,* 19 (2–3), pp 151–82.

Brenner, N. and Theodore, N. (eds) (2002) *Spaces of Neoliberalism: Urban Restructuring in North America and Western Europe.* Oxford: Wiley-Blackwell.

Bridge, G. and Watson, S. (eds) (2010) *The Blackwell City Reader.* 2nd ed. Chichester: Wiley-Blackwell.

Briggs, A. (1963) *Victorian Cities.* Harmondsworth: Penguin.

Brooks, P. C. (1969) *Research in Archives: The Use of Unpublished Primary Sources.* Chicago: University of Chicago Press.

Brown, A. and Kristiansen, A. (2009) *Urban Policies and the Right to the City Rights, responsibilities and citizenship.* Nairobi: UNESCO UN-Habitat.

Brownill, S. (2011) *Docklands Redevelopment: Looking Back, Looking Forwards*, accessed online at oisd.brookes.ac.uk/spatialplanning.

Brownill, S. and O'Hara, G. (2015) From planning to opportunism? Re-examining the creation of the London Docklands Development Corporation, *Planning Perspectives*, DOI 10.1080/02665433.2014.989894.

Brunet-Jailly, E. (2008) Vancouver the Sustainable City, *Journal of Urban Affairs*, 30 (4), pp 375–88.

Bryant, A. and Charmaz, K. (2010) Grounded Theory in historical perspective: Methods and practices, in: Bryant, A. and Charmaz, K. (eds) *The Sage Handbook of Grounded Theory*, London: Sage.

Bryman, A. (2012) *Social Research Methods.* 4th ed. Oxford: Oxford University Press.

Burk, A. L. (2011) *Speaking for a Long Time: Public Space and Social Memory in Vancouver.* Vancouver: University of British Columbia Press.

Burnett, K. (2014) Commodifying poverty: gentrification and consumption in Vancouver's Downtown Eastside, *Urban Geography*, 35 (2), pp 157–76.

Buser, M. (2012) The production of space in metropolitan regions: A Lefebvrian analysis of governance and spatial change, *Planning Theory*, 11 (3), pp 279–98.

Button, M. (2003) Private security and the policing of quasi-public space, *International Journal of the Sociology of Law*, 3 (3), pp 227–37.

Carmona, N. (1999) Three generations of urban renewal policies: analysis and policy implications, *Geoforum*, 30 (2), pp 145–58.

Carp, J. (2009) "Ground-Truthing" representations of social space: Using Lefebvre's conceptual triad, *Journal of Planning Education and Research*, 28 (2), pp 129–42.

Carter, J. (1978) *Lowell National Historical Park Statement on Signing HR 11662 Into Law*, accessed online at presidency.ucsb.edu.

Chow, L., Kudzius, B. and Scott, D. (2009) *Carol Street Greenway Public Realm Improvements & Community Development.* Annual Conference of the Transportation Association of Canada Vancouver, BC.

Clapson, M. and Larkham, P. J. (eds) (2013) *The Blitz and Its Legacy: Wartime Destruction to Post-War Reconstruction.* Farnham: Ashgate.

Cochrane, A., Peck, J. and Tickell, A. (1996) Manchester Plays Games: Exploring Politics of Globalisation, *Urban Studies*, 33 (3), pp 1319–36.

Coolidge, J. (1993) *Mill and mansion: architecture and society in Lowell, Massachusetts, 1820–1865.* Boston, MA: University of Massachusetts Press.

Couch, C., Sykes, O. and Börstinghaus, W. (2011) Thirty years of urban regeneration in Britain, Germany and France: The importance of context and path dependency, *Progress in Planning*, 75 (1), pp 1–52.

Coupland, D. (2009) *City Of Glass.* Vancouver: Douglas & McIntyre.

Cran, B. and Jerome, G. (2008) *Hope in Shadows: Stories and Photographs of Vancouver's Downtown Eastside.* Vancouver: Arsenal Pulp Press and Pivot Legal Society.

Davis, M. (1990) *City of Quartz: Excavating the Future of Los Angeles.* London: Verso.

Davis, M. (2006) *City of Quartz: Excavating the Future of Los Angeles.* 2nd ed. London: Verso.

Dear, M. (2005) Comparative urbanism, *Urban Geography*, 26 (3), pp 247–51.

Deas, I., Robson, B. and Bradford, M. (2000) Re-thinking the urban development corporation 'experiment': the case of Central Manchester, Leeds and Bristol, *Progress in Planning*, 54 (1), pp 1–72.

Degen, M. (2003) Fighting for the global catwalk: formalizing public life in Castlefield (Manchester) and diluting public life in el Raval (Barcelona), *International Journal of Urban and Regional Research*, 27 (4), pp 867–80.

Degen, M. (2008) *Sensing Cities: Regenerating Public Life in Barcelona and Manchester.* London: Routledge.

Dennis, R. (2008) *Cities in Modernity: Representations and Productions of Metropolitan Space, 1840–1930.* Cambridge: Cambridge University Press.

Denzin, N. K. (1970) *The Research Act: A Theoretical Introduction to Sociological Methods.* New York: McGraw Hill.

DoE (1977) *Policy for the Inner Cities (White Paper) Cmnd 6845.* London, NAE: HMSO.

Dowling, N. (2006) Blockade stops canal traffic, *Manchester Evening News*, 27 November.

Douet, J. (ed) (2014) *Industrial Heritage Re-Tooled.* Walnut Creek, CA: Left Coast Press Inc.

Dublin, T. (1992) *Lowell: The Story of an Industrial City.* Washington DC: US Department of the Interior.

Duignan, P. (1993) *The United States: A Hopeful Future.* Hoover Institution, Stanford University.

Eade, J. and Mele, C. (2002) *Understanding City: Contemporary and Future Perspective*, Oxford: John Wiley & Sons.

Elden, S. (2004) *Understanding Henri Lefebvre: Theory and the Possible.* London: Continuum.

Eliot, K. (2008) Demonstration of squatters turns into mass occupation ['Karen Eliot' is the pseudonym adopted by many urban activists], accessed online at indymedia.org.uk.

Fernandes, E. (2007) Constructing the 'Right To the City' in Brazil, *Social & Legal Studies 2007*, 16 (2), pp 201–19.

Ferris, S. (2015) *Street Sex Work and Canadian Cities: Resisting a Dangerous Order.* Edmonton: University of Alberta Press.

Fincher, R. and Iveson, K. (2008) *Planning and Diversity in the City: Redistribution, Recognition and Encounter.* Basingstoke: Palgrave Macmillan.

Fitzgerald, T. (2015) Manchester needs a New-York-style city centre park, say experts, *Manchester Evening News*, 29 January.

Foresta, R. A. (1984) *America's National Parks and Their Keepers.* Washington DC: RFF Press.

Franck, K. and Stevens, Q. (eds) (2006) *Loose Space: Possibility and Diversity in Urban Life.* London: Routledge.

Frangopulo, N. J. (ed) (1962) *Rich Inheritance: A Guide to the History of Manchester.* Manchester: Manchester Education Committee.

Frenchman, D. and Lane, J. J. (2008) *Assessment of Preservation and Development in Lowell National Historical Park at its 30-Year Anniversary.* Washington DC: LNHP.

Fyfe, N. (1996) Contested visions of a modern city: planning and poetry in post war Glasgow, *Environment and Planning A*, 28 (3), pp 387–403.

Gall, L. D. (1991) The Heritage Factor in Lowell's Revitalization, in: Weible, R. (ed) *The Continuing Revolution: A History of Lowell, Massachusetts.* Lowell, MA: Lowell Historical Society.

Gehl, J. (2011) *Life Between Buildings: Using Public Space.* 6th ed. Washington, DC: Island Press.

General Manager of Engineering Services (2006) *Report to the Standing Committee on Planning and Environment*, Vancouver City Council, 27 June.

Gittell, R. (1992) *Renewing Cities.* Princeton, NJ: Princeton University Press.

Goldstein, C. M. (2000) Many voices, true stories, and the experiences we are creating in industrial history museums: Reinterpreting Lowell, Massachusetts, *The Public Historian*, 22 (3), pp 129–37.

Goonewardena, K., Kipfer, S., Milgrom, R. and Schmid, C. (eds) (2008) *Space Difference and Everyday Life: Reading Henri Lefebvre.* London: Taylor Francis.

Gottdiener, M. (1985) *The Social Production of Urban Space.* Austin: University of Texas.

Graham, S. (2011) *Cities Under Siege: The New Military Urbanism.* London: Verso.

Grant, J. L. (2009) Experiential planning: A practitioner's account of Vancouver's success, *Journal of the American Planning Association*, 75 (3), pp. 358–70.

Gray, K. and Gray, S. F. (1999) Civil rights, civil wrongs and quasi-public space, *European Human Rights Law Review*, 1 (4), pp 46–102.

Gregory, D. (1994) *Geographical Imaginations.* Oxford: Blackwell.

Groth, J. and Corijn, E. (2005) Reclaiming urbanity: Indeterminate spaces, informal actors and urban agenda setting, *Urban Studies*, 42 (3), pp 503–26.

Gutstein, D. (1975) *Vancouver Ltd.* Toronto: James Lorimer & Company Ltd.

Hall, T., Hubbard, P. and Short, J. R. (eds) (2008) *The Sage Companion to the City.* London: Sage.

Hall, S. (1997) The Work of Representation, in: Hall, S. (ed) *Representation: Cultural Representations and Signifying Practices*, London: Sage.

Hall, S. (2011) The Neoliberal Revolution, *Cultural Studies*, 25(6): pp 705–28.

Hall, P. (2014) *Cities of Tomorrow: An Intellectual History of Urban Planning and Design in the Twentieth Century.* 4th ed. Oxford: Wiley-Blackwell.

Hall, T. and Hubbard, P. (eds) (1998) *The Entrepreneurial City: Geographies of Politics, Regime and Representation.* London: Wiley-Academy.

Halvorsen, S. (2015) Encountering Occupy London: boundary making and the territoriality of urban activism, *Environment and Planning D: Society and Space*, 33 (2), pp 314–30.

Hambleton, R. (1991) The regeneration of US and British cities, *Local Government Studies*, 17 (5), pp 53–65.

Haran, M., Newell, G., Adair, A., McGreal, S. and Berry, J. (2011) The performance of UK regeneration property within a mixed asset portfolio, *Journal of Property Research*, 28 (1), pp 75–95.

Hardwick, W. G. (1974) *Vancouver.* Don Mills, Ont: Collier Macmillan.

Harvey, D. (1989b) *The Condition of Postmodernity: An Enquiry into the Origins of Cultural Change.* Oxford: Basil Blackwell.

Harvey, D. (2000) *Spaces of Hope.* Oxford: Blackwell.

Harvey, D. (2008) The right to the city, *New Left Review*, 53 (Sep/Oct), pp 23–40.

Harvey, D. (2012) *Rebel Cities: From the Right to the City to the Urban Revolution*. New York: Verso Books.

Haslam, D. (2007) Manchester – a culture capital? *The New Statesman*, June, accessed online at davehaslam.com.

Hasson, S. and Ley, D. (1997) Neighborhood organizations, the welfare state, and citizenship rights, *Urban Affairs Review*, 33 (1), pp 28–58.

Hayes, D. (2006) *Historical Atlas of Vancouver and the Lower Fraser Valley*. Vancouver: Douglas & McIntyre.

Healey, P. (2007) *Urban Complexity and Spatial Strategies*. London: Routledge.

Hebbert, M. (2009) Manchester: Making it happen, in: Punter, J. (ed) *Urban Design and the British Urban Renaissance*, London: Routledge.

Heseltine, M. (1987) *Where There's a Will*. London: Hutchinson.

Heseltine, M. (2000) *Life in the Jungle*. London: Hodder & Stoughton.

Heseltine, M. (2012) *No Stone Unturned: In Pursuit of Growth*. London: Department for Business, Innovation and Skills.

Hodos, J. I. (2011) *Second Cities: Globalization and Local Politics in Manchester and Philadelphia*. Philadelphia, PA: Temple University Press.

Hou, J. (ed) (2010) *Insurgent Public Space: Guerrilla Urbanism and the Remaking of Contemporary Cities*. London: Routledge.

Howell, P. (2001) Book Review: The production of public space by Light, A. and Smith, J. M. *Cultural Geographies*, 8 (2), pp. 223–25.

Hubbard, P., Faire, L. and Lilley, K. D. (2003) Contesting the modern city: reconstruction and everyday life in post-war Coventry, *Planning Perspectives*, 18 (4), pp 377–97.

Hussain, F. (2011) A fresh future for Vancouver's back alleys, *Vancouver Observer*, 16 July, accessed online at www.vancouverobserver.com.

Hutton, T. A. (2004) Post-industrialism, post-modernism and the reproduction of Vancouver's central area: Retheorising the 21st-century city, *Urban Studies*, 41 (10), pp 1953–82.

Hylton, S. (2010) *A History of Manchester*. 2nd ed. Chichester: Phillimore & Company.

Imrie, R. and Thomas, H. (eds) (1999) *British Urban Policy: An Evaluation of the Urban Development Corporations*. London: Sage.

Isin, E. (2000) Introduction: democracy, citizenship, and the city, in: Isin, E. (ed) *Democracy, Citizenship and the Global City*, Cambridge MA: Blackwell.

Jones, A. J. H. (2014) *On South Bank: The Production of Public Space*. Farnham: Ashgate.

Kalman, H. and Ward, R. (2012) *Exploring Vancouver: The Architectural Guide*. Vancouver: Douglas & McIntyre.

Kazimierczak, J. (2014) Revitalization and its impact on public space organization: A case study of Manchester in UK, Lyon in France and Łódź in Poland , *Journal of Land use, Mobility and Environment*, Special Issue (June), pp 545–56.

Keith, M. (2013) Urban regeneration and the city of experts, in: Leary, M. E. and McCarthy, J. (eds) *The Routledge Companion to Urban Regeneration*, London and New York: Routledge.

Keith, M. and Pile, S. (1993) Introduction Part 1: The Politics of Place, in: Keith, M. and Pile, S. (eds.) *Place and the Politics of Identity*. London: Routledge.

Keith, M. and Rogers, A. (1991) Hollow promises? Policy, theory and practice in the inner city, in: Keith, M. and Rogers, A. (eds) *Hollow Promises?: Rhetoric and Reality in the Inner City*, London: Mansell.

Keller, L. (2011) *Triumph of Order: Democracy and Public Space in New York and London*. New York: Columbia University Press.

Ketelaar, E. (2008) Archives as spaces of memory, *Journal of the Society of Archivists*, 29(1), pp 9–27.

Kidd, A. J. (2006) *Manchester: A History.* 4th ed. Edinburgh: Edinburgh University Press.

Kidd, D. (1992) Offbeat, In-Step: Vancouver Co-operative Radio , in: Girard, B. (ed) *A Passion for Radio: Radio Waves and Community*, Montreal: Black Rose Books.

King, A. D. (1991) *Urbanism, Colonialism and the World-Economy.* New York: Sage.

King, R. (2006) *Detonation: Rebirth of a City.* Warrington: Clear Publications.

Klemek, C. (2012) *The Transatlantic Collapse of Urban Renewal: Postwar Urbanism from New York to Berlin.* Chicago: University of Chicago Press.

Kofman, E. and Lebas, E. (1996) Introduction: Lost in Transposition – Time Space and the City, in: Kofman, E. and Lebas, E. (eds) *Writings on Cities: Henri Lefebvre*, Oxford: Blackwell.

Kolb, D. (2008) *Sprawling Places.* Athens, GA: University of Georgia Press.

Lannan, K. (2014) Federal grant will fund Lowell Riverwalk extension, *Lowell Sun*, 25 April.Larner, W. (2000) Neo-liberalism: Policy, ideology, governmentality, *Studies in Political Economy*, 63 (Autumn), pp 5–26.

Latham, A. (2003) Researching and writing everyday accounts of the city: An introduction to the diary-photo diary-interview method, in: Knowles, C. and Sweetman, P. (eds) *Picturing the Social Landscape: Visual Methods and the Sociological Imagination*, London: Routledge.

Laurence, R. (2009) Vancouver artist Stan Douglas revisits the 1971 Gastown Riot, 29 December, accessed online at straight.com.

Leary, M. E. (2008) Gin and tonic or oil and water: The entrepreneurial city and sustainable managerial regeneration in Manchester, *Local Economy*, 23 (3), pp 222–33.

Leary, M. E. (2009) The Production of space through a shrine and vendetta in Manchester: Lefebvre's spatial triad and the regeneration of a place renamed Castlefield, *Planning Theory & Practice*, 10 (2), pp 189–212.

Leary, M. E. (2011) The Production of Urban Public Space: A Lefebvrian Analysis of Castlefield, Manchester. PhD Thesis, Goldsmiths College, University of London.

Leary, M. E. (2013a) A Lefebvrian Analysis of the production of glorious, gruesome public space in Manchester, *Progress in Planning*, 85, pp 1–52.

Leary, M. E. (2013b) Emerging reconceptualisations of urban regeneration, in: Leary, M. E. and McCarthy, J. (eds) *The Routledge Companion to Urban Regeneration*, London and New York: Routledge.

Leary, M. E. and McCarthy, J. (eds) (2013) *The Routledge Companion to Urban Regeneration*. London and New York: Routledge.

Lees, L. (ed) (2004) *The Emancipatory City: paradoxes and possibilities.* London: Sage.

Lees, L. (2014) The Urban Injustices of New Labour's "New Urban Renewal": The Case of the Aylesbury Estate in London, *Antipode*, 46 (4), pp 921–47.

Lefebvre, H. (1991 [1974]) *The Production of Space.* Oxford: Blackwell.

Lefebvre, H. (1996 [1968]) The Right to the City, in: Kofman, E. and Lebas, E. (eds) *Writings on Cities*, Cambridge, MA: Blackwell.

Lefebvre, H. (1995 [1960]) Seventh Prelude: Notes on the New Town, in: Lefebvre, H. (ed) *Introduction to Modernity: Twelve Preludes*, London: Verso.

Lefebvre, H. (2003 [1970]) *The Urban Revolution.* Minneapolis, MN: University of Minnesota Press.

LeGates, R. T. and Stout, F. (eds) (2011) *The City Reader.* 5th ed. London: Routledge.

Lehtovuori, P. (2010) *Experience and Conflict: The Production of Urban Space.* Aldershot: Ashgate.

Ley, D. (1980) Liberal Ideology and the Postindustrial City, *Annals of the Association of American Geographers*, 70 (2), pp 238–58.

Ley, D. and Dobson, C. (2008) Are There Limits to Gentrification? The Contexts of Impeded Gentrification in Vancouver, *Urban Studies*, 45 (12), pp 2471–98.

Light, A. and Smith, J. M. (eds) (1998) *The Production of Public Space*. Lanham, Maryland: Rowman & Littlefield.

Lovering, J. (2007) The relationship between urban regeneration and neo-liberalism: two presumptuous theories and a research agenda, *International Planning Studies*, 12 (4), pp 343–66.

Low, S. and Smith, N. (2006) Introduction: The Imperative of Public Space, in: Low, S. and Smith, N. (eds) *The Politics of Public Space*, London: Routledge.

Lowell Historical Society (2005) *Lowell: The Mill City*. Arcadia Publishing.

Lyser, D. (2001) Do you really live here? Thoughts on insider research, *The Geographical Review*, Jan–April, pp 441–4.

Mace, A., Gallent, N., Hall, P., Porsch, L., Braun, R. and Pfeiffer, U. (2004) *Shrinking to Grow? The Urban Regeneration Challenge in Leipzig and Manchester*. London: The Institute of Community Studies.

Mackie, J. (2014) Leaders of Portland Hotel Society resign in battle over funding, *Vancouver Sun*, 19 March, accessed online at www.vancouversun.com.

Madanipour, A. (2003) *Public and Private Spaces of the City*. London: Routledge.

Madanipour, A., Knierbein, S. and Degros, A. (eds) (2013) *Public Space and the Challenges of Urban Transformation in Europe*. London: Routledge.

Madgin, R. (2009) *Heritage, Culture and Conservation: Managing the Urban Renaissance*. Saarbrücken: VDM Verlag.

Madgin, R. (2010) Reconceptualising the historic urban environment: Conservation and regeneration in Castlefield, Manchester, 1960–2009, *Planning Perspectives*, 25 (1), pp 29–48.

Makepeace, C. (2004) *Manchester: Past and Present*. Stroud: Sutton Publishing Ltd.

Malmo-Levine, D. (2007) Vansterdam Livin', *Cannabis Culture*, Fall, pp 68, accessed online at cannabisculture.com.

Malone, P. M. and Parrott, C. A. (1998) Greenways in the industrial city: Parks and promenades along the Lowell Canals, *Journal of the Society for Industrial Archaeology*, 24 (1), pp 19–40.

Mann, K. (1992) Castlefield's Canalside, *Landscape Design*, April (209), pp 33–7.

Mansbridge, F. (2015) *Vancouver Then and Now*. San Diego, CA: Thunder Bay Press.

Marion, P. (2011) Lowell Folk Festival Time Machine, 12 February, accessed online at RichardHowe.com.

Marion, P. (2014a) *Mill Power: The Origin and Impact of Lowell National Historical Park*. New York: Rowman and Littlefield.

MCC (1984) *City Centre Local Plan*. Manchester City Council.

MCC (2004) *Manchester: Shaping the City*. Manchester: RIBA/MCC.

MCC (2008) Castlefield Conservation Area Statement, accessed online at www.manchester.gov.uk.

McCann, E. J. (1999) Race, protest, and public space: Contextualizing Lefebvre in the U.S. city, *Antipode*, 31 (2), pp 163–84.

Meller, H. (1997) *Towns, Plans and Society in Modern Britain*. Cambridge: Cambridge University Press.

Mellor, R. (1997) Cool times for a changing city, in: Jewson, N. and MacGregor, S. (eds) *Transforming Cities: Contested Governance and New Spatial Divisions*, London: Routledge.

Mellor, R. (2002) Hypocritical City: cycles of urban exclusion, in: Peck, J. and Ward, K. (eds.) *City of Revolution*. Manchester: Manchester University Press.

Merrifield, A. (1993) Place and space: a Lefebvrian reconciliation, *Transactions of the Institute of British Geographers*, 18 (4), pp 516–31.

Merrifield, A. (2011) The right to the city and beyond: Notes on a Lefebvrian re-conceptualization, *City*, 15 (3–4), pp 473–81.

Minchin, T. J. (2013) *Empty Mills: The Fight Against Imports and the Decline of the U.S. Textile Industry*. New York: Rowman & Littlefield Publishers.

Mitchell, D. (1995) The end of public space? People's Park, definitions of the public and democracy, *Annals of the Association of American Geographers*, 85 (1), pp 108–33.

Mitchell, D. (2013) The liberalization of free speech: Or, how protest in public space is silenced, in: Miller, B., Beaumont, J. and Nicholls, W. (eds) *Spaces of Contention: Spatialities and Social Movements*, Farnham: Ashgate.

Mould, O. (2015) *Urban Subversion and the Creative City*. London: Routledge.

Nevell, M. (2008) *Manchester: The Hidden History*. Stroud: The History Press.

Norkunas, M. (2002) *Monuments and Memory: History and Representation in Lowell, Massachusetts*. Smithsonian Institution Scholarly Press.

Oakley, S. (2014) A Lefebvrian analysis of redeveloping derelict urban docklands for high-density consumption living, Australia, *Housing Studies*, 29 (2), pp 235–50.

O'Connor, J. and Wynne, D. (eds) (1996) *From the Margins to the Centre: Cultural Production and Consumption in the Post-industrial City*. Aldershot: Ashgate Publishing.

Office of the Mayor (2006) *Project Civil Society.* Vancouver City Council.

Pagano, M. A. and Bowman, A. O'M. (1997) *Cityscapes and Capital: The Politics of Urban Development.* Baltimore, MA: Johns Hopkins University Press.

Park, R. E. (1984 [1925]) The Growth of the City: An Introduction to a Research Project, in: Park, R. E. and Burgess, E. W. (eds) *The City: Suggestions for Investigation of Human Behavior in the Urban Environment,* Chicago: University of Chicago Press.

Parkinson, J. R. (2014) *Democracy and Public Space: The Physical Sites of Democratic Performance.* Oxford: Oxford University Press.

Parkinson, M. (1993) A new strategy for Britain's cities? *Policy Studies,* 14 (2), pp 5–13.

Parkinson, M. and Wilks, S. R. M. (1983) Managing urban decline – the case of the inner city partnerships, *Local Government Studies,* 9 (5), pp 23–39.

Parkinson-Bailey, J. (2000) *Manchester: An Architectural History.* Manchester: Manchester University Press.

Peck, J. (2010) *Constructions of Neoliberal Reason.* Oxford: Oxford University Press.

Peck, J. and Tickell, A. (1995) Business goes local: dissecting the 'business agenda' in Manchester, *International Journal of Urban and Regional Research,* 19 (1), pp 55–78.

Peck, J. and Ward, K. (eds) (2002) *City of Revolution: Restructuring Manchester.* Manchester: Manchester University Press.

Pickvance, C. (1995) Comparative analysis, causality and case studies in urban studies, in: Rogers, A. and Vertovec, S. (eds) *The Urban Context: Ethnicity, Social Networks and Situational Analysis,* Oxford: Berg.

Pinch, P. (2015) Waterspace planning and the River Thames in London, *The London Journal,* 40 (3).

Prior, L. (2008) Repositioning Documents in Social Research, *Sociology,* 42 (5), pp 821–36.

Punter, J. (2003) *The Vancouver Achievement: Urban Planning and Design.* Vancouver: UBC Press.

Quilley, S. (1999) Entrepreneurial Manchester: The genesis of elite consensus, *Antipode,* 31 (2), pp 185–211.

Quilley, S. (2002) Entrepreneurial turns: municipal socialism and after, in: Peck, J. and Ward, K. (eds) *City of Revolution: Restructuring Manchester,* Manchester: Manchester University Press.

Raco, M. (2005) Sustainable development, rolled-out neoliberalism and sustainable communities, *Antipode,* 37 (2), pp 324–47.

Rahn, M. (1997) Festival at Lowell Series, *Journal of American Folklore*, 110 (436), pp 205–08.

Ranasinghe, P. (2011) Public disorder and its relation to the community–civility–consumption triad: A case study on the uses and users of contemporary urban public space, *Urban Studies*, 48 (9), pp 1925–43.

Redhead, B. (1993) *Manchester: A Celebration*. London: Andre Deutsch.

Richardson, B. (1972) *The Future of Canadian Cities*. Toronto: New Press.

Robinson, H. H. (1898) *Loom and Spindle or Life Among the Early Mill Girls*. New York: T. Y. Crowell.

Robinson, J. (2011) Cities in a world of cities: the comparative gesture, *International Journal of Urban and Regional Research*, 35, pp 1–23.

Roche, F. L. (1977) New towns' contribution to inner areas, *Town and Country Planning*, 45 (4).

Roche, F. L. and Thomas, W. (1978) *Renewing the Inner Areas: The Task and the Means (16 November)*. NAE, AT 41/319.

Ryan, L. A. (1991) The Remaking of Lowell and Its Histories: 1965–83, in: Weible, R. (ed) *The Continuing Revolution: A History of Lowell, Massachusetts*, Lowell, MA: Lowell Historical Society.

Ryan, R. (2007) *Dpercussion @ Castlefield*. Manchester Evening News, 5 August.

Samuel, R. (2012) *Theatres of Memory: Past and Present in Contemporary Culture*. 2nd ed. London: Verso.

Schofield, J. (2000) Evaluating Castlefield Urban Heritage Park from the consumer perspective: destination attribute importance, visitor perception and satisfaction, *Tourism Analysis*, 5 (2–4), pp 183–9.

Sellars, R. W. (2007) The National Park System and the Historic American Past: A Brief Overview and Reflection, *The George Wright Forum*, 24 (1), pp 8–22.

Shepherd, A. (2012) Walking in the air: Castlefield's own High Line Park, *Independent*, 28 October.

Shields, R. (1999) *Lefebvre, Love, and Struggle: spatial dialectics*. London: Taylor & Francis.

Simmel, G. (1994 [1909]) Bridge and Door, *Theory, Culture & Society*, 11 (1), pp 5–10.

Slattery, J. (2015) Vancouver named unhappiest city in Canada, VanCityBuzz, accessed online at http://www.vancitybuzz.com.

Smith, N. (2003) 'Preface' to *The Urban Revolution by Henri Lefebvre*. Minneapolis, MN: University of Minnesota Press.

Soja, E. (1989) *Postmodern Geographies: The Reassertion of Space in Critical Social Theory*. London: Verso.

Soja, E. (1996) *Thirdspace: Journeys to Los Angeles and other Real-and-Imagined Places*, Oxford: Blackwell.

· Soja, E. (2010) *Seeking Spatial Justice.* Minneapolis, MN: University of Minnesota Press.

Sommers, J. (2001) The Place of the Poor: Poverty, Space and the Politics of Representation in Downtown Vancouver, 1950–1997. PhD Thesis, Simon Fraser University.

Sorkin, M. (ed) (1992) *Variations on a Theme Park: The New American City and the End of Public Space.* New York: Hill and Wang.

Staeheli, L. A. and Mitchell, D. (2007) USA's Destiny? Regulating Space and Creating Community in American Shopping Malls, *Urban Studies*, 43 (5/6), pp 977–92.

Stamp, G. (2007) *Britain's Lost Cities.* London: Aurum Press Ltd.

Stanek, L. (2011) *Henri Lefebvre on Space: Architecture, Urban Research, and the Production of Theory.* Minneapolis: University of Minnesota Press.

Stanek, L., Moravánszky, A. and Christian Schmid, C. (eds) (2014) *Urban Revolution Now: Henri Lefebvre in Social Research and Architecture.* Aldershot: Ashgate Publishing.

Stanton, C. (2006) *The Lowell Experiment: Public History in a Postindustrial City.* University of Massachusetts Press.

Stevens, Q. (2007) *The Ludic City: Exploring the potential of public spaces.* London: Routledge.

Stewart, P. and Riddell, C. (2010) *Barnaby Grimes: Phantom of Blood Alley.* Oxford: David Fickling Books.

Tallon, A. (2013) *Urban Regeneration in the UK.* 2nd ed. London: Routledge.

Taylor, A. J. P. (1977) Manchester, in: Taylor, A. J. P. (ed) *Essays in English History*, London: Hamish Hamilton.

Tonkiss, F. (2013) *Cities by Design: The Social Life of Urban Form.* London: Polity Press.

Unwin, T. (2000) A waste of space? Towards a critique of the social production of space…, *Transactions of the Institute of British Geographers*, 25 (1), pp 11–29.

Vancouver Public Space Network (2014) Big Ideas for the City: A Laneway Strategy, 12 April, accessed online at vancouverpublicspace. ca.

VCC (2013) *DTES Local Area Plan Overview.* Vancouver: VCC.

VCC (2014) *Downtown Eastside Local Area Plan.* Vancouver: VCC.

Venugopal, R. (2015) Neoliberalism as Concept , *Economy and Society*, 44 (2), pp 165–87.

Vormann, B. (2015) *Global Port Cities in North America: Urbanization Processes and Global Production Networks*. London/New York: Routledge.

Wacquant, L. J. D. (1992) The Structure and Logic of Bourdieu's Sociology, in: Bourdieu, P. and Wacquant, L. J. D. (eds) *An Invitation to Reflexive Sociology*, Oxford: Blackwell Publishers.

Ward, K. (2010) Towards a relational comparative approach to the study of cities, *Progress in Human Geography*, 34 (4), pp 471–87.

Watson, S. (2009) The magic of the marketplace: Sociality in a neglected public space, *Urban Studies*, 46 (8), pp 1577–91.

Weible, R. (ed) (1991) *The continuing revolution: A history of Lowell, Massachusetts*. Lowell, MA: Lowell Historical Society.

Weible, R. (2011) Visions and Reality: Reconsidering the Creation and Development of Lowell's National Park, 1966–1992, *The Public Historian*, 33 (2), pp 67–93.

Welker, G. (2014) Federal grant to support trolley-plan design work, *Lowell Sun*, 12 March, accessed online at http://www.lowellsun.com.

Whitby Bird Spokesman (2009) *Merchants Bridge*. online access at Department of Civil Engineering, University of Portsmouth www. civl.port.ac.uk accessed, November 2009.

Will, G. (1988) 'Daddy, Who Was Kerouac?', *Newsweek*, 4 July .

Williams, E. (1994 [1944]) *Capitalism and Slavery*. Chapel Hill: University of North Carolina Press.

Williams, G. (2003) *The Enterprising City Centre: Manchester's Development Challenge*. London: Taylor & Francis Ltd.

Wilson, E. (1996) *Vancouver Nightmare*. London: Bodley Head.

Yafa, S. (2005) *Big Cotton: How a Humble Fiber Created Fortunes, Wrecked Civilizations, and Put America on the Map*. New York: Viking Penguin.

Yin, R. K. (2013) *Case Study Research: Design and Methods*. 5th ed. London: Sage.

Zukin, S. (2006) David Harvey on Cities, in: Castree, N. and Gregory, D. (eds) *David Harvey: A Critical Reader*. Oxford: Blackwell Publishing.

Primary data sources

Alexander, J. (1995) *Federal Design Achievement Awards 1995*. US Department of the Interior, accessed online at http://archive.org/.

Andras, R. (1971) Letter from Minister of State for Urban Affairs to Mayor Thomas Campbell, Vancouver, 25 May. PABC, GR 1548 Box 17.

Arsenault, M. (2014) Email exchange; a former Lowell Sun journalist, currently at the Boston Globe, 29 April.

Atkin, J. (2014) Email correspondence; he is an experienced and highly knowledgeable Gastown tour guide, 16 August.

Aucella, P. (2012b) He was interviewed at LNHP HQ, 26 July, for about one hour.

Bahr, B. (1984) *Boott Cotton Mills: Survey for the Historic American Engineering Record*. Washington, LNHPA: NPS, Dept of the Interior.

Bannerman, G. (1971) Gastown project tactics questioned, Vancouver *Province*, 7 July, VCA.

Barnes, P. (1964) *Lowell Capital Backs Corporations*. 25 July, Lowell Sun, NoA.

Barrett, L. W. and Wright, J. E. (1969) *Script of a delegation presentation to Vancouver city council, Standing Committee of Planning, Development and Transportation, 11 July*. VCA, Location 22-B-1, File 1.

Basford, R. (1971) *Letter from Canadian Minister of Consumer and Corporate Affairs to Alderman E C Sweeney, chairman, Special Committee of Council, Gastown/Chinatown Historical Areas, 4 February*. PABC, GR 1548 Box 17.

BBC (2001) Thousands join anti-war protest, accessed online at news.bbc.co.uk/, accessed September 2009.

BBC (2004) D:Percussion at Castlefield. 7 August, accessed online at bbc.co.uk/manchester.

BCC (1968) *Letter from Chinatown historic preservation activists to the Vancouver Mayor and city council, 23 August*. VCA, Series 20, Location 22-B-1, File 1.

Bernstein, H. S. (2009) Chief Executive of Manchester City Council 1990–present. In the 1980s he was Assistant Chief Executive. He was interviewed on 2 July at his office in the Town Hall. Pat Bartoli, Head of Regeneration, also attended the interview, which lasted about an hour.

Birmingham and Wood (1971) *Consultants Report on East Gastown Beautification Project*. VCA, Location 120-E-1 File 285.

Birmingham and Wood, Hopping Kovach & Grinell (1971) *Consultants Report on the East Gastown Beautification Project*. VCA, Location 120-E-1 File 285.

Birmingham and Wood, Hopping/Kovach/Grinnell and Bing Marr & Associates (1969) *Restoration Report: The Case for Renewed Life in the Old City*. VCA, Location 120-E-1 File 285.

Black, C. (1971) Urban park work continues, *Lowell Sun*, 3 January, NoA.

Black, C. (1973) Model Cities: Seven years and six million dollars after initial okay Lowell's unique project in Acre faces final days, *Lowell Sun*, 22 July, NoA.

Black, C. (1974) Bill to create urban park commission passed, *Lowell Sun*, 18 December, NoA.

Bohlen, C. (1974a) Model Cities has brought $9.1 million into Lowell, *Lowell Sun*, 8 July, NoA.

Bohlen, C. (1974b) Congressmen praise park project, *Lowell Sun*, 27 April, NoA.

Bohlen, C. (1974c) Urban Park funding – a moment of triumph, *Lowell Sun*, 20 August, NoA.

Britton, S. (1987) *Response to Kerouac commemorative chilly*, 30 April, NoA.

Brown, R. G. (1979) *Memo from the Secretary of the DoE's Planning Advisory Group to members of the Group with attached inner city regeneration paper by Thomas and Roche*. March (day unknown), NAE, AT 41/319.

Bula, F. (2011) Gastown dreamer looks lovingly upon creation, *The Globe and Mail*, 5 January, accessed online at theglobeandmail.com.

Campbell, D. (1970) *Letter from BC Minister of Municipal Affairs to Mr H P Capozzi MLA, 17 March*. PABC, GR 1548 Box 17.

Campbell, T. J. (1971) *Briefing Paper from Vancouver City Mayor to the Canadian Federal Minister of Housing and Urban Affairs, Robert Andras, 30 April*. PABC, GR 1548 Box 17.

Chance, I. O. and Pevsner, N. (1973) A Manchester Station, *The Sunday Times*, 12 March, BLNA.

Charlton, A. A. (1981) *Letter from Acting Director, Heritage Conservation Branch, Ministry of Provincial Secretary, Victoria, BC, to Vancouver Mayor, Michael Harcourt, 26 August*. PABC, GR 1548 Box 17.

Chippendale, P. (1972) Old station that BR neglects, *Guardian*, 15 June, GrGA, Liverpool Road Station file.

City Development Authority (1973) *Historic Districts Study Committee Final Report*. CLHA.

CMDC (1989) *Development Strategy for Central Manchester*. GONWA, uncatalogued records.

Comrie, C. (1991) *Memo from NWRO officer to Mrs Meek (DoE) 'Evaluation of Environmental Improvement Projects'*. GONWA, PNW/5624/605/3.

Cook, A. (1974) Urban park pledged $10M by state, *Lowell Sun*, 20 August, NoA.

Cook, J. (2012) Research interview with the Executive Director of the Lowell Development and Financial Corporation and the Executive Director of The Lowell Plan, Inc, since 1990. He was Lowell City Director of the Division of Planning and Development in 1986. Interview held at the offices of the Lowell Plan for about one hour, 30 July.

Corrie, W. (1978) *Letter from the MOWP Chairman (DoE) to Mr G A Harrison Chief Executive GMC, 7 November*.

Crighton, T. (1997) *The Last Streetfighter: The History of the Georgia Straight Newspaper*. Produced by Baton Broadcasting Inc/Vancouver Television, accessed online at www.youtube.com, August 2013.

Cross, M. M. (1970) *Letter from Deputy Director of Planning, Vancouver to Mr R W Davidson, Purchasing Agent, Vancouver General Hospital*. 30 January, VCA, Location 925-C-6.

CSC (1982a) *Castlefield Tourism Development Plan*. GMCRO, Location BA1717 Box 1250 (undated but date deduced from various CSC Minutes).

CSC (1982b) *Minutes of a meeting of the CSC, 14 December*. GMCRO, Location BA1717 Box 1250.

CTIG (1969) *Letter from Chinatown Improvement Group to the Vancouver Mayor, Tom Campbell and city council, 10 January*. VCA.

Daily Mail (2009) Corrie's Roy Cropper ends up in the canal after fighting back against Tony Gordon, 29 September.

DNR (1974) *A proposal for an Urban State Park in Lowell, Massachusetts*. Massachusetts Department of Natural Resources, Office of Planning, CLHA.

DNR (1976) *Lowell Heritage State Park: Press Kit and Memorandum of Understanding between the Commonwealth of Massachusetts and Lowell City Council*, CLHA.

Donna and Joe (2010) Research interview (1.5 hours) with two founder members of MNB at the On the Eighth Day café in Manchester, 10 June (not their real names).

Dover, D. (1996) *House of Commons speech during the Royal Ordnance (Chorley) debate, in: House of Commons speech during the Royal Ordnance (Chorley) debate*. Hansard, HC Deb 13 March vol 273 cc1081–8, accessed at publications.parliament.uk.

Dubs, L. (1996) *House of Lords speech during the Central Manchester Development corporation (Area and Constitution) Order 1996 debate*. Hansard, House of Lords Debates, 18 March, vol 570 cc 1113–6, accessed at publications.parliament.uk.

Duffy, M. (1979) Castlefield: Treasures in a city's backyard (Castlefield Special Part 1 of 3), *Manchester Evening News*, 29 October, BLNA.

East Gastown Petitioners (1969) *Petition from Easter Gastown property owners to William Graham, Director of Planning, Vancouver City, 15 November*. VCA, Location 22-B-1, File 1.

ECOTEC (1988) *Central Manchester Development Corporation: Development Strategy*. Commissioned by CMDC, GONWA, uncatalogued records.

Faust, F. (1981) *Executive Director, Lowell Historic Preservation Committee, Letter to Mary Costello, of the Lowell Sun*. 28 October, LNHPA, Blue Dye House/Lowell Sun Garage file (1).

Ferrers, E. (1996) *House of Lords speech during the Central Manchester Development Corporation (Area and Constitution) Order 1996 debate*. Hansard, House of Lords Debates, 18 March, vol 570 cc 1113–6, accessed at publications.parliament.uk/ in 2008.

Flanders, V. (1972a) AMNO board accepts plans for canal project, *Lowell Sun*, 7 November, NoA.

Flanders, V. (1972b) Model Cities is beginning to show: Some are just beginning… *Lowell Sun*, 12 November, NoA.

Flanders, V. (1973) Lowell cultural center planned, *Lowell Sun*, 23 April, NoA.

Foreman, J. (1976) Lowell Museum making heritage real: living history is its goal, *Lowell Sun*, three page special, 18 January, NoA.

Francis, D. (1990) City unveils a 'world-class' urban park. *Lowell Sun*, 2 July, NAaB, LHPC Records, box 4.

Freeman, H. L. (1972) Oldest station that BR neglects, *Sunday Times*, 2 July, GrGA, Liverpool Road Station file.

Ganong, K. B. (1971) *Letter from Vancouver manager, CMHC to Gerald Sutton Brown, Commissioner, Vancouver Board of Administration, 4 August*. VCA.

Gardiner, S. (1973) How to Destroy a Great City: The Rape of Manchester, 25 February, *Observer*, DRPA.

Gervais, R. (2014) Email exchange with the British co-director and co-writer of the film *The Invention of Lying*, 10 May.

Glennie, I. M. (1973) *Memo from HBC Secretary to Mr Lewin, HBC Property Surveyor*. 10 May, NAE, HLG 126/1702.

Glennie, I. M. (1974) *Memo to Mr Anthony, HBC Surveyor*. 3 July, NAE, HLG 126/1702.

Glester, J. (1989) *Letter from CMDC CEO to DoE (London) civil servant.* 10 April, GONWA, PNW/5264/623/6.

Glester, J. (2008) He was a civil servant for many years rising by the 1980s to a senior position in the GONW in Manchester. He was the CEO of the CMDC throughout its eight year life. He was interviewed for about two hours at the City Inn Hotel, Manchester, 16 October.

GMC (1979) *Minutes of Liverpool Road Station 26 April meeting at County Hall.* 21 May, MSIA.

Golec, P. (2008) *Lowell community activist, transcript of interview by Mehmed Ali, 16 April.* Oral History Collection, UMASS Lowell, CLHA.

Graham, W. (1971) *Memo from Director of Planning to The chairman and members, Vancouver City Planning Commission, 2 December.* VCA.

GTV (1981) *Yesterday's Dust, Tomorrow's Dreams – script marked 'Confidential'.* GMCRO, Location BA1717 Box 1250.

GTV (1982) *Yesterday's Dust, Tomorrow's Dreams.* DVD, GTVA (Leeds).

GMC (1978) *Minutes of meeting to discuss the Liverpool Road Station restoration and conversion to a science museum.* 21 February, MSIA, LRSS file.

Hall, Jonathan (2010) Research telephone interview, 26 July, which lasted about half an hour. He worked for the Civic Trust for the North West in the early 1970s and currently is a lecturer in Planning and Sustainable Development at University College Cork.

Hall, J. C. and Rhodes, D. (1972) *Castlefield: Past Present and Future: A pilot study by the Civic Trust for the Northwest.* CTNW, DRPA.

Harrison, G. A. (1978) *Letter from GMC Chief Executive to Mr W Corrie, DoE NW Regional Office Manchester – marked <u>STRICTLY CONFIDENTIAL</u>.* 27 October, GMCRO, NAE, HLG 156/810.

Hawcroft, F. (1978) *Letter from Keeper of the Whitworth Gallery to Eleanor Murray, Secretary Georgian Group.* 24 February, GrGA, Liverpool Road Station file.

Hendricks, M. (1969) *Letter from the operator of the Vancouver Antique Flea Market, to Vancouver city council.* VCA, Location 22-B-1, File 1.

Heseltine, M. (1979) *Memo from the SoS DoE to Margaret Thatcher, British Prime Minister – marked 'confidential', July (day unknown).* NAE, File AT 41/319.

Heseltine, Michael (2007) He was junior minister in the DoE 1970–72, DoE Secretary of State 1979–83 and 1990–92 and Deputy Prime Minister 1995–97. He was interviewed (for about one hour) by telephone on 15 December; an email exchanged followed.

Heseltine, M. (2009) He was interviewed (for about one hour) at his Hammersmith Haymarket Publishing Office on 18 February.

Howard, L. (1965) Should The Dutton St. 'Row Houses' Be Saved? *Lowell Sun*, 3 July, LSA.

Howe, R. (2008) Pat Mogan's Vision for Lowell, accessed online at www.richardhowe.com.

HSC (1995) *Dr Patrick J Mogan: Visionary & Realist.* HSC/Page One Productions, accessed online at youtube.com.

HSC (1991) *Roots of an Urban Cultural Park.* Produced by HSC, accessed online at youtube.com.

Hudson, K. (2009) Email correspondence; Chair of the Campaign for Nuclear Disarmament, 6 May.

Jones, P. (2010) Email communication with freelance photographer working in the Manchester area who often works with the Lesbian Gay Bi-sexual Transgender community, 16 April.

Jones, G. D. B. and Rhodes, D. (1978) *Historic Castlefield.* DRPA.

Joseph, K. (1979) *Memo from SOS DTI to the British Prime Minister regarding, 30 July – marked CONFIDENTIAL.* NAE, AT 41/319.

Kalman, H. (1969) *Letter from Instructor, Department of Fine Arts, UBC to the Vancouver City Clerk,* 28 April, VCA, Location 22-B-1.

Kalman, H. (2014a) Email correspondence, Professor of Architectural History UBC. He was one of the original shareholders in the Stanley and New Fountain Hotels redevelopment company, Cordova Redevelopment Corporation, in the 1960s, 24 November.

Kalman, H. (2014b) Email correspondence, 27 August.

Karabatsos, L. (2014) Research email from the former director of the Lowell Museum. 23 May.

Keate, E. (1971) *Letter from President Gastown Merchants' Association to Mayor Thomas Campbell, Vancouver, 28 October.* VCA.

Kennedy, E. (1972) *Letter from Massachusetts senator to Michael Southworth.* 23 June, MSPA.

Kick it Out (2003) *Manchester kick's it out,* accessed online at kickitout. org/, September 2009.

Killam, L. (1970b) *Letter from president, Town Group Ltd to Bill Graham, Director of Planning Vancouver, 26, January.* VCA, Location 925-C-6, File 1.

Lafleur, M. (2006) *Trouble preserving canals.* 26 October, Lowell Sun, NoA.

Lavoie, D. (1988) Nearly two decades after his death, a city gives Jack Kerouac what life didn't – recognition, *Lowell Sun*, 22 June, NoA.

Lawson, G. H. (1970) *Letter from Vancouver Deputy City Engineer to Mr Sid Erikson, Ross and Howard Iron Works Co Ltd, Vancouver.* 18 November, VCA.

Lecky, J. M. (1968) *Letter from the chairman of the Vancouver Town Planning Commission to Vancouver city Mayor Tom Campbell, 29 October.* VCA, Series 20, Location 22-B-1, File 1.

Lee, G. (1972) *Letter from Chairman, Water Street Improvement Committee to Mr W E Graham, Director, City Planning Vancouver, 21. November.* VCA, Location 10-C-6 File 37.

Lesser, D. (1969) *Script of presentation by the President of IDEAS to the Vancouver Standing Committee of Planning, Development, and Transportation, 3 July.* VCA, Location 22-B-1, File 1.

Lezberg, M. (1999) *Former President of Locks and Canals Company, transcript of interview by Mehmed Ali, 30 September.* Oral History Collection, UMASS Lowell, CLHA.

LHCDC (1977) *Report of the Lowell Historic Canal District Commission [The Brown Book].* US Government Printing Office, Washington DC, CLHA.

LHPC (1978) *Minutes of the first (informal) meeting of the LHPC, held in the Trustees' Room Cumnock Hall, University of Lowell, 14 December.* NAaB, LHPCR box 1.

LHPC (1980) *Preservation Plan.* Department of the Interior, LNHPA.

LHPC (1989) *Preservation Plan Amendment.* US Department of the Interior, CLHA.

Lipchitz, W. (2004) *Deputy Executive Director, Community Teamwork, Inc and long time political friend of Paul Tsongas, transcript of interview by Mehmed Ali, 27 July.* Oral History Collection, UMASS Lowell, CLHA.

Low-Beer, F. (1969) *Letter from President, Community Arts Council of Vancouver to Mayor Thomas J. Campbell, 23 June.* VCA, Series 20, Location 22-B-1, File 1.

Lowell Sun (1967) Editorial: Model City Approval, 17 November, NoA.

Lowell Sun (1970) Model Cities Agency proposes national park for Lowell area, 23 October, NoA.

Lowell Sun (1973a) Urban park planners optimistic, 2 January, NoA.

Lowell Sun (1973b) Historic District Commission Approved, 29 August, NoA.

Lowell Sun (1974) Editorial: Urban Park, *Lowell Sun*, 2 January, NoA.

Lowell Sun (1985) Kerouac may tell city's 'human story', LSA.

Lowell Sun (1989) Editorial: Canalway progress, *Lowell Sun*, 8 July, LNHPA Newspaper cuttings.

Lowell Sun (1997) Editorial: Coming Home, *Lowell Sun*, 20 January, LNHPA, newspaper cuttings file.

MacKechnie, E. (1968) *Handwritten letter from a prominent member of VCAC to His Worship the Mayor of Vancouver, 30 September.* VCA, Location 22-B-1, File 2.

Mah, T. and Chang, F. (1970) *Report to the Vancouver Mayor and city council presented in person by the Co-chairmen of the Chinatown Improvement Group, 7 July.* VCA, Location 114-D-1, File 133.

Manchester Corporation (1945) *City of Manchester Plan 1945.* London: Jarrold and Sons Ltd, MLSA.

Manchester Corporation (1973) *Minutes of a meeting at Manchester Town Hall.* 6 June, NAE, HLG 126/1702.

Manchester Corporation (1974) *Minutes of a meeting at Manchester Town Hall.* 18 June, NAE, HLG 126/1702.

Manchester Guardian (1852) *Knott Mill Fair, Manchester*, 14 April, accessed online at www.fairground-heritage.org.uk.

Mann, Kevin (2010) Email research correspondence (2 January). He worked for Groundwork Trust in the 1980s and 1990s and led the environmental improvements and bridge building projects for CMDC in the early 1990s.

Marion, P. (1988) Stones that speak of Kerouac, and Lowell, *Lowell Sun*, 23 June, NoA.

Marion, P. (2012) Walking tour and extended conversation before, during and after lunch with former LHPC Director of Cultural Affairs in the 1980s. Currently Executive Director, Community Relations and Co-Director, Center for Arts and Ideas, UMass Lowell, 7 April.

Marion, P. (2014b) Email communication with LHPC Director of Cultural Affairs (and assistant) in the 1980s, Currently Executive Director, Community Relations and Co-Director, Center for Arts and Ideas, UMass Lowell, 1 June.

Marion, P. (2014c) Email communication, 24 November.

Marshall, W. (2014) Telephone interview (about one hour) with former Conservation and Urban Design Manager, Manchester City Council. He retired in 2010 after 38 years, 13 November.

Martin Randolph (1970) *Report by City Engineer to VCC, 23 February.* VCA, Location 925-C-6, File 1.

Maund, Robert (2008) He worked for Manchester Corporation as a town planner over 1960–74, after which he joined the GMC's newly established planning department where he worked until 1985. He was interviewed at his home in Ayrshire on 24 October. The interview was an extended conversation that started in the morning and resumed again after lunch.

MCC (1974) *Minutes of a LRS meeting at Manchester Town Hall, 18 June.* NAE, HLG 126/1702.

MCC (1988) *Minutes of an informal meeting at MCC.* 26 May, GONWA, PNW/5624/606/1.

McClarnan, G. (2010) He is CEO and founder in the early 1990s of the arts and media company Sparklestreet and a Manchester based arts promoter and entrepreneur. He was interviewed by telephone for about 30 minutes on 15 January.

McLeod, L. (2008) Email communication; Librarian, Christie's Archives, London, 5 March.

MNB (2008) *From No Borders Manchester,* accessed online at libcom. org/, February 2010.

MNB Activist (2010) Email communication with MNB anonymous source, 12 May.

MOWP (1978) *Draft Inner Area Programme 1979/80–1981/82.* September, NAE, HLG 156/810.

MSWP (1978) *Draft Inner Area Programme 1979/80 - 1981/82.* (September), NAE, HLG 156/810.

Munson, P. (1981) *Report by an Eric Thrun Associates Ltd lighting engineer to the Townsite Committee, 29, July.* VCA, PD 847.

Murray, E. (1977) *Letter for Georgian Group Secretary to Sir Peter Parker, Chairman BR.* 10 March, NAE, AN 111/637.

New York Times (1992) Editorial; The Mills Weren't Made of Marble. 7 September, accessed online at www.nytimes.com, December 2013.

Newham Recorder (1979) Docklands Plan Boost, 9 August, NAE, AT 41/319.

Nicholson, H. D. (1970) *Letter from Assistant City Engineer, (Electrical), to City Projects Engineer, 28 July.* VCA, Location 925-C-6, File 1.

Noon, R. (1990) *The Lowell Regatta Festival Committee.* The Local, newsletter of the Lowell Office of Cultural Affairs, Aug/Sep, online at ecommunity.uml.edu/ accessed August 2012.

Ogden, G. (1973) *Letter to Geoffrey Rippon, Secretary of State, Department of the Environment, 6 April.* NAE, HLG 126/1702.

O'Hearn, J. (1983) *Letter to Mr Fred Faust, cc Senator Paul Tsongas.* 20 December, LNHPA, Blue Dye House/Sun Garage file (1).

Papirno, E. (1972) *Plans would place emphasis on historic, ethnic landmarks.* 20 August, Lowell Sun, NoA.

Parker, A. (c1978) Comments on the Gastown Project, in: Vancouver City Planning Department (ed) *Gastown Rehabilitation Project,* VCA, Location 22-B-1, File 2.

Parker, J. W. (1970) *Gastown Brief from Chairman, Townsite Committee presented to VCC, 7 July.* VCA.

Parrott, C. (1988) *Letter from the LHPC chief architect to James O'Hearn, general manager Lowell Sun, 3 February,* LNHPA, Blue Dye House File.

Parrott, C. (2012a) Research interview with chief architect LNHP 1980–present. Member of the Historic American Building survey team 1974-75 that catalogued and assessed the condition of Lowell's historic buildings and structures. He started working for the LHPC in 1980 and moved across to LNHP in 1995. Interviewed at LNHP HQ and walking around the Boott Mills courtyard, 5 April.

Parrott, C. (2012b) Research interview, at LNHP HQ and walking around the Boott Mills courtyard, the turbine hall and the Riverwalk, 30 July.

Parrott, C. (2014a) Research email correspondence, 2 June.

Parrott, C. (2014b) Research email correspondence, 5 June.

Parrott, C. and Sanders, J. (1995) *Lowell. Then and Now: Restoring the Legacy of a Mill City.* Lowell Historic Preservation Commission, LNHPA.

Parsons, A. (1972) A boat trip via Lowell canals, *Lowell Sun*, 1 October, NoA.

Peng, C. (1969) *Letter from Consul General, The Republic of China to Vancouver Mayor, Thomas Campbell, 11 June.* VCA, Location 22-B-1, File 1.

Peskin, S. (1986) *Memo to Brown & Rowe, Landscape Architects and Planners, 13 January.* LNHPA, Boardinghouse Park file.

Phillips, F. (1972) Locks and Canals want $5000, *Lowell Sun*, 31 July, NoA.

Phillips, F. (1975) Locks, Canals, pays $700,000, *Lowell Sun*, 2 April, NoA.

Pieda Ltd (1991) Evaluation of Environmental Improvement Projects: Working Paper 4, Central Manchester Pilot Case Study.

Pizzi, P. (1988) Buddhist influence on Kerouac influenced sculptors granite work, *Lowell Sun*, 22 June, LSA.

Pollock, J. M. (1980) *Letter from chairman The Townsite Committee to Mr MG Thomson, Mercantile Mortgage Co Ltd Vancouver, 27 November.* PABC.

Province (1971) Gastown project inquiry sought, 17 July, VCA.

Pugh, R. (1990) The making of Little Venice, *Manchester Evening News*, 4 September, MENA, Castlefield file.

Rhodes, D. (2008) He worked as a conservation officer for the Civic Trust for the Northwest 1971–73. He was a historic buildings conservation officer at MCC, 1974–84. He was interviewed at his home in Harrogate on 15 July 2008. The interview was an extended conversation starting in the morning and continuing over and after lunch.

Rhodes, D. (2009) Research interview at the Victory Services Club in London W1, 8 July.

Rippon, G. (1973) *Letter from the Secretary of State, DoE to Sir Robert Cary MP, 27 April*. NAE, HLG 126/1702.

Robson, B., Bradford, M., Deas, I., Fielder, A. and Franklin, S. (1997) *The Impact of Urban Development Corporations in Leeds, Bristol and Central Manchester: Final Report to the DoE*. GOMWA, PNW/5624/605/3.

Rochon, L. (2005) It sends out a terrible message, *The Globe and Mail*, 25 June, accessed online at http://www.theglobeandmail.com.

Scholz, F. (1972) Morse seeks urban national Park in Lowell, *Lowell Sun*, 25 April, NoA.

Scholz, F. (1974) The city's major tax delinquents, *Lowell Sun*, 3 December, NoA.

Schubarth, C. (1976) Urban National Park progressing rapidly, *Lowell Sun*, 16 May, NoA.

Sigesmund, A. (1972) *Letter from co-director Cordova Redevelopment Corp Ltd to Max Cross, deputy city planner, VCC, 7 February*. VCA, Ref 84-E-4.

Southworth, M. (1992) How Park Originated, *The New York Times*, 22 September, accessed online at www.nytimes.com.

Southworth, M. (2014a) Research email correspondence, Professor Emeritus in both the Departments of City and Regional Planning and Landscape Architecture and Environmental Planning, UC Berkeley, 18 April.

Southworth, M. (2014b) Research email correspondence, 19 April.

Southworth, M. (2014c) Research email correspondence, 29 April.

Southworth, M. and Balster, L. (1970) *Memo to Pat Mogan and members of the Model Cities Education Component Historical Committee, 14 December*. CLHA, Box 15 F12.

Southworth, M. and Zien, J. (1971) *Memo from consultants to Lowell Model Cities, to Ed Larter, owner of Wannalancit Mills, 1 February. Ideas for developing Lowell mills, in particular the Wannalancit (Suffolk) complex, for education and community use*. CLHA, Box 23 F10.

Spaxman, R. (2012) Interview with Principal of the Spaxman Consulting Group, former Vancouver Director of Planning 1972–87, at the Belagio Café, Hornby Street, Vancouver, 17 January.

Stringer, G. M. (2009) Currently a Manchester MP (since 1997), he became a councillor in 1979 and leader of Manchester City Council 1984–96. He was interviewed at the House of Commons on 2 June for about 1.5 hours. He was not tainted by the MPs' expenses scandal of 2008–09.

Sullivan, J. (1978) *Secretary, LHPC, Minutes of the first informal meeting of the Lowell Historic Preservation Commission, held at the Trustees' Room, Cumnock Hall, University of Lowell, 14 December.* NAaB, LHPCR, box 1.

Sweeney, E. C. (1970) *Letter from Vancouver Alderman and Chairman, Special Committee of Council, Gastown/Chinatown Historical Areas to the Hon Wesley Drew Black, Provincial Secretary, BC, 8 October.* VCA, Ref 114-D-1.

Sylvester, D. (1976) Pat Mogan made the scoffers into believers – with time, *Lowell Sun*, 31 October, NoA.

Tavares, J. (1998) *Director of the Lowell Model Cities Agency, interview 20 July with Mehmed Ali, for UMASS Lowell, Center for Lowell History.* CLHA.

Baltimore Sun (1992) City Fair's Death, 13 June, online archives.

The Business Community of Chinatown (1968) *Letter signed by three members, to the Vancouver Mayor and city council.* 23 August, VCA, Series 20, Location 22-B-1.

The Mule (2008) Manchester Reclaimed. *The Mule*, 19 May, alternative newspaper published in Manchester, accessed online at manchestermule.com/, June 2010.

Thomson, M. G. (1969) *Letter from the Chairman of the Townsite Committee to Vancouver Mayor Tom Campbell, May (day unknown).* VCA.

Trudeau, P. (1975 [c1978]) Letter from Prime Minister of Canada to the Gastown Merchants Association, in: Vancouver City Planning Department (ed) *Gastown Rehabilitation Project,* VCA.

Tuttle, N. (2005) Lowell has it all: City is perfect setting for suspense, says mystery writer Mark Arsenault, *Lowell Sun*, 26 March.

Unger, M. (1990) Playful sculptures reflect spirit of Lowell, 15 July, *The Boston Sunday Globe*, LNHPA.

Vancouver City Planning Department (c1978) *Gastown Rehabilitation Project.* VCA, PD 2968.

VCC (1970) *City Council minutes 1 August,* accessed online at https://archive.org.

VCC (1971) *Vancouver city council minutes 27 July*, accessed online at archive.org/stream.

Vogel, R. (1972) *Letter from the Curator, Division of Mechanical and Civil Engineering, Smithsonian Institution, The National Museum of History and Technology to Dennis Coffey, Secretary, Historic Districts Study Committee.* 3 April, CLHA, Human Services Corporation file.

Wallace, K. and Phillips, F. (1975) Locks, Canals may fall to Teamsters, *Lowell Sun*, 27 April, NoA.

Walter, C. (1986) *Memo from Superintendent, LNHP to Sarah Peskin, Planning Director LHPC.* 14 February, LNHPA, Boarding House Park file (1).

Walter, C. (1991) *Letter from LNHP superintendent to Louis Saab, Principal, Saab Realty.* 4 June, LNHPA, Boarding House Park file (1).

Ward, R. (1998) Heritage Lost and Faked while Advances Made in High Tech Design, 28 December, *Vancouver Sun*, NoA.

Washington Bureau (1973) Cronin files bill to create Lowell's Urban National Cultural Park, *Lowell Sun*, 2 January, NoA.

Washington Bureau (1967) LOWELL LOSES MODEL CITY BID: Hub, Cambridge, Springfield Chosen for Massachusetts, *Lowell Sun*, 25 February, NoA.

Weaver, K. R. (1970) *Letter from Executive Director, Vancouver General Hospital, to Mr M Cross, Deputy Director of City Planning, 2 March.* VCA, Location 925-C-6, File 1.

Webb, M. (2007) *Email communication: with Mike Webb, Publicity Manager*, Peel Holdings, 15 July

Whitaker, J. (1771) *The History of Manchester in Four Books: Book the First.* London: J Murray, MLSA.

Willis, D. K. (1982) Renovating cities of the Old World with New World ideas, *Christian Science Monitor*, 9 August, accessed online at csmonitor.com.

Wittenauer, G. (1989) *Letter from LHPC Boarding House Park Construction Supervisor, to Clarissa Rowe, Partner, Brown and Rowe, 18 October.* LNHPA, Boardinghouse Park, file (4).

Index